AMERICAN FARM POLICY, 1948–1973

*Published with assistance
from the Minnesota
Agricultural Experiment Station*

AMERICAN
FARM
POLICY,
1948-1973

by
Willard W. Cochrane
and
Mary E. Ryan

UNIVERSITY OF MINNESOTA PRESS □ MINNEAPOLIS

Library of Congress Catalog Card Number 75-32671

ISBN 0-8166-0783-4

Contents

Preface   vii

Glossary of Terms   ix

PART I. TOWARD AN UNDERSTANDING OF FARM POLICY

Chapter 1. The Agro-Economic Setting   3

Chapter 2. Policy Goals and Directions   21

Chapter 3. The Evolution of Policies and Programs   72

Chapter 4. A Look at the Legislative and Administrative Processes   103

PART II. THE HISTORICAL RECORD

Chapter 5. Farm Price and Income Legislation   131

Chapter 6. Program Operations: Major Commodities   175

Chapter 7. Program Operations: Land Retirement, Exports, and
          Food   256

Chapter 8. Program Interrelations and Costs   295

PART III. CONSEQUENCES AND APPRAISAL

Chapter 9. Program Analysis and Consequences   359

Chapter 10. Program Appraisal and Implications for the Future   383

          Notes   401

          Index   417

Preface

This is basically a reference book. It seeks to record and explain what we did in the United States in the farm policy area between 1948 and 1973. Part I provides a setting for the policy developments, describes the evolution and general content of the programs, and explores the policy formulation process. Part II, The Historical Record, is the core of the book. In this part we describe in some detail the farm policy legislation that was enacted during the period and the operations of the more important programs that were in effect during the period 1948–73. Part II focuses on program mechanics, program magnitudes, program interrelations, and program costs.

Part III of the book contains some interpretation and appraisal of the farm policies and programs of the period 1948–73. But the principal purpose of the book is to record as accurately as possible the farm policy of the United States from 1948 to 1973. Thus, the book focuses on the policy actions of the government, the direct consequences of those actions, and the leading actors in the drama, not on policy analyses or policy literature of the period. The book is designed to inform the student and analyst what we did and how we did it, in the farm policy area, between 1948 and 1973.

The program data presented in the book come almost entirely from materials published by divisions of the U.S. Department of Agriculture. Descriptions of program features and operations are based primarily on USDA materials, but much of that material takes the form of mimeographed releases which after a few years become difficult if not impossible to retrieve. In sum, the farm policy record presented in this volume is based almost entirely on the wealth of data and information disseminated by the USDA over the years with regard to farm policies and programs.

We received assistance from many persons in the preparation of this volume. But we would like to acknowledge the assistance of three individuals in particular. William H. Meyers did the original data digging and research that became the export section of chapter 7. Howard L. Engstrom compiled and refined most of the cost data that ended up in tables 8-1 to 8-26 in chapter 8. Mary Strait edited and typed the long and difficult manuscript.

Financial support for the project under which this volume was produced was provided by the Agricultural Experiment Station, Institute of Agriculture, University of Minnesota. The Department of Agricultural and Applied Economics of the University of Minnesota provided the facilities and the pleasant intellectual environment in which the book was written.

Finally, we wish to offer the usual disclaimer concerning our sole responsibility for the contents of the book.

Willard W. Cochrane
Mary E. Ryan
St. Paul, Minnesota
April 1975

Glossary of Terms

The terms described here have specific meanings in relation to farm programs.* Because they occur frequently in the text that follows, the glossary is placed here to facilitate reference for the reader. The program components or features described in this glossary were not necessarily in operation throughout the entire 1948–73 period. Chapters 6 and 7 specify whether a particular program feature applied in a given year and for what commodities.

Acreage Allotments

The principal function of acreage allotments was to control output. Each year when they applied the secretary of agriculture was required to proclaim acreage allotments for specified crops unless he suspended them under emergency powers. (Allotments were suspended during and immediately after World War II and in the Korean War period.) The size of the national allotment was determined by the amount of acreage needed to produce a crop which, together with the carryover and imports, would provide a supply equal to a normal year's domestic consumption and exports, plus an allowance for reserve. The national allotment was apportioned to states, counties, and farms on the basis of past production and other factors. National minimums were often specified by law for allotment crops, thus preventing downward adjustments below the minimum level even if supplies were expected to be excessive. Compliance with acreage allotments was usually required as a condition for obtaining price supports, but no penalties were imposed for noncompliance unless marketing quotas also applied. In some years acreage

*Many of these descriptions are adapted from a more comprehensive list. See U.S. Department of Agriculture, *Glossary of Terms Used in ASCS and Related Programs*, Agriculture Handbook 371, November 1969.

allotments were employed as a basis for computing government payments to producers.

Base Acreage

Base acreage, like acreage allotments, was a means to control output and to allocate government payments. The apportionment of base acreage was determined from historical planting practices. Base acreage was used to compute allowable planting and acreage diversion in qualifying for benefits under government commodity programs.

Basic Crops or Basic Commodities

Corn, cotton, peanuts, rice, tobacco, and wheat were declared by law to be the basic crops. According to this designation, price supports were mandatory for these six commodities.

Complier and Noncomplier
or Cooperator and Noncooperator

These terms refer to compliance with the provisions of a government program. Compliers (or cooperators) complied with the provisions and hence qualified for program benefits. Noncompliers (or noncooperators) were not eligible for program benefits. Moreover, when marketing quotas applied, noncompliers were subject to penalties.

Conserving Base

A conserving base was a specified amount or share of cropland historically devoted to conserving uses or the amount of conservation land recommended by good farming practices.

Conserving Use

A conserving use was a cultural practice or use approved under requirements of commodity programs or of general cropland retirement programs. These uses included permanent or rotation cover of grasses and legumes; summer or winter cover crops consisting principally of small grains, annual legumes, or annual grasses; small grain cover crops when used for any purpose other than grain; idle cropland including clean tillage and summer fallowed cropland; and volunteer cover. The specific uses that qualified in this category differed somewhat among programs and from year to year. In general, a broader range of uses qualified for conserving-base acreage than for diverted acreage.

Cross Compliance

This term refers to commodity program requirements that restricted program benefits to those who complied with all commodity programs applicable to a given farm.

Diverted Acreage

This was acreage withdrawn from crop production and devoted to approved conserving uses under production adjustment programs. In some years planting of nonsurplus crops was allowed on diverted acreage.

Government Payments

Payments to producers were authorized under various federal government programs. They included commodity price support payments, payments for diverting land from crop production to conserving uses or to nonsurplus crops, payments to implement conservation practices, etc. Government payments have been variously called direct payments, compensatory payments, income payments, diversion payments, set-aside payments, and deficiency payments.

Mandatory Price Support

The law directed the secretary of agriculture to support prices of some commodities within a specific range or at a specific level. Support was mandatory for the basic crops and for several other commodities.

Marketing Quotas

Marketing quotas were used in conjunction with acreage allotments as a more stringent means of controlling output. When the expected supply for a year exceeded estimated use by a specified amount, marketing quotas had to be proclaimed by the secretary of agriculture for certain crops. Before a quota became effective it had to be approved by two-thirds of the producers of the commodity voting in a referendum. When marketing quotas were approved, compliance with acreage allotments was compulsory; noncomplying producers not only lost price supports but were subject to penalties. If marketing quotas were disapproved, the level of price supports was lowered substantially for those who complied with acreage allotments.

Parity Price*

The definition of the parity price for an agricultural commodity in 1973 was the dollars-and-cents price, determined by a formula, that would give the

*For details on calculating parity prices and analyses of parity indexes at three points in the study period see U.S., Congress, Senate, *Parity Handbook: A Reference Manual on Parity Price*,

commodity the same buying power, in terms of goods and services bought by farmers, that the commodity had in the 1910–14 base period, updated by an adjustment factor. The adjustment divided the commodity's most recent 10-year-average farm price by the ratio of the general level of prices for all farm commodities during the 10-year period to the general level of prices received for all commodities during the 1910–14 base period. In earlier years different formulas were employed. The parity price of a commodity is an overall standard. It applies to the average of the various locations, grades, qualities, and classes.

Payment in Kind (PIK)

PIK refers to payment in commodities in lieu of currency. PIK was used by CCC for export and domestic commodity programs. PIK certificates were issued to producers, buyers, or exporters. They stated a dollar value, redeemable for specified commodities and products from CCC stocks or in face value cash equivalent.

Permissive Support

The secretary of agriculture had considerable discretion in setting the level of price supports for commodities designated as permissive. Support was authorized by law but was or was not undertaken at the discretion of the secretary. In determining whether support would be undertaken and at what level to set supports, the secretary was to consider the following factors: (1) the supply of the commodity in relation to the demand; (2) levels at which prices of other commodities were being supported; (3) the availability of funds; (4) the perishability of the commodity; (5) the importance of the commodity to agriculture and the national economy; (6) the ability to dispose of stocks which would be acquired through price support operations; (7) the need for offsetting temporary losses from export markets; and (8) the ability and willingness of producers to keep supplies in line with demand.

Price Support Loans

Commodity loans have been made by the government to farmers or farmers' cooperative marketing associations to provide floors under market

---

Index of Prices Paid by Farmers, and Index of Prices Received, S. Doc. 129, 82nd Congress, 2nd session, May 13, 1952; *Possible Methods of Improving the Parity Formula*, S. Doc. 18, 85th Congress, 1st session, 1957; and *Parity Returns Position of Farmers*, S. Doc. 44, 90th Congress, 1st session, August 10, 1967. Senate Document 44 is a report of a study of the parity income of farmers, required by Section 705 of the Food and Agriculture Act of 1965. It summarizes the history and significance of parity and analyzes alternative criteria for measuring parity returns of commercial farms.

prices. Loans were secured by a commodity stored in approved facilities, on or off the farm. The loans were nonrecourse. This meant that the government would accept the commodity as full satisfaction for the loan at the farmer's discretion. If the farmer chose to repay the loan he could do so at any time before maturity, for most commodities. If the loan was redeemed, interest and service charges were added to the face value of the loan. This nonrecourse feature allowed farmers to gain from any price rise with no risk of loss.

When supply conditions warranted, the USDA offered loan extension, or "reseal" privileges. This permitted withholding of surplus commodities for longer periods of time. Storage costs accruing during reseal periods were paid by the government. This enabled farmers who stored their commodities under loan to earn income for storage.

Loans performed several functions: (1) they provided farmers a cash return for the commodity at the support level, (2) they strengthened market prices of the commodity through withdrawal of supplies from the market especially at harvest (this was the original and principal purpose of the loan programs), and (3) they tended to even out marketing because farmers who obtained loans on their crops at harvesttime could market the crops over the season. Frequently loans were the first step in the government acquisition of commodities under price support operations.

For most commodity programs, in many years, producers had to comply with planting restrictions to obtain price support loans. Yet, insofar as loan operations maintained market prices above equilibrium levels, noncompliers benefited because they sold their production at the supported market prices. Market prices could drop below loan levels when program participation is low and thus supplies withheld from the market are small.

Purchase Agreements or Purchases

Purchases of commodities by the government were means of supporting prices by reducing the supply in the market. When purchase agreement programs applied, the Commodity Credit Corporation (the government) was required to buy offered commodities from eligible producers. The transaction price was the loan rate. Purchase procedures supplied price protection similar to loans except that the farmer did not receive payments under purchase programs until the commodity was delivered to the government. Purchases provided producers who did not have immediate need for cash or who could not meet loan storage requirements a less complex form of price protection than the loan program. Purchase agreements required an advance formal agreement between the farmer and the CCC; other purchase programs did not require any advance arrangement.

For some commodities, notably dairy products, the government initiated purchase operations to assure market prices at the support level. Purchases of dairy products were made from processors rather than from producers. Purchase programs of this type were called "direct purchase programs." They were not continuous programs but were instituted by the government when markets were depressed.

Set-Aside Acreage

Acreage withdrawn from crop production and devoted to approved conserving uses under production adjustment programs is termed "set aside." Planting of nonsurplus crops, haying, and grazing could be permitted on set-aside acreage.

PART I

Toward an Understanding
of Farm Policy

CHAPTER 1

The Agro-Economic Setting

American farm policy developments in the post–World War II period can be understood and rationalized only in terms of the agro-economic conditions of that period. It was a highly dynamic period, a wondrously productive period, but most often an economically painful period for farmers. Let us, therefore, explore the period in some detail in order to provide perspective for the policy development that occurred.

A Dynamic Farm Economy

The yields per acre of the nation's three major crops, wheat, corn, and cotton, increased as follows over the period 1945–73:

	Yield per Acre Harvested		
Crop Year	Wheat (Bushels)	Corn (Bushels)	Cotton (Pounds)
Average for 1945–49	16.9	36.0	270
Average for 1972–73	32.2	94.2	513

The yield increases for most of the lesser crops were as great as, or greater than, those indicated above for wheat, corn, and cotton. Thus, average crop production per acre in the United States increased importantly (see figure 1-1).

Science unlocked the door to a sustained increase in agricultural productivity during the period 1948–73. Research laboratories and experiment stations produced a steady flow of output-increasing technologies and farmers adopted them and put them into practice on a wide scale. The result was an extraordinary increase in farm output (see figure 1-2). Total farm output increased from an index value of 100 in 1950 to 158 in 1973. And since the total input of productive resources held about constant over this period, output per unit of input increased almost as much as farm output itself (see figure 1-2). In other words, the gain in output over this period resulted almost exclusively from increased productivity — increased resource efficiency.

It is important to understand the nature of this important gain in productive efficiency. Farmers increasingly substituted fertilizer, machinery, gasoline

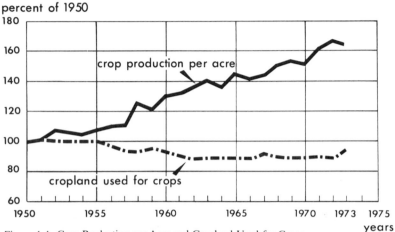

Figure 1-1. Crop Production per Acre and Cropland Used for Crops

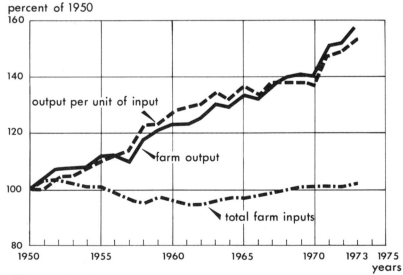

Figure 1-2. Farm Productivity

and electricity, and other nonfarm-produced inputs for human labor and land
in the production of food and fiber (see figure 1-3). But they did not substitute
the same kinds and units of nonfarm-produced inputs for human labor and
land; they substituted new and improved — more productive — units of
nonfarm-produced inputs for human labor and land, and thereby increased,
year after year, output per unit of input.

In a larger sense, what happened is the following. Farmers substituted
cheap fossil fuels, transformed into such productive inputs as fertilizers, tractors, milking machines, and harvesting equipment, for expensive, relatively
inefficient human labor. As a result, the energy output of major food crops,
measured in calories per unit of energy input, declined over this period.[1] In
physical terms, there was a decline in the efficiency of producing digestible
energy through crops over the period 1948–73. But because fossil fuels were
so cheap in price, there was an important gain in the efficiency of producing
crops measured in economic terms. Thus, the period 1948–73 may be charac-
terized as one of a massive transference of cheap fossil fuels into agriculture in
the form of new and improved technologies which had the effect of increasing
output per unit of input importantly and increasing total farm output greatly.

The production success story just described gave rise to difficult problems
in adjustment of human resources and chronically depressed farm prices and
incomes. Prices received by farmers for crops declined following the Korean
War and held reasonably constant from 1953 to 1967 (see figure 1-4), whereas
prices received for livestock sagged rather substantially. This should not

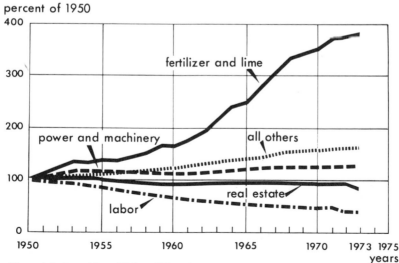

Figure 1-3. Quantities of Selected Farm Inputs

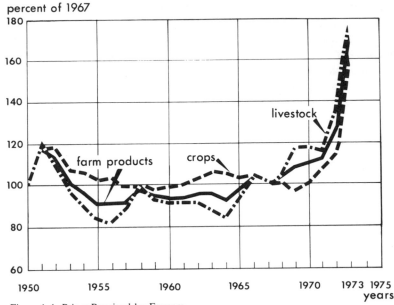

Figure 1-4. Prices Received by Farmers

surprise us, since the prices of all important crops were supported by government programs and most livestock products were not. It is generally agreed
that farm prices would have averaged considerably lower over these years if
the government price support programs had not been in operation. Estimates
range from 10 to 25 percent lower, depending upon the assumptions made and
the exact years involved. But few analysts dispute the conclusion that farm
prices rode on government price support programs during much of the time
during the decades of the 1950s and 1960s, and would have tumbled sharply if
those programs had been withdrawn.

Following 1967, farm prices began to move upward, and in 1973 they shot
skyward. The surge in farm prices in 1973 was of a magnitude never before
experienced in the United States except during wars or their aftermath. It was
a totally new experience and raises the question in everyone's mind of what
comes next.

Despite revolutionary developments in production in parts of the less-
developed world, the upward movement in farm prices during the years
1967–73 in the United States reflects a general tightening of world food
supplies — particularly grain supplies. Except for the year 1972, in which
world grain production declined modestly, this tightening did not result from
production reverses. It resulted from a rapid increase in the demand in the

developed world for meats and for the raw materials from which to produce those meat products. This latter development in conjunction with environmental and energy considerations set the stage for a new economic era for world agriculture in general and American farm producers in particular. The age of surpluses and low farm prices may have come to an end in the early 1970s. The signs point in that direction, but it is much too early to draw any firm conclusions.

Prices paid by farmers behaved differently from prices received. Prices paid by farmers started rising in 1956 and rose steadily throughout the late 1950s, all of the 1960s, and into the 1970s. Thus, for much of the 1950s and 1960s, farm producers were squeezed between stable product prices and rising input prices. What saved them, insofar as they were saved, was the increased efficiencies of production in this period.

We see what happened to average farm income, gross and net, for the period 1948–73 in table 1-1. With a few annual dips, average gross income per farm climbed steadily over the entire period, as output per farm increased and prices received by farmers held reasonably steady. Average net income per farm did not develop so favorably; it rose substantially during the Korean War period, leveled off during most of the 1950s, climbed slowly during the 1960s, and then spurted upward in 1972–73 with the runaway movement in farm product prices. The great roller-coaster-like movements in aggregate net farm income over the long period 1910–73 may be seen in figure 1-5; we see also in that figure the close relation between movements in net farm income and movements in farm prices.

In respect to income, most of the period 1948–73 was not a happy one for farmers. They saw these great increases in productivity result in increased output, constant product prices, and very slowly rising net incomes. Most farmers felt cheated by this development; they were unable to benefit in terms of income from the great gains in productivity that resulted from their efforts.

The material on average income just reviewed provides at best a broad general description of the economic position of individual farmers. Much was happening to farmers and their farms that is not reflected in these averages. In the first place there was a great decline in the total number of farms between 1948 and 1973. Looking at table 1-1 again, we see that the total number of farms in 1948 was not greatly different from that of the period 1910–14. But the number of farms declined from 5,803,000 in 1948 to 2,844,000 in 1973. And as we might guess, this contraction did not take place easily or painlessly. It took place through the painful process of forced retirement and business failure, in which thousands of inefficient medium to small farmers went out of business. It took place through a process in which the larger, more efficient farmers with strong asset positions acquired the productive resources

Table 1-1. Number of Farms and Average Farm Income per Farm (Averages for the Five-Year Periods 1910–14, 1925–29, and 1935–39, and Annual Figures for 1948 through 1973)

Five-Year Period or Year	Number of Farms[a] (in thousands)	Realized Gross Income per Farm				Production Expenses per Farm	Operators' Realized Net Income per Farm
		Cash Receipts from Marketings	Government Payments	Realized Nonmoney Income	Total		
1910–14	6,429	$ 922	0	$ 266	$ 1,188	$ 590	$ 598
1925–29	6,475	1,687	0	410	2,097	1,161	936
1935–39	6,631	1,206	$ 72	307	1,585	880	706
1948	5,803	5,209	44	730	5,983	3,238	2,745
1949	5,722	4,859	32	636	5,527	3,142	2,385
1950	5,648	5,039	50	629	5,718	3,445	2,273
1951	5,428	6,054	53	728	6,835	4,118	2,717
1952	5,198	6,258	53	775	7,086	4,385	2,701
1953	4,984	6,221	43	773	7,037	4,307	2,730
1954	4,798	6,217	54	750	7,021	4,545	2,476
1955	4,654	6,337	49	761	7,147	4,764	2,383
1956	4,514	6,735	123	766	7,624	5,030	2,594
1957	4,372	6,797	232	787	7,816	5,422	2,394
1958	4,233	7,904	257	848	9,009	6,093	2,916
1959	4,097	8,212	166	866	9,244	6,641	2,603
1960	3,963	8,643	177	895	9,715	6,919	2,796
1961	3,825	9,192	390	929	10,511	7,471	3,040
1962	3,692	9,877	473	950	11,300	8,191	3,109

Table 1-1 — *continued*

	Number of Farms[a] (in thousands)	Realized Gross Income per Farm				Production Expenses per Farm	Operators' Realized Net Income per Farm
Five-Year Period or Year		Cash Receipts from Marketings	Government Payments	Realized Nonmoney Income	Total		
1963	3,572	10,491	475	999	11,965	8,823	3,142
1964	3,457	10,798	631	1,046	12,475	9,175	3,300
1965	3,356	11,729	734	1,098	13,561	9,988	3,573
1966	3,257	13,336	1,006	1,181	15,523	11,182	4,341
1967	3,162	13,542	974	1,259	15,775	12,106	3,669
1968	3,071	14,388	1,127	1,335	16,850	12,872	3,978
1969	2,999	16,064	1,265	1,455	18,784	14,064	4,720
1970	2,954	17,107	1,258	1,473	19,838	15,088	4,750
1971	2,909	18,171	1,081	1,589	20,841	16,364	4,477
1972	2,870	21,254	1,380	1,741	24,375	18,270	6,105
1973	2,844	31,151	917	2,031	34,099	22,767	11,332

Source: U.S. Department of Agriculture, Economic Research Service, *Farm Income Situation*, FIS-224, July 1974, Table 3H, p. 46.

[a] A farm is defined according to the census. That definition is: "Farms are places on which agricultural operations larger than a specified minimum were conducted at any time during the census year."

9

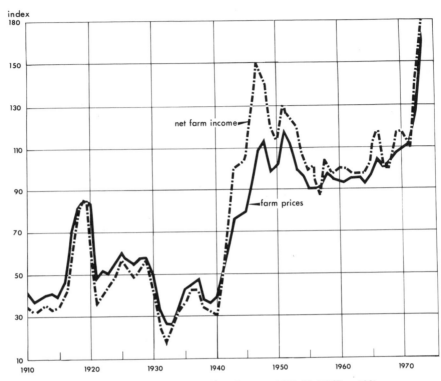

Figure 1-5. Indices of Farm Prices and Net Farm Income, 1910–73 (1967 = 100)

of the smaller, inefficient farmers in financial difficulty. There is no way that such a process can be made pleasant to the families being dispossessed.

The results of this contraction process may be observed in table 1-2. We see that the number of farms with product sales of $10,000 or more per year increased importantly between 1949 and 1969 — from 497,000 to 1,073,000. During the same period the total number of small commercial farms with sales between $2,500 and $10,000 per year declined from 1,683,000 to 675,000. And the low-production farms with sales less than $2,500 declined in total numbers by almost 2 million over the period 1949–69. Small farmers went out of business in droves in the decades of the 1950s and 1960s.

It would be a mistake, however, to conclude that the large corporate farm, with absentee ownership and hired management, became the dominant form of farm organization during this period as the family farm type of organization ceased to exist. Basically, what happened during the period is that the larger, more successful family farmers bought out the smaller, less successful family

Table 1-2. Number of Farms by Economic Class and Percentage Distribution in the United States, for Selected Years 1949–69

Economic Class	Number of Farms (in thousands)					Percentage Distribution				
	1949	1954	1959	1964	1969	1949	1954	1959	1964	1969
All farms...........	5,247	4,798	4,097	3,442	2,971	100	100	100	100	100
Commercial farms........	2,180	2,192	2,175	1,898	1,748	41.5	45.7	53.1	55.1	58.8
Farms with sales less than $2,500 ...	3,067	2,606	1,922	1,544	1,223	58.5	54.3	46.9	44.9	41.2
Commercial farms........	2,180	2,192	2,175	1,898	1,748	41.5	45.7	53.1	55.1	58.8
$40,000 or more	48	63	106	146	211	0.9	1.3	2.6	4.2	7.1
$20,000 to $39,999	107	137	219	268	357	2.0	2.9	5.3	7.8	12.0
$10,000 to $19,999	342	398	503	482	505	6.5	8.3	12.3	14.0	17.0
$ 5,000 to $ 9,999	739	725	693	533	389	14.1	15.1	16.9	15.5	13.1
$ 2,500 to $ 4,999	944	869	654	469	286	18.0	18.1	16.0	13.6	9.6

Source: U.S. Department of Agriculture, Economic Research Service, *The Expanding and the Contracting Sectors of American Agriculture*, Agriculture Economic Report 74, May 1965, Table 15, p. 24–25 (for the years 1949–59); *Farm Income Situation*, FIS-216, July 1970, Table 1D, p. 68 (for the years 1964, 1969).

farmers. As a result, the representative family farm grew larger in terms of production assets and product sales over the period.

A second result of the contraction in the number of farms over the period 1948–73 should be noted. The share of total product sold was steadily concentrated into the hands of the larger farmers. Farms with sales over $10,000 per year sold 50.2 percent of the total product of agriculture in 1949 and 88.5 percent in 1969.

The employment and productivity changes in agriculture in the decades of the 1950s and 1960s are placed in perspective in table 1-3. American agriculture was an expanding industry in terms of employment up to 1910. Between 1910 and 1920 American agriculture crossed a great watershed. Since 1920 it has been a contracting industry in terms of employment. Since 1920 farm entrepreneurs have increasingly substituted nonfarm-produced machines, equipment, and power for human labor, and that substitution process increased with a roar in the decades of the 1950s and 1960s.

Further, that substitution process did not dampen down agriculture's capacity to produce. We see in table 1-3 the dramatic gains in farm output that resulted from the substitution of more and more nonfarm-produced capital, embodied in increasingly technologically efficient forms, for human labor. We see also the spectacular gains in worker productivity that resulted from that substitution process in table 1-3.

The process of development that occurred in American agriculture in the 1950s and 1960s should be properly viewed as a continuation of a process which got underway between 1910 and 1920. But in the late 1950s and 1960s the process accelerated greatly with wondrous and frightening results. What the decades of the 1970s and 1980s will bring remains to be seen. But there are several indicators which suggest that America may in the 1970s be crossing another great development watershed.

The Chronic Farm Problem: Excess Productive Capacity

Each farmer who failed and went out of business during the period 1948–73 no doubt had an explanation in terms of a cause, or set of causes, specific to his situation: bad weather in his area, low prices for his crop, or a bad business decision. And certainly over that long period the producers of some commodities have suffered more from lower prices, or sharply fluctuating prices, than producers of other commodities. The agricultural industry, like any other industry, is subject to a range of conditions and is made up of business managers with widely varying capacities. But these specific conditions and situations in agriculture have been compounded by one overriding problem — the problem of general excess productive capacity.

Table 1-3. Changes in Farm Employment, Production, and Output per Worker, 1870–1970
(1870 = 100 for All Indexes)

Year	Farm Employment		Farm Output		Output per Worker	
	Number[a] (in Millions)	Percentage Change in Past Decade	Index[b]	Percentage Change in Past Decade	Index	Percentage Change in Past Decade
1870	8.0		100		100	
1880	10.1	26	155	55	123	23
1890	11.7	16	185	19	127	3
1900	12.8	10	240	30	150	18
1910	13.6	6	250	4	147	−2
1920	13.4	−1	279	12	166	13
1930	12.5	−7	315	13	202	22
1940	11.0	−12	351	11	254	26
1950	9.9	−10	437	25	352	39
1960	7.1	−28	527	21	592	68
1970	4.5	−37	605	15	1,077	82

[a]The figures for 1870 to 1900 are based on data from U.S. Bureau of the Census, Population Series P-9, No. 11. From 1910 to 1960 the figures are from U.S. Department of Agriculture, Agricultural Marketing Service, *Average Annual Farm Employment*. The figures for 1970 were estimated by the Economic Research Service on the basis of trends.

[b]Three-year averages are centered on the year indicated. Index estimates of output were obtained from the Agricultural Adjustment Research Branch, Farm Production Economics Division, U.S. Department of Agriculture.

Farm output ran ahead of the growth in domestic demand during most of the long period 1930–70 in the United States. During the war years of the 1940s and the period of rehabilitation that followed, this imbalance created no problem; first our allies and later the defeated countries swallowed up the American surplus of food and fiber products and cried for more.[2] But during the 1930s, the 1950s, and again in the 1960s, food and fiber supplies pressed against domestic demand, causing farm prices to fall disastrously in the 1930s, government stocks to build up in the 1950s, under price support, and large control programs to be imposed in the 1960s in order to contain the outturn of farm products. Except in wartime there have been too many resources producing too much product — excess production capacity — on American farms since 1930; this is the basic problem of the commercial farm sector.

During the 1950s farm output increased about 2.1 percent a year despite programs to limit production. During the same period population in the United States increased about 1.7 percent a year. That is, total farm output increased about one-half of 1 percent faster than population growth during the 1950s.

Per capita food consumption remained almost constant during this period; thus increased per capita food consumption did not absorb any significant part of the excess production. Commercial exports did increase, and did absorb a part of the excess. Foreign food aid (Food for Peace) came into being in 1954 and helped absorb an important part of the excess. But increased exports did not succeed in absorbing all the domestic farm surplus.

Government-owned stocks of farm commodities grew from about $1.3 billion in 1952 to $7.7 billion in 1959, as the government acquired stocks in price-supporting operations. Between 1959 and 1970 the government stock position improved modestly, but this occurred through expanded production control programs which kept an increased number of productive acres out of production.

We know that it was not because farmers maintained the status quo that the excess productive capacity of the national farm plant continued over the long period 1930–70. Millions of them left farming between 1930 and 1970, and the number of acres devoted to crops declined importantly after 1949. But new and improved capital and practices so effectively substituted for labor and land in the 1950s and 1960s that total output continued to increase — and to increase enough to hold the farm economy in a chronic state of surplus.

What was the extent of this continuous excess productive capacity of the national farm plant? Several studies that measured the excess productive capacity or the surplus production of the national farm plant for the 1950s are available.[3] One places the estimate as low as 5 percent of total production. Other estimates run as high as 8 and 9 percent. A part of this discrepancy in the size of estimates is due to the different assumptions of the various studies, but a part is due to the study of different periods. Excess productive capacity increased during most of the 1950s, reaching a peak in 1958–59. It may therefore be concluded that between 5 and 9 percent of total farm production each year during the 1950s was surplus — production that could not find a commercial home at the supported farm price level.

Surplus production, or excess productive capacity, must be measured at some price level above the free, equilibrium price level, for at the free, equilibrium price level there is no surplus. At the equilibrium price, supply equals demand. But some idea of the magnitude of surplus farm production at the level of support prices in the 1950s may be obtained by considering to what level farm prices would have had to drop in order to wipe out a surplus of, say 7 percent (the median of the estimates above). With an elasticity of aggregate demand for all farm products of $-.3$ at retail, farm product prices would have had to fall by over 20 percent at retail and by 40 percent or more at the farm level. Measured in price terms the excess productive capacity of the national farm plant in the 1950s was breathtaking.

A later study of excess capacity in American agriculture by Tyner and Tweeten throws additional light on the problem.[4] Taking account of commodity acquisitions by the CCC (the government), commodities that would have been produced on land withdrawn from production under various control programs, and all government subsidized exports, these investigators conclude that surplus production in 1961–62 amounted to as much as 10 percent of total production. Then, taking into account certain value received by the United States from subsidized farm exports, they conclude that a realistic estimate of surplus farm production for 1961–62 would be 7 percent of total production. This means that the excess productive capacity of the national farm plant for the early 1960s was just about the same as that for the middle 1950s, namely 7 percent.

The question thus arises — why was there chronic excess productive capacity in farming over the long period 1950–70? Why were there too many resources producing too much product at a reasonable level of prices year in and year out?

This chronic condition grew out of four related circumstances: (1) the high value that American society placed on scientific research and technological development; (2) the market organization or structure within which farmers operated; (3) the extreme inelasticity of the aggregate demand for food; and (4) the inability of resources previously committed to farm production to shift easily and readily out of farming. These are the components of a general theory which explains the chronic excess capacity in American farming during the 1950s and 1960s.[5]

The American people did not in this period single out agriculture in general and farming in particular to carry the burden of scientific and technological advances; Americans prize science and technology highly, expect it, and demand it in all segments of the economy. And they got rapid scientific and technological developments in agriculture, and their widespread adoption in farming in the United States between 1950 and 1970. Society supported the research and development effort; the new and improved technologies poured forth; farmers adopted them eagerly and rapidly; and the capacity of the farm production plant expanded importantly.

The market structure under which the typical farmer operates is highly conducive to the adoption of new and improved technologies on farms. The typical farmer operates in a market so large that he can have no perceptible influence on it and must take as given to him the prices generated there; he is a price taker. Confronted with this situation, he reasons, "I can't influence price, but I can influence my own costs. I can get my costs down." So the typical farmer is always searching for some way to get his costs down. By definition, an improved technology is cost-reducing (that is, it increases output per unit of input). The typical farmer is thus on the lookout for new, cost-reducing technologies; built into the market organization of farming is a powerful incentive for adopting new and improved technologies—the incentive of reducing costs on the individual farm. And it works: farmers generally adopt new and improved technologies to reduce costs; this widespread adoption increases farm output in the aggregate, and as a result farm technological advance pushes total output before it in an expanding action.

If the demand for food were highly elastic all would be well in farming: the bountiful and expanding supplies of food that farmers want to produce would sell in the market at only slightly reduced prices, gross incomes to farmers in the aggregate and individually would increase, and the surplus resources would be employed to produce the additional product that would be taken by consumers at only slightly reduced prices. If the aggregate demand for food were elastic, farming would be an expanding industry as more men and more land were combined with improved technological practices to produce an increased total product that sold for such modest price decreases that gross receipts to farmers would increase as a result. This is the happy situation confronting an industry with an elastic demand for its product.

But the aggregate demand for food is not elastic; it is inelastic and extremely so. For this reason, a little too much total output drives down the farm price level in a dramatic fashion. In other words, with a severely inelastic demand confronting the producers of food, it is very easy to develop a condition of excess capacity, or surplus production; a small surplus can have an extreme effect on farm prices and gross farm income.

The severely inelastic aggregate demand for food would not be devastating, however, if the aggregate supply of farm food products were elastic. If the aggregate supply were elastic, then with a surplus situation and a downward movement in farm prices, productive resources would quickly move out of farming, production would be reduced, and a bottom would be placed under the price decline. Through an adjustment in resource use the surplus would be eliminated and the drastic price decline avoided. But the aggregate supply of farm food products is inelastic and extremely so. It is inelastic because productive resources cannot easily and readily leave farming and move to other industries in response to changes in the farm price level. Farm labor is tied to family patterns of living, with increases and decreases in response to family growth cycles rather than to price level changes, except when the whole family decides to move. Farm land cannot pick up and move to urban areas when farm prices fall; it shifts into nonfarm uses only when those uses come to it. Capital sunk into farm buildings, irrigation and drainage works, tractors, and combines does not move easily or have ready uses in nonfarm industries. Most resources employed in farming move only slowly, as equipment and the like are worn out and not replaced, or as human resources come of age and break away from the family. Consequently, the short-run aggregate supply of farm food products is highly inelastic and provides no brake to falling prices in a surplus situation.

What we had in farming during the 1950s and 1960s is, then, the following: (1) a generous publicly supported research and development effort which turned out a great array of new and improved technological practices year after year; (2) the widespread adoption of these technologies by farmers, resulting in a sustained increase in the aggregate production of farm food products; (3) expanding supplies which pressed against a slowly expanding and inelastic aggregate demand for food and as a result created a strong downward pressure on farm prices; (4) a downward movement in farm food product prices which was unable to induce the reduction in marketable supplies required to put a brake on falling prices because resources employed in farming move sluggishly in response to changes in price level. As a result of the interaction of these forces, the inflow of new and improved technologies exceeded the outflow of conventional resources employed in farming year after year and created a chronic price-depressing surplus. This is the general theory of a chronically maladjusted farm sector which applied with great force over the long period 1950–70.

The physical farm surpluses were kept off the market by two devices: the withdrawal of land from production through government programs and the acquisition of supplies by government at support price levels. Farm prices therefore did not fall disastrously in the 1950s and 1960s as the result of excess productive capacity; the excess productive capacity was contained in one way or another by government programs. The rest of this volume will be concerned with describing, measuring, interpreting, and appraising the government programs noted above. But before we turn to that larger task, let us consider the hopes and aspirations of farm people in this highly dynamic development process of which they have been both prime movers and principal recipients.

The Quest for Economic Justice

The quest for economic justice on the part of farm people in the United States antedates by many decades the period 1948–73. The great farmers' movements of the 1870s and 1880s and Populist political uprising of the 1890s were direct efforts on the part of farmers to control their economic destiny and to rid themselves of the depressed conditions which plagued them. Those efforts resulted in some modest successes and some monumental failures. Again in the 1920s farmers sought relief from economic depression. This time they turned first to collective bargaining as preached by Aaron Sapiro and then to government action in the form of the McNary-Haugen domestic allotment plan. But both efforts came to naught. Then in the 1930s farmers experienced their first real success in raising prices and reducing surpluses through collective action; the Agricultural Adjustment Act of 1933 was the vehicle of this first success. But we will say no more about these early efforts, since they are well chronicled by Murray Benedict.[6]

Farmers came out of World War II fearful that the bottom would fall out of farm prices and incomes as it did following World War I, and much of the policy and legislative effort of the government during the latter years of World War II was directed toward assuring farmers that the bottom would not fall out of farm prices and incomes with the advent of peace. These fears were calmed to some degree by the so-called Steagall Amendment, which guaranteed that most farm commodities would be supported at 90 percent of parity (with certain specific exceptions) for two years after the cessation of hostilities. This amendment in conjunction with post–World War II food shortages in Europe and Asia and the Korean War held farm prices in the United States up to acceptable levels till 1953 (with the exception of the 1949–50 crop year). Thus, after nearly twelve consecutive years of farm prosperity (1941–52) some farmers, perhaps even many, had reached the conclusion that farm depressions were a thing of the past, and it was time to get government out of agriculture. Falling prices and depressed incomes in 1953 and 1954 caused some farmers to reconsider their free-market position. They knew that something had gone wrong with the farm economy once again — but what?

The reliable and representative price series — the index of prices received and the index of prices paid — developed by the U.S. Department of Agriculture in the 1920s, together with the parity concept, provided farmers with measures of their economic disadvantage. This kind of economic information, together with the empirical fact that their less able neighbors were going out of business all about them, caused farmers to be both frustrated and angry and drove them to demand corrective action from their government. But what kind of corrective action? — that was the question.

Some farmers accepted the excess capacity argument advanced earlier in this chapter and were willing to accept a systematic set of production controls to adjust supplies to demand. Others believed that many consumers did not have enough to eat, and if a way could be found to expand their food consumption, the price-depressing surpluses would melt away. Others blamed bankers, or politicians, or foreign competition for the problem. Minnesota farmers often blamed their economic troubles onto the importation of Canadian grains, western ranchers onto the importation of Australian beef, dairymen onto the importation of New Zealand butter, and so on down the list of commodities. Still others believed that the problem was temporary and that farmers should act vigorously to get government out of their businesses. In fact, there were almost as many theories about the causes of low prices and depressed incomes in the 1950s and 1960s as there were farmers.

Perhaps a majority of commercial farmers in the 1950s and 1960s dimly perceived that, to cope with the general surplus situation, some kind of collective action was called for, either controlling production or expanding consumption at home and abroad. But even this conclusion cannot be made without qualification, since during this period the largest single farm organization, the American Farm Bureau, persistently and stridently called for a return to the free market as a means of solving the problem of surplus.

But this much is clear. Farmers were dissatisfied with the government programs that they had, and they were loud in criticism of those programs. Singly and in groups they told their congressmen, and anyone else who would listen, how they thought the price support and resource adjustment programs should be modified. But no single policy position advocated by farmers stood out with logical clarity and with majority support. What the Congress heard, and what each administration heard when it would listen, was a babble of discontent from farming areas.

The clear and forceful policy position that emerged in the Populist uprising, the McNary-Haugen era, and the early days of the New Deal failed to emerge in the 1950s and 1960s. Thus, the quest for economic justice on the part of farmers dissipated itself among the warring farm factions and contending organizational groups. As a result farmers received assistance, but it was one of two kinds: a grab bag of economic "goodies" put together by the Congress in an effort to please everyone, or a program that formed part of an administration's national economic strategy. The hopes and aspirations of farmers themselves were lost in the national policy-making process because their policy views were so varied in objective, so disparate in means, and so fragmented in support. Why this was the case is not clear. Perhaps it is to be explained by the heterogeneity of farm people in the United States with respect to ethnic background and to regional differences in the agricultural art. But whatever the reason, the range of views about what ought to be done to improve farm prices and incomes in the 1950s and 1960s was very, very wide and hence did not and could not exert a positive force in the policy-making process.

This is not to say that the farm policies and programs that took shape in the period 1948–73 would have been better, in some sense, if farmers had spoken with one voice, or that the policies and programs that emerged were niggardly in their support of commercial farmers. If farmers had been unified in their support of some one policy and program, the result could easily have turned out worse, in some sense, than what did take place, and no more economic support to farmers might have been forthcoming than the support they received. But it is to say that what they got would have been their own policies and programs, or at least a modified version of them. As it turned out, farmers got, in the way of policy solutions, what someone else thought was best for them.

What happened is that farm policy formation and program development passed over into the hands of experts. These experts are of two general kinds: (1) experts at effecting compromises among contending parties, and (2) experts at formulating economic features consistent with the economic and political strategy of the particular administration involved. Thus, the quest for economic justice for farmers has been transformed from one of direct involvement on the part of farmers to one of accepting or vetoing that formulation of economic justice concocted by the experts. The heterogeneity of modern-day society and the complexity of governmental processes perhaps made this transformation inevitable. In any case it did occur, and farm people in the 1950s and 1960s and now in the 1970s have for the most part accepted a limited, but not unimportant, role in policy formulation: complaining and evidencing discontent, waiting and watching, and approving or vetoing that which the experts have wrought.

The remainder of this volume will be concerned primarily with describing in prose and numbers the results of this policy-making process. We turn now to a review of the policy goals and direction, often conflicting in nature, that were advanced during the period 1948–73.

CHAPTER 2

Policy Goals and Directions

Although it is widely agreed, and has long been held, that the fundamental goal of farm policy is to maintain a prosperous, productive farm sector with a family-farm type of organization, differences arise — important differences — with regard to the means for achieving that broad policy goal. Should equitable farm incomes and the family-farm structure be obtained solely through the marketplace or through direct governmental assistance, or by some combination of the two? This question is at the heart of most farm policy debates and influences the selection and evaluation of particular policy proposals. Moreover, responses to this question have changed through time to reflect changing attitudes on the extent and nature of governmental intervention in the marketplace. As the economy has grown in complexity and specialization has increased, it has become increasingly accepted that the government not only has a role but also has a responsibility to actively assist whatever segments of the nation are adversely affected by the forces of development.

In general terms American farm policy, in its development since the end of World War II, has reflected the social attitude noted above. But the tide of opinion regarding farm policy, hence the direction of farm policy, has shifted importantly over the years. Further, a myriad of policy ideas — objectives and program mechanics — have flowed into the farm policy debates, beginning with the Truman administration and concluding with the Nixon years. Therefore, as we seek to identify and describe the important farm policy goals and directions for the period 1948–73, we find it necessary to introduce into the discussion, and sort through, the varied and often conflicting policy ideas that were voiced during the period. And this we do here against the backdrop of major policy debates in the political arena.

21

This chapter thus seeks to describe the broad spectrum of policy ideas that interacted to produce the central trends, or general directions of American farm policy in the period 1948–73. Its purpose is not to describe the end policy product — specific legislative acts and specific programs. Specific legislative acts and specific programs that evolved out of the mélange noted above, what they did and how they relate to one another, are the subject of succeeding chapters.

But first we present a brief prologue to take account of events and developments that were precursors of policy developments in the period 1948–73.

Prologue

Nearly all postwar farm policies are rooted in earlier times — differing in specifics, perhaps, but similar in principle.[1] Even in colonial days, for instance, control of supply was practiced in an attempt to maintain desired prices for tobacco. But experience with modern farm programs begins with the period following World War I. Export demand for U.S. farm products contracted drastically in 1920 because European importing nations lacked dollars with which to buy needed American products. Farm prices fell precipitously, ushering in two decades of depressed farm prices and income. Excess capacity began to plague the industry and was intensified as tractors rapidly replaced horses, adding another impetus to output capability. This period of crisis for American agriculture stimulated a new appraisal of farm policies and programs, along with a reassessment of overall economic policies.

Until then, it was the prevailing view that government should not intervene directly in economic matters; the role of government was seen to be one of simply assuring an equitably functioning marketplace. But the crises developing in the nation led to a growing recognition that market forces often create inequities and socioeconomic ills which a responsible government cannot tolerate. The view that government should intervene in the marketplace to correct or prevent injustices ensuing from the operation of a free market gained adherents.

This modification of public opinion and the distressed condition of the farm economy were responsible for the appearance and serious consideration of several new measures during the 1920s to boost farm prices through government action. Two merit attention. First, the McNary-Haugen proposal would have established a government corporation to buy farm commodities for export. The volume of government purchases would have been geared to maintain a certain level of domestic market prices; export sales would have been made at whatever price they would bring. In essence it was an export "dumping'' scheme. Various versions were considered in five sessions of the Congress; two passed both houses only to be vetoed by President Coolidge. The second item that was a precursor of future proposals was the establishment of a Federal Farm Board in 1929. The board was empowered to assist farmers' marketing organizations and to finance loans for purchase of surplus commodities in order to raise prices. Insufficient funding and the deteriorated nonfarm economy prevented actions of the magnitude required to make an appreciable impact on farm prices.

These first steps of the 1920s were succeeded by more ambitious programs during the 1930s as part of President Roosevelt's New Deal attack against the Great Depression. Consumer incomes dropped, shrinking demand for all products which in turn contributed to further mounting of burdensome stocks of farm products.

The Commodity Credit Corporation was created to carry out commodity loan and storage operations as a means of supporting prices of farm products. Government land rental and acreage control attempts were instituted to reduce production of surplus crops. Payments to farmers from the government were authorized for soil conservation practices and as income supplements. Machinery was designed to regulate markets of perishable products by means of marketing agreements and orders. The supply control features of these programs were modeled after industry, which generally gears production to match demand. Other programs were instituted to aid consumers and to stimulate demand. They included direct distribution of surplus food, the school lunch program, a low-cost milk program, and a limited food stamp program for low-income families. Many ideas first implemented during these crucial times remain in programs today. In fact, the Agricultural Act of 1938 is still the nation's basic price support and production control legislation, amended and revised repeatedly.

The agricultural crisis of the 1920s and 1930s was alleviated by the advent of World War II. Demand for farm products cut into U.S. surpluses and drove prices to high levels. Military service and employment opportunities in war industries, especially in north central and western states, absorbed urban unemployed and attracted rural underemployed men and women. Total farm population dropped from 30.5 to 24.4 million between 1940 and 1945, the greatest outmigration in our nation's history.[2] Farm prosperity returned. Yet USDA officials somewhat reluctantly abandoned the depression policies to control or reduce production because they feared overexpansion and the consequent problems when wartime demand would cease. The catastrophic price and income situations following World War I were still fresh in their memories. Farmers, however, reacted readily to rising market prices by investing in new equipment to cut costs and to expand output. Gradually policy makers induced all-out production by price incentives and appeals to patriotism.

A New Era Begins

Long before the guns of World War II were silenced, planning for postwar agricultural adjustment began. The wartime objective of all-out production was generally recognized as inappropriate for a peacetime economy. Extraordinary demand had been created for U.S. food and fiber by military requirements and by the destruction of foreign farm output and distribution systems in war zones. These abnormal markets were expected to collapse when peace returned. If U.S. farm production did not contract simultaneously, or if alternate outlets were not found, prices would plummet in the face of large surpluses. But no easy solution for maintaining an economically healthy agricultural sector was readily forthcoming.

The Steagall Amendment had been enacted in 1941 to protect farm prices from an immediate postwar drop. This stopgap legislation pegged prices of many farm commodities at high levels until two years after hostilities were officially declared to have ceased. Such a declaration was issued by President Truman on December 31, 1946, so the amendment expired on December 31, 1948.[3]

Meanwhile, several groups studied long-run agricultural problems and policies. Among these were a committee of the Association of Land-Grant Colleges and Universities, a U.S. Department of Agriculture committee, and a congressional committee chaired by William Colmer, a member of the House from Mississippi.[4] Reports of these three committees contain many similarities. All recognized the importance of (1) a full-employment economy to create strong demand for farm output and to provide jobs for the agricultural underemployed who wished to leave farming, (2) buoyant international commerce to stimulate foreign markets for U.S. farm products, and (3) production adjustments within the farm sector and labor shifts out of farming consistent with changing demand and new technology. Excess capacity to produce was perceived as an underlying problem but the magnitude of the problem was not yet recognized. Cotton and wheat were singled out as commodities particularly in need of adjustment in quantity and/or location of production. Each report noted that special measures would be necessary during a depression: there was agreement that farmers would need income supplements and that some consumers would require aid to buy farm products. All recommended programs to conserve natural resources, to improve nutrition and expand domestic consumption (especially for low-income consumers), and to raise the quality of rural life.

Differences among the reports lie in the scope of solutions examined and the relative emphasis given to the various alternatives. The Land Grant report stressed measures which would provide farmers with opportunities to establish economically viable farm units or to seek nonfarm employment. Direct governmental involvement in the determination of agricultural production and prices was viewed as undesirable after wartime measures were phased out. In contrast, the USDA committee declared that flexible price supports could be important policy tools for guiding production away from surplus products toward desired commodities. The department report made note, but did not emphasize, that potential productivity advances ensuing from adaptation of new technology would intensify present adjustment problems. Also, special needs of farmers in certain geographic regions — such as the Cotton South, the Great Plains wheat area, Appalachia, and the cutover region in the Lake states — were identified. The Colmer committee's position on price supports fell between those of the other two groups. This congressional committee considered price supports as undesirable tools to achieve agricultural adjustment, but it did propose the use of supports as floors under commodity prices. The report explicitly identified unique problems of commercial farmers, low-resource–low-income producers, part-time farmers, and nonfarming rural residents.

Many agricultural economists also addressed themselves to postwar farm policy issues. A contest, sponsored by the American Farm Economic Association in 1945, produced over 300 essays on the subject of agricultural price policy. The association president's summary reveals the prevalent themes. He wrote:

Among the prize winning papers there was a strong accent on the desirability of general measures that would maintain a vigorous and prosperous general economy, greater freedom in prices of individual commodities than is possible under existing price support legislation, some type of "forward pricing" in order to guide production, and government supplementary payments to maintain total returns from individual products or total overall farm income. In some papers the suggestion was made that these payments be tied to some overall measure of economic activity or income.

The general trend of thought was toward freer markets accompanied by measures to support some minimum level of farm income. Although not specifically developed in all of the papers the justifications for this procedure are (1) it would permit the price structure to perform its normal functions of guiding production and distribution of commodities and (2) it would provide a minimum level of income to farmers in depression periods for continuing production of needed goods (foods and fibers) at a time when the industrial sector of the economy is shrinking.[5]

This period of intensive and extensive analysis of farm problems and program ideas both within and outside of government provided more information about U.S. agriculture to more people than ever before. And, though none of these study groups formalized their conclusions into legislative packages, many of the principles endorsed and ideas espoused emerged at later dates in farm program proposals. It should be noticed that not one of the reports recommended a continuation of the high, rigid price supports of wartime or the reintroduction of prewar attempts to control production. Such policies were considered antithetic to the principles of full employment and contrary to efficient allocation of resources.

This chorus of voices almost universally proposed some form of flexible price supports and favored direct income payments to farmers under distressed circumstances. Yet despite this wide approval in professional circles, these two features were to create storms in agricultural circles for many years to come. Moreover, some of the measures outlined in these reports were politically sensitive. In particular, recommendations in the USDA report for adjustment of cotton production were strongly attacked by southern farmers and their congressional representatives, contributing to a growing antipathy between the Congress and the USDA's Bureau of Agricultural Economics (BAE).

Policy debates preceding enactment of the Agricultural Act of 1948. The urgent need to replace terminating wartime measures sparked action within the USDA and by agricultural committees in the Congress late in 1946. Farm policy discussions at this time were carried out within an environment of strong export demand created by postwar food shortages abroad; they were also influenced by the recently passed Employment Act of 1946, which committed the federal government to a policy of full employment at home. This situation calmed fears of surpluses and prevented downward pressure on farm prices, enveloping many farm policy makers in an aura of hope.[6]

In December 1946, Secretary of Agriculture Clinton P. Anderson appointed Charles F. Brannan to head a committee charged with shaping a farm program. Resultant proposals were presented to the Congress during 1947 hearings on long-range agricultural policy. In introducing the department's ideas, Secretary Anderson told House Agricultural Committee members, "I want to outline what I believe to be the one practical policy for American agriculture—a policy of organized, sustained and realistic abundance. I want to show you the opportunity we have now, at long last, to establish and maintain a balance between consumption and the sound capacity output of our agricultural plant. . . . What our studies and experience boil down to is one simple fact: By supplying only the reasonable needs of our own people and reasonably expected export and industrial markets, we can not only market as much agricultural production as we have now, but can actually expand."[7]

Proponents of this and similar hopeful policies became known as "advocates of abundance." In their opinions the abundant output of U.S. farms was not, and should not be, a problem. They believed that a problem would arise only if consumers lacked purchasing power to buy all that was produced. This view departed sharply from the principles embodied in the New Deal programs then on the books, which sought to raise prices, hence farm incomes, by reducing supplies — creating a scarcity.

Edward A. O'Neal, president of the American Farm Bureau Federation, remained an adherent of the New Deal scarcity economics. In Senate testimony he emphasized concern for agricultural surpluses when a peacetime economy returned. He said, "we must recognize that burdensome surpluses again may wreck farm prices."[8] He endorsed the basic tenets of the Agricultural Act of 1938, which supported farm incomes by price guarantees and restricted production.[9] But official Federation policies were to change with the presidency in December 1947. O'Neal, a southerner, was succeeded by a midwesterner, Allan B. Kline. Kline's views reflected the grain livestock farmers' opposition to high price supports and restricted production. High feed prices increased livestock production costs and thus, understandably, were unpopular among livestock producers. Policies of high price supports had been popular with cotton and tobacco farmers in the South who believed that their incomes would be unacceptably low with free-market pricing.

Under Kline, the Farm Bureau supported variable price supports to balance supply with demand and to protect against extreme price declines, but it advocated production controls only if surpluses became excessive. These recommendations were consistent with the views of the three study groups noted earlier favoring a shift away from high, rigid price supports. But on the issue of direct payments to farmers, the Farm Bureau deviated. A resolution adopted at its December 1948 annual convention stated: "We feel that compensatory income or price payments are not a desirable way of supporting farm prices or of bringing income into agriculture."[10]

Early in 1948 a rare consensus prevailed among the farm organizations, the Democratic administration, and many Republican congressmen, for flexible (or variable) price supports. Even James Patton, president of the Farmers Union, shifted from his long-held high support posture to join the majority.[11] Opposition was strongest among southern Democrats who foresaw excess capacity as the crucial problem and believed that the "scarcity" approach of high price supports with restriction of output was essential to ensure acceptable farm incomes. The two views were combined, but not reconciled, in the Agriculture Act of 1948, also called the Hope-Aiken bill after its key congressional sponsors. The act extended for one year high-level price supports for many major commodities. After that, flexible price supports were to become effective.[12] After combining the two divergent views of farm price policy in one piece of legislation, the 80th Congress adjourned and its members departed for their respective party conventions.

Hindsight reveals that the prophets of burdensome surplus were most accurate. However, even they did not adequately anticipate the skyrocketing output which was to flow from the nation's farms as new technology was adopted ever more widely. A USDA study of future trends, prepared in 1948 for the House Committee on Agriculture, predicted farm output increases of one-fifth to one-fourth over the next twenty-five years. The realized rate was nearly double that envisioned. In the twenty-year period beginning with 1950, output climbed 38 percent.

The 1948 presidential campaign. Farm policy did not emerge as an important issue in the 1948 presidential campaign until autumn. Both the Democratic and Republican platforms endorsed flexible price supports and expansion of existing auxiliary programs, such as soil conservation and agricultural research. But a bumper corn crop brought falling prices and an end to midwestern farmers' lethargy concerning future farm prosperity. The Democrats seized the issue. Charles F. Brannan, who had succeeded Anderson as secretary of agriculture in May 1948, campaigned vigorously for Truman. Both Brannan and Truman claimed that the Democratic party was the farmer's friend and that the election of Dewey and a Republican Congress would bring a return of depression miseries to rural America. On September 18, 1948, in Dexter, Iowa, Truman delivered a major farm address to spectators and participants at the national plowing contest. He said, "How well you must remember the depression of the Nineteen Thirties. The Republicans gave you that greatest of all depressions, when hogs went down to three cents and corn was so cheap that you burnt it up." [13] Dewey spoke in Des Moines, Iowa, two days later but he did not rebut Truman's charge or address himself to farmers' immediate price concerns. The *New York Times* classified Dewey's speech as "an exposition of his general philosophy of government and the principles that guide his approach to governmental problems." [14] His lofty focus may be seen in this quotation: "As we chart our course for the years ahead, we must find the stars by which to sail. We must look to the fundamentals of our country. They're easy to find. . . . The roots of our country are not material. They are moral and spiritual. . . . Our magnificent America is the end result of the deep convictions of a great people devoted above everything else to faith in their God and the liberty and precious importance of every single human being." [15]

The relative merits of the idealistic versus "give 'em hell" appeals are disputable. But the fact remains that farm state voters contributed importantly to Truman's subsequent victory at the polls.

The 81st Congress. A Democratic Congress and administration reopened the farm policy debate in 1949. The action was stimulated by falling farm prices, campaign rhetoric, and southern Democrats' vehement opposition to the flexible price support provisions due to become effective on January 1, 1950, under the Hope-Aiken bill.

Congressional agricultural committee chairmen requested a new program from the USDA. In response, Secretary Brannan commissioned a series of departmental seminars to aid in formulating a program. The resulting proposal strongly bore Brannan's mark. It elucidated his philosophy of positive government and his goals of income equity for farmers and adequate, cheap food for all consumers. Supply and demand were allowed to determine market prices but acceptable incomes for family farmers were to be guaranteed by supplemental payments made to them by government when necessary.[16] Brannan presented his program to a joint hearing of the House Committee on Agriculture and the Senate Committee on Agriculture and Forestry, April 7, 1949.[17]

After Brannan's efforts at a major overhaul of the farm programs were defeated, the Agricultural Act of 1949 was enacted, modifying provisions of the Hope-Aiken bill but not altering the basic method of sustaining farm incomes by means of supported prices. Public discussion of the Brannan Plan continued even after its defeat, and subsided only with the onset of the Korean War in June 1950. Once again wartime demand mitigated the pressures of low prices and mounting surpluses, notably wheat.

During the Korean War farm spokesmen claimed that farm products should be exempt from price control ceilings imposed on other sectors of the economy to curtail inflation. Ceilings were assailed as unfair to farmers as well as unsound economic policy. The Farm Bureau phrased its objections thus: "They [price, wage and ration controls] interfere with production; impair the flexibility of our economy; reduce our capacity to expand output; require huge administrative staffs; and invite black markets."[18] The wartime market crises eased in 1952, reducing inflationary forces throughout the economy and shifting the focus of agricultural debates from price controls back to price supports. The war had only postponed the day of reckoning. In a presidential election year, however, the Congress was not ready to reexamine the entire farm question thoroughly; high price support legislation was extended through 1954 — two years into the next administration.

Thus ended a debate-filled interval in which new, imaginative farm policy ideas were widely discussed and examined, and none were enacted into law. The Congress was not convinced that free-market prices supplemented by income payments would yield adequate farm incomes at acceptable government costs. Price supports coupled with some cursory attempts at supply control remained as the politically acceptable farm policy.

A New Dimension in Farm Policy (1952–60)

"A technological explosion is occurring on American farms. Production per farm worker has doubled in the last 15 years. This creates a new dimension in farm policy and makes it virtually impossible to curtail agricultural output with the type of controls acceptable in our society." [19] In this letter Ezra Taft Benson, President Eisenhower's secretary of agriculture, delineated one of the major forces shaping the farm economy in the 1950s — catapulting productive capacity. This force led to supplies so excessive that public and private storage facilities overflowed. Meanwhile the farm work force shrank at a record rate. These trends created greater stresses within the agricultural sector than had ever before been experienced.

Another pervasive influence during this period was fear of communism. Any and all governmental involvement in the economic life of the nation was subject to the charge of being communistic. How this fear was related to farm policy was displayed by the secretary in an evaluation of the Brannan Plan. He wrote: "This philosophy that the government knows how to operate farms better than the farmers themselves is more than an academic theory. It is almost exactly the concept by which the Communist economies operate over nearly half of the earth." [20] This influence diminished as the 1950s waned but in the early years of the decade the Communist specter was frequently and rather effectively evoked to denigrate government action and aid. During the 1952 campaign its presence was especially evident.

The 1952 presidential election. The ideological issue was raised in the Republican platform which charged "the present Administration with seeking to destroy the farmer's freedom. . . . We condemn the Brannan Plan which aims to control the farmer and to socialize agriculture." [21] On the question of farm prices, the platform stated: "We favor a farm program aimed at full parity prices for all farm products in the market place. . . . We do not believe in restrictions on the American farmer's ability to produce." [22] Conversely the Democrats hailed existing high price supports and prescribed extending income protection to farmers producing perishables and other non-supported commodities. This position marked a shift from the Democrats' stand in 1948 when they along with the Republicans favored flexible supports.

The two platforms indicate different farm policy emphases but the planks were not precise enough to permit comparison of concrete program proposals. And to the surprise of many, the two presidential candidates, Eisenhower and Stevenson, appeared to take similar stands when both addressed a farm audience at the National Plowing Contest in Kasson, Minnesota. The essence of their speeches was captured by *New York Times* headlines: "Candidates bid for farm votes; Eisenhower favors full parity, but Stevenson cites GOP record.''[23] Eisenhower declared with vehemence that he stood behind ''the price support law now on the books . . . to continue through 1954 the price supports on basic commodities at 90 percent of parity.'' He went on to say that a fair share for farmers ''is not merely 90 percent of parity — it is full parity.''[24] These remarks were widely interpreted as going beyond the Republican platform by embracing high support levels. After Eisenhower's speech, Stevenson was left with little to challenge. He could only attack the past records of Republican congressmen and raise questions about their platform. Since both candidates seemed to favor the then current high supports, farm policy was abrogated as an election issue.

Farmers aided the Republican sweep of the executive and congressional offices, but, according to political analysts, the Korean War, not farm problems, was their primary concern. Although farm income had dropped from a 1951 peak, an alarming level had not yet been reached.

New policy directions emerge. Any uncertainties about the new administration's farm policy that may have existed during the campaign were soon to be dispelled. A change of direction was signified by Mr. Benson in his first speech as secretary of agriculture. The *New York Times* reported that he ''apparently set the tone for a major shift in the Government's over-all farm policies from what he called dependence on 'Government bounty' to a 'free market' economy.''[25] Ideas in the secretary's address were also contained in a ''General Statement on Agricultural Policy'' issued a few days earlier to members of the Congress and the press. The statement set forth Benson's guidelines for administering the U.S. Department of Agriculture and for formulating policy. These excerpts reveal Benson's underlying philosophy of government.

> The supreme test of any government policy, agricultural or other, should be ''How will it affect the character, morale, and well-being of our people?'' . . .
> . . . It [freedom] must be continually guarded as something more precious than life itself. It is doubtful if any man can be politically free who depends upon the state for sustenance. . . .
> Our agricultural policy should aim to obtain in the market place full parity prices of farm products and parity incomes for farm people. . . .
> In the administration of this Department, the guiding purpose will be to strengthen the individual integrity, freedom, and the very moral fiber of each citizen.[26]

Mr. Benson approached his task as secretary of agriculture with missionary zeal. He hoped to exert moral leadership consistent with his values, of which freedom was foremost. Such a view was not embodied in the existing agricultural legislation or in the Brannan Plan advanced by the previous administration. Both of the latter implicitly required some sacrifice of a farmer's economic freedom in order to gain a greater measure of economic justice and security. Benson presumably could see no justifiable compromise of freedom.

It would be a year before Benson's ideas were translated into farm program proposals. Then new legislation would be expected to replace the high-support measures scheduled to terminate at the end of Eisenhower's second year in office. In the interim, surpluses were accumulating and farm incomes were shrinking. There was a drop in net farm income of $2.5 billion between 1952 and 1954 while the value of CCC-owned stocks increased from $0.9 to $4.0 billion. Wheat was the major problem. The carryover swelled from a postwar low of 256 million bushels on July 1, 1952, to a new record high of 933 million bushels two years later. The situation demanded immediate and vigorous action.

Extension of flexible price supports to major storable commodities. Proposed new legislation was placed before the Congress in the president's farm message on January 11, 1954. He requested greater authority to employ flexible price supports in order to reduce incentives for overproduction, a freeze on stocks to prevent past surpluses from depressing future prices, and a special study of problems experienced by low-income, low-resource farmers. Later an export program, "Food for Peace," was introduced as a means to reduce surpluses through food aid programs for friendly less-developed nations. Although this last idea had been discussed in the Congress during 1953, it had not received administration endorsement until now.[27]

Food for Peace (P.L. 480) met little opposition and was enacted in July 1954. Bitter controversy, however, greeted the proposed shift to flexible price supports for the major crops. The conflict between the administration and the Congress was sufficiently compromised to enact the Agricultural Act of 1954. Under this act flexible price supports finally would become effective for the major crops, after years of dispute. The range of permissible adjustment, however, was less than the president desired. The compromise did not allow the strong action required by the farm income-surplus plight — neither control provisions nor economic disincentives were adequate to sufficiently curtail production.

Congress versus the executive. Congressional campaigns in the autumn of 1954 found Democrats forecasting dire straits for farmers stemming from flexible supports and Republicans lauding the Agricultural Act of 1954 as a means to "realistically adjust farm production to markets."[28] Democrats took control of both houses, but again farm issues did not seem to be among the major concerns of the electorate.

In the remaining two years of President Eisenhower's first term the conflict intensified between the new Congress and the Republican executive. The Congress passed measures in 1955 and 1956 to reinstate high, rigid price supports and the president vetoed both bills. At the end of the first term of the Eisenhower-Benson administration a virtual stalemate existed between the Congress and the executive on the issue of price supports.

Though no legislative steps were taken in 1955 or 1956 to protect farm incomes or to prevent overproduction, two new approaches to farm problems surfaced. One was the Soil Bank. This program aimed at the reduction of output through short- and long-term retirement of tilled land. In essence it authorized the government to rent cropland which was to be withdrawn from production. This approach was not entirely without precedent. It resembled the soil conservation programs, begun in the 1930s, which authorized payments for conservation practices on farmland. New, under the Soil Bank, was an official acknowledgment that too much land was employed in agricultural production. Until now most attention to the excess capacity problem of agriculture had centered on excess labor. Withdrawal of land from production for the stated purpose of reducing acreage in surplus crops had not previously been viewed as a politically acceptable idea.

The second innovation was an interdepartmental Committee for Rural Development created by the president to focus concern on the needs of the rural poor. It was the outgrowth of a study on problems of low-income farmers first proposed in the president's 1954 farm message. Among other proposals the study report recommended health, education, and welfare measures to alleviate the problems of rural poverty. This approach clearly separated problems and policies for low-resource farms from those for commercial agriculture. Again, this idea had its origin in earlier years. The need for separate approaches had been pointed out by the Colmer study in 1946, among others. Appropriations for rural development programs were meager and the impact small.

Another idea which gained adherents during the mid-fifties was the limitation of government payments according to farm size. Earlier Brannan had suggested payment restrictions as a means of protecting family farms. Now this idea gained bipartisan support for the additional reason of reducing government outlays. Nonetheless, strong opposition by southern Democrats prevented enactment of any meaningful payment limitation at this time. This issue gained momentum in the sixties.

The presidential election of 1956 sharpened official differences between the parties on their approaches to farm income problems. The Democrats pledged backing for high support levels, with production controls if necessary, and for direct payments to farmers when required for income maintenance. The Republican platform defended flexible support provisions as essential to avoid excess production and emphasized market expansion efforts to stimulate demand.

The breach widens. The ensuing four years of Eisenhower's administration saw a widening of the breach between the Congress and the executive. Although Democrats retained control of both chambers, the differences on farm policy did not follow party lines. Republican congressmen from farm states joined Democrats in sponsoring bills to prohibit dropping price supports as scheduled by current provisions, only to be met with administration opposition. The Republican farm revolt peaked on February 20, 1958, when "thirty farm area Republican Congressmen caucused and subsequently called on Secretary Benson and, in effect, asked for his resignation."[29] They believed present policies would cost the party congressional seats in the autumn election. In fact, Democrats did win important farm seats in November 1958.

Congressional wrath with Secretary Benson became acute. Agricultural committees in both chambers blamed him for the administration's farm policies, which they disavowed. The intensity of feeling is revealed in the following comments made by the agricultural committee chairmen when the secretary appeared respectively at House and Senate hearings. In rebuking the secretary, Representative Harold Cooley stated that he (Cooley) did "not believe that the facts and figures and statistics in your Department will support your philosophy and your reasoning that lower prices bring about lower production."[30] Senator Allen Ellender also castigated the secretary by sarcastically remarking, "Of course, if you put all the farmers out of business, by making price supports so low they can't go along, you might not get enough for the people of this country to eat, either."[31] Later Mr. Cooley continued his attack on administration policies in an address to the entire House. He depicted the plight of agriculture "after 4 long years of steady and devastating deterioration" as "still growing progressively worse," while "Secretary Benson was winning the great battle to bring down prices and to lower farm income."[32] He further censured the secretary by asserting, "Never on any occasion has he championed the cause of farmers."[33]

Policies advanced by the most influential farm organizations during this period, the Farm Bureau and the Farmers Union, closely paralleled those of the administration and congressional agricultural committees respectively. Throughout the 1950s the Farm Bureau prescribed "the principle of using changes in price support levels to encourage needed production adjustments and aid in moving excess supplies into market channels."[34] Its leaders echoed administration praise of free markets: "With less interference from government, the marketing system will be freer to operate effectively and efficiently. This will encourage the expansion of market outlets and the production of quality products in line with market demand. Thus we can better meet competition at home and abroad and gradually eliminate government regulation of individual farming operations."[35] Toward the end of the decade the Farm

Bureau leaders became increasingly aware of agriculture's growing excess capacity as output per man-hour and output per acre soared. They recognized the need of governmental action to redress the imbalance between supply and demand and were instrumental in convincing the administration it should advocate the Soil Bank to reduce production and P.L. 480 for expanding exports.

The leaders of the Farmers Union also recommended acreage reduction and food aid measures somewhat like those embodied in the latter two administration measures but their major emphasis was on firm price and income support. "We are definitely opposed to any type of variable, flexible or sliding scale price supports that brings lower support levels in response to more abundant farm production, regardless of whether the bottom of the scale is 60 percent of parity, 75 percent of parity or some other level." [36] They recommended "enactment of mandatory Federal farm income protection legislation at 100 percent of fair parity for the family farm production of all farm commodities. Means of protection should include production payments in workable combinations with price supporting loans, purchase agreements, purchases and other methods." [37] In 1958 their policy statement began to emphasize "bargaining power," the need for farmers to organize like business and labor to protect and promote farmers' interests in the marketplace. This idea would become the principal thrust of many farm spokesmen during the 1960s.

The 1950s ended with surpluses, distressed farm incomes, large-scale noncommercial government exports, and skyrocketing productivity advances. Output per farm worker had increased 68 percent during the decade while average annual net farm income slipped to $12 billion in 1957–59 from $15 billion in the war-influenced first years of the fifties. The decline in income occurred despite massive removal of farm products from commercial markets. The value of government-owned stocks increased to over $6 billion and shipments under P.L. 480 were valued at more than $1 billion in each year since 1956.

The Hard Choice

Dramatic attempts to redirect farm policy took place during the first half of the 1960s. Action was stimulated by the intensifying farm income and surplus problems and by a new element in the boiling farm policy cauldron — mounting pressures to reduce the costs of farm programs. An urbanized nation and Congress were losing sympathy for farmers and becoming impatient with their problems and the high federal expenditures for agriculture. Secretary Benson and others had emphasized the high costs repeatedly in speeches throughout the nation. In his final report to the American people, Benson said that "9 billion of taxpayers' dollars [are] tied up in surplus farm products" and that carrying charges on the surpluses was more than $1 billion a year; he called the problem "*not* just a farm problem — it is a national problem."[38] Scandals associated with storage of surplus commodities further aggravated the situation. Congressmen from rural districts and other farm leaders knew that something must be done.

Farm policy analyses. While legislative inaction and deepening problems were capturing public attention during the late 1950s, farm issues and policy alternatives received widespread examination by congressional committees, by presidential hopefuls, by agricultural economists in and out of government, and by others with an interest in farming. As a result of such pursuits these years became somewhat of a watershed period for the economic appraisal of the chronic excess-capacity, farm-income problem. A decade earlier agricultural economists had nearly unanimously recommended reliance on market prices to allocate productive resources while hailing flexible price supports as the best means to prevent extreme price variations. A full employment economy was expected to yield acceptable farm incomes provided that adjustment programs were employed (1) to assist those who wished to leave farming, (2) to guide farm production away from surplus commodities, and (3) to provide low-income consumers with the means for obtaining adequate diets. But it was now realized by many that advances in productivity were so widespread and rapid that the capacity to produce was growing faster than demand could be expanded, resulting in a chronic downward pressure on prices, in spite of the great exodus of workers and land from agricultural production and the emphasis on foreign food aid. This condition could be corrected by moving to a free market, but the wringing-out process in terms of business failure and asset devaluation would be more painful and prolonged than society was willing to accept. Hence, many agricultural economists and farm leaders concluded that movement to a free market was no longer a viable policy option.

One of the authors of this book was among those who changed his policy recommendations from the mid-forties to the late fifties as the impact of the technological explosion on U.S. farms became increasingly apparent. In 1945 Cochrane proposed that "individual commodity prices . . . be permitted to seek their own level" and that "two general type programs . . . be included to mitigate the economic consequence of a free market system."[39] The general programs were consumption adjustment and production adjustment programs to make the free-market situation tolerable to consumers and producers. By 1957 Cochrane thought that no one knew "how low support levels would have to go, but," he concluded, "they would have to go much lower and stay there a long time to bring production back into line with demand." Furthermore, he believed that "no political party in modern times could live through the social and economic unrest that the above action would entail."

He contended that the Eisenhower-Benson administration "in lowering price support levels to the neighborhood of 82 percent of parity has reached the lower limits of political tolerance with respect to farm prices." [40] In the 1945 statement Cochrane recognized that adjustment problems were an unavoidable consequence of price fluctuations in a relatively free market, but the resultant problems were not considered insurmountable. Twelve years later, however, he expected economic and social chaos to attend free-market pricing.

Elsewhere Cochrane proposed a solution. Under the assumption that society was unwilling to pay indefinitely for supported farm incomes and for costs of surpluses resulting from inadequately curtailed production, effective supply control seemed the only realistic alternative. He outlined a plan, later to be called "supply management," for gearing production of each commodity to estimated demand at an agreed-upon price. The price would be set to assure an acceptable income for producers. Under most circumstances farm incomes would derive solely from the sale of commodities in the marketplace; government loans and support payments would be provided only as insurance against price and income declines when market prices slipped below desired levels. The market price would be maintained by strict supply control, preventing surplus accumulation, and thereby eliminating a further source of government costs. The approach was likened to a public utility inasmuch as the government would set prices determined to be fair to producers and consumers and would oversee production and marketing to ensure that enough but not too much was marketed. [41]

Two subcommittees of the Senate-House Joint Economic Committee also studied rural problems in 1958 and 1959. One dealt with rural poverty as part of a broader study of low-income problems in the nation and the other devoted attention to needs of commercial agriculture. The latter subcommittee reported that "the failure of demand for farm products to expand as rapidly as farm productivity, together with other factors, is likely to exert strong pressures toward persistent surpluses of farm products, fewer employment opportunities in farming, a need for important adjustments in individual farm operations, and generally unfavorable income in commercial agriculture." [42] And in its judgment "production control will continue to be a main reliance for improvement of farm income. But controls will need to be more effective than those used in the past and permit more interfarm adjustment of production." [43]

Another analysis of agricultural policies prepared for congressional consideration stated that "if the general policy decision is to maintain or somewhat improve current incomes for farmers, particularly the 2 million commercial farmers who produce over 90 percent of our farm products, programs enabling farmers to produce at less than capacity or increased Government payments will be needed." This report also concluded that "farm prices and income would fall sharply if current farm price support, production control, and conservation reserve programs were dropped and not replaced by an alternative program or combination of programs . . . net income per commercial farm with sales of $2,500 or more in 1965 would be 30 percent lower than in 1959."[44]

Farm policy was also discussed at the American Farm Economic Association meeting in December 1959 where the free-market solution to the "farm problem" championed by the Eisenhower-Benson administration was defended and criticized. The defense, presented by Don Paarlberg, special assistant to the president and former assistant secretary of agriculture under Benson, followed lines of the classical economic argument sketched in the previous section.[45] In his critique, Robert L. Clodius called the policy a failure. "It should be evident," he said, "that the policy of flexing support prices downward and moving toward the free market has not reduced production enough, increased consumption, reduced surplus stocks, and solved the farm problem. . . . The only policy the Administration prefers in 1959 is flexing support prices still lower and moving righteously toward an agriculture free of controls. After observing that gasoline poured on a fire makes a bigger blaze, would any reasonable person advocate gasoline for fire fighting? This is the paradox that the Administration's view of agriculture presents and one that I hope to explain by pointing out that the Administration is not unreasonable; it is simply wrong."[46] Clodius went on to argue that the existing market structure did not fit the competitive model assumed by a free-market solution. He then proposed another course: a system of production goals based on marketing quotas which would be designed to meet estimated domestic and foreign demand at reasonable prices. His plan resembled Cochrane's public utility approach for solving income problems of commercial farmers. A discussant of the two papers, James T. Bonnen, claimed that "the bulk of farmers are likely to be shattered economically and politically by the end of Mr. Benson's short run."[47] As evidence Bonnen cited recent USDA and Iowa studies which estimated 25 to 40 percent declines in income to agriculture if free-market pricing prevailed.

Subsequent studies indicated similar income consequences and it was observed that thereafter "politicians ceased to advocate an immediate return to free prices, even though the theme was still popular with some constituents."[48] Another expression of disenchantment with the free market came in a speech by an Iowa farmer at the National Farm Institute in February 1960. "It is time for us farmers to take a hard look at the free competitive market as a method for regulating price, production and incomes in modern American agriculture. . . . For myself," he said, "I don't believe the natural adjustment processes of the free market will ever allow farmers to achieve equity in the exchange of their products for the products of modern corporate industry or modern organized labor. We should use the market for the functions that it can perform well. But for the immediate future I do not see how we can avoid fairly drastic measures to bring our exploding production under control." [49]

Threading through all these reports and statements is an acknowledgment that the free market was inadequate for achieving acceptable farm incomes at a time when supply increases flowing from new technology were outracing demand growth. This conclusion was not universally shared, however, as the 1960 presidential campaign would bring out. [50]

The 1960 presidential campaign. "*The farm issue boils down to production & marketing controls*, and price guarantees. Kennedy would have them; Nixon wouldn't, or only to a limited degree. The difference is sharp, and important. It goes to the very heart of the explosion in farm production, and to the basic difference between the parties: More gov't intervention, or less." [51] This synopsis pinpoints the key difference between Kennedy's and Nixon's solutions to the income problem of commercial farmers but it does not reveal the basic difference between the two in their assessments of the problem — Nixon viewed the income problem of farmers as temporary, Kennedy did not.

In a policy statement on agriculture Kennedy referred to "the small but chronic surplus in agriculture now depressing prices and incomes." [52] In contrast, Nixon was "staking all on ending surpluses within four years, and then letting farmers operate in free markets with a minimum of gov't. aid." His approach was similar to Benson's but differed in "that he'd give more protection to farm income during the trek back to free enterprise." [53] Proposals for domestic and foreign food distribution, farm credit, research, the rural poor, and other auxiliary agricultural programs did not appear to differ significantly between the two presidential candidates.

As was customary, platforms indicated in broad terms the direction and goals of farm policy for each party. "The Democratic platform included the widest pledge of assistance to farmers made in the postwar period, with emphasis on raising farm income. . . . The Republican platform . . . avoided pledges of high supports and emphasized the desirability of more individual freedom for the farmer with a 'minimum of federal interference and control.'" [54]

Vice-President Nixon elaborated on the themes of freedom and opposition to government controls in his farm addresses during the campaign: "what we want is to work toward a program of freedom from controls — get away from all this [sic] Federal Government activities — as far as our farm program is concerned. . . . After we get the surpluses reduced to manageable proportions then the farmers can regain their freedom to grow what they wish for markets freed of the burden of accumulated stocks of commodities." [55]

Farm policy guidelines set forth by Kennedy were founded on the supply management concepts advanced by Cochrane, who was Kennedy's farm adviser. Production control was at the heart of supply management and, of necessity, entailed some relinquishment of farmers' freedom to make all their own production decisions. But Kennedy did not consider the required sacrifice of freedom irrational or undesirable. Quite the contrary, it was his view that "men agree among themselves to limit their unrestricted 'freedom' in some field in order to achieve some other goal that is highly valued. . . . To give up freedom of action for nothing is nonsense. But to circumscribe to some degree complete freedom to act in one field, to achieve a highly prized and generally accepted goal is, I repeat, the act of rational and civilized men."[56]

Kennedy spelled out his program in general terms. Equitable incomes would be assured through supply management programs developed with the aid of producer groups and approved by them. But Kennedy knew that he was offering farmers a hard choice. In describing his program he said:

It gives you no assurances that you can have high incomes *and* unlimited production and no controls, without regard to the taxpayer. . . . we pledge ourselves to securing full parity of income . . . which gives average producers a return on their invested capital, labor and management equal to that which similar, or comparable, resources earn in non-farm employment. . . . But a basic instrument of assuring parity of income will be supply management controls — including the use of marketing quotas, land retirement with product diversion and other devices — to be used either together or separately, depending upon the needs of the specific commodity and the desires of the producers.[57]

Kennedy's cognizance of urban pressures to reduce farm program costs was one element, albeit an important one, in his dedication to supply management as a solution for farm price and income problems. He said, "total governmental expenditures for agriculture could be reduced by at least one billion per year at the same time as we achieve lasting solutions to several farm and farm related problems."[58]

The Democratic victory at the polls brought the new president and Congress to power when corn and wheat prices were at postwar lows and carryovers at all-time highs. It was too late in the season to introduce new wheat legislation since winter wheat was already sown, but legislation dealing with feed grains could be enacted before 1961 planting began. Under the direction of the new secretary of agriculture, Orville Freeman, USDA policy advisers drafted feed grain legislation. The administration sent a bill covering corn and grain sorghum to the Congress less than one month after the new team took office. It was known as the "emergency" Feed Grains Bill, and it was intended to be just that — a temporary provision for an emergency situation while permanent legislation was worked out.[59]

Kennedy long-range program. On March 16, 1961, still only a few weeks after inauguration day, the president sent a special message to the Congress containing his proposal for permanent agricultural legislation. It was designed to facilitate the supply management programs that Kennedy had outlined during the campaign. The central and most controversial feature of the bill subsequently submitted to the Congress was a procedural change which transferred to the executive the responsibility for drafting farm programs, granting the Congress veto but not amending power. The proposal relied heavily upon producer committees for determining the advisability of a program, and, if desired, for formulating the program provisions. The procedural change was defended as necessary in order to establish commodity programs which would effectively control supply, provide adequate farm incomes, and entail only modest expenditures. The bill died in committee.

When it became apparent that the procedural change would not be approved, the administration worked out a temporary alternative with the congressional agriculture committees. The revision extended for one year the "emergency" Feed Grains Bill, initiated a generally similar one-year measure for wheat, which included voluntary acreage reduction for payment, and continued for longer periods nondisputed items such as the Wool Bill and Food for Peace authorizations. The revised Agricultural Act of 1961 passed both houses with bipartisan support early in August. It was described by the leading adversary as "a major victory for those groups representing the vast majority of farmers who opposed the administration's scheme to control all farm commodities"[60] and by the administration "as the most constructive and promising farm legislation in many years."[61]

This seeming contradiction was due in part to a concentration on the procedural issue in congressional hearings and by the press which masked the significance of the new policy direction given impetus by the feed grain and wheat provisions. The policy change was observed by Wayne Darrow's *Washington Farmletter*:

Don't be deceived about how much Secretary Freeman lost. Examine what he gained. He was upheld in his supply-management idea in feed grain and wheat programs. . . .

Congress recognizes production control is the heart of the problem, the sine qua non — without which nothing. It denied him the procedures he sought to expedite controls, but acknowledged the principle.

The whole farm act breathes an agrarianism alien to Benson ideas. Whether you like it or not, the advocates of more government in agriculture won the battle. This will become more apparent the next few years.[62]

The administration abandoned efforts to persuade the Congress to delegate farm program formulation responsibilities to the Department of Agriculture after the unsuccessful 1961 airing. Instead, in 1962, the administration presented the Congress with a wide-ranging bill, entitled the Food and Agriculture Act of 1962. It contained several conservation and land-use features designed to develop farmland for recreational and other nonfarm purposes, an array of provisions to alleviate rural poverty both on farms and in rural communities, expanded domestic and foreign food aid programs, along with mandatory supply management programs for the most troublesome commodities at that time — wheat, feed grains, and dairy products. The title and scope of the act purposely emphasized concerns beyond the farm gate — in particular those of consumers and rural communities. There were two principal reasons for this strategy: first, a broader base of political support for farm legislation was sought, to counteract declining farm population, by emphasizing USDA benefits for nonfarm people; and second, the USDA wished to expand services to rural communities whose problems were increasing as off-farm migration continued.

Program costs were one of the main constraints confronting program formulators. Reduction of farm program expenditures was a top priority item of the Kennedy administration, so consultation with and approval by the Budget Bureau were a prerequisite at each step in the decision-making process. An opposing pressure was exerted by farm groups sympathetic with the administration. They pressed for more costly measures with higher income goals and program features attractive enough to be reasonably popular among their farmer constitutents. A third constraint on program formulators, to assuage urban congressmen, was the need to assure little or no increase in food prices as a consequence of farm income support programs.

Amid these conflicting pressures, the Food and Agriculture Act of 1962 was debated. The Farm Bureau and Republican congressmen in both chambers fought the bill. Loss of economic freedom was their chief argument. Republicans from farm areas who had joined Democrats in opposing Benson's policies now united with their party colleagues against the supply management programs. Grudging congressional approval was finally won for a bill containing voluntary provisions for feed grains and mandatory controls only for wheat. The act was signed by the president in September 1962. Because of its late passage the new wheat program would not become effective until the 1964 crop year. The 1962 wheat program was extended to cover the 1963 crop.

The wheat referendum. The new wheat bill was a major legislative innovation. Passage itself, though, was little cause for relaxation and celebration by the administration because successful enactment was only the first hurdle on the path toward a supply management program for wheat. Before becoming operative, the program required approval by two-thirds of the wheat producers voting in a referendum. If not approved, a less restrictive program offering much lower price supports would apply. The choice was popularly phrased as $1.00 or $2.00 wheat. Preceding the referendum, scheduled for May 1963, proponents and opponents engaged in strenuous drives to win votes.

The administration launched a large-scale campaign to inform the farmers of the program and of the referendum. Its assumption was that a "yes" vote was the logical outcome if the two alternatives were understood by farmers. Within the USDA, however, there was not unanimous agreement on the nature of its role or the extent of backing that the department should give. Some thought the department should promote the program while others believed a neutral stance should be maintained. After some initial selling efforts, department spokesmen essentially engaged in an informational campaign.

Critics also plunged into the fray with vigor. Their primary weapon was to deny that the choice was really as stated in the referendum. If the referendum were defeated, they argued, Congress would not permit wheat prices to drop as scheduled but would enact another, more satisfactory program. The Farm Bureau led the opposition forces. Much of its effort was directed toward small-acreage wheat farmers previously exempt from acreage restrictions. It charged that farmers were being asked to surrender their freedom to an unprecedented extent. One of the bureau's leaflets stated: "The real issue in the Wheat Referendum is . . . 'Freedom to Farm.' " A resolution passed at the bureau's 1962 annual meeting said: "In 1963 wheat producers have the responsibility to make the most important decision with respect to the future of the nation's farm business that any group of farmers has ever faced. The basic issue before them is whether American agriculture is to remain free or whether we shall turn to a system of farming by government directives." [63]

Organized support came through a National Wheat Committee formed by groups favoring the program. These included the Grange, the Farmers Union, the Grain Terminal Association (a grain storage and marketing cooperative), and the National Association of Wheat Growers. Their campaign stressed the basic premise of the supply management advocates: farmers could not "expect Government to maintain support prices at a satisfactory price level on ALL the wheat that American farmers can produce, even on the 55 million acres defined as the MINIMUM NATIONAL ALLOTMENT." [64] They were less well organized and financed and less devoted to their cause than the "vote no" enthusiasts. One reason was that some felt the income goals of the program were too low to be acceptable to farmers.

Political analysts of the issue described the referendum as follows:

Circumstances were in the Farm Bureau's favor in the endeavor to make farmers act out of desire for freedom rather than on the basis of the ostensible referendum issues. The referendum was coming at the end of a three-year string of good crops in the commercial wheat area, so many farmers could afford the luxury of voting "no." It also followed eight straight years of acreage controls, during which many farmers had accumulated grievances against local administrators of the program, and all had been obliged to watch productive land lying idle, and to plow up beautiful green wheat acreages (used for pasture) just before the wheat began to bud.

To aggravate farmer frustration with controls, the Farm Bureau dubbed the new wheat program "the tightest, strictest, most complete control plan ever considered for a major farm commodity," a statement which other observers said was untrue. "That is extreme language and it is careless language," said an editorial in the respected *Des Moines Register*, which was reprinted by supporters of the program and distributed all across the country. Farm Bureau speakers, to prove their point, came up with eight new "controls," but the proponents replied by noting five new "flexibilities," and when Congress authorized the free interchange of wheat and feed-grains allotments in an expected though last-minute action, little basis remained for the Farm Bureau's strong words.[65]

An unusually large turnout of voters defeated the proposed wheat program in referendum. In commenting on the referendum, Democratic leaders could hardly disguise their resentment at the verdict. Chairman Ellender said, "Democracy has spoken and wheat farmers have voted themselves out of a program. I wish them well." Secretary Freeman observed: "The point of view which prevailed in the referendum is entitled to a full and fair trial." [66] He then sat back to await developments.

Winter wheat was planted in the autumn of 1963 with the virtually free-market price provision in force. A redeeming measure, however, was well en route through the Congress, just as the opposition had predicted. Hadwiger and Talbot say that "the idea for the new program originated with a Freeman staff member but had to be smuggled out of the USDA because Freeman had placed a moratorium on staff work on any new proposals following the referendum."[67]

Two other noteworthy events intervened before a new wheat bill emerged from congressional committees. First, wheat sales to Russia were authorized and, second, President Kennedy was assassinated and succeeded by Lyndon Johnson. Relaxation of trade barriers with Communist countries was initially approved by John F. Kennedy and after his death the policy was reaffirmed by President Johnson. Many Republican spokesmen criticized the move and attempted to block the sale through congressional maneuvers. Richard Nixon remarked, "What we're doing is subsidizing Khrushchev at a time when he is in deep economic trouble. . . . It pulls his economy out of a very great hole and allows him to divert the Russian economy into space and into military activities that he otherwise would have to keep in agriculture." [68] Obstructing efforts failed, and the sale was consummated, opening a new potential market for U.S. commodities.

Johnson's first year. Lyndon B. Johnson assumed the presidency about three years after the Democrats had replaced the Republicans in the White House. During these years total government costs for storage and handling of agricultural commodities had been diminished because of substantial reductions in government-owned stocks of wheat and feed grains. Moreover, there was a reversal in the post–Korean War downward trend of farm income — annual net farm income averaged $12.5 billion for 1961–63 compared with $11.9 billion for the last three years of the Eisenhower administration. On the debit side, the goal to lower government outlays for agricultural programs had not been achieved; however, that possibility had been premised upon enactment of the strict supply-management programs, now defeated. Net USDA expenditures associated with price support programs totaled $7.0 billion for Benson's last three years and $7.5 billion for Freeman's first three years. Though net spending changed little, the funds were directed to different recipients in the two periods. Under Benson large costs borne by the government were incurred by the grain trade for handling the enormous surpluses. Now more government payments were going to farmers. Farm income derived from government payments climbed from $2.5 billion to $4.9 billion in the two three-year periods under consideration. This occurred while cash receipts from farm marketing likewise increased, boosting farm income even more.

When Johnson took command, bills for cotton and wheat were brewing in the Congress. Generally acceptable feed grain legislation was already enacted covering 1964 and 1965 crops so feed grains presented no imminent concern. In his first farm message to the Congress, the new president urged prompt passage of cotton and wheat measures. His stated farm program objectives were "to maintain and improve farm income, strengthening the family farm in particular" and "to use our food abundance to raise the standard of living both at home and around the world." [69] He additionally emphasized the need to improve conditions of the rural poor. This was linked to one of Johnson's major domestic thrusts — the War on Poverty.

Less than three months after the Congress received the message a bill containing cotton and wheat programs for 1964 and 1965 was signed into law. Passage of the bill was attributed to four major factors: the combination of wheat and cotton measures to unite southern and midwestern Democrats; the backing from the textile industry because of a subsidy for domestic cotton; the support from urban congressmen, gained by linking this bill with a measure expanding the Food Stamp Program; and pressure from the White House.[70]

Late in the summer, only a few months before the presidential election, the anti-poverty bill and a meat import quota act were passed. The former included special provisions for mitigating rural poverty. The idea that problems of the rural poor could not be solved by programs for commercial agriculture had been gaining recognition but it had not yet come of age. Two more years would pass before the president would appoint a public commission to study rural poverty, thus singling out the problem for national attention.

The meat import issue had surfaced a few years earlier as rising imports from New Zealand and Australia alarmed U.S. livestock producers. The new act required that the secretary of agriculture impose quotas on imports to protect the domestic producers' share of the market. This move toward protectionism conflicted with the administration's general trade policies and, furthermore, aggravated a rift within agriculture. Producers and marketers of export commodities feared that demand for their products would be curtailed by other nations in retaliation for this action by the United States. The dispute between opponents and proponents of free trade remains a burning issue into the 1970s.

Farm issues did not loom large in the presidential campaign of 1964. There was no crisis of farm prices or incomes to inflame agricultural interests and, as surpluses shrank, nonfarm ire concerning overflowing government storehouses had subsided. Moreover, politicians and farm leaders presumed that the contracting farm population, less than 7 percent of the nation in 1964, was losing political muscle.

The party platforms indicated diverse positions on agriculture, yet neither party delineated a new farm program. The theme of freedom from government controls was once again repeated by the Republicans while the Democrats reiterated the three goals President Johnson had spelled out in his farm message earlier in the year: higher incomes for farmers, lower prices for consumers, and improvement in the living conditions of the rural poor. The Democratic farm plank also mentioned reduction of federal costs.

President Johnson did not deliver a major farm address during the campaign but frequently praised farm programs among other Democratic legislative accomplishments in his speeches. He relied mainly upon his running mate, Senator Hubert H. Humphrey, to win rural Midwest votes. Humphrey campaigned strongly in predominately agricultural communities, but only his speech at the National Plowing Contest in North Dakota concentrated primarily on farm policy. He indicated that the administration would abandon efforts to enact compulsory production controls, seeking instead to improve voluntary programs. Mostly, however, he attacked past Republican policies and raised doubts about the devotion to agricultural interests of the GOP standardbearer, Senator Barry Goldwater.

The Republicans also paid considerable attention to rural voters in the Midwest. This area had traditionally been a Republican stronghold, but dedication had wavered during the depression and in the Benson years. In

Goldwater's book *The Conscience of a Conservative*, he had proposed ending farm programs, including support of government-operated rural electrification and flood control projects. The latter two government programs were widely approved by farmers of all political persuasions; hence the Republicans found it necessary to assure farm voters that no drastic changes would be undertaken. Goldwater preceded Humphrey on the platform at the plowing contest but, according to the *New York Times*, "devoted less than half of his speech in North Dakota to that problem [farm policy]. . . . He called price support programs 'absurd' and 'self-defeating' . . . he said he believed that a 'gradual decline' of supports would be good for farmers. . . . The bulk of his agricultural remarks," in the opinion of the *Times* reporter, "comprised a denunciation of the Democratic party's farm programs and of the Secretary of Agriculture."[71]

The voters returned a Democratic executive and Congress, now with a decisive majority in both chambers.

The Food and Agriculture Act of 1965. One of the major victories scored by the Johnson administration and the new 89th Congress was passage of an omnibus four-year farm bill covering cotton, wheat, feed grains, rice, dairy products, and wool, along with long-term cropland retirement provisions. Passage marked the end of vociferous, and often inflammatory, congressional debate for nearly two decades. In each session the Congress had been confronted with an expiring farm bill for one or another of these commodities or with a low-price, surplus crisis that demanded attention. For the next four years the Congress would be freed of annual reexamination of these farm programs, unless some unforeseen event intervened, since the bill granted the secretary of agriculture enough flexibility to adjust commodity programs to satisfy farm income and budgetary objectives. A synopsis of the legislative history of this omnibus bill follows.

The president had introduced his ideas for farm legislation in a message to the Congress on February 4, 1965. As in 1964, he stressed the "need to separate the social problems of rural America from the economic problems of commercial agriculture" and the goal of "a workable balance between supply and demand at lower costs to the Government."[72] He recommended continuation and improvement of the existing commodity programs, remarking:

> Our farm programs must always be adapted to the requirements of the future. Today they should be focused more precisely on the opportunity for parity of income for America's family farmers and lower Government costs. But we must recognize that farm programs will be necessary as long as advance in agricultural technology continues to outpace the growth of population at home and markets abroad. . . .
>
> Our objective must be for the farmer to get improved income out of the marketplace, with less cost to the Government.[73]

Notice that the reduction of farm program costs remained a paramount goal.

The Kiplinger Agricultural Letter interpreted the message as a tough line for commercial agriculture. "What Johnson wants," it stated, "is to gut the USDA's big spending programs on commodities. He stays convinced that big farmers don't need them. . . . This means moving the gov't out of commodity markets gradually, slowly, so as not to panic farmers, jolt economy, rile farm congressmen. And that means important piecemeal changes over the next few years, during which time gov't farm program spending will continue to run high."[74]

In the draft bill sent to Congress by the administration program cost reductions were to be achieved by transferring to consumers some costs formerly borne by taxpayers. The domestic food markets for wheat and rice were to absorb supported prices for these commodities, while production for export would be protected at about world market prices, entailing little or no government expense. Strong opposition defeated these efforts to pass along total costs to consumers. After a cost reduction feature for wool also met with defeat, more expensive programs were approved for all three commodities. Other provisions advanced by the administration were accepted with little controversy, and a cotton bill formulated by congressional agricultural committees was added to the original package.

The final bill continued and extended the general form of supply control and income support instruments first combined in the emergency feed grain program for 1961. Positive experience with the feed grain program and the negative political realities learned about mandatory controls from the wheat referendum made this type of voluntary control politically acceptable. This broad and complex bill sailed through the Congress with relative ease in contrast with vehement struggles over past agricultural legislation. While the bill was under congressional consideration, Don Paarlberg, a member of the previous and the subsequent Republican administrations, observed that "Democrats have not been pointing to the farm program with very much pride and Republicans have not been viewing with much alarm. This forbearance makes reasonable legislation eventually more probable. With neither party forcing the other into a corner, both can be more flexible and some accommodation becomes more readily possible."[75] After one year in operation, the 1965 act was praised for its accomplishments even by traditional opponents to governmental involvement in any economic matter. For example, the following assessment appeared in an article in *Fortune*:

In some respects, supply management has performed pretty well. Certainly, it offers a more rational way to deal with overproduction than the programs that preceded it. Instead of letting unwanted grain accumulate and run up immoderate storage bills for the government, supply management has held down output by keeping land out of cultivation — about 60 million acres in 1966. By letting crops move at market-determined prices, it has strengthened the importance of the marketplace. The more realistic market prices, in turn, helped reduce surpluses by encouraging foreign purchases of U.S. farm commodities.

The costs of supply management to the Treasury have been very high — and would have been even higher if the increased exports had not helped to bring supply and demand into balance. But the money is going out in different ways. Direct payments to farmers have gone up sharply within the past few years, largely for diverting land from crops, but the price supports extended on crops have gone down, and so, of course, have storage costs. Under supply management, then, more government money goes to farmers and less to storage operators. That, even critics admit, at least seems more rational.[76]

But the act was not perfect. Weaknesses received scrutiny from those favoring the general principles of supply control and farm income support as well as from critics. According to James T. Bonnen the legislation contained a built-in economic and political dilemma:

With voluntary programs, the unrelenting pressure of significant annual increases in yields means that budget costs go up each year — even if you are only maintaining the same level of farm income. Each year politicians are faced with a "Hobson's choice" between greater budgetary costs or higher prices to the consumer (via certificate type systems), or — failing increases in either budget or prices — lower total farm income. If in the process of making political choices it is decided that farm program budgets must be reduced, then farm income must fall as a direct consequence, unless the costs of these programs can be transferred to the consumer. This is the economic dilemma. It is also a political dilemma since each of these variables — budget, consumer costs, and farm income — involves politically potent interests.[77]

Earlier Cochrane had cited the same phenomena and proceeded to predict a collision between program costs and governmental budget limitations.

. . . if this collision course argument is correct, then one thing is certain. The urban voter must give way with respect to budget objectives, or the farmer must give way with respect to the present level of price support under a system of voluntary controls. For 10 years the urban voter has been beating a Fabian retreat with regard to farm program costs. But I for one believe that the retreat is about over. Thus, I believe that farmers will be forced, in the next 3 to 10 years, to accept some major changes in the present policy of price and income protection.[78]

A period of relative calm. After the heated disputes began in 1948 over the Brannan Plan, a storm of controversy about farm programs raged in the Congress and in farm communities throughout the nation; but following enactment of the 1965 act the protagonists in the grueling farm policy debate relaxed to some extent, perhaps more exhausted than contented. But reality also supported the calm. The new four-year legislation did prove reasonably successful in maintaining acceptable farm incomes. Total net farm income crept upward slowly while the continuing outward flow of population from agriculture meant a fairly rapid advance in per family incomes. Median money income of farm families climbed from $2,875 in 1960 to $4,119 in 1965 and further increased to $5,769 by 1968. Meanwhile the number of farm families shrank from 3.8 to 2.6 million. The overall price level of farm output also began to trend upward slightly, after nearly a decade of stagnation.

Farm policy, however, cannot be given full credit for the improvements in farm prices and incomes. Strong export demand, particularly in the middle 1960s, siphoned off excess supplies, removing from the market the threat of accumulated surpluses. The principal source of export market strength came from extraordinary import demand in India, where drought caused two successive crop failures.

The world food crisis. Besides its immediate impact on trade, the threatened famine in India created a stir within U.S. agricultural circles. The fear of widespread starvation while U.S. agricultural productivity was held in check stimulated many to call for abolishment of production controls. Those with humanitarian motives, opponents to controls in general, and those who would profit by expansion of output in the United States, such as farm supply industries, urged unlimited production. These were welcome words to many in the USDA and the Congress who saw dual benefits flowing from unleashing U.S. agricultural productive capacity — a solution to the income plight of U.S. farmers and a contribution to world peace. Secretary Freeman became a leading spokesman for this appealing cause. In October 1966 he said:

. . . the encouraging advances in per capita food production among the developing countries that encouraged us during the 1950's have been reversed.

As of today, we are not winning the war against hunger. The grim, Apocalyptic figure of Famine gallops across the earth, casting an ominous, lengthening shadow over the immediate years ahead.

Virtually all the studies since World War II have underestimated population growth and, hence, the demand for food, and they have overestimated the developing countries' ability to accept improved techniques for food production. The net result is increasing food deficits throughout two-thirds of the world. Once, not so long ago, we discussed the food-people problem as though it were a problem of the future. It is not. It is here now.[79]

Controls were eased but not eliminated for 1967 crops. Yet the secretary did not believe that the United States and other developed nations could be the breadbaskets for the world indefinitely. He pleaded for crash programs to aid developing countries in controlling population growth and in accelerating their food production. Without such efforts he predicted an ominous future.

With fully four-fifths of the 3 billion people-increase projected by the turn of the century added to the developing countries, where food already is in short supply, we can then expect to find by the Year 2000:

A world where the developed nations sacrifice compassion on the altar of survival — feeding only themselves as they huddle behind arms-and-tariff-protected borders.

A world where the trickling food supply of the hungriest lands runs dry before it reaches everyone . . . and millions succumb to starvation. . . .

When this occurs, the developed nations that did not act when there was still time to act will learn the harshest lesson of all — that there is no peace, there can be no security in a world where population smothers the land and hunger takes to the streets.[80]

While the world food crisis captured headlines, U.S. food aid policies were receiving an intensive examination in the Congress. Since the inception of P.L. 480 in 1954, the objective of surplus disposal had predominated. In 1966 the act was amended to shift the focus to foreign aid goals. Consistent with the secretary's assessment of the world food situation the new policy encouraged recipient countries to become self-sufficient by improving their own agricultural productivity and by controlling population growth.

The furor over the use of American food to feed the world's hungry was relatively short-lived. Output advances, flowing from Green Revolution developments and improved weather, sharply reduced import demand for food grains in Asia, stifling the hopes of those who pressed for all-out production in the United States. This issue, however, reemerged in the 1970s when grain production fell short of needs in many nations.

Other issues. Other noteworthy events of the mid-1960s included reports to the president from three commissions he had appointed earlier: the National Commission on Food Marketing, the National Advisory Commission on Food and Fiber, and the National Advisory Commission on Rural Poverty. These reports and the technical studies which accompanied them provided the basis for many future policy analyses and proposals.

The study of the food industry by the National Commission on Food Marketing was precipitated by congressional concern over a widening spread between prices consumers paid for food and prices received by farmers. The final report suggested that some reduction in the farm-retail price spread might be possible if all marketing firms introduced efficiencies not universally practiced, but the spread would remain wide because processing and distribution functions cannot be eliminated without reducing services desired by consumers. Moreover, inflationary forces were found to have a greater effect at the retail level than at the farm level, further enlarging the farm-retail gap.

The appearance of the food marketing report coincided with a public outcry over rising food prices. Food prices rose rapidly in 1965 and 1966, sparking boycotts of supermarkets by housewives in several cities throughout the nation. The charges focused mainly on promotional schemes employed by retailers. The consumers blamed trading stamps, contests, and advertising for high food prices. These advertising and promotional activities were among the issues examined by the marketing commission.

It was the opinion of the majority of commission members that "while some of the selling function — advertising, sales promotion, salesmen — is socially productive, most of the costs incurred to sway consumers toward one seller or product rather than another add little of value to the food consumers buy. The selling function could not be eliminated in most instances, but in principle, it might be substantially reduced without impairing the value of final products to consumers."[81] Despite these and other suggestions for improving the industry, the commission concluded "that the contribution of the food industry to a high and rising level of living in the United States was fully comparable with that of other leading sectors of the economy."[82]

The Food and Fiber Commission was appointed "to make a penetrating and long-range appraisal of our agricultural and related foreign trade policies in terms of the national interest, the welfare of our rural Americans, the well-being of our farmers, the needs of our workers, and the interests of our consumers."[83]

The commission concluded:

. . . the time has arrived for a major shift in the direction of U.S. food and fiber policy.

Our burdensome surpluses have largely disappeared.

Foreign demand for food is growing rapidly.

Technology and capital will continue to flow into agriculture, and the necessary changes in farm employment, farm size, and production patterns will lag behind unless more positive efforts are made to encourage the inevitable adjustments.[84]

It recommended that

. . . the United States adapt its policies to accomplish a market-oriented agriculture. . . .

A market-oriented agricultural policy would aim at improving the farmer's income in the long run by reducing the overcapacity of the industry. Positive steps would be taken by Government to encourage adjustment of cropland and to help the people who are leaving agriculture anyway, under any policy, to make better incomes in nonfarm occupations. Government assistance to farmers would be furnished in ways which least interfere with the functioning of markets.[85]

Among suggestions for commercial farm policy:

The commission recommends that price supports be set modestly below a moving average of world market prices. . . .

Under present conditions of surplus production capacity, it is clear that most farmers cannot earn parity incomes through the market alone. . . .

Direct payments can be made to farmers to protect their incomes with less interference to the market than with high price supports, export subsidies, and import quotas.

THE MAJORITY OF THE COMMISSION RECOMMENDS, THEREFORE, THAT DIRECT COMMODITY PAYMENTS BE MADE TO FARM PRODUCERS TO ENABLE EFFICIENT COMMERCIAL FARMERS TO RECEIVE PARITY INCOMES, WHEN RETURNS FROM THE MARKET DO NOT PROVIDE SUCH INCOMES.[86]

In addition to recommendations concerning commercial farm policy, the report included proposals to alleviate adjustment problems of low-income rural residents and noncommercial farm families, to expand agricultural trade, and to reorient aid programs for less-developed nations toward improving indigenous production capacity and away from perennial reliance on food aid.

Major disagreement occurred within the commission over the role of commodity programs in a "market-oriented agriculture." The majority, composed mostly of producers and agricultural economists, foresaw an indefinite need for government assistance because they believed that pressures to increase supply were likely to continually exceed forces stimulating demand and, even if excess capacity could be eliminated, they concluded that "standby programs providing for price supports at or near world price levels, supply adjustment mechanisms, and income deficiency payments should be provided for."[87] Business executives from food and fiber firms, three university administrators, and representatives from some commodity associations constituted the minority. They disapproved of price supports as a long-run policy, believing that only market forces should determine prices. In their view incomes could be protected by supplemental government payments similar to unemployment compensation, if farmers experienced a temporary income deficiency.

The Commission on Rural Poverty documented the plight of 14 million poor living in substandard conditions in rural areas throughout the nation. "Most of the rural poor," it found, "do not live on farms."[88] The commission reaffirmed that commercial farm programs do not serve the poor in rural areas and it went on to cite how some agricultural programs actually aggravated the situation for noncommercial farmers and other rural residents. In the commission's judgment past programs directed toward low-income rural families had been inadequately financed and general social welfare and labor legislation had ignored or discriminated against the nonurban populace. Its recommendations included a wide range of policies and actions to change and improve rural institutions, and to provide means of improving living conditions for rural residents.

Several other farm issues came to the fore in the mid-sixties which have aroused increasing attention since then. One is concern about environmental effects caused by the use of agricultural chemicals and by farm practices such as land drainage and feed lot runoffs. Another is farm bargaining. Some farm groups believe that farm prices could be raised if farmers had more power in the marketplace. They have proposed a variety of measures generally similar to labor laws which would establish a framework for government-supervised bargaining between buyers and sellers of farm products. The National Farmers Organization (NFO) captured headlines for this issue by organizing withholding actions for milk and livestock in some midwestern states. A third issue involves working conditions of farm labor and rights of workers to organize into unions. And lastly, domestic food programs came under attack, highlighted during the 1968 Poor People's March to Washington, D.C. None of these issues is yet resolved.

A Low Profile for Farm Policy

The 1965 act reconsidered. During the summer of 1968, the Congress debated extension of the Food and Agriculture Act of 1965 beyond 1969, its expiration date. Permanent extension had been proposed by President Johnson, and he was backed by a coalition of about twenty farm groups. The coalition, formed at the instigation of the Grange, included the Farmers Union, the National Farmers Organization, and several commodity groups. Leaders of these farm organizations were willing to disregard some disagreements and work together, in order to attempt passage of sympathetic farm legislation which they believed would become increasingly difficult as the Congress became more and more urban-oriented. Of the major farm organizations, only the Farm Bureau did not join this new united front. Instead, the bureau lobbied against any extension of the existing act. Congressional Republicans also opposed long-term extension but eventually accepted a one-year continuation since this would allow the next administration, which they hoped would be Republican, enough time to draft a new measure without a pressing deadline.

Many amendments were proposed. Among the main revisions was one to impose payment limitations. With considerable justification advocates of limitations claimed that payments larger than $20,000 to any one farmer were indefensible as a necessary income support. Those opposing the limitation agreed. Nonetheless, they upheld the existing practice, asserting that effective output control required participation in programs by large producers and that payment restrictions would make it unprofitable for large producers to comply with voluntary supply control programs. The payments limitation question was not resolved in 1968; a compromise solution was reached in 1970.

An unamended version of the 1965 act seemed the only possibility in an election year. But the Congress remained deadlocked until word came from Nixon's campaign headquarters that he would accept a one-year extension.

The unamended bill to extend the act for one year cleared the Congress late in September. Nearly everyone understood that this merely postponed any serious consideration of farm legislation until a new administration was installed in January 1969.

The 1968 election. Farm policy was not an issue in the 1968 presidential campaign. Because extension of the 1965 act was still under debate when party platforms were being drafted and campaigning begun, it was difficult to delineate a clear-cut farm issue. Republicans could not vehemently attack a farm program which they might help to pass and the Democrats could not chastise the Republicans for a stand not taken. Then, after Nixon favored the extension, no viable issue was left.

Moreover, the intensity of problems in the commercial farm sector remained at a relatively low point. As mentioned, incomes for farm families had climbed steadily during the 1960s, narrowing the gap between farm and nonfarm incomes. Per capita income of the farm population rose to about three-fourths of nonfarm per capita income in the late 1960s compared with about one-half a decade earlier. Commenting on farm problems during that period, Lauren Soth, editorial page editor of the *Des Moines Register*, said: "Even those of us in farming and in close communication with farming must admit that the business problems of agriculture really are not pressing."[89]

What pressures there were to change significantly farm policy arose not from the farm sector but from those who paid for government programs, especially the urban taxpayers. But even these pressures, manifested in the Congress by the efforts to curtail government payments to large farmers, did not create enough concern to make farm policy an election issue in 1968.

The farm plank in the Democratic platform recommended that current programs be continued and improved, without specifying what improvements should be made. The Republican platform was even more vague. It called for "farm policies and programs which will enable producers to receive fair prices in relation to the prices they must pay for other products."[90] In accord with the general platform emphasis on the need to control inflation, the farm plank stressed reduction of farm production costs. Despite the lack of a specific farm program proposal, it was obvious that the position of the 1968 Republicans diverged from their stand in 1964 and previous postwar presidential campaigns. Until now they had repeatedly called for the removal of government from agriculture.

Neither Mr. Nixon nor Vice-President Humphrey devoted a major speech to farm problems or programs. Agriculture Secretary Freeman, the principal Democratic spokesman on farm issues, recited accomplishments of Democratic administrations and challenged Nixon to spell out his plans. Although Nixon never presented a program he expressed displeasure with the current law. After eight years' absence, the Republicans recaptured the White House but the Democrats retained control of the Congress, setting the stage for future legislative struggles.

Speculation on future policy directions. When the new administration took office, farm policy observers had no clear signals on what course new policy might take. President Nixon's appointment of Clifford Hardin as the new secretary of agriculture left future farm policy directions unknown because Secretary Hardin was not identified with any particular program. Neither the president nor the secretary came into office with any commitment on farm commodity policy. The uncertainty felt in Washington was expressed by the *Farm Journal*:

"He's a Hard Man to Shoot At." That's what both friend and foe in Washington, D.C. are saying about the new Secretary of Agriculture, Clifford M. Hardin. "How can you shoot at him when you don't know where he stands on anything — and when he might even be on your side?" say likely critics. But Republicans who want to support him have qualms, too: "How can you go all-out for a guy when you don't know what his position will be?" . . .

Republican Farm Congressmen are confused. Nobody has told them what the Nixon Administration will do on farm matters. Some influential farm Republicans on the Hill weren't even consulted on the choice of Secretary of Agriculture. One says of the Nixon team: "I don't know who they think is going to be ram-rodding their program up here in Congress."[91]

Despite the lack of a definitive policy, there was a general and understandable feeling by the new "team" that they had to do something different from what the preceding Democratic administration had done. Some indication of Mr. Hardin's position began to emerge during Senate questioning preceding his confirmation as secretary. "The Senate group made clear they felt farmers would continue to need price support. Hardin agreed, adding that he hoped farm income would be not only maintained, 'but hopefully improved.' Regulation of production, he said, will continue to be needed. Hardin noted again that he and his aides mean to spend at least a year in developing new approaches to farm problems."[92]

In response to further questions from the Senate committee the new secretary said no drastic changes would be made in programs for 1969 and 1970 but for the future "Hardin hinted that extensive land retirement might be one answer. Committee members warned him that such a program would need to be worked out very carefully if farmers and rural economies were not to suffer. The new secretary agreed."[93]

Policy formulation. The secretary appointed a committee within the USDA to review programs and to prepare policy recommendations. He also scheduled seven "Look and Listen" conferences in farm areas scattered throughout the nation to obtain reaction from the public on farm problems and programs. But this scholarly approach to policy formulation was unsatisfactory to some farm leaders who were anxious to speed up the process. In an editorial entitled "Let's Get Moving," the *Farm Journal* described the situation as follows:

This Act [the 1965 Act] expires with the 1970 crop season, and if there is to be any real change in farm programs, it's urgent that we get started on the job.

Farmers need plenty of lead time to change their management and bring their long-range plans in line with program changes. Legislative machinery, even when started, is interminably slow to turn. So we need to get things moving down in Washington, and soon.

But things are almost on dead center in the nation's capital. . . . The House and Senate Agriculture committees are controlled by the Democratic Party. This leadership is now saying: "We have a new Administration and a new Secretary of Agriculture. It is only fair to give them time to come up with their farm proposals. . . .

The ranking Republican on the House Agriculture Committee, Page Belcher of Oklahoma, is saying: "With a new Administration just barely in town, I don't think I should comment on farm policy." The ranking Republican on the Senate Agriculture Committee, George Aiken of Vermont, says: "There's no hurry. Give the new team time to come up with a farm plan." . . .

The upshot is that both the Democrats and the Republicans in Congress are spinning their wheels on the new farm program. Unless they get off the dime, we could run so far into 1970 that we'd have to settle for another one-year extension of programs that have let farm parity fall to depression lows and let payments climb to record highs.[94]

But it seemed that the administration intended to avoid taking a leadership role in farm policy and program development. Don Paarlberg, Secretary Hardin's chief agricultural economist, confirmed that the department wished to play a relatively passive role. He said that the secretary wished "to make available the considerable resources of his Department in the development of program alternatives that will be helpful to farmers and acceptable to the Congress. Note that the secretary does not consider himself the sole architect of farm policy. That is a role shared, as he sees it, by the farm organizations, by the Department of Agriculture, and, above all, by the elected representatives of the people."[95]

But the belief that the Congress should legislate and that the executive branch should only administer the acts of the Congress was not shared by all. A member of the staff of the Council of Economic Advisers (CEA) wrote:

Despite any desire the Secretary may have to stay off the legislative firing line, ultimately it becomes his responsibility to forward or recommend legislation he or the "Administration" favors. He cannot be only an analyst of proposals put up by Congress. While it is the responsibility of the legislature to enact legislation, it is also the responsibility of each agency head to initiate for his particular clientele laws that speak for their interests, and do so in such a way that his proposals are compatible with the economic, social, and political health of the nation.[96]

Program ideas emerge. During the spring months of 1969 rumors abounded that a massive land retirement program was being given top consideration. The secretary had alluded to such a plan in two appearances before Senate committees but no formal proposal was presented by the administration. As the months wore on, the idea slipped into oblivion, apparently abandoned. A year later Don Paarlberg described the episode:

> Long range land retirement . . . has much better economic credentials than it has political attractiveness. . . . This year the Department of Agriculture floated a trial balloon in the form of a suggested Easement Program. This was shot down by the cattlemen, who feared grazing on the retired acres, by businessmen, who feared a decline in the agricultural service industries, by tenants who feared loss of their leases, and by agrarians everywhere, who feared depopulation of the countryside. Within living memory this nation populated the West, put millions of acres to the plow, and considered this a great triumph. This history is not easy to reverse.[97]

Unwilling to wait any longer for direction from the administration, Congressman William R. Poage, chairman of the House Agriculture Committee, scheduled hearings to begin in July 1969. The committee planned to wed farm program and food stamp hearings, as it had in 1965 and 1968, in order to gain support for farm programs from urban congressmen who favored food stamp legislation. Secretary Hardin was invited to present the first testimony. Since food stamp and farm programs were combined, Hardin opted to concentrate his remarks on the food stamp program. This tactic was consistent with the attention devoted to food programs by the Nixon administration, in response to national outrage on hunger in America. The president had sent a special message to the Congress in May, prescribing measures to alleviate hunger and malnutrition. But no presidential message on farm programs had been issued nor was one forthcoming.

The secretary did promise that recommendations for commodity programs would follow soon and he hinted at their content. He said, "While our studies are not yet ready, it is possible to say that our suggestions will embrace two major components: 1. *Long range resource adjustment* involving voluntary land retirement coupled with programs to assist rural people in making the changes associated with new opportunities. 2. *Modification of commodity programs* so as to make them more equitable, more effective, less costly, and more acceptable."[98]

Farm organizations also testified at the hearings. The Farm Bureau presented a land retirement scheme embracing many of the ideas which the administration had suggested informally earlier in the year. Its plan would ultimately lead to the removal of government from agriculture. The coalition of the Farmers Union, the Grange, the National Farmers Organization, and other farm organizations proposed continuation and expansion of the existing farm program with improved farm income goals. Support and opposition to these two extremes polarized mostly along party lines within the House committee and each group found the other's position completely unacceptable. The administration opposed the coalition bill chiefly on the grounds of the built-in escalating treasury costs when the Office of Management and Budget (OMB) and other administration leaders were urging reduction of farm program costs.

While the hearings were getting underway, Secretary Hardin suggested to Mr. Poage that a series of off-the-record seminars be held with members of the House committee and USDA policy advisers to work out "like rational gentlemen" what was best for agriculture. In these sessions grounds for agreement were being sought between the Republican administration and the Agriculture Committee controlled by southern Democrats. Both parties were anxious to arrive at a compromise acceptable to the Congress. Chairman Poage pressed Secretary Hardin to come in with an administration bill but the secretary continued to urge that the committee draft a bill. Despite this difference, the conciliatory attitude of both parties contrasted sharply with the situation during the 1950s when there was the same division of power between the parties. Then Republican Secretary Benson and the Democratic congressional leaders had exchanged heated rhetoric and the result was a legislative stalemate.

Looking back on the negotiations, which began in the summer of 1969, a writer for the *Minneapolis Tribune* analyzed the policy formulation strategy. He said:

The farm bill strategists — mainly Hardin, Poage and Belcher [senior Republican committee member] — have taken their time and walked cautiously in fashioning a farm bill because they are in political trouble of an unprecedented nature.

They agree that unless the administration and farm protectors on both sides of the committee aisle can agree on a bill, they will have little chance of pushing it through a House that is increasingly urban-oriented and increasingly concerned that more money is spent on declining numbers of farmers than on such things as federal aid to elementary and secondary education and the Office of Economic Opportunity's war on poverty.

In a letter to President Nixon last week farm bureau president Charles Shuman accused him of not keeping campaign promises to reduce farmers' dependence on the government.

And it is true that Hardin has been most pliable. But he knows the committee farmers aren't willing to take a cut.

For their part, both Belcher and Poage know that neither the administration nor the farm critics in Congress will accept a more costly program.

So the result, essentially, has been a steady negotiation toward retention of the status quo.

The three-sided unity that Hardin, Poage and Belcher seek appears possible but is no certainty.[99]

Late in the summer of 1969 several happenings began to solidify the morass of confusion of the preceding weeks of informal meetings. Notably, the secretary was relieved of budgetary pressures to reduce farm program costs and Mr. Poage insisted that the secretary bring an administration program to the committee. The cost issue was settled at the White House level among officials of the USDA, CEA, and OMB. Mr. Hardin was assured that farm costs at recent levels were acceptable. In September the secretary reappeared before committee hearings to present what he termed "two approaches" for commodity programs, one called a set-aside program and the other a domestic allotment and diversion program. Both plans continued direct payments as income supports and loans as base price guarantees, but relaxed the planting restrictions currently in force. The set-aside program was slightly more stringent than the allotment program and it was given chief consideration. The set-aside proposal provided commodity loans and income support or diversion payments for farmers who idled a certain amount of their cropland, without restrictions on planting the remaining acreage.

The administration was seeking a farm bill which would entail minimum costs, maximum use of market prices, maximum freedom for the individual farmer, and vigorous promotion of export markets, while moving away from price supports for protecting farm incomes and from the use of the 1910–14 parity ratio as a guideline. It further wished to achieve major shifts in land use and to employ noncommodity programs to relieve the plight of the rural poor.

The Agriculture Act of 1970. Until about December 1969 a standoff prevailed between the House Agriculture Committee and the USDA. Then it appeared that the committee was finally willing to accept the basic idea of the set-aside scheme and that the administration appeared ready for the first time to take a position and back it.[100] But despite this tentative agreement, the road to final passage was strewn with obstacles.

Major opposition against the principles embodied in the set-aside program was launched by the coalition of farm organizations during 1970. The coalition argued that farm income can be maintained only with high government price supports and tight production controls. It strongly denounced efforts to ease government controls and to lower prices to free-market levels while vehemently insisting on retention of the parity concept for government support of farm prices.

Meanwhile the farm press was speculating on the very real possibility of no new bill after the extended 1965 act expired. No farm group supported the set-aside proposal and, since it entailed a compromise by both the House committee and the USDA, neither of the latter was enthusiastic about the measure. Moreover it was essential to deal with the question of payment limitations as part of this bill. This thorny issue had aroused so much bad publicity for farm programs that it was a political must to curtail or reduce payments to wealthy farmers, viewed by many as exorbitant.

The Agriculture Act of 1970 was finally enacted at the end of November 1970. It can be said that the result was a bill nobody wanted, nobody claimed parentage of, and nobody was proud of. Nonetheless, it was hailed by the secretary as a "break with the past by enabling farmers to employ their land and capital resources in planting the crops they can best produce. At the same time, the Act continues the protection of farm income through payments and loans." [101] The coalition, and other proponents of minimum price guarantees for farmers, had succeeded in retaining price floors for cotton, wheat, and feed grains, and in basing price supports on some measure of parity; however, the new bill moved away from the principle of fairly rigid supply control toward more flexibility. Yet the new law did not move far enough in that direction to satisfy those opposed to government controls on agricultural production. For instance, the Farm Bureau stated: "We believe that this law is not in the best interest of farmers and consumers." [102]

Revitalized interest in the farm voter. The 1970 congressional election came after the new farm bill had passed the House but while it was still being debated in the Senate. Some Republicans who favored the new, less restrictive legislation were defeated or involved in close races while critics garnered rural votes. As a result, the *Washington Farmletter* predicted that farmers will "be courted with more than usual vigor by both Republicans and Democrats between now and the Presidential election." [103] And *The Kiplinger Agricultural Letter* raised a question about Hardin's security in his job as secretary of agriculture.[104] In its opinion, political pressures to please midwestern farmers who had supported Nixon in 1968 would conflict with administration efforts to keep food prices low in order to stop inflation. This dilemma persisted for a year, climaxed by Hardin's resignation in the fall of 1971 and the appointment of Earl Butz to succeed him.

The new secretary took office confronted with low corn prices, resulting from a bumper crop under the first year of the set-aside program. Midwestern farmers were angry. Butz immediately announced that he would begin to buy corn to buoy the depressed market price. He soon became an outspoken advocate of raising farm prices. He was quoted as saying that "THE PRESIDENT told me he wanted a vigorous spokesman for agriculture and I told him he may have gotten a more vigorous one than he wanted. . . . When I came in, people were saying that the farm vote was lost (to Nixon), and I'm delighted to say, it's turned around." [105]

The Early 1970s

Food prices in a general inflation. As previously noted, farm prices sagged in the summer and fall of 1971 as the result of a bumper crop. In part, the bumper crop was the result of good weather and, in part, the result of a looser system of controls under the act of 1970. But whereas the agricultural sector was in a price-income slump, the economy generally was growing rapidly and experiencing a strong upward movement in prices. In short, the country was in the midst of a prolonged price inflation. In an effort to control the upward spiral of prices and costs, President Nixon on August 15, 1971, announced a ninety-day freeze on prices, rents, wages, and salaries. But this freeze specifically exempted the prices of raw agricultural products. The Nixon administration thence moved through a series of price control phases between 1971 and 1973:

1. *Phase I*: Announced on August 15, 1971 — it imposed a ninety-day freeze on prices and wages (with the price of raw agricultural products exempted).
2. *Phase II*: Announced from November 8 to 11, 1971 — it set guidelines of 5.5 percent increases for wages and 2.5 percent increases in prices. Raw food products were exempt at the first point of sale.
3. *Phase III-A*: Announced January 11, 1973 — mandatory controls were ended and replaced by a voluntary system.
4. *Phase III-B*: Announced June 13, 1973 — it imposed a sixty-day price freeze while Phase IV controls were being drawn up.
5. *Phase IV*: Announced July 18, 1973 — it lifted the price freeze as of August 12, 1973, and set forth proposals for moving the economy out of the price freeze on a sector-by-sector basis, beginning with food.

The events leading up to Phase IV as well as the procedures of Phase IV as they relate to food prices were described by the *Congressional Quarterly* as follows:

> With food price increases evidently inevitable, President Nixon July 18 exempted all foods except beef from the price freeze he imposed on June 13.
> The President set up a two-stage program for phasing the food industry into Phase IV controls designed to allow price increases sufficient to stimulate production needed to overcome supply shortages created or worsened by the freeze on food prices. . . .
> The President acknowledged that his June 13 price freeze has played havoc with agricultural supplies. "If price restraint was needed anywhere" during the first part of 1973, "it was needed for food," Nixon said. But since ceilings were imposed, he went on, "food has given the clearest evidence of the harm that controls do to supplies."
> In dealing with the food price pressures, the President concluded: "We must pick our way carefully between a food price policy so rigid as to cut production sharply and a food price policy so loose as to give us an unnecessary and intolerable bulge."
> *The Bulge.* To moderate that bulge, the President kept the ceiling on beef prices and

limited price increases for other foods dollar-for-dollar to the increases in raw agricultural product prices. By allowing such increases, the controls are expected to encourage production by raising the prices that processors and distributors are willing to pay farmers. . . .

After Sept. 12, the second stage of Phase IV food price controls will terminate the beef price ceiling and allow processors and distributors to raise their prices dollar-for-dollar for other cost increases as well as for raw product price increases.[106]

The "on-again, off-again" price control actions of the Nixon administration had two consequences for food supply availability which were not beneficial to consumers or producers. First, leaving raw product prices free and freezing retail food prices had the effect of squeezing handling margins and driving certain food products off the retail shelves. Second, the uncertainty about when food price ceilings would be imposed or lifted caused farm producers to be cautious and conservative about expanding production and on occasion to hold back marketable supplies in an effort to force government to remove the price ceilings. Overall, the price controlling actions of the Nixon administration were probably counterproductive in terms of halting the price inflation; and in 1972–73, international developments destroyed the Phase IV operation with respect to stabilizing food prices. Farm and food prices shot skyward in response to the exploding international demand for grains, oilseeds and products, and livestock and meat products.

A new theory regarding the farm voter. Although the number of farms and farmers continued to decline in the late 1960s and early 1970s, the political behavior of farm people was assigned a new and enlarged role. The theory gained currency in 1971 and 1972 that farm people tended to vote as a block, and at the margin, this block voting could swing an election in the direction that the block voted. It was thus argued that a relatively few farmers, voting as a block, in many midwestern states largely controlled which way those states would go. And, of course, the party in power was in the best position to court the farmer for his votes. John Schnittker, in a perceptive discussion of farm politics in Washington, describes the efforts of the Nixon administration as follows:

Clearly the Nixon team has bought the idea that farmer discontent was an important factor in the last election, that it could lose the Farm Belt and the election in 1972, and that no effort should be spared to counter this dangerous trend. The President sponsored a corny Farmers' Day on the White House grounds in May at a cost of hundreds of thousands of dollars. Signs now point to an unprecedented opening of the public treasury next year to buy back the farm vote. Raising milk prices again will increase butter and cheese surpluses, and will add some $200 million to the next deficit. . . .

Nixon's political priorities for 1972 became clear if one compares his recent efforts to let school children go hungry with the hasty decision made in October, under pressure from falling prices and angry farmers, to double spending on corn and wheat programs in 1972. . . .

The same week the Administration gave up its fight to cut school lunch funds, it decided to raise federal payments to grain farmers by as much as $1 billion next year. Secretary of Agriculture Clifford Hardin candidly told newsmen he hoped the enriched feed grain program would help the Nixon Administration politically.[107]

An emerging export strategy. But special treatment for farmers was really not needed in 1972. Farm product prices were rising from strong demand forces in the market. And the strongest of these forces was the growing exports of agricultural products — particularly grains and oilseeds and oilseed products. Agricultural commodity exports increased in value from $7.8 billion in fiscal 1971 to $12.9 billion in fiscal 1973. Who needs friends in government when market demand is expanding like that!

Recognizing a good thing, the Nixon administration adopted this expansion of agricultural exports as the cornerstone of its farm policy. A sustained increase in farm commodity exports would, it was argued, place an effective support under farm prices in the form of a strong market demand and eliminate the need for traditional price supports and production controls. It was, and remains, an attractive policy package.

This policy strategy was outlined in the Republican party platform at the national convention at Miami Beach. The agricultural section of the platform read in part as follows:

Farmers are benefitting markedly from our successful efforts to expand exports — notably a $750 million sale of United States grains to the Soviet Union, with prospects of much more. Last year we negotiated a similar sale amounting to $135 million.

For the future, we pledge to intensify our efforts to:

Achieve a $10 billion annual export market by opening new foreign markets, while continuing to fight for fair treatment for American farm products in our traditional markets.[108]

Additionally the Republicans in Miami promised farmers that they, if elected to office, would slow down inflation, assist farmers in bargaining for fair prices, and keep farm prices exempt from price control while they remained silent on the never popular subject of production control. It was an attractive platform which the Democrats could not match.

Many people no doubt had a hand in developing the farm export strategy of the Nixon administration, and certainly, events played an important determining role. But the man most often credited for its development is Peter Flanigan, White House assistant. It was under his guidance and direction that the basic study in the USDA outlining the potentialities of such a strategy was done.

The Flanigan report was a comprehensive examination of international agricultural trade with emphasis on policy recommendations for enhancing the U.S. position. It reviewed farm and trade policies of the major agricultural trading nations and reported that high price supports were the essential features of farm policies in Japan and the European Community and that in several countries no limits on production were required for obtaining government guaranteed prices. The report stated that such policies stimulate production, leading directly to surpluses, import barriers, and subsidized exports. It was observed that these consequences conflicted with the goal to expand international trade. To resolve this conflict, the report recommended moving away from high price supports and adopting payment programs, if needed, to meet farm income objectives, although it was recognized that such a change posed political problems.

Considerable attention was devoted to a study of the grain-feed-livestock sector to determine what benefits and costs would likely flow to the United States from worldwide liberalization of trade, assuming that trading countries had market-oriented domestic policies. (Other commodities were considered in less depth.) Projections were made for all U.S. agricultural exports and imports in 1980 with and without trade liberalization. The conclusions were as follows:

. . . the benefits to the United States from trade liberalization are substantial. The potential gains are threefold: a substantial improvement in the balance of payments; an important reduction in government expenditure; and a significant increase in net farm income.

U.S. agricultural exports would rise sharply from the estimated $8.9 billion in 1980 (with no change in policies) to $18.4 billion; imports would rise from $7.7 billion to $9.0 billion. The net balance of trade would thus be improved by about $8 billion.

However, if present agricultural trade policies are continued, only a small increase in exports is projected for the year 1980 and the net balance of trade from agriculture would drop by nearly a billion dollars from fiscal year 1971. These large gains in U.S. exports and in the net balance of trade [noted in the preceding paragraph] come almost exclusively from the feed-livestock sector. . . .

. . . Almost two-thirds of the total increase would be in grains and soybeans — 53 million additional metric tons of feedgrains and 285 million bushels of soybeans. The remainder is from animal products; increased exports of beef are the principal factor although modest increases are projected for other animal products except dairy.

On the import side, there would be an increase of a billion dollars, entirely accounted for by dairy products. It is assumed that the United States would continue to import processing-type beef even though our net balance of trade in beef would shift sharply to an export position. . . .

Recommendations

1. The potential benefits from liberalization of agricultural trade are so great that agriculture definitely warrants inclusion in any future round of multilateral trade negotiations.

2. Such negotiations should be broadly-based, involving both agricultural and industrial trade and monetary reform.

3. In agriculture, the negotiations should concentrate on the grain-feed livestock

sector, in which we would seek to eliminate barriers to international trade in the entire sector through negotiating a commodities agreement.

4. Product-by-product negotiations for other politically or economically sensitive commodities should be entered into for the purpose of obtaining whatever specific concessions would be meaningful for the commodities involved.

5. We should make clear to our trading partners right from the start that we are seriously prepared to withdraw from GATT protective levels if we cannot arrive at a satisfactory trade and monetary settlement, including liberalization of the grain-feed-livestock sector along with appropriate additional settlements for other agricultural commodities.[109]

Hopes for an early round of multilateral trade negotiations, as of December 1973, were not bright; in fact, they were dead. Nonetheless, the Nixon administration continued to push farm commodity exports as the principal solution to the long-run farm problem of excess production capacity, and it continued to be a highly viable policy solution. Farm commodity exports ran at record-breaking levels throughout 1973.

The Russian grain deal. Record levels of farm commodity exports were not, however, an unmixed blessing for the Nixon administration and the American people. While they acted to hold up farm prices and help with the balance of payments, they also acted to push food prices even higher and thus contributed to the problem of inflation. No single export action contributed more to this bag of mixed blessings than the great Russian grain deal in the summer of 1972. The Soviet Union experienced a poor grain crop in the winter of 1971–72. This it had experienced before, but this time it elected to offset its production losses and maintain the dietary levels of its people by purchasing large quantitites of grain in the world market. In the summer of 1972, the United States had large reserve (or surplus) stocks of wheat and feed grains and a secretary of agriculture in an administration eager to eliminate those stocks and expand agricultural exports. Soviet buyers came to the United States and contracted to purchase $750 million worth of United States–produced grain from several private American exporting companies. Secretary Butz said it was the largest grain deal in history; and it probably was. But the full implications and consequences of the deal were still reverberating across the land as the year 1973 came to an end.

Joseph Albright, in an article entitled "The Full Story of How *Америка* Got Burned and the Russians Got Bread: Some Deal," makes this assessment:

> The Russian sale, in itself, was not big enough to create a food shortage. But it had a shock effect in every other grain-purchasing nation, particularly since both Canada and Australia were very short of exportable wheat. Orders began flowing in from Europe and Japan, as these traditional grain buyers pressed to get in their orders while the United States Agriculture Department was still holding the world price at the low level of $60 a ton. Then, later in the year, they kept buying to get in their orders while there was any wheat, corn or soybeans left at all. . . .

The biggest winners were the Russians. They began the summer of 1972 in a tepid bargaining position, with empty granaries and bad growing weather. Nevertheless, they walked away with contracts for enough grain to offset their own crop shortfall, with enough left over to continue Russian grain exports to Eastern Europe and build a grain stockpile for 1973. Most of their purchase was of wheat, which the United States Agriculture Department promoted for them at a discount below the going world price. . . .

The clear losers in the grain deal were the supermarket-shopping, tax-paying American bystanders. On one hand, their combined grocery bills rose perhaps $5-billion because of it. On the other hand, the Agriculture Department spent $300-million in export subsidies to hold the price of wheat abroad to a needlessly low price. . . .

The best explanation of the mishandling of the grain deal is more prosaic than nefarious. . . .

Secretary Butz maintains he did not learn of the huge proportions of the grain deal until mid-September, 1972. If he didn't, clearly he should have done more to find out. But, like every Secretary of Agriculture, Butz had his sights set on pushing up farm prices during an election year. The trouble with Butz was that he had tunnel vision: He did not worry about the grain deal beyond its impact on the farm vote in November.[110]

From news stories such as that quoted above, sharp congressional criticism of the Soviet grain deal, cries of anguish from grain producers who failed to profit from the deal, and the impact of rising food prices on consumers, strong pressures developed for the federal government to develop an export-monitoring system as a minimum and a firm export food policy, replete with export controls, as a maximum. A monitoring system was quickly developed and put in effect by the federal government following the Soviet grain sale to keep all interested parties fully informed of export developments. But the formulation of a firm export food policy was a very different matter. Views on what should constitute the principal features of such a policy ranged from doing nothing to instituting a comprehensive system of export controls. As the year 1973 ended, with farm and food prices soaring, the debate over the need for, and the content of, a food export policy widened and became more intense.

The Agricultural Act of 1973. It was in the context of sharply rising farm and food prices and later skyrocketing prices that the Agricultural Act of 1970 expired and a new agricultural act was passed into law. In such a context, it was not easy to pass new farm legislation, and some thought that there would not be any new legislation. The *Congressional Quarterly* reported:

The farm price support program, which is having its 40th birthday May 12, faces the perils of Pauline in the 93rd Congress, as it seeks a new lease on life. The soaring price of food alone — up 3.2 per cent in March — would seem to place it in mortal danger, with attention focused more on whether to impose ceilings on farm prices rather than to maintain floors. . . .

Perils of Pauline

The timing would seem to be ideal for those who want to kill the farm program or dismantle it:

Housewives are angry about soaring food prices that are leading the worst inflation since the Korean War.

High U.S. incomes have kept domestic demand strong.

Overseas demand for U.S. farm products continues high, especially since the devaluation of the dollar Feb. 12.

Bad weather in many farm states threatens 1973 crops.

Once-bulging U.S. storage bins are nearly empty.

A determined Nixon administration is anxious to reduce the government role in agriculture and to cut federal spending.

Farm income is expected to reach a record $21-billion in 1973. Parity, a measure of a farmers' [sic] well-being, stood at 86 per cent in March — the highest level in 15 years.

The farm population has shrunk to 5 per cent, compared to more than 20 per cent 40 years ago, and the farm bloc in Congress in [sic] greatly diminished.[111]

But the *Congressional Quarterly* also noted in the same issue that there were several pluses for new farm legislation. It listed them as follows:

Pluses for Farm Program

Nevertheless, the farm program has a lot going for it:

A consensus exists that minimum price support tools should be retained as insurance against farm income collapse.

Agriculture remains the nation's largest single industry, holding assets of $371-billion — about two-thirds of the value of the capital assets of all U.S. corporations — and employing 4.4 million workers.

The agricultural-rural contingent in Congress is larger than appears on the surface.

Northern and southern Democrats in Congress can find common ground on the issue of congressional versus presidential powers, as well as on farm policy.

Agriculture has an effective lobby.

High-ranking midwestern Republicans favor extension of the existing farm program.

The administration may be ready for a retreat from confrontation politics by the time the farm bill comes to the forefront.

Members of Congress from farm states, Secretary of Agriculture Earl L. Butz and farm organizations testified almost unanimously before the Senate and House Agriculture committees that the 1970 version of the farm program should be extended.[112]

Out of the interaction of these forces, positive and negative, bearing on the new farm legislation, a new farm bill haltingly took shape. The chaos in the House of Representatives during the passage of the new farm bill is described as follows:

"Mr. Speaker, a parliamentary inquiry."

"The gentleman will state his parliamentary inquiry."

"Mr. Speaker, my parliamentary inquiry is whether there is any way we can now determine what the first amendment was that we voted on."

That conversation actually took place on the House floor July 19, as the House stumbled through more than eight hours of debate before passing a farm bill providing price support programs for wheat, feed grains and cotton for the next four years.

Making the inquiry was Rep. James G. O'Hara (D Mich.), one of the ablest students of parliamentary procedure in all of Congress.

By the time O'Hara made his inquiry, the farm bill had been amended, re-amended and de-amended so many times that hardly anyone knew what it contained. "I cannot recall a period of more sustained chaos on the House floor on any issue," Rep. Paul Findley (R Ill.) noted after the vote. It wasn't until the next day that the House parliamentarian issued the final ruling that determined the contents of the farm bill.[113]

But out of this chaos emerged the Agriculture and Consumer Protection Act of 1973. And it may turn out to be the best piece of farm legislation that the Congress has ever passed in the long history of farm price and income legislation. It is flexible with regard to the use of production controls. It drops the antiquated parity price goal. And it moves forthrightly into a deficiency payments scheme for protecting farm income.[114]

Other issues. The following issues related to farm policy received considerable attention during the early 1970s: farm bargaining, farm labor relations, corporate farming, rural development, and governmental reorganization. In the interest of space, we will discuss only one — governmental reorganization.

In his message to the Congress on January 22, 1971, President Nixon recommended a major reorganization of the executive branch of the government. He proposed that the Departments of State, Treasury, Defense, and Justice remain unchanged but that all other departments be consolidated into four new super departments: Human Resources, Community Development, Natural Resources, and Economic Development.[115] The president's proposal meant, of course, that the Department of Agriculture would cease to exist, and that most of its functions would be transferred to the four new departments mentioned above.

Many people with a background in government agreed with President Nixon on this issue. Charles L. Schultze, former director of the Bureau of the Budget, stated that "the President's proposals are in my view fundamentally reasonable." But farm people and farm leaders, almost to a man, opposed the reorganization plan. They felt, and probably rightly so, that the affairs of agriculture and farm people would be lost in these new, huge, consolidated departments. Farm organizations and groups of all ideologies and all shades of views fought the president's reorganization plan as it applied to the Department of Agriculture.

Later in 1971 in connection with the nomination of Earl Butz for secretary of agriculture, President Nixon stated that the Department of Agriculture would be kept with full cabinet status. It seems likely that in the process of nominating Earl Butz for secretary of agriculture and in wooing the farm votes for the presidential election in 1972 (noted earlier), the president promised the very aggressive Mr. Butz that the USDA would not be reorganized out of existence. In any event, all the talk of eliminating the Department of Agriculture emanating from the White House died with the appointment of Earl Butz as secretary of agriculture.

But talk of reorganizing the Department of Agriculture has not ended, and it will not be because real problems exist with regard to the present organization of that federal department. The National Planning Association summarized the state of debate regarding the USDA in the fall of 1972 and then went on to make some recommendations of its own. It argues along the following lines:

> Agricultural economists and other observers of the rural scene have argued for at least two decades that the U.S. Department of Agriculture has done a poor job of administering to the needs of small, low-production farmers. Spokesmen for the black community and other minority groups have long argued that the interests and needs of these groups have been neglected by the USDA. And spokesmen for consumer oriented groups frequently argue that the USDA fails to adequately represent and protect the interests of consumers in the food field. Thus, there is widespread dissatisfaction with the U.S. Department of Agriculture as it is presently structured and operated.
>
> On the other hand, it should be recognized that the USDA has been highly successful in conducting and supporting agricultural production research, in developing new production technologies, in extending those technologies to commercial farmers, and in providing services required by modern farm units, but external to individual units (e.g., market, news, plant and animal disease control). As a result, the commercial sector of agriculture is highly productive, dramatically dynamic, and of tremendous benefit to consumers. Further, the USDA has been effective in stabilizing prices and incomes for the commercial sector, and in representing the interests of commercial farmers in many and varied problem areas. Thus, the USDA has a highly successful record working with and for commercial agriculture. . . .
>
> The Agriculture Committee of the National Planning Association thus recommends that an essentially new department, replacing the USDA, be created to deal with the issues and problems of rural welfare, rural development and commercial agriculture. It is true that much of the staff of this new department would come from the old USDA, but the missions of this new department would differ radically from those of the old USDA, as would its structure.
>
> This new department would have three primary missions:
>
> 1. The improvement of social conditions and services in rural areas (e.g., housing, education, health).
>
> 2. The development of nonfarm economic and social activities in rural areas (our concept of development here is broad and inclusive, ranging from the establishment of a factory in a market town to new rural-urban, living-working communities, to the establishment of recreation and wildlife facilities).
>
> 3. The continued support and development of commercial farming.[116]

A Concluding Note

It is interesting to observe that, as the number of farmers has declined and the number of representatives in the Congress from farming districts has dwindled, the influence of farmers and interest in their problems have not eroded away. The role of agriculture in national policy debates is changing, but it has not disappeared. The farm bill of 1973 has the word ''Consumer'' in its title, and the technique of protecting farm income through high-level price supports is gone. But farm incomes up to a $20,000 limit are still being protected. The Department of Agriculture is still in being, although its operations and vistas are changing. It is much more concerned with the administration of food programs and rural development than it once was.

Problems concerned with food, agricultural production, and rural welfare and rural environment remain important problems to the American people; hence they are assigned a high priority in policy discussions and action. Policy directions and goals with respect to food, agriculture, and rural areas are continually changing, but not their importance; hence they continue to hold center stage in national policy debates and action.

CHAPTER 3

The Evolution of Policies and Programs

The ideas and goals that entered into the farm policy debates in the period 1948–73 were reviewed in the preceding chapter, and the broad directions in which farm policies moved were sketched. In this chapter we seek to describe more specifically the policies and programs that evolved, the nature of policy struggles that took place, and the content of the program compromises that emerged. The main steps in the evolution of programs are traced as key program features were introduced and modified during the 1948–73 period. The policy and program formulation process is viewed by examining the efforts of three secretaries of agriculture. The principal features of the basic policy compromise, which took place in the 1960s, are presented. And lastly, the economic content of the programs is analyzed.

This chapter is not presented as a complete history of farm policy from 1948 to 1973; but it does seek to present the essential program elements of American farm policy as they evolved over this period.

The Point of Departure

The support of individual commodity prices by government became commonplace during World War II.[1] In 1945, for example, price support was announced for 166 farm commodities. Under legislation passed during World War II the U.S. Department of Agriculture was required to support the prices of the six basic commodities (corn, wheat, cotton, tobacco, rice, and peanuts) at 90 percent of parity in most cases.[2] The USDA was further required by law to support the prices of the 14 Steagall Amendment commodities (manufacturing milk, butterfat, chickens, eggs, turkeys, hogs, dry peas, dry beans, soybeans for oil, flaxseed for oil, peanuts for oil, American Egyptian cotton, Irish

72

potatoes, and sweet potatoes) at 90 percent of parity through 1948. And by precedent the USDA was expected to support the price of other nonbasic commodities (e.g., barley, oats, rye, dried fruit, and various seed crops) at or near 90 percent of parity through 1948.

The basic farm price and income program in 1948 took the following form:

1. The federal government was required to support the prices of most important farm commodities at 90 percent of parity.

2. The support price level was effectuated, when necessary, by the use of nonrecourse loans for storable commodities and the purchase of semi- or fully-processed products in the case of nonstorable farm commodities.

3. When stock acquisitions of the federal government became burdensome, or excessive, the USDA was authorized to employ various devices: the distribution of food to the poor and needy domestically, the distribution of food through the School Lunch Program, and the subsidization of exports on the demand side; the imposition of marketing quotas and acreage allotments to control production on the supply side.

But in fact, actions under points 2 and 3 above were rarely undertaken during the war and postwar years, 1941–48, because the extraordinary demand for food created first by war and second by reconstruction held prices of most commodities above the mandatory support levels most of the time; potatoes were the one crop that was chronically in trouble in the immediate postwar years.[3] The basic role of price support programs during the period 1941–48 was to provide farm producers with insurance against price declines — to assure producers that prices would not decline drastically between planting time and harvesttime; rarely did the price support programs become operational.

Program Evolution

The Truman period.[4] In many ways 1948 was a pivotal year. Wartime price supports expired December 31, 1948. Without additional legislation the level of farm price support would revert to the provisions of the 1938 Agricultural Act, and the price support provisions of the latter act were frighteningly low. The great wartime and postwar boom in farm prices leveled off in 1948. There were unmistakable signs in 1948 that the world was returning to some kind of peacetime normalcy.

In the immediate postwar years two opposing camps emerged with respect to what shape new farm legislation should take. President Edward O'Neal of the American Farm Bureau Federation was, until his retirement in late 1947, the unofficial but powerful leader of one camp; its lieutenants were prominent farm congressmen from the South and Great Plains (for example, Congressman Clifford Hope from Kansas and Congressman Stephen Pace from

Georgia); the troops were large commercial farmers and their commodity spokesmen around the country. They were fearful that the bottom would once again fall out of farm prices, as had happened in 1920–21; hence it was determined to commit the federal government to supporting farm prices at a high level (e.g., at 90 percent of parity) to protect farm incomes. This group was united in its belief about what was likely to happen to farm prices if strong supporting action by government was not undertaken, hence in its determination to place a high support floor under the high prices that existed in 1948.

The official leader of the second camp was Secretary of Agriculture Clinton Anderson; the lieutenants were Senator George Aiken of Vermont, certain prominent agricultural economists of that day (e.g., John D. Black), and certain government officials with long memories; the troops were nonfarm citizens and organizations. This group was unified by one thought: it did not want a continuation of high level price supports. The position of Secretary Anderson seemed to be that demand would remain strong and that high level price supports were not needed to protect farm income. The agricultural economists, guided in large measure by static equilibrium theory, believed that farm prices should be free, or at least flexible, to direct resources into their most efficient uses. The public officials could remember how poorly production controls had worked in the 1930s, as well as the unhappy experience of the Federal Farm Board, and were fearful that a major break in farm prices would destroy farm programs as the government accumulated inventory in an effort to hold prices at 90 percent of parity. The nonfarm troops simply wanted lower food prices.

The struggle which ensued in the Congress between these warring camps produced a curious compromise. It was an agricultural act with two separate and distinct parts: one part to satisfy camp one and a second part to satisfy camp two.

One part of the act simply extended wartime price support levels at 90 percent of parity through 1949 for the basic commodities and for dairy products, hogs, chickens, and eggs. The second part instituted the concept of flexible price supports in which the level of price support on the basic commodities in 1950 and thereafter would be set at 75 percent of parity for a normal supply with adjustments downward as the supply exceeded the defined normal level and upward as supply fell below normal. Basic commodities were to receive mandatory price support according to the scale below (sometimes referred to derisively as the sliding scale). In connection with the flexible provision, support prices for nonbasic commodities would be permitted at levels not to exceed 90 percent of parity, but not be required. The parity formula was also revised and modernized for use beginning in 1950.

Estimated Supply	Level of Support (in percentage of parity)
Not more than 70% of normal	90
More than 70% but not more than 82%	85
More than 82% but not more than 94%	80
More than 94% but not more than 100%	75
More than 100% but not more than 118%	70
More than 118% but not more than 130%	65
More than 130% of normal	60

Those agricultural economists who could bear the thought of any farm price and income program in 1948 were cheered by the long-term aspects of the act of 1948. George Brandow made the following appraisal of the 1948 act:

1. A permanent program is definitely intended. A withdrawal of government from the farm price field will not happen.

2. More than "depression only" action is contemplated. The program will be used more in depression than in prosperity, but it will always be operating.

3. Government assistance to farmers will be largely through price support rather than through direct payments to farmers.

4. Main reliance for supporting prices at desired levels will be placed on control of supply. This will take various forms: government loans for withholding crops from market, acreage controls, marketing quotas, and restrictions of sales under marketing agreements.

5. All sorts of subsidiary devices to support prices will be tried if necessary. These include subsidization of uneconomic uses of products, subsidies to consumers, export dumping, curtailment of imports, and the like. . . .

Both changes introduced by the new Act — adoption of variable price supports and revision of parity — are desirable. Price relationships when supports are in effect are likely to conform more with economic requirements than price relationships did under past or present programs.

The implied confidence of the new Act in production and marketing controls is disturbing. The rather disorganized but, on the whole, tremendous effort at production control in the 1930's accomplished relatively little. It is doubtful whether any controls acceptable to farmers can adjust production well enough to make price supports work in hard times. . . .

The best hope for the program is that continued prosperity will make price supports unnecessary except in occasional years or on a few products. . . .[5]

But those who found hope in the long-term aspects of the Agricultural Act of 1948 met with bitter disappointment on October 31, 1949. With farm prices falling in 1949, the forces in favor of high and rigid price support won another partial victory. The act of 1949 set the price support level for basic commodities at 90 percent of parity for 1950, and between 80 and 90 percent of parity for 1951, if producers had not disapproved marketing quotas or marketing quotas were in effect. Proponents of high price support coupled with acreage production control measures for the crops involved were winning the annual battle of price support in the Congress.

John D. Black, a leading advocate of flexible price support, wrote as follows in December 1949:

> It was evident even while the Act of 1948 was being jammed through the closing hours of the 80th Congress that the proponents of rigid 90 per cent of parity intended to extend the rigid 90 per cent provisions of Title I in the following Congress. This they have already succeeded in doing for 1950–51, and it is already apparent that they fully intend to keep the liberalizations provided for 1951–52 from going into effect when the time comes. The actual "firm" achievement may therefore be very limited indeed.[6]

Dr. Black assessed the future correctly. The Defense Production Acts of 1950, 1951, and 1952 required that the prices of basic commodities be supported at 90 percent of parity in 1951, 1952, and 1953, and during 1952 proponents of high price supports in the Congress passed farm legislation making price support at 90 percent of parity mandatory for the basic commodities for crops harvested in 1954 if the producers had not disapproved marketing quotas. This legislation also extended through 1955 the requirement that the effective parity price for the basic commodities should be the parity price computed under the new or old formula, whichever was higher.

The Eisenhower period. It could be, and it was, argued that commercial farmers with the aid of congressional leaders were riding roughshod over the interests of the general public. But all policy analysts were not of that view. Bushrod W. Allin, an institutionalist in the tradition of John R. Commons, argued as follows before a group of cooperative leaders in 1953:

> In every period in our past history we have moved out of a wartime situation into what may be called a more normal peacetime situation. Government demand for military purposes has shrunk sufficiently to cause a contraction in the supply of dollars and a reduction in prices. It was in connection with this type of an adjustment that agitation for the present parity price support system began. It was designed to correct a disparity in prices, and by disparity we mean the level of farm prices had sunk to a point where the purchasing power per unit of farm products was less than farmers regarded as fair and reasonable. . . . it seems to me virtually certain that the Federal Government will continue into the indefinite future assuming responsibility for assisting farmers in protecting themselves against excessive swings in the prices of their products. In deciding precisely what will be done, it is my opinion the principle of *workability* will be the controlling principle. For example, I see little prospect that tobacco growers, tobacco consumers or the tobacco industry will ask for the abolition of the tobacco price-support program. Questions will continue to arise concerning both the level of supports and the mechanics. We will probably face important decisions in this respect, especially in connection with our programs for other export crops. The greatest area of uncertainty concerns many of our perishable commodities. We have not yet discovered both workable and generally acceptable methods for them.[7]

But trouble was building up in the period 1952–54 for the three great commodities: wheat, feed grains, and cotton. Yields per acre were increasing rapidly, exports were at a low level, production controls were failing to hold supplies in balance with demand at the support levels of 90 percent of parity, government stocks were accumulating rapidly, and net farm incomes were sagging. By 1954 something had to be done.

To cope with the related problems of low-level exports and mounting stocks in government hands, the Agricultural Trade Development and Assistance Act was approved in July 1954; this act is now better known as P.L. 480.[8] This act, which provided the authority for disposing of surplus agricultural products through sales for nonconvertible foreign currency and other concessional means, became a powerful instrument for increasing exports of agricultural commodities. Exports under P.L. 480 and other government programs increased from $449 million in 1952 to $1.9 billion in 1957, and averaged well over a billion dollars a year from 1955 to 1973. In short, P.L. 480 turned out to be a powerful mechanism for increasing the total demand for American farm products; it may well have saved farmers and their programs from complete disaster in the late 1950s.

The Republican administration under the vigorous leadership of Secretary of Agriculture Ezra Taft Benson, supported by the American Farm Bureau and a Republican Congress, was determined to move to a system of flexible price supports. They reasoned that the surging flow of farm products to market could be slowed and brought into balance with demand by lowering the level of farm price support. The coalition won a limited victory in August 1954 with the passage of the Agricultural Act of 1954, which authorized the use of flexible price supports for the basic commodities ranging from 82.5 percent of parity to 90 percent for 1955, and from 75 percent of parity to 90 percent in 1956 and thereafter; an exception was made for tobacco, which was to be supported at 90 percent of parity so long as marketing quotas were in effect. This act also provided for production payments as a means of supporting incomes of wool producers; one important idea of the Brannan Plan had now become operational.[9]

A modest lowering of the loan rate for wheat, feed grains, and cotton in 1955–56, in conjunction with the administration's aversion to strict production control, did not, however, stem the tide of agricultural output. Total farm output took another important upward jump in 1955, and except for momentary pause in 1957 continued to trend upward throughout the 1950s. Thus, once again pressed by the increasing productivity of agriculture, which under the existing commodity programs was resulting in increased stocks of wheat, feed grains, and cotton in government hands and lower net farm incomes generally, farm leaders went looking for a new farm program with the capacity to cope with their problems. This they thought they found in the Soil Bank concept, which was established in the Agricultural Act of 1956.

The Soil Bank had two parts.[10] One was an Acreage Reserve Program,

which operated in 1956, 1957, and 1958. In 1957, some 21 million acres were
"banked" in the Acreage Reserve Program; no crop could be harvested or
pastured on those acres. The second part of the Soil Bank, the Conservation
Reserve, was designed to assist producers to reduce the production of crops
through shifting acreages of cropland to long-range conservation uses. The
first acres went into this program in 1956 and the last acres came out in 1972;
a maximum of 28.6 million acres were under this program in 1960. Whole
farms could be "banked" under the Conservation Reserve Program after
1957, but tradesmen and community leaders in low-production areas where
this provision was popular with farmers became highly critical and highly
vocal in their criticisms of the whole farm provision of the Soil Bank. For
various reasons the Acreage Reserve Program was permitted to drop after
1958, and the Conservation Reserve was not pushed after 1959. Those reasons include (1) their lack of success in reducing total output, (2) the high cost
of removing a crop acre from production, (3) nonfarm voters' opposition to
paying farmers for doing nothing, and (4) the "whole farm" criticism in
many rural areas.

Serious efforts to reduce the production of wheat, cotton, and feed grains
through the imposition of control programs were abandoned in 1959 and
1960. Under legislation obtained in 1954 and 1958 dealing with the permissible range of price support, Secretary Benson sought to curb the flow of the
major commodities to market through the lowering of the level of price
support. Levels of price support for wheat, cotton, and corn in 1959 and 1960
were, for example, as shown in the tabulation.

	Percentage of Parity	
Product	1959	1960
Wheat	77	75
Cotton	80	75
Corn	66	65

But this was not a successful strategy. Total farm output increased significantly in 1959 and 1960. Carryover stocks of wheat and feed grains
reached excessive levels in 1960, and stocks of cotton ended their brief
decline of 1957–58. Most important, net farm income continued to be depressed. The implications of general excess production capacity in American
agriculture became clear to anyone who was willing to look or listen in
1959–60. There were simply too many resources, and continuingly improved
resources, producing too much total product for the commercial market. And
any reasonable decline in the level of farm prices could not correct the situation. What to do about the chronic problem of general excess production

capacity in agriculture — that was the problem confronting the nation in 1960.

The Kennedy-Johnson period. The Kennedy-Freeman administration understood full well the general nature and the persistence of the excess capacity problem of American agriculture. It also understood, or thought it understood, some other things: first, that a highly urbanized society will not support large and continuing expenditures on agricultural programs; and, second, that a highly urbanized society will not tolerate government policies which lead directly to rising food prices.[11] Given the chronic excess capacity problem in agriculture and its adverse income implications for farmers and the constraints noted above — what then was the Kennedy-Freeman administration to propose in the way of a new and effective farm policy?

It proposed, in the first place, to expand demand as fully as possible by (1) meeting the food needs of the poor and underprivileged at home, (2) providing food aid to the poor and downtrodden abroad, and (3) expanding commercial exports wherever possible. To this end it initiated the Food Stamp Plan and pushed all kinds of domestic food programs; it supported and expanded the coverage of P.L. 480 programs initiated in the Eisenhower administration; and it developed a trade expansion agenda and the Kennedy round of trade negotiations.

But this it knew would not suffice in the short run and probably not in the long run. Thus it argued for, and proposed, a system of mandatory supply management devices — ranging from acreage controls to marketing orders — to adjust supply to demand at prices determined by the Congress to be fair to producers and consumers alike.[12] Before the Kennedy-Freeman administration could develop its long-range supply management agenda, however, it had to turn to an immediate and acute problem. Stocks of feed grains in government hands on January 1, 1961, had reached a level where under the current pattern of inflow and outgo, an additional bushel of feed grain taken over by the government would incur storage costs greater than the original value of the grain. Stocks of feed grain had to be brought down, and there was time to reduce production in 1961 if an effective program could be developed. A feed grain program was developed and enacted into law in March 1961. It was a voluntary program in which participants were guaranteed a price support rate of $1.20 per bushel for corn[13] if they would divert to soil-conserving uses a minimum of 20 percent and running up to a maximum of 50 percent of their base acreage in return for a payment designed to maintain or increase modestly their gross income from farming. Nonparticipants were offered nothing. Interestingly, almost everyone liked the program: farmers did, tradesmen and community leaders did, and politicians did. Some economists regarded it as damaging to the nation, but even most economists found it, on balance, to be beneficial. And in spite of a significant increase in the yields of corn and other feed grains in 1961,[14] the program did cut production in 1961, it did reduce stocks in government hands the following year, and it did reduce program costs in fiscal 1962 by some $350 million from fiscal 1961. By almost any standard the emergency feed grain program of 1961 was a success.

With the feed grain problem contained by an emergency program, the administration turned its attention to the long-run problem of (1) raising farm incomes and (2) lowering government program costs while the price of food was not increased significantly to consumers. It hoped to do this through a system of mandatory supply management devices in which payments to farmers for controlling production were sharply reduced or eliminated and farmers achieved their economic reward in the marketplace. In reality there was no solution to this problem, since the administration would not permit product prices in the market to increase significantly as a result of reductions in supply offered on the market. But this did not keep the administration from trying. It made a determined effort in 1961 and again in 1962; each failed (these efforts are discussed in greater detail later in this chapter).

Following each failure the administration turned to voluntary control programs along the pattern established in the emergency feed grain program. The Agricultural Act of 1961, approved August 8, 1961, provided for the idling of wheat and feed grain cropland on a voluntary basis for the 1962 crop; each wheat and feed grain farmer was given the option of withdrawing a part of his cropland from production in return for guaranteed price support and a land diversion payment. Other provisions of the act included the authorization for marketing orders for peanuts, turkeys, cherries and cranberries, and apples under special conditions. It also extended the Wool Act of 1954 and P.L. 480.

The Food and Agricultural Act of 1962 built on the voluntary acreage diversion principle, with one exception, wheat. Under this act, the antiquated 55-million-acre minimum national allotment for wheat was permanently abolished, and the secretary of agriculture could set acreage allotments for wheat at whatever level he deemed appropriate to achieve the supply-price objectives of each year's program. Farmers were given the choice in referendum between two systems of price support for the management of supplies. The first program alternative provided for the payment of penalties by those farmers overplanting their acreage allotment and the issuance of marketing certificates to each cooperating farmer based on his estimated share of wheat used in domestic human consumption and a portion moving in commercial export. That wheat covered by marketing certificates would be supported at between 65 and 90 percent of parity (for 1964, support would be $2.00 per bushel). The remaining wheat produced by each farmer on his acreage allotment would sell at the feed wheat price. The second program alternative imposed no penalties for overplanting, and, of course, no price support for those overplanting. But those farmers complying with the announced allotments would receive price support at only 50 percent of parity. The second alternative was very close to a free-market alternative.

The first alternative was defeated in referendum on May 21, 1963.[15] In the first alternative farmers were in effect offered price support very little higher than they had been receiving in the past, no government payment for reducing production, and strict mandatory controls. Seeing little in the way of price or income gain in the first alternative, but being forced to accept unpalatable control provisions, farmers in essence bet that the government would never let the second alternative become a reality and voted the first alternative down. And they bet right. The Congress with the support of the administration passed the Agricultural Act of 1964 in April 1964, which kept the second alternative from becoming effective.

But certain other provisions of the Food and Agricultural Act of 1962 should be noted. In the case of feed grains, the price support level was dropped to near the world price level and the approximate difference between the old higher support level ($1.20 per bushel for corn in 1962) and the new lower support level ($1.07 per bushel in 1963) was paid to the farmer in the form of a price support payment ($0.18 per bushel for corn) on the farmer's normal production (allotment acreage times a yield trend). In addition the feed grain producer received a diversion payment for land withdrawn from production as he had in 1961 and 1962.

The program feature described above combining the concepts of price support at or near equilibrium levels and production payments had important implications. It permitted export crops to move into international markets without subsidy; it provided a mechanism for holding down prices to the domestic consumer; and it provided a means for supporting producers' incomes. Only the federal budget suffered. Because of its many desirable features it established a precedent for future programs in wheat and cotton, and it became a central feature of the Food and Agricultural Act of 1965.

With the defeat of the mandatory control alternative in the wheat referendum in May 1963 and the acceptance of production payments in the feed grain program in 1963, the stage was set for a voluntary program involving a low level of price support in combination with production payments for cotton and wheat. And this was partially accomplished in the Agricultural Act of 1964. In the case of wheat, producers who complied with their acreage allotments and agreed to divert additional land into nonproductive uses were in 1964 eligible for price support at $1.30 per bushel, domestic marketing certificates valued at 70 cents per bushel, export marketing certificates valued at 25 cents per bushel, and a land diversion payment. In the case of cotton, the secretary of agriculture was authorized to make subsidy payments to handlers and the textile mills to bring the price of cotton consumed in the United States down to the export price. Each farmer complying with his regular allotment would have his crop supported in 1964 at 30 cents a pound (or at about 73 percent of parity). As we see, production payments to cotton producers were hidden in subsidies paid to the mills for the 1964 and 1965 crop years.

The Food and Agricultural Act of 1965 represents the final stage in farm program development during the Kennedy-Johnson period. All aspects of mandatory production control are gone from that act. It extended the voluntary feed grain program with low-level price support and production payments, as well as land diversion payments in certain circumstances, through 1969. Similar voluntary programs for wheat and cotton were provided in which the market price of those commodities was supported at or near world equilibrium levels, and incomes to producers participating in acreage control programs were supported through various kinds of direct payment to those producers. Voluntary production control programs with low levels of price support and direct payments to producers had carried the day in the major commodities. And these program features of the Food and Agricultural Act of 1965 remained essentially unchanged for five years — through the last four years of the Johnson administration and the first year of the Nixon administration.

The Nixon period. The Republican administration which took office in January 1969 was not committed to any specific line of action with regard to farm price and income policy. After a while it became clear that the new secretary of agriculture, Clifford M. Hardin, really did not want to take the leadership in formulating a new farm program; in his view it was the responsibility of the Congress to write the new farm legislation.

In the leadership vacuum which ensued, a program package began to take shape that was not too different from that incorporated in the Food and Agricultural Act of 1965 — a not unexpected development since the principal experience of the congressmen writing the new legislation had been with the Food and Agricultural Act of 1965; and, on balance, the experience of politicians and farmers with the Act of 1965 was satisfactory, if not good. But two new ideas worked their way into the emerging legislation. One had to do with the way in which acreage controls were applied to individual farms, the other with a limit on the size of government payment that any farmer could receive. The first of these ideas emerged from the inner recesses of the USDA; the second was articulated by Congressman Paul Findley of Illinois on behalf of nonfarm taxpayers.

The Agricultural Act of 1970 suspended marketing quotas, acreage allotments, and base acreages for wheat, cotton, and feed grains and provided that producers of those crops be required to *set aside* a designated number of acres from productive uses in order to qualify for price support and program payments. Having set aside a designated number of acres, the farmer was then free to produce any amount of crop not subject to marketing quotas on the remainder of his farm. This provision eliminated in part the difficult problem of maintaining equitable acreage bases for each crop on each farm on which acreage diversions applied, and it provided the farmer with greater flexibility in his farming operation. But it did not eliminate completely the need for acreage bases on each farm since they were still required in order to compute program payments to complying farmers. The control mechanism on individual farms was loosened and eased since (1) control over the supply of individual crops was abandoned, and (2) many farmers had some pasture and other land not previously controlled by the commodity programs which could be brought into production under the set-aside control mechanism. Thus, the question remained whether the set-aside control mechanism would prove effective in a period of heavy overproduction.

The second new provision was straightforward in concept, although exceedingly difficult to administer equitably. It put a limitation of $55,000 on the amount of program payments that any producer of wheat, cotton, or feed grains could receive from the federal government under each commodity program. This provision too has its good and bad sides. Since the commodity programs were designed to assist farmers earn a parity of income, not make the rich farmers richer, the limitation makes good sense on the grounds of equity. But the payments are made in large measure to control production in situations of excess production capacity, thus payment limitations might in certain situations complicate the objective of supply management.

It is difficult to appraise the effectiveness, or the full implications, of these two program features as yet. Neither has been fully tested. But as of the middle 1970s it would appear that the set-aside provision will become one of those many interesting "gimmicks" in the long history of farm price and income programs which passes into disuse. The payment limitation provision, however, seems destined for an increasingly prominent role in farm policy.

The Agriculture and Consumer Protection Act of 1973 barely falls within the historical scope of this book. It was passed on August 10, 1973, in the midst of the greatest peacetime boom in farm prices in the history of the United States, yet certain of its key features bore little or no relation to that great upswing in farm prices (e.g., the level and duration of the commodity loan rates and target prices); and certain features not included (e.g., an effective reserve stock program) would suggest that the legislation might have been written in the Middle Ages rather than in 1973. Also at the time the act was moving through the Congress there was much rhetoric in and out of the administration, and particularly from the vigorous and vocal secretary of agriculture, Earl L. Butz, to the effect that "now is the time to get government out of agriculture — now is the time to set agriculture free." And, of course, an extraordinarily strong foreign demand for grains and oilseed products in 1972–73 did cause domestic farm prices to soar high above traditional price support levels, and suggest to any policy maker with a "lick of sense," that production controls in the grains and possibly other crops should be lifted in 1974 and possibly 1975 to increase the production of needed commodities, to rebuild world stocks, and to bring food prices down to reasonable levels again. But neither the rhetoric nor the situation in 1973 seems to have made much impression on the framers of farm legislation.

The Agriculture and Consumer Protection Act of 1973 was a logical exten-sion of the acts of 1965 and 1970. The voluntary features of the programs were maintained. The basic principle of setting levels of price support at or near world equilibrium levels was maintained. The payment principle was further institutionalized by the clear provision that deficiency payments would be paid to producers whenever market prices fell below certain target prices set by the Congress. Although the set-aside control feature was maintained, the act also provided for control by individual commodities if the situation called for a tighter system of controls. And the payment limitation established in the act of 1970 at $55,000 per commodity for an individual producer was lowered to a total of $20,000 per person in the act of 1973.

In time, at least two aspects of the price-income guarantee mechanism will need to undergo modification and reformulation. First, setting target prices four years in advance in a highly uncertain world can only lead to trouble. For the target prices to be useful and relevant, they should be set for only one year ahead under guidelines provided by the Congress. Second, with the parity price principle dead, the Congress must develop guidelines for setting both the target prices and the loan rate; they cannot, year after year, be simply "pulled out of the hat" as the Congress did in 1973.

The Agriculture and Consumer Protection Act of 1973 has one overriding deficiency. It makes no provision for a reserve stock program to be used to stabilize farm and food prices. In the highly volatile world of food and agriculture of the 1970s, this is a grave omission, and one that events — extreme price fluctuations — will almost certainly force the Congress to deal with.

The clear enunciation of a support system which makes use of a loan rate, a target price, and deficiency payments was new in the act of 1973. But the basic program embodied in the act of 1973 was the same program as that which came together in the act of 1965 — with a few new wrinkles. The fact that the market developments around the world in 1972 and 1973 made the program nonoperational in 1974 does not mean that the program is either eliminated or rendered unnecessary. The program is authorized, and will become operational once again whenever market developments around the world result in declining farm prices and incomes.

A note on food aid programs, domestic and foreign. Domestic food programs designed to increase the per capita consumption of food among the poor and the needy increased in importance throughout the 1960s and early 1970s. The growth of the Food Stamp Plan was only a little short of miraculous; the expenditure level for it stood at $13 million in fiscal 1962, rose to $173 million in 1968, rose to $551 million in 1970 and then to $2,136 million in 1973. The poor people liked the program, urban politicians found something to like about farm programs, and the retail food trade liked the program; thus, it became an important instrumentality for expanding the demand for food in the United States. The School Lunch Program expanded both with respect to student coverage and the number of meals served free or at reduced cost during this same period.

Foreign food aid under P.L. 480 remained important throughout the 1960s but declined somewhat in the early 1970s. Total expenditures by the federal government under P.L. 480 stood at $1.1 billion in 1961, rose to a high of $1.5 billion in 1965, and slowly declined to $0.9 billion in 1973.

The authorizations for demand expansion programs such as P.L. 480 and the Stamp Plan often were not a part of the agricultural legislative packages during the 1960s, but they were a major and constituent part of the total farm policy. It should be recognized further that these programs ceased to be crude surplus disposal programs in the 1960s and increasingly became demand expansion programs, in which the magnitudes of the programs were determined to an increasing degree by the needs of poor and needy people at home and abroad rather than by the size of the surplus stocks in government hands. The integration of food programs with farm programs in a national food and agricultural policy came close to achievement in the Agriculture and Consumer Protection Act of 1973, which included authorizations for the Food Stamp Plan, commodity distribution to institutions and the needy, and P.L. 480.

The Basic Compromise

American farm policy and the specific programs that evolved over the period 1948–73 did not come into being by either design or accident. The policy and its program elements were the product of a prolonged struggle and a series of compromises. Many and diverse interest groups participated in the struggle and compromises; the struggle was many-sided and the compromises many-dimensional. Farm policy and the specific programs that took shape in the period 1948–73 might properly be viewed as an uneasy, continually evolving compromise among diverse and contending interest groups.

Consumers sought policies and programs that would result in lower food prices. Taxpayers and their spokesmen sought reduced program expenditures and costs. Welfare agencies looked with favor on government food surpluses, since such a state of affairs resulted in their obtaining free of charge, or at least cheaply, food stocks to distribute to the poor at home and abroad. Agribusiness firms favored, and lobbied for, wide-open agricultural production, since this expanded the market for their products and increased the volume of products which they might process or handle. Organized labor was willing to support farm programs *if* farmers and their representatives would support friendly labor legislation. And so it went.[16]

The people most concerned, farmers, were divided into many factions with regard to farm policy. Some farmers, often the larger, more successful commercial farmers, were opposed to all forms of government intervention in the farm economy. Some farmers of this persuasion did not fully understand the nature of the market forces involved, others did but believed that they could beat the treadmill; but all believed deeply, even religiously, in a free-market philosophy. The American Farm Bureau Federation was the chief spokesman for this group. Some farmers believed fervently in high-level price supports, sometimes in conjunction with production control, sometimes not. The National Farmers Union was the chief spokesman for this group. Other farmers vacillated between favoring governmental intervention in the form of price and income support programs and opposing them, depending on events and circumstances. The National Grange could not be said to represent such a group, but it did tend to vacillate with it. (The National Farmers Organization did not emerge as a spokesman for one segment of farm policy opinion until late in the period under review here.)

Commodity organizations tended generally to favor commodity programs, and certainly they worked hard to present the producer point of view in program formulation and operation. Professional workers in agriculture, like their farmer clients, were badly divided on farm policy: production specialists tended to favor any policy that increased output and opposed policies that interfered with output maximization; agricultural economists became increasingly friendly toward farm price and income support programs over the period, as the general excess capacity problem deepened and widened. Farm politicians in the Congress tended to mirror the policy views of their constituents as closely as they were able to discern those views.

Pushing and hauling, struggle and compromise, went on year after year over farm policy issues, large and small, among the interest groups mentioned above. But at the center of the struggle — at the eye of the storm, so to speak — always were to be found two contending parties: (1) congressional leaders from farm districts and farm states and (2) the secretary of agriculture representing the administration. The approach and objective of these parties to farm policy involve a fundamental difference. Farm congressmen have the objective of protecting and enhancing the economic position of farm people in their respective districts and states. The secretary of agriculture on the other hand is concerned with such national considerations as security, international trade, abundant food supplies, consumer needs, the incomes of all farmers, and government costs. Because of these differing and often conflicting objectives, clashes between these two parties in the farm policy area are usually prolonged, often intense, and sometimes bitter. Let us review the struggles of three different secretaries of agriculture with Congress. Although this review retraces some of the policies and programs treated previously, it examines the policy formulation process from another vantage point and thereby provides additional insights into the shaping of policies and programs. It will help us understand the basic compromise which emerged in the late 1960s.

The Brannan effort. On April 7, 1949, Secretary Brannan presented the administration's position on farm policy to a joint hearing of the House and Senate Committees on Agriculture. His recommendations, which came to be known as the Brannan Plan, burst like a bomb across the farm policy scene. This was the case for a number of reasons. First, Charles Brannan did not look the part of a fighting liberal; on the contrary, a close friend is supposed to have said Charlie Brannan "looked very much like a tired banker."[17] Second, Secretary Brannan was viewed in political circles as a protégé of the conservative Democrat and former Secretary of Agriculture Clinton P. Anderson. Third, the Brannan Plan really did contain some new and novel ideas.

After the election of Harry S. Truman to the presidency in the fall of 1948, Secretary Brannan moved quickly to formulate an administrative position on farm economic policy. He began by appointing some 20 department officials to a seminar group, chaired by O. V. Wells, to probe the more important farm policy issues of the day.[18] This seminar group met in the first of eight sessions on January 26, 1949; it concluded its work on March 3. To promote discussion, Secretary Brannan participated mainly by listening, but in the sixth session he presented his views on the goals and elements of a good farm price and income policy. Shortly after the eighth and final seminar session Secretary Brannan appointed a five-man task force to prepare a policy statement.[19] After much hard work, some disagreement, strong guidance from the secretary, and considerable rewriting, the group came up with the policy statement which Secretary Brannan presented to the Congress on April 7, 1949.[20]

Whether Secretary Brannan and his chief political adviser, Wesley McCune, realized the extent to which the Brannan recommendations broke with past developments and represented an innovative approach, it is difficult to say. But O. V. Wells and John Baker certainly recognized the radical nature of the Brannan recommendations since both had been deeply involved in farm policy debates of the 1940s and both were astute political economists. What were the new ideas contained in the Brannan Plan?[21] Basically, they were four in number:

1. An income standard to replace the old 1910–14 parity price standard.
2. Production, or income payments, to support gross returns to producers of perishable commodities (price support programs would be continued for producers of storable commodities).
3. A new list of farm commodities (including the important animal products) to replace the old so-called basic commodity list.
4. No price or income support on production above a certain limit — that limit to be determined by the size of the typical family farm.

In retrospect, all the new policy ideas in the Brannan Plan would seem to have merit. As a nation, we have been moving in the direction of points 2 and 4 for some time. We have tried on numerous occasions to develop an income support standard to replace the ancient parity price standard, but without operational success. And the idea of replacing a list of so-called basic commodities, which included peanuts and rice, with a list of ten of the most important income-producing commodities in American agriculture needs no defense — then or now. Why, then, were the Brannan proposals beaten down in the Congress?

There were probably many specific and personal reasons why the Brannan Plan met defeat in the Congress. But we would mention three general causes. First, commercial farmers, particularly the larger commercial farmers, who are well represented in Washington, were violently opposed to points 2 and 4. They did not want to see the extent of their income subsidy exposed to public view as it would be under the production payment proposal; it was in their economic interest to keep the income subsidy to them hidden as it is in a price support program. And most of all, they did not want to see any limit on price and income support, which would certainly affect them adversely. Thus, the large commercial farmers and their Washington representatives fought the Brannan Plan with skill, vigor, and success.

Second, Secretary Brannan proposed an income support standard so high that it drove away his natural allies. He set his income standard essentially at the income levels achieved by farmers in the World War II period and created a mechanism which would maintain that level and raise it as the price level increased. Most agricultural economists, who were basically sympathetic to the program ideas of the Brannan Plan, were appalled by the level of income support proposed.[22] And congressmen who were friendly to the basic provisions of the Brannan Plan were appalled by estimates of the governmental costs of the program ranging from $3 billion to $8 billion per year. To an important degree Secretary Brannan lost his entire program by asking for too much in the way of farm income support.

Third, the Republican party was badly frightened by the political appeal of the Brannan Plan — high prices and incomes to farmers and low food prices to the laboring man. One political observer is reported to have said with regard to the Brannan Plan, "If the Democrats get it through, they are in for life."[23] Thus the Republicans closed ranks against the Brannan Plan and fought it as a united, although minority, party.

But the Brannan proposals were not easily defeated in the Congress. President Truman marshaled the forces of his administration in support of the Brannan Plan, and Congressman Pace of Georgia introduced the administration bill, which included some but not all of the important provisions of the original Brannan Plan, in June 1949. The administration bill was, however, defeated in the House and Senate in the summer of 1949. This defeat did not cool the ardor of the administration for the Brannan proposals. With President Truman's support, a major effort was made again in 1950 to enact the Brannan Plan into law. And for a brief period it looked as if the political forces might coalesce behind the Brannan proposals — when farm prices were low and falling in the winter of 1949–50. But with an upward surge in farm prices in the summer of 1950 and with the invasion of South Korea by North Korea, the last hopes for passage of the Brannan proposals into law were snuffed out.[24]

The Benson effort. Secretary Benson, like his predecessor Charles Brannan, had some firm ideas regarding the desirable directions in which farm price and income policy should move. In his first press conference he issued a "General Statement on Agricultural Policy" which set the tone and style of his administration. In part this statement said:

> The objective of agriculture is to provide consumers with high quality food and fiber at reasonable prices, improve the productivity of basic land resources, and contribute to higher levels of human nutrition and of living. The reward for these contributions must be an income that will provide the opportunity for a constantly rising level of living for farm people fairly related to that of other large productive groups of the nation.
>
> Our agricultural policy should aim to obtain in the market place full parity prices of farm products and parity incomes for farm people so that farmers will have freedom to operate efficiently and to adjust their production to changing consumer demands in an expanding economy. This objective cannot be assured by government programs alone. . . .

Price supports should provide insurance against disaster to the farm-producing plant and help to stabilize national food supplies. But price supports which tend to prevent production shifts toward a balanced supply in terms of demand and which encourage uneconomic production and result in continuing heavy surpluses and subsidies should be avoided. . . .

The principles of economic freedom are applicable to farm problems. We seek a minimum of restrictions on farm production and marketing to permit the maximum of dependence on free market prices as the best guides to production and consumption. Farmers should not be placed in a position of working for government bounty rather than producing for a free market. . . .

Our agricultural policy will emphasize the further development of both domestic and foreign markets for farm products. We will seek ways and means of improving the operation of free markets. We envision increased efficiency in marketing and distribution as well as in production, more complete crop and market reports, improved grading and inspection services, and an expanded educational program for better human nutrition. In these ways, as in others, we can serve the best interests of consumers as well as farmers.[25]

But Secretary Benson was not ready to make specific recommendations to the Congress. He wanted to review the situation with farm leaders and probe the farm price-income problem in depth. This he did in 1953. He traveled far and wide, discussed farm policy with many leaders across the nation, and called upon the land-grant colleges for studies of various aspects of the price and income problem.

The administration's position on farm price and income policy, as developed by Secretary Benson, was outlined in a presidential message to the Congress on January 11, 1954. In general terms, the Benson proposals moved in the direction of getting government out of agriculture. This would be accomplished by the sliding scale provision in which the level of price support would decline as supplies increased. In other words, the level of price support, just as market price, would reflect the supply situation — moving inversely with it. This was the heart of the Benson policy proposal. Some of the more important provisions in the administration's new program were as follows:

Authorize the insulation from commercial markets of up to $2.5 billion worth of existing farm commodity surpluses, excluding them from carryover calculations affecting price-support levels.

Strengthen the Department of Agriculture's program for developing foreign markets.

Allow modern parity to take effect as scheduled Jan. 1, 1956, for wheat, corn, cotton, and peanuts, but limit changes from old parity formula to five percentage points per year.

Permit flexible price supports, ranging from 75 percent to 90 percent of parity, to take effect — with modifications — on five of the six basic commodities, as scheduled for Jan. 1, 1955.

For tobacco, the sixth basic commodity, continue support at 90 percent of parity when marketing quotas are in effect.

Continue the secretary of agriculture's authority to raise price supports above 90 percent of parity when such action is required by considerations of national welfare or security.

For commodities under flexible supports, vary support level inversely one percentage point for each change of two percentage points in supply, except for corn, on which supports would vary inversely to supply at one-for-one ratio.

Raise level of normal carryover for corn from 10 percent to 15 percent of domestic use plus exports.

Abolish marketing quotas for corn.

Continue discretionary price supports at up to 90 percent of parity for non-basic feed grains.

Authorize no direct price supports for meat animals.[26]

Congressional reaction to the sliding scale system of price support was mixed and to some degree along party lines, but farm congressmen from both parties were wary of the idea. Farm Bureau Federation leadership, on the other hand, was pleased with the general idea. The Congress wrangled over the sliding scale provision during the first half of 1954 and then passed the Agricultural Act of 1954 in August of that year.

The Agricultural Act of 1954 represented a compromise between the administration and farm congressmen wherein a sliding scale system of price support ranging from 82½ to 90 percent of parity was adopted for the basic commodities (excepting tobacco) for the year 1955, and support levels between 75 and 90 percent of parity thereafter.

With continued commodity surpluses and low farm prices, the Congress acted in early 1956 to pass H.R. 12, which repudiated the sliding scale of price support for basic crops and called for a restoration of price support at 90 percent of parity for the basic crops. This act was passed on April 11, 1956, and vetoed by the president on April 16. The Congress failed to override the presidential veto, but as a result of congressional pressure, the administration raised levels of price support on most grains by 5 to 6 percentage points in 1956. And so the struggle continued throughout the 1950s between the administration and the Congress over the level of price support.

In the end, Secretary Benson got his way with respect to levels of price support. He lowered the level of price support for wheat to 75 percent of parity on the 1958 crop, for corn to 77 percent of parity on the 1957 crop and on down to 65 percent of parity for the 1960 crop, and for cotton to 78 percent of parity on the 1957 crop. But price support at these lower levels did not reduce output — did not even slow down the rate of expansion — as he had hoped and expected. Stocks in government hands continued to mount, net farm incomes continued to decline, and the final years of the Benson secretaryship were bitter years in which farmers and congressmen angrily denounced the secretary and called for his resignation, and he in turn lashed back at his tormentors.[27] Agricultural distress and discontent were widespread and the agricultural administration was near a state of shambles as the year 1960 drew to an end.

The Freeman effort. As he took office in January 1961, Secretary Freeman believed strongly that farm incomes should be increased and that with the aid of government they could be increased. President Kennedy held the same general views as his secretary of agriculture regarding the desirability of increasing farm incomes, but he was also most anxious to reduce the cost of farm programs to the federal government. How was this miracle — raise farm incomes, reduce program costs — to be achieved? It was to be achieved through the mechanism of mandatory supply control. In general terms, the administration sought to raise farm prices and farm incomes by reducing the supplies of farm products offered on the market through the vehicle of self-imposed, mandatory production controls. Government would, through the granting of monopoly power to a commodity group, enable it to control, or manage, its supplies and as a result drive up prices in the marketplace to some defined, desirable levels — but not too high a level. This was the basic Kennedy-Freeman approach to the farm price-income problem.

After dealing with mounting surplus stocks of feed grains with an emergency program, the Kennedy administration turned to its long-range general program. President Kennedy in a special message to the Congress outlined the principal provisions of his long-range general program on March 16, 1961. The basic objectives of the program were (1) to raise farmer income and (2) to reduce government costs.

The technique to achieve these ends was "supply management" — a stringent system of sales and production quotas that would prevent surpluses from reaching the market and thereby drive farm market prices up above support levels. The quotas were to be based on an individual farmer's history of production. The increase in market price would mean few Government price-support acquisitions would be necessary, and therefore CCC would not acquire expensive inventories with heavy carrying costs . . .

The basic technique proposed by Mr. Kennedy was similar to production control techniques in effect since 1933. But it differed radically from existing legislation in a number of respects. It proposed to use quantity limits wherever possible instead of acreage allotments. So-called marketing quotas, as established in 1938, were based on acreage allotments, and a farmer's quota was simply as much as he could grow on his allotment. This form of production limitation had been vitiated by substantial increases in yields per acre over the years, coupled with minimum acreage allotments which prevented reduction of allotments to the sizes needed to avoid surpluses. What the new President proposed, in effect, was to hand out marketing quotas in terms of bushels of wheat, for example, that might be marketed; in that case a farmer would have no incentive to pour on fertilizer, labor and machinery in order to boost production on a given acreage. . . .

A second major difference between the existing system and Mr. Kennedy's proposal was that the new President wished to make the technique of supply control available to all farm commodities, compared with the handful (cotton, rice, peanuts, wheat, tobacco) now subject to marketing quotas (based on acreage allotments) and the larger number (but still relatively few) subject to marketing orders (e.g. — certain fruits and vegetables; see Agricultural Marketing Agreement Act of 1937).

The President did not propose installing the new system immediately for all or any commodities. What he proposed was that Congress, by amendments to existing basic laws, first create legal authority for the supply management technique to be used for any crop. Next, Congress would create a set of procedures whereby committees of producers of each commodity would meet and draft income-support programs, which might include the supply-management techniques best adapted to their crop. If agreed to by two-thirds of the producers in a referendum, the individual crop programs would then be submitted to Congress, which would have the power to veto any program (but not alter it) by majority vote in either chamber within 60 days.

Mr. Kennedy also made several other important requests — expansion of surplus disposal operations, both for domestic welfare and to needy foreign peoples, more aid to areas of rural poverty through a rural Area Redevelopment Program, expansion of farm credit facilities and rural housing program. But the supply management proposal was the heart of his long-range program for solving the farm problem.[28]

But whereas farm congressmen greeted the emergency feed grain program, with its features of voluntary controls, production payments, and higher levels of price support, with enthusiastic support, they greeted the long-range program with solid resistance. The idea of mandatory production controls was clearly repugnant to them. To accept mandatory controls, first without a system of payment to farmers and second with a set of enabling procedures which had the effect of reducing their political power, was too much. The Kennedy-Freeman mandatory supply management approach died in committee in both chambers of the Congress.

To obtain the legislative authorizations that it sought in the areas of surplus disposal and rural development and to cope with the continuing surplus situation in wheat and feed grains, the Kennedy-Freeman administration retreated to a system of voluntary controls and production payments for wheat and feed grains in the omnibus Agricultural Act of 1961 (passed August 8, 1961). But the administration came back to the Congress in 1962 with a proposed program involving mandatory controls for wheat, feed grains, and dairy products wherein farmers would derive their benefits in the form of higher prices in the marketplace resulting from the operation of the control programs — *not from payments to producers by government.* In the legislative struggle that ensued, the concept of mandatory controls was beaten down for both feed grains and dairy products, but the administration saved the mandatory control feature for wheat beginning with the 1964 crop. As is well known, however, the mandatory control program for the 1964 wheat crop was defeated by wheat producers in referendum in the spring of 1963. With this defeat, the long struggle on the part of the Kennedy administration to find an effective, *but low-cost,* solution to the excess capacity problem of American agriculture was over. The objective of voluntary control programs with production payments espoused by farmers overrode the objective of reduced program costs advanced by the administration.

Key policy developments. The policy struggles discussed above produced some important results. Although Secretary Brannan lost his battle for a whole new farm program, the idea of employing production payments to support farm income gained conceptual recognition and growing numbers of supporters as a result of the submission of the Brannan Plan. Thus, in 1954, when a way was being sought to increase incomes to wool growers as an incentive to increase wool production in the United States, without raising wool prices above world levels, the production payment idea was adopted for wool in the agricultural act of that year. And the Kennedy administration made increasing use of payments to producers in the early 1960s as a means of supporting producer incomes. Support for production payments as a means of protecting and enhancing producer incomes gained strength steadily from the Brannan Plan experience onward.

If the agricultural sector of a nation is experiencing rapid technological advance and thus rapid increases in aggregate output, if its producers are unwilling to impose strict production controls on themselves, and if the sector has a large exportable surplus, a policy of high-level price support — significantly above the world price — will, short of a miracle, become an unworkable policy. The "if" conditions outlined above, it will be noted, fit almost perfectly the situation in the United States in the 1950s. Thus, it is not surprising that the policy collapsed. Secretary Benson oversold his flexible price support policy in that it could not cure the general surplus problem and the farm income problem at one and the same time (and within the range of permissible price support flexibility granted by the Congress, it could do neither). But Secretary Benson was right on one point — *the level of price support had to come down.* And his pursuit of this extremely unpopular policy among farmers and farm politicians led eventually to a situation in which the commodity programs could once again be formulated in workable, or manageable, terms.

The Kennedy administration lost its fight for strict mandatory controls in which the government costs of farm programs might be reduced significantly. But in losing, it pioneered a system of voluntary controls, which were workable in the sense that (1) they were acceptable and (2) they had the capacity to reduce production. The experience in the Kennedy years further demonstrated that any farm policy which seeks to hold farm prices and incomes above equilibrium levels must, if it is to be continued over a period of years, have coupled with it a system of *effective* supply management devices.

With these policy lessons, experiences, and results, all acquired through prolonged struggles, and often intense struggles, the stage was set for fashioning an effective, workable, reasonably acceptable, although still costly, farm policy.

The basic compromise, circa 1965–70. The basic policy compromise of the period 1965–70 included more than the Food and Agricultural Act of 1965, although that act provided much of its central structure. As our phrasing indicates, it was a compromise — a compromise of many dimensions — among interest groups with varied and often conflicting objectives. But through a testing in the political fires it emerged, not perfect, but able to cope with the central problem of commercial agriculture in the United States in the 1950s and 1960s, *general excess production capacity.* For two decades too many resources were engaged in producing too many food and fiber products; in the basic compromise the nation found a workable, acceptable solution to that general problem. Let us set down the constituent parts of the compromise:

1. Expansion of the aggregate demand for farm products by pursuing a foreign commercial policy aimed at expanding world trade.
2. Expansion of the aggregate demand for food domestically by the implementation of programs designed to increase food consumption among the poor and other vulnerable groups.
3. Expansion of the aggregate demand for food and fiber products by the implementation of foreign aid programs designed to increase food and fiber shipments to less developed countries.
4. Provision of stability to commercial agriculture (i.e., protect commercial farmers against unpredictable, short-run declines in farm prices) by supporting the prices of major farm commodities at or near world levels.
5. Increase of farm incomes above equilibrium levels for producers of major crops by making direct income payments to those producers who participate in any control programs that may be in effect.[29]
6. Control of production by means of acreage control measures wherein supplies of each major commodity are adjusted to total requirements (domestic commercial, plus foreign commercial, plus domestic food aid, plus foreign food aid, plus storage needs).

7. Voluntary control of production where individual producers have the option of participating or not, and receive a land diversion payment for participation.

8. Maintenance of a reserve stock of grains and certain other storable commodities, but one not clearly defined, to protect the nation against unforeseen emergencies.

The Food and Agricultural Act of 1965 directed the secretary of agriculture in some cases to set price support, or income, payments at specific levels; in other cases it defined a range within which he was free to determine the specific levels. Diversion payment rates were typically left to the discretion of the secretary. Other acts and budget appropriations determined the magnitude of expenditures on food programs, domestic and foreign. Thus, the level and extent of price and income support provided commercial farmers under the basic compromise were determined in part by the Congress and in part by the administration. Gross expenditures by the federal government on all the programs involved ranged from a low of $4.8 billion in 1967 to a high of $7.6 billion in 1970.[30]

To the basic policy compromise for the period 1966–70 three new or clarifying ideas were added by the acts of 1970 and 1973: (1) the set-aside control device, (2) the payment limitation principle, and (3) the clear enunciation of the principle of price support at or near world levels and income support through the use of payments to producers in the form of (a) an announced loan rate, (b) an announced income target price, and (c) the use of deficiency payments whenever the market price falls below the target price. None of these program concepts changes the basic policy compromise; they refine it, make it more explicit, and attempt to make it more equitable.

Economic Content of the Programs

The economic content — substance and effects — of the evolving farm programs as they affected a single commodity is depicted in figures 3-1, 3-2, 3-3, and 3-4. The lines DD and SS in figure 3-1 may be said to represent the demand for and the supply of some major commodity X (say, wheat), where no government programs are at work. The resulting equilibrium price of commodity X is OM. In figure 3-1, the high price support model, the loan rate is represented as ON price, which makes the effective demand for commodity X perfectly elastic to the right of line DD at ON price. Various program features cause the demand and supply curves to shift positions. The operation of domestic food assistance programs and foreign food aid programs causes the demand for commodity X to expand to position D_aD_a. The operation of acreage control programs causes the supply of commodity X to contract to position S_aS_a.[31]

But the adjustments in demand and supply resulting from the operation of the programs, represented in figure 3-1, do not clear the market of commodity X at the supported price ON. Thus, the government is required to take over, to acquire stocks, of AB amount to hold the market price of commodity X up to the support price ON. And this is in fact what happened in 1953–55; the government acquired large stocks of grains, cotton, and other commodities in its effort to support farm market prices above equilibrium levels. Gross returns to producers are represented by the shaded area, ON-OB.

In figure 3-2, the Benson model, the demand for and supply for commodity X are represented by the lines DD and SS, unchanged from figure 3-1. But several other important developments of the Benson years are represented in figure 3-2. In accordance with the policy views and legislative achievements of the Eisenhower-Benson administration the loan rate is lowered to ON_1 amount in figure 3-2. In conformity with the continuance and expansion of certain domestic and foreign food assistance programs the demand for commodity X is expanded to position D_aD_a. The weak efforts to control production in the Benson years were overridden by rapid and widespread farm technological advance, which is represented in figure 3-2 by an expansion in the supply curve to $S_{at}S_{at}$. Thus, in the Benson model the government is required to take over A_1B_1 amount of commodity X to hold the market price of that commodity up to the lowered loan level ON_1. An expansion in supply, powered by rapid and widespread farm technological advance, overrode the effect of a limited reduction in the level of price support, and forced the government to continue to accumulate stocks to support farm prices, even at lower levels. The shaded box formed by ON_1-OB_1 represents producers' gross returns from this commodity.

A differently conceived effort to cope with the farm price and income problem is represented in figure 3-3, the Kennedy-Freeman proposal. In this proposal, the basic demand for and supply of commodity X are represented by lines DD and SS as in the previous two figures. In figure 3-3, the loan rate is increased modestly to ON_2 price (increased modestly over ON_1 represented in figure 3-2). In figure 3-3 the demand for commodity X expands to position D_aD_a, as in the previous two models, as the result of the operation of domestic and foreign food assistance programs. The Kennedy-Freeman proposal, it will be recalled, called for tight, mandatory production controls sufficiently effective to override the expansionary effects of farm technological advance and thus adjust supply to the expanded demand D_aD_a at the level of price support. This is represented in figure 3-3 by the shift of the supply curve first to the

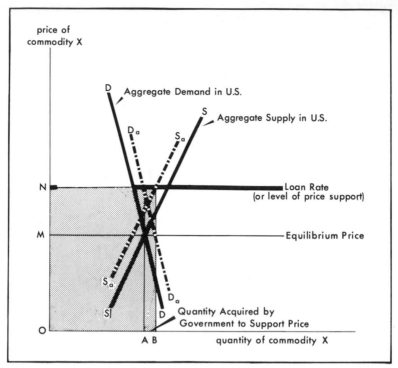

Figure 3-1. The Economic Effects of Farm Programs: The High Price Support Model, circa 1954

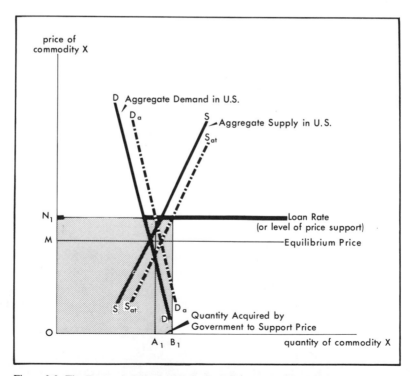

Figure 3-2. The Economic Effects of Farm Programs: The Benson Model

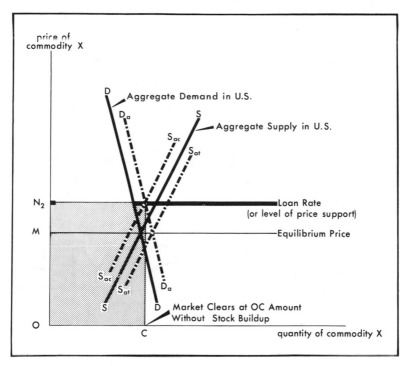

Figure 3-3. The Economic Effects of Farm Programs: The Kennedy-Freeman Proposal

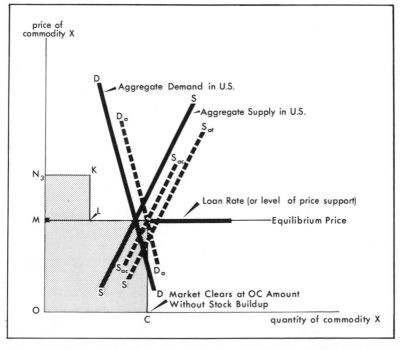

Figure 3-4. The Economic Effects of Farm Programs: The Compromise Model, 1965–72

expanded position $S_{at}S_{at}$ and then back to the market-clearing position $S_{ac}S_{ac}$. Under the Kennedy-Freeman proposal the market would clear at OC amount and at price ON_2, which is also the level of price support. Farmers' gross returns are equal to the shaded area, ON_2-OC.

It will be observed in the Kennedy-Freeman proposal, figure 3-3, that farmers were asked to effect a significant reduction in supply through the acceptance of tight mandatory production controls, for which they would have received only a small gain in price (compare ON_2 of figure 3-3 with ON_1 of figure 3-2). Under the Kennedy-Freeman proposal, farmers would not have been permitted to employ mandatory production controls to drive the supply curve $S_{ac}S_{ac}$ up the inelastic demand curve D_aD_a and realize some price above ON_2 and the corresponding larger gross revenue. Thus seeing no obvious income benefit to themselves from the acceptance of mandatory controls, farmers rejected tight mandatory controls both with the help of their representatives in the Congress and the referendum in the field.

The basic farm policy compromise described in the previous section is represented in figure 3-4. The basic demand for and supply of commodity X is shown in figure 3-4 by the lines DD and SS as in the previous three figures. The loan rate is lowered to OM price, or the market equilibrium price. Once again the demand for commodity X expands to D_aD_a through the operation of domestic and foreign food assistance programs. First the supply of commodity X expands to position $S_{at}S_{at}$ through the force of farm technological advance, and, second, the supply curve contracts to position $S_{ac}S_{ac}$ through a system of voluntary controls in which farmers are paid to participate in the production control program. The payments are made to farmers in part to maintain their incomes where loan rates have been lowered and in part to induce them to participate in the "voluntary" production control program. The total payments received by participating farmers (price support payments plus land-idling payments) are represented in figure 3-4 by the box N_3KLM. In the compromise model the market clears at OC amount and at the equilibrium price OM. Farmers' gross returns in this model are equal to the shaded area OM-OC plus the payment box N_3KLM.

In the compromise model, figure 3-4, the price support mechanism ceases to be a price–income-enhancing mechanism and converts into a price-stabilization mechanism. Price supports are used to stabilize product prices at the market equilibrium level and thereby assure farmers that the bottom will not fall out of their price structure. Production controls are employed to prevent the accumulation of stocks and thereby force the market equilibrium price to decline in a future period and pull the level of price support with it. The income supplement to commercial farmers is made in the form of payments from the public treasury, and those payments are modified from year to year to reflect the amounts needed to (1) induce farmers to participate in the control programs and (2) provide them with some measure of a fair income.

In sum, we have in figures 3-1, 3-2, 3-3, and 3-4 a graphic interpretation of the farm price and income programs, and their economic effects, that evolved over the period 1948–73. In some respects they were similar. They all sought to expand demand, and they were all confounded by rapid and widespread technological advance of farming. Yet philosophically and ideologically, the Eisenhower-Benson and Kennedy-Freeman approaches were very dissimilar. Those two administrations viewed the food and agricultural sector very differently and approached it very differently.

The basic compromise, like most compromises, is not elegant in economic terms. But from 1965 to 1972 it worked reasonably well. It facilitated the integration of the agricultural sector of the United States with the world market. It operated to stabilize prices to both domestic producers and consumers. It effected a reasonable adjustment of supplies to demand in a highly uncertain, dynamic world. And it contributed to a gradual decline in government-owned stocks. Finally, it continued to protect and support the incomes of farmers. All this we can see or visualize in the graphic presentation of figure 3-4.

A Closing Note

By the end of 1973 administration spokesmen were arguing that a fundamental change had occurred in American farm policy. Agriculture, they argued, was no longer government managed and government directed; it was now market oriented and market directed. How could they argue thusly? The basic policy compromise for the period 1966–70, described above, was still in place. True, some of the program elements had been modified and refined somewhat by the acts of 1970 and 1973, but the principal program features of the basic policy compromise were still authorized in law.

What happened is as follows. Some dramatic physical events and some important changes in market forces around the world in 1972–73 lifted prices and incomes in the agricultural sector of the United States far above the pricing triggers (target prices and loan rates) authorized for the programs in 1973. In terms of figure 3-4, foreign commercial demand for commodity X expanded dramatically, causing the demand curve DD to jump far, far to the right. This great expansion in DD in 1972–73 caused the market price for commodity X to shoot skyward, far, far above the old equilibrium price and loan rate shown in figure 3-4. Market prices in 1973–74 were so far above the equilibrium price shown in figure 3-4 that, given the scale of figure 3-4, they could not be shown on the same chart.

As a result the farm programs became inoperative in 1974, and market prices generated in a worldwide context became the principal guides to re-source use in American agriculture in 1973 and 1974. American farm policy did not change; the world changed in 1972 and 1973. Time will tell whether prices and incomes of American agriculture will fall back to their pre-1973 levels and the programs will once again become operative at that level; or whether the pricing triggers of the programs will be raised to the post-1973 price and income levels and the programs will once again become operative at that level; or whether a wide gulf will be maintained between the level of program-pricing triggers and the actual level of farm prices and incomes, and the agricultural sector in fact will operate in a free market as the programs wither away from disuse.

CHAPTER 4

A Look at the Legislative and Administrative Processes

It is our purpose in this chapter to examine and gain an appreciation of the legislative and administrative processes that produced the policies and programs that are the subject of this volume. We cannot in this volume, for reasons of space, review the legislative history of each piece of farm legislation or detail the many reorganizations of the U.S. Department of Agriculture over the period 1948–73. Further, the central focus of this volume is not on public administration or the legislative process. It is on the substance of farm policy — the intent of policies, the content of programs, and the operations and results of programs. But one can understand the policies and programs of the period 1948–73 much better if he has some knowledge of the conditions under which they were enacted into law and subsequently administered.

We will then inquire into the legislative and administrative processes in the farm policy area as they existed in the 1960s and early 1970s and develop a generalized pattern of behavior for that period. The reader should recognize, and will in part from the discussion, that the patterns of legislative and administrative behavior presented here evolved over a long period of time and will continue to change in the 1970s and 1980s. But the material in this chapter should give the reader a good appreciation of the workings of the legislative and administrative processes in the period in history in which the Agricultural Acts of 1965, 1970, and 1973 were passed and implemented.

It should be recognized further that the legislative and administrative styles of Democratic and Republican administrations differed to an important degree in the agricultural policy area during the period 1948–73. Democratic administrations were more at home with the staff and the organization of the U.S. Department of Agriculture than Republican administrations, since a Democratic administration created the modern USDA over the long period 1933–48.

103

Hence, Democratic administrations have been inclined to use the technical staff of the USDA more fully and unreservedly in the development of legislation than Republican administrations. The Democrats too have been more willing to take the career staff into their confidence in the administration of programs than have the Republicans — and probably for the same reason, namely, the Democrats are inclined to think that the career staff are their own people.

The differing ideologies of the two parties with respect to farm policies have also influenced the legislative and administrative styles of their respective administrations. The strong desire on the part of Republican administrations to get government out of agriculture and to let the market play a more influential role has influenced the legislative style of Republican administrations as well as the content of their legislative proposals. An administration that proposes to reduce or eliminate a government program, and possibly the agency that is administering it, must be careful and cautious in developing and submitting its legislative proposals if it is to avoid building opposition to its proposals. Democratic administrations, on the other hand, which have little or no ideological bias against developing and using government programs to achieve certain economic and social objectives, have typically found career government workers and existing government agencies willing and happy to help develop new programs and expand or modify old ones. Thus, Democratic administrations tend to lean heavily on the professional and career staffs of existing agencies in the development and submission of legislative proposals in the farm policy area.

It would be a mistake to make too much of these points in thinking about and appraising the legislative and administrative activities of agricultural administrations of different political persuasions. Both must find the ways and means to convert their policy ideas into legislation, and both must administer the laws as enacted. Nonetheless, the attitudes and styles of secretaries of agriculture and their political staffs do differ importantly, and they do differ by political parties and for some of the reasons given above. Readers should keep this in mind as they look at the generalized, nonstylized pictures of legislative and administrative processes for the agricultural sector presented below.

The Legislative Process

The changing role of administrations. The president of the United States and his secretary of agriculture were not active agents of economic policy formation in the agricultural sector at the turn of the twentieth century. This was true primarily because it was not deemed proper for government to interfere with the forces of the market at that time — with the possible exception of the manipulation of the external tariff. "Tama Jim" Wilson, secretary of agriculture from 1897 to 1913, was concerned primarily with developing a strong research and extension program in the Department of Agriculture; he was not concerned with the formulation of economic policies and programs for agriculture, since government was not concerned.

But times and conditions change. Hard times in agriculture in the 1920s forced elected officials in government to think about economic policies for agriculture. By a concurrent resolution, the House and the Senate created a Joint Commission of Agricultural Inquiry in June 1921 to study the agricultural depression and make recommendations for dealing with it.[1] One year later Secretary of Agriculture Henry C. Wallace called a national conference to inquire further into the causes of the agricultural depression. Secretary Wallace also created in 1922 the Bureau of Agricultural Economics to study the economic problems of agriculture on a systematic and continuing basis. And from 1924 to 1928 the Congress and President Coolidge wrestled over legislation designed to intervene in the market and support domestic farm prices, the McNary-Haugen Bill.

President Coolidge succeeded in defeating the McNary-Haugen legislation, but in the process he and his administration became deeply involved in farm policy formulation. And so it would remain from the Coolidge to the Nixon administrations. President Hoover in 1929 took personal charge of formulating a farm program to deal with the farm depression and piloted that program through the Congress against strong opposition; his program was enacted in the Agricultural Marketing Act of 1929. Thus, the precedent was set, not only for involvement in policy formulation, but for presenting the administration's views on farm policy to the Congress in the form of a program.

When President Roosevelt and his secretary of agriculture, Henry A. Wallace, took office in 1933 they had positive views for dealing with the now worsened agricultural depression. They submitted those views to the Congress in the form of legislation, and with relatively minor modifications those views were enacted in the Agricultural Adjustment Act of 1933, which created the Agricultural Adjustment Administration.[2] What had established precedent in the Hoover administration now became a tradition in the Roosevelt administration. Whenever old legislation expired or new legislation was needed in the farm policy area, the administration expected to propose such legislation, and the Congress expected to receive such proposed legislation.

The emergent legislative procedure. Over the long period 1933–68 it thus became accepted procedure for the secretary of agriculture to initiate new price and income legislation for the farm sector. This does not mean that the Congress has simply become a "rubber stamp" in this policy area; we reviewed the long and fierce struggles waged between three secretaries of agriculture and the Congress over farm policy in the previous chapter. But it does mean that the Congress has come to accept the procedure wherein the secretary of agriculture initiates new program ideas with respect to farm price and income policy.

The general acceptance of this procedure is made clear by the relationship that developed between Secretary Clifford M. Hardin and the Congress in the period 1969–70. Secretary Hardin tried to revert to the pre-1933 relationship by asking the Congress to write the new legislation required by the expiration of the existing law. This the Congress would not do or could not do (we shall argue the latter shortly); hence it looked for an extended period in 1969–70 as if an impasse had been reached with regard to new farm policy legislation. But finally the secretary gave the Congress some policy guidance with regard to the administration's wishes and loaned some of his experienced staff to the congressional committees of agriculture with the result that the Agricultural Act of 1970 was finally put together in a coherent package. The somewhat old-fashioned view of Secretary Hardin with respect to the proper relation between the executive and legislative branches of the government created an important void in the farm policy legislative process in 1969–70.

Why, it may be asked, has the secretary of agriculture so readily usurped the key initiating role with regard to farm policy legislation and why has the Congress so readily acquiesced in the usurpation? The answer, we believe, rests in the legal, administrative, and economic complexity of farm price and income legislation and the need for a skilled and experienced staff to deal with those complexities. Any piece of farm price and income legislation has direct effects on the commodities involved with respect to quantities, prices, and costs that are difficult to estimate. Further, there are many and varied indirect effects on other commodities, resource use, and size and structure of farms that are even more difficult to estimate and appraise. The program provisions as they impinge on farm operators must be equitable as between operators, and administerable as they relate to individual farmers, if the program is to operate successfully in the field. Finally, each new piece of legislation represents amendments to some earlier act. New legislation is created, or written, by adding on to earlier acts some new language here and cutting some old language there.

Even without concern for the moment with the good or bad aspects of the objectives of a piece of price-income legislation, it is no easy task to specify the program features of that legislation which will in fact result in the achievement of those objectives. Skill and experience are required by at least three kinds of professionals in the drafting of new legislation if that legislation is to yield the intended results in practice: economists who understand and are able to measure the relevant economic relations in the farm economy; program administrators who understand farmers and their problems, hence include program features which can be effectively administered; and lawyers who know the received law in sufficient detail and the legislative history so intimately that they are able to amend the organic law to achieve the desired results.

This skill and talent has been built into the concerned agencies in the USDA over many decades, and it exists nowhere else. Thus we argue that new farm price and income legislation gets written in the only place where it can be written, namely, the U.S. Department of Agriculture. Only in the USDA do we find the staff with the capacity in the necessary areas to draft legislation which can in fact produce the results intended by those initiating the legislation.

Perhaps the agricultural committees of the Congress could build a staff with sufficient skill and experience to draft effective legislation in the complex area of farm price and income legislation. But they have not. And they could do so now only with considerable effort and at considerable expense. Thus, the work of developing new program ideas and incorporating those ideas into legislation has devolved upon the research, legal, and administrative staffs of the U.S. Department of Agriculture. The secretary provides the policy guidance in the form of program goals and objectives, and his technical staffs construct the program features which can achieve those goals, or perhaps even tell the secretary that his goals are unattainable, given certain constraints (e.g., a budget limit).

The legislative initiating process circa 1965–70. The secretary of agriculture and his immediate advisers, in consultation with the president and his immediate advisers, decide upon certain farm policy goals. The secretary next calls upon his economists and program administrators to construct a program, or to set forth the program alternatives, for achieving those goals. In the process of building a program, estimates of costs, production, and prices will be generated, as well as estimates of secondary effects on commodity substitutes, resource use, and farm numbers and size. In this process, the original goals of the secretary may be compromised in various ways. Through an intricate refinement process of discussion, estimation, compromise, and reformulation, a farm program is built. At this juncture the secretary will call upon the lawyers and request them to cast the program in a legislative form; this process may also lead to program changes and compromise. Finally an internal draft of new legislation is prepared, which if enacted, would have a high probability of producing the results originally sought by the secretary.[3]

But this is only the beginning. Next the secretary will want to try out his legislative proposal on interested and concerned parties. These will include White House staffers, farm organization and commodity representatives, farm congressional leaders, and agribusiness leaders. The White House will be interested in program costs and effects on food prices and foreign trade, among other things. Farm organization and commodity representatives will be interested in possible commodity price results, farm income results, and possible conflicts between program provisions and the public stand of these organizations. Farm congressmen will be interested in the implications for their constituents and whether the legislative package can be passed, and agribusiness leaders will be concerned with the volume of product produced, hence the volume of producer goods to be sold to farmers and the volume of the farm product to be processed.

After the legislative proposal has been reviewed with these interested parties it is highly likely that it will be modified further. Certainly the legislative proposal must be acceptable to the White House if it is to be transmitted to the Congress by the president. And certainly it must have the support of some of the more important farm organizations and commodity groups, as well as congressional leaders, if it is to stand a chance of being passed by the Congress. Thus, much tailoring of the legislative proposal is likely to take place in order to improve the chances of its passage by the Congress. It is at this stage that political considerations influence the proposal to an important degree.

We digress at this point to emphasize that the steps and stages described here do not, in fact, occur in the same orderly fashion as our discussion. There is much backing and filling in the preparation of a legislative proposal at each step and stage. An important new idea may enter the proposal as the result of a luncheon between the secretary of agriculture and a key congressional leader; or an important idea may drop out of the proposal as the result of a farm leader's visit to the White House. The development of a farm legislative proposal is a wonderously complex and unpredictable process. Now back to our orderly discussion of a disorderly process.

In the next stage the proposed legislation is transmitted to the White House for official review by the Bureau of the Budget and the Council of Economic Advisers. The Bureau of the Budget reviews the proposed legislation for consistency with the federal budget and the programs of other agencies. The council reviews the proposed legislation for consistency with the general economic policies of the nation. Since the proposed legislation will have already been reviewed by these agencies informally, as well as for political clearance in the White House, it is unlikely that any major modifications will be made in it at this stage. As the secretary explains the proposed legislation to the president and gains final clearance for its transmittal to the Congress, the secretary in reality commits himself to the estimates and judgments that have been made regarding the consequences that flow from its enactment (e.g., governmental costs, price results, farmer reaction). The secretary's standing in the White House will be determined in large measure by whether the estimated results turn out to be correct. The president does not expect to be deceived by his chief agricultural officer with respect to the budget or the reaction of voters, and a president is not likely to tolerate a cabinet officer who leads him astray. Thus, the relationship established between a secretary and his president at this stage regarding an important piece of legislation is likely to have an important bearing on future relationships.

The next and final stage in the legislative initiating process is the transmittal of the legislative proposal to the Congress by the president and its introduction into the congressional legislative process. The first draft of the presidential letter of transmittal will almost certainly have been prepared in the USDA. It does two principal things: (1) describes the purposes and mechanics of the proposal in nonlegal language and (2) builds a persuasive argument for its early passage into legislation. The final draft of the message is likely to show the special trademark of the president's staff. The letter of transmittal is, of course, intended to catch the eyes of the press as well as congressmen and will attempt to build support for the legislative proposal through the communications media.

If the legislative proposal is an important one (as we have assumed here), and the houses of Congress are controlled by the party of the president, then the chairman of the committee concerned will be consulted with regard to who should introduce the administration proposal and under what conditions. It is likely that the committee chairman himself will be asked to introduce the bill and to pilot it through the congressional legislative steps. The secretary's program proposal is now in legislative bill form, has a sponsor, and is before the Congress. The initiating phase is complete.

The role of the Congress in farm policy formulation. As the federal government has played a more positive role in the farm economy in the way of supporting, or enhancing, prices and incomes, the initiation of such policies has shifted, as we noted above, from the Congress to the administration. The logic of this shift is not difficult to understand when we consider the role of the individual congressman in the political process. True, he is a member of a legislative body with the responsibility for making legislative decisions (i.e., transforming certain ideas into law, or rejecting certain ideas). But he is only one member of that legislative body. And in the American system he represents one small area of the country: a district, if he is a member of the House, or a state, if he is a member of the Senate. As a representative of a district or a state, then, he is concerned with representing the interests of the people who elected him from his district or state.

What does this mean? It means that his number one goal, as a congressman, is in doing those things and achieving those objectives that *his* constituents want done. This means knowing the problems of his local area, the aspirations of the people in his area, and the needs of his area. Now the problems, aspirations, and needs of his area may be similar to those of the rest of the nation, in which case the task of lawmaking is made easy. But more often this is not the case. And with respect to the agricultural economy it typically is not the case. The economic, social, and technical problems confronting cotton, peanut, or tobacco farmers in Georgia are likely to be very different from those of apple growers in Washington or feed-lot operators in Nebraska-Colorado.

Thus, the viewpoint that a representative from one of these areas brings to the Congress with respect to farm price and income policy is a partial or limited view — limited to the problems of his geographical area. In the case of a congressman from a farming district, or state, this view is concerned with crop and livestock problems of his area and how to deal with those problems. And he will be judged by his constituents on how well he represents their local problems and finds solutions to them. In this political context a farm congressman is not likely to spend much of his time and scarce resources on the development of a national farm program. He prefers, much prefers, that a responsible government agency or major farm organization do the time-consuming staff work that is involved in developing a national farm program, and that the program be introduced into the legislative process by some congressional friend of the administration, or of the farm organization. In this process, the farm congressman will study the program in terms of its effects on his farmer constituents and seek to amend it so as to make it more consistent with the needs and objectives of his farmer constituents. This is the role that the congressman who wishes to survive prefers to play. The formulation of a national program he will leave to those with national responsibilities. What he wants is the opportunity to cut and piece the national program to fit the needs of the farmers in his area. If the program in the bill, as amended by him, will help his farmers, he will be for it; if it is indifferent he will be indifferent; if it hurts his farmers he will be against it.

But how is the farm congressman going to get his desired amendment adopted in committee, and how are the farm congressmen going to get their bill adopted by an urban-dominated Congress? In each case, a minority party is seeking to achieve a particular legislative objective in which a majority must concur. The answer runs as follows: the minority parties achieve their legislative objectives through an informal process of bargaining. The farm congressman from Georgia who seeks a special program feature for peanuts will agree to support a program feature sought by an Iowa congressman with regard to corn and a Kansas congressman with regard to wheat in return for their support of his peanut provision. By such a bargaining process majorities are built in committee to report bills onto the floor of the House or Senate, and by such a bargaining process majorities are built in the full House and Senate to pass the legislation that may be involved.

To some degree congressmen follow party lines in building these majorities, but only to a degree. In farm legislation, for example, it is common for a midwestern farm congressman from the Republican party to support a program provision sought by a southern farm congressman from the Democratic party in return for the southerner's support on some other issue. And this crossing of party lines occurs regularly both in committee and on the floor of the House or Senate. This process of building temporary majorities through individual and group bargaining to pass legislation important to a local area or region was termed by John C. Calhoun as the Doctrine of the Concurrent Majority, and it is still a regularly employed procedure of the American Congress.[4] Majorities come and go — forming around an issue through compromise and bargaining and then dissolving once the issue is decided.

Operating procedures and policy formulation. The principal work of the Congress is conducted in committees. A bill introduced into one chamber or another of the congress is immediately assigned to a committee with responsibility in its subject area, and the committee involved will in large measure decide its fate: whether to reject it by letting it die in committee; whether to hold hearings on it; whether to amend it; or whether to approve it and report it back to the House or Senate for further legislative action. As one former member of the House wrote to a constituent, "Congress is a collection of committees that come together in a chamber periodically to approve one another's actions."[5]

The Senate Committee on Agriculture and Forestry in the 92nd Congress contained 14 members — eight Democrats and six Republicans. It had six subcommittees; they were (1) Environment, Soil Conservation, and Forestry, (2) Agricultural Credit and Rural Electrification, (3) Agricultural Production, Marketing, and Stabilization of Prices, (4) Agricultural Research and General Legislation, (5) Agricultural Exports, and (6) Rural Development. The titles of these subcommittees describe reasonably accurately the jurisdiction of the full Committee on Agriculture and Forestry. The chairman of this committee in the 92nd Congress was Herman E. Talmadge of Georgia.

The Committee on Agriculture in the House of Representatives in the 92nd Congress was composed of 36 members — 22 Democrats and 14 Republicans. It had ten subcommittees; they were (1) Cotton, (2) Dairy and Poultry, (3) Forests, (4) Livestock and Grains, (5) Oilseeds and Rice, (6) Tobacco, (7) Conservation and Credit, (8) Department Operations, (9) Domestic Marketing and Consumer Relations, and (10) Family Farms and Rural Development. Again the titles of the subcommittees are an indication of the nature and scope of the jurisdiction of the full House Committee on Agriculture. The chairman of the full committee in the 92nd Congress was William R. Poage of Texas.[6]

The committees described above are authorizing committees; they authorize legislation. But almost every piece of legislation passed by the Congress and signed into law by the president requires an appropriation of funds to implement it. The appropriation of funds in both chambers of Congress comes under the jurisdiction of the Appropriations committees of those chambers. The work of taking testimony, reviewing budgets, and recommending a particular budget for agricultural programs is conducted by an 11-member subcommittee of the Appropriations Committee of the House. Needless to say, this agricultural subcommittee on appropriations wields great power, since a program, or governmental operation, without a budget appropriation for practical purposes does not exist. And a program or operation that is inadequately funded will in all probability be poorly or weakly implemented. Policy formulation may be the exclusive province of the authorizing committees, but implementation is dependent upon favorable action by the relevant appropriations subcommittee.

The committee structure and system of conducting the business of the Congress is ideally suited to the *partial, incremental approach* to policy formulation generally, and to agricultural policy formulation in particular. This is true for a number of reasons. First, committee chairmanships, hence positions of leadership, have not in the past been achieved through party regularity, but rather through seniority. Second, members with similar basic interests are brought together in working groups (i.e., subcommittees) and these common areas of interest tend to transcend party interests and goals. Third, the working arrangements of subcommittees tend to be informal, at least relatively so, and the work of subcommittees takes place in executive sessions not open to the public or the press — out of the public eye. For these reasons political bargains among subcommittee members, regardless of party, are easily and conveniently arranged.

A congressman thus finds it relatively easy (1) to bring before a working subcommittee an amendment to a bill adding a provision beneficial to his district, or state, or deleting a provision that is harmful to his local area, and (2) to work out an arrangement with his colleagues for their support of his amendment in return for his support of theirs in this or some other bill. In other words, the informal procedures and the easy, closed-to-the-public sessions of the working subcommittees lend themselves to (1) the representation of special and area interests and (2) bargaining processes wherein the objectives of those special or area interests are realized.

The committee and subcommittee structure and system of conducting business further lends itself to the representation of special interests by individuals and organizations in the congressman's district, or state, and by groups and organizations that maintain offices in Washington. Procedures for taking testimony on bills give special interests and groups with a formal invitation to present their views on pending legislation, which more often than not amounts to a partial view. Typically, a special-interest group will be seeking to add or delete a particular provision in a bill in order that the interests of that group will be favorably affected by the legislation. But more important than the formal hearing procedure in the influencing of pending legislation in a partial or incremental way is the informal representation of local and special-interest groups to congressmen in the subcommittee. Representatives of local and special interests can at the time a bill is being reviewed and reworked in subcommittee — when the bill is in a state of flux and out of the public view — most easily achieve partial and special amendments. This period in the life of a bill was designed, it would seem, for achieving the special purposes of special interests, and they make the most of it.

Once the bill has been reported out of committee and moves onto the floor of the House or the Senate, the process of amendment becomes more difficult — party discipline becomes more important, personal bargaining less so, and the national interest becomes important relative to special and local interests. Bargaining over issues and votes continues as a bill is debated on the floor, but that bargaining relates more to major groups and regions and less to personal arrangements wherein support for one local provision is traded for support on another local provision. The increased visibility of a bill, as it is debated on the floor, tends to raise the level of debate and widen the bargaining process.

The tone of the preceding discussion may have implied that the partial, or local, or incremental approach to policy formulation through the legislative process in the Congress is all bad. But this is not the case. Rationalistic, national price and income programs may in certain situations deal with the problems of and the needs of farmers in a given local area in a completely unsatisfactory manner. National policy formulators have a way of ignoring the unique characteristics and problems of local areas in their drive to achieve such national objectives as lower program costs, higher farm prices, or more effective control of production; hence the national policy may create new and possibly even worse problems for such areas. A congressman who knows his district, or his state, and understands the implications of a national farm policy for his district or state, may amend the legislation as it relates to his local area so that the program effects are beneficial to his farmers rather than harmful, without in any way weakening the national program. The interest which a congressman has in his area together with his intimate knowledge of it may convert an intolerable program situation for his area into a tolerable one. Thus, without question the congressman has a legitimate role to play in the formulation of national farm policies in the way of helping to tailor an operating program to the special needs and problems of his area.

At the other end of the continuum relating to special provisions, special concessions, and special amendments, however, we find legislative products which are ineffective in achieving their policy objectives because they are shot full of loopholes and exceptions. At this end of the continuum a new piece of legislation becomes a grab bag of "goodies" for local and special interests that is incapable of dealing satisfactorily with the problems confronting farmers. We do not suggest that every piece of farm policy legislation passed by the Congress approaches such a state of ineffectiveness. Or even that most do. But we do suggest that unless such disciplining forces as program costs, or party discipline, or presidential leadership are at work to maintain the essential integrity and internal consistency of a national farm policy, it can be picked to pieces through local and special-interest amendments. The danger is always present in the congressional legislative process that a strong program will be rendered ineffective through the local, or partial, approach to policy formulation.

Some special problems. A combination of congressional characteristics — representation on a geographical basis, the committee system, and the seniority convention — operates to produce farm price and income legislation that treats certain commodities with tender, loving care. Historically, membership in the House Committee on Agriculture has been heavily weighted with southerners who have much seniority; consequently the problems of cotton, tobacco, and peanuts have received solicitous attention. And through a friendly working relationship between southern farm Democrats and midwestern farm Republicans, feed grains too have received generous support. The composition of the Senate Agricultural Committee has been such as to lend further support to the commodities listed above and in addition provide a friendly hearing to producers of wheat, sugar, and dairy products. Thus, the principal agricultural crops, as well as dairy products, have had their champions on the House and Senate Agricultural committees who have "looked after the interests" of these commodities and who, through the amendment process in committee, have helped enact legislation that was more generous in support of these commodities than otherwise would have been the case. Each commodity program contains provisions easing the impact of the program on producers of those commodities, as well as providing delightful "goodies" that would not be there if it had not been for the work of their champions on the committees.

As a corollary of this partial approach to farm policy formulation, which for agriculture turns out to be a geographical-commodity approach, the public cost of farm programs is certainly increased over what a rationalistic, national approach might call for. This is the case because few congressmen are concerned with the total cost of the program; the prime concern of each farm congressman is to enrich, or sweeten, the commodity program as it relates to constituents in his district. And this he can do by offering to support more generous program provisions for a commodity in which one of his congressional colleagues is interested in return for the latter's support for his own more generous provision. The amendment process in committee and subcommittee operates to provide more generous support for commodities all around, hence operates to raise the cost of the total national program.

It might be suggested that the Appropriations committees of the House and Senate would provide a check to this cost escalation process. And in some cases they may. But typically they do not. They do not, because the members of the agricultural subcommittees of the Appropriations committees have in the past come from the same general geographic areas as the commodity champions on the authorization committees; the agricultural appropriations subcommittees tend to reinforce through the funding process the favorable commodity decisions already taken in the authorization committees.

The check on the public cost of farm programs, if it is to come, must come on the floor of the House or Senate from urban-oriented congressmen. But under the rules by which the House operates and the tradition under which the Senate operates, it is exceedingly difficult to make important substantive changes on the floor of either chamber. The content of the bill has been forged in committee, and except for deletions, that content will not be altered importantly on the floor. Barring an uprising in the House or the Senate in which major provisions are eliminated or program expenditures are slashed in an across-the-board manner, it is unlikely that the cost of farm programs will be reduced by actions taken on the floor of the House or the Senate. Barring a major upheaval, it is too late.

But whereas the interests of the major commodity groups are well represented in the congress, the interests of certain other groups have been poorly represented: low-production farmers, hired farm workers, minority groups, and nonfarm rural families living in poverty. Action in the Congress on behalf of the downtrodden from rural areas has been minimal to nonexistent. Why should this be? Why should the income needs of those from rural areas most in want be ignored in farm price-income legislative activity in the Congress? The answer is straightforward. Congressmen represent the views and interests of those persons and groups who can reach their congressmen and state their case in persuasive terms. This the big farm producers can do individually and in groups. This the poor and the downtrodden in rural areas cannot do. They lack the funds, they lack the experience, and most often they lack the ability to do so. Their wants and needs simply do not get transmitted to their congressional representatives; hence their congressional representatives fail to represent their interests in the Congress.

The state of affairs described above is, in the 1970s, changing somewhat. The dispossessed in rural areas are finding ways to represent themselves to their congressional representatives. The blacks in the rural South are beginning to vote. Migrant farm labor is being organized. And poor, low-production farmers have broadened their horizons through more and better education, and have increased their social experience through increased non-farm employment. Thus, congressmen from rural areas are beginning to hear from constituents that they could safely ignore in the past (e.g., the blacks) and from constituents they really did not know existed (e.g., poor, low-production farmers). As this occurs these same congressmen will become ready and anxious to represent the needs of these people in the legislative process in the way discussed earlier in this chapter. Their jobs will depend on it.

The House and Senate Agricultural committees are changing in another way. Urban-oriented congressmen with an interest in food problems and food programs are increasingly asking to be appointed to the Agricultural committees, and are being appointed to them. So slowly the Agricultural committees of the Congress are being transformed into committees concerned with food and agricultural problems.

Special interests and farm policy formulation. We have seen in the previous sections how special interests relate to the administration and the congress in the legislative process. But it should be instructive at this point to look more carefully at the structure and operations of special interest groups that seek to influence farm policy.[7] There are three broad categories of interest groups that are concerned with farm policy. They are the general farm organizations, the commodity interest groups, and all others.

There are three general farm organizations with memberships distributed across the nation and two regional organizations. The American Farm Bureau Federation is the largest of the general farm organizations, claiming more than two million members, and it is the most conservative in outlook. The National Farmers Union is much smaller and much more liberal in outlook than the Farm Bureau, with a sprinkling of members across the nation but with the heaviest concentration of its membership located in the Great Plains. The Grange, more correctly called the National Grange of the Patrons of Husbandry, falls somewhere between the Farm Bureau and the Farmers Union in economic outlook and has its greatest concentration of members on the East and West coasts. The National Farmers Organization is a militantly radical organization with its membership located almost exclusively in the Upper Midwest. The Midcontinent Farmers Association has its organizational seat in the state of Missouri and laps over into adjoining states; it is probably the most regional in outlook of these five farm organizations.

The American Farm Bureau has from time to time developed general legislative proposals and promoted them in the Congress. Since World War II such proposals have typically included provisions to lower the level of price support, relax or eliminate production controls, and generally get government out of agriculture. The Farmers Union, sometimes with the cooperation of the Grange, too has developed and sponsored general farm legislation. Most often such legislation has included provisions designed to raise levels of price support, control production, and subsidize food consumption at home and abroad.

Rarely has one of these general farm organizations, or coalition of organizations, been able to muster enough strength in the Congress to pass its piece of general farm legislation. But by developing a general farm policy legislative proposal, introducing it into the Congress, and keeping it under consideration in the Congress, a farm organization accomplishes two limited objectives: it establishes a policy position around which it can rally friends and allies to combat administration proposals of which it disapproves; and by establishing a policy position in the Congress, the organization is in a better position to introduce amendments to general farm legislation that does have sufficient support to win passage. Thus, a general farm organization by developing and sponsoring a legislative proposal in the Congress is able to influence legislation enacted into law even where it is not able to pass its own proposal in total.

In the period under review, 1948–73, certain of the general farm organizations have tended to ally themselves with political administrations and operate as lobbyists on behalf of their administration ally in moving a legislative proposal through the Congress. The Farm Bureau has worked closely with Republican administrations, the Farmers Union with Democratic administrations. In this way the general farm organization often acts as an arm of a political administration in the farm policy legislative process, rather than as an independent interest group.

There are almost as many commodity interest groups represented in Washington, D.C., as there are farm commodities. Some of the less important commodities in terms of total returns, say the honey producers, may be represented only by a lawyer, who works only part time for them, and serves as a representative for other interest groups as well. But some commodity groups have competent and modest-sized technical and administrative staffs located either in Washington or with ready access to Washington, working full time the year around to look after the special interests of their producer members. Among these commodity groups are the cotton growers, the wheat producers, the sugar beet producers, the cattlemen, and the milk producers.

The commodity interest group is typically a highly effective lobbying group. Since the membership of a commodity group is homogeneous with respect to economic activity, it tends to be unified with respect to economic objectives. The Washington representatives of such groups usually understand the technological requirements of their producer members and are able to translate such requirements into program features with the capacity to achieve the expressed objectives of the program. Finally, the Washington staff representatives are always on hand to interpret the wishes and needs of their producer members to administration officials who may be initiating a legislative proposal, to help an uninformed congressman unravel the intricacies of a commodity program, or to help a congressman with a campaign contribution at election time. For these reasons commodity interest groups tend to be highly influential in getting those program features sought by their membership regarding their commodity included in a price and income legislative proposal before the Congress. Commodity groups have the technical knowledge, the desire, and the persistency to get their wants incorporated into farm policy legislation.

The third category of agricultural interest group is a disparate grouping. In it we find such widely varying interest groups as vegetable canners, labor unions, charitable food distribution organizations, fertilizer associations, feed and grain dealers, religious organizations, environmental groups, and so on down the line. Having some interest in the food and agricultural sector, each is represented in Washington to watch over legislation that has some bearing on its agricultural interest. Some of these interest groups have competent technical and administrative staffs, have lots of money to spend, and are highly influential. Others have little lobbying know-how, have little money to spend, and exert little or no influence. But the varied and disparate interests are all there, all working to make any piece of farm policy legislation enacted into law conform to their particular needs and wants: surplus foods for the charitable institutions, the recognition of the right of farm workers to bargain collectively for the labor unions, bans against the use of DDT for the environmental groups, soil-conserving programs for the limestone producers, and on and on.

The gamut which a piece of farm policy legislation must run with respect to special interest involvement from the time it is initiated in the U.S. Department of Agriculture until it is enacted into law in the Congress is almost incomprehensible to anyone who has not experienced it or observed it at close range. It would seem to be an unending process in which modifications, revisions, and amendments are infinite. And perhaps this is the way it must be if the varied and disparate interests of the American people are to be represented in the farm policy and programs of the nation. In any event it is the way things are.

The role of economists and other professionals. Graduate students in agricultural economics sometimes gain the impression that farm policy is written by their professors. This is a highly erroneous impression. Very few professional agricultural economists have had an important direct influence on American farm policy. John D. Black had considerable influence on food and agricultural policy in the 1930s and 1940s. Walter W. Wilcox may have had more direct influence on American farm policy in the 1950s and 1960s than any other professional economist. The senior author of this volume had some direct influence on farm policy in the late 1950s and early 1960s; but he had some failures too. In the period 1960–73 three professional economists have had considerable influence on American farm policy; they are, without any attempt here to rank their influence, George E. Brandow, D. Gale Johnson, and John A. Schnittker. And off and on, and in some strange ways, J. K. Galbraith has had a significant influence on food and agriculture over the long period 1940–65. But having recognized this handful of men, one runs out of names pretty fast.

It is interesting to observe that the man who has had the greatest influence on his colleagues and his profession, T. W. Schultz, has had little direct influence on American farm policy. Why should this be? It is, we argue, because Schultz, when he sought to influence farm policy directly, was unwilling to take account of, or adjust to, political realities in his policy recommendations and proposals. Now what do we mean by political realities? First, they are not necessarily bad or evil. They are, or represent, the hopes, aspirations, and objectives of different people and groups in society. They include such things in the food and agricultural sector as income support for the family farm, food security for the nation, protection for sugar beet producers, protection for wool growers, improved working conditions and minimum wages for hired field workers, and social security benefits for independent family farmers. Some of these political objectives are lofty in concept, some humanitarian, and some selfish and irresponsible. But each creates problems for the economist as it runs up against his ideal construct, namely, "that the economic system should be organized to produce the bill of goods and services desired by society at minimum cost." The economist who holds the view that this latter objective (i.e., his objective) is more important than some of the social and political objectives listed earlier and above, and the many more that could be listed, and hence should supersede them, will have great difficulty influencing farm policy, or any other kind of policy. This is so because *farm policy attempts to achieve a compromise among the many dif-*

ferent and conflicting objectives held by groups in society with respect to the farm sector.

The economist cannot in the policy arena say, "Make my economic objective dominant, or I won't play." If he does, he won't play. But he can say, "I will help, or work with, decision makers to effect a compromise among the different and conflicting goals held by society which is (1) acceptable in that it gives all of the power groups in society enough of what they want so that they will accept the compromise, (2) workable in that the program features of the compromise have the capacity to achieve the objectives of the compromise, and (3) tolerable in that the real costs of the compromise are not greater than the society is willing to bear." Not many economists appear to be interested in working with decision makers in such a manner. They are not interested in becoming political economists. Hence, as we have seen, not many economists have had much direct influence on farm policy formulation.

We have used the phrase "direct influence" above for a special reason. Many economists in government and out are *involved* in the policy formulation process by way of estimating parameters of the economic system and estimating the economic consequences of pursuing alternative courses of action. The estimation of reliable estimates of the elasticity of demand for various farm products and their aggregates greatly influenced the direction of farm policy in the 1950s and 1960s. And the estimation of the production effects of different levels of price support was an important part of each major policy revision between 1948 and 1973. Thus, agricultural economists have played an important role in policy formation over the years. But it has been an indirect role. Most agricultural economists have either not wanted to be involved in the policy-compromising process itself, or have not understood the nature of the role they must play if they want to influence policy directly.

Other social scientists — sociologists, anthropologists, and political scientists — have had little influence on farm policy, either directly or indirectly. Why this is the case is not entirely clear. Intuitively, one would think that rural sociologists and political scientists would have a contribution to make to the formulation of farm policy. We have two tentative explanations to offer for their lack of influence. First, the other social scientists, just as the economists, have not discovered a way of remaining scientists and entering into the rough and tumble of policy compromise at one and the same time. And desiring to maintain their credentials as scientists they have refrained from entering the policy, or more appropriately, the political, fray. Second, the kind of quantitative work in which sociologists and political scientists typically engage is not as useful to policy decision makers as that done by agricultural economists. In other words, decision makers in the farm policy area are more interested in the price-income-supply consequences of alternative courses of action than they are in the divorce rate or voter registration consequences of those same alternative courses of action. As a result, sociologists and political scientists generally do not get called upon to provide quantitative estimates of the consequences of alternative farm programs.

One broad category of scientists probably influenced farm policy more in the period 1948–73 than any other professional group — and largely without recognizing the fact. We refer to that broad group of agricultural production scientists — agronomists, plant pathologists, horticulturists, animal nutritionists, soil scientists, agricultural engineers — whose work resulted in the continuing production revolution of American agriculture in the 1950s and 1960s. These were the men who developed the new production practices which greatly increased the productivity of American agriculture. These were the men who, through their research efforts, made the agricultural treadmill possible.

If farm technological advance had been slower in the 1950s and 1960s than it was, and all else constant, the prices received by farmers would have been higher, the returns to producers greater, and the real cost of food to consumers higher. Policy problems and policy solutions would no doubt have been much different from what they were. In this sense the agricultural production scientist had a profound influence on American farm policy.

The Implementation of Policies and Programs: The Key Role of the Commodity Credit Corporation

Once policies and programs that have as their purpose the influencing of farm prices and incomes are enacted into law, they are in almost every case referred to the Department of Agriculture for implementation — execution and administration.[8] As the chief executive officer of the USDA the ultimate responsibility for faithfully and effectively implementing the policies and programs enacted into law falls on the secretary of agriculture. He is responsible for overseeing directly, or through his assistants, the work of program implementation by the agency in the USDA designated in the legislation, or suggested by legislative history, for carrying out the purposes and intent of the legislation. The secretary is also likely to call upon his various staff services — legal, economic, statistical, and informational — to assist in the implementation of policies and programs enacted into law. Thus, many people and many service units in the USDA are likely to become involved in the implementation of a particular farm program, e.g., the support of producer milk prices at a specific percentage of parity.[9] The support of milk prices might, for example, in some way concern the following agencies (see figure 4-1): Office of the General Counsel; Office of Communication; Agricultural Marketing Service;

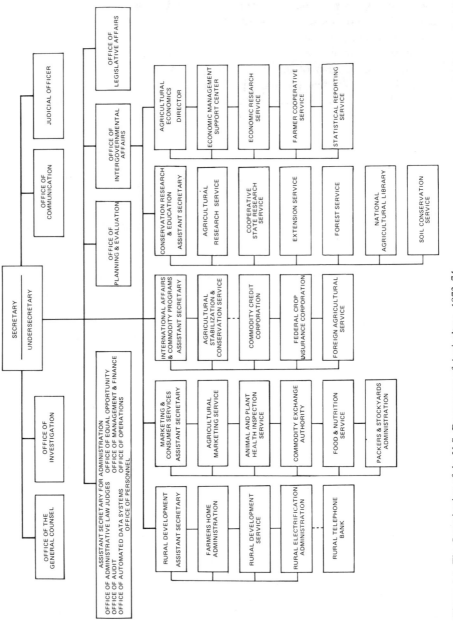

Figure 4-1. The Organization of the U.S. Department of Agriculture, 1973–74

Food and Nutrition Service; Agricultural Stabilization and Conservation Service; Foreign Agricultural Service; Economic Research Service. But one agency of the U.S. Department of Agriculture (somewhat vaguely positioned in figure 4-1) becomes involved in the implementation of every price and income program affecting farmers, if there is some expenditure of funds. It is the ubiquitous Commodity Credit Corporation (CCC).

The CCC has been, and remains, an institution of very great importance in the day-to-day and week-to-week operation of the many and varied farm programs. In reality the CCC plays the role of an army general headquarters with an almost limitless budget in the operation of farm programs. It is here that information regarding new demand and supply developments is received; it is here that plans are discussed and decisions made to cope with those demand-supply developments within the terms of the existing legislation; and it is here that funds are dispensed to implement the program and actions decided upon. The CCC is a highly flexible agency of government that can move in many different directions — to acquire stocks, dispose of stocks, support prices, or make payments to farmers — within the limits of the law, to effect the various price and income objectives of the law.[10] In simple language the CCC was given the authority and the financial resources by the Congress to do whatever it had to do to support the prices and incomes of American farmers.

Until the general excess capacity problem of American agriculture was explicitly recognized in the 1960s, a production-restraining, or price-supporting action taken in one part of the agricultural sector most often resulted in a supply-price response in another part of the sector. Farm program operations thus generally moved from price support, to stock acquisition, to storage, to acreage control in one crop, to increased stock acquisitions in a second crop or product purchases in the market, to increased storage, to product disposal to the poor and the needy at home and abroad. The mechanism in the USDA which permitted the government to move quickly and effectively from one operation to the next as the need arose was the CCC. Before 1960, the CCC was the mechanism whereby the government was able to take successive actions to manage an explosive supply situation; after 1960 it was the mechanism whereby the government was able to take successive actions to contain a potentially explosive supply situation.

More specifically, the CCC has functioned as the fiscal agency of the U.S. government for commodity and other farm programs since its inception in 1933.[11] The CCC charter gives it authority to "buy, sell, make loans, store, transfer, export and otherwise engage in commodity operations." These functions entail financing activities and operations for physically handling commodities. The CCC has no operating personnel; its programs are and have been carried out by personnel and facilities of the Agricultural Stabilization and Conservation Service (ASCS), Agricultural Marketing Service, Foreign Agricultural Service, and their predecessor agencies. Its charter directs the CCC to use to the extent possible private trade and financial facilities for transportation, processing, storing, and merchandising commodities. But authority is granted the CCC to own real property for business operations.

Management. Management of the CCC is vested in a board of directors, subject to the general supervision and direction of the secretary of agriculture, who is an ex officio director and chairman of the board. The board consists of six members (usually composed of the undersecretary of agriculture, the four assistant secretaries, and the economic adviser to the secretary), in addition to the secretary, who are appointed by the president of the United States by and with the advice and consent of the Senate.

In addition, there is a bipartisan advisory board of five members appointed by the president to survey the general policies of the CCC and to advise the secretary with respect thereto. The advisory board cannot be composed of more than three members of the same political party. The board is required to meet at the call of the secretary at least every 90 days.

The secretary is directed to appoint officers and employees for the conduct of business of the CCC, define their authority and duties, delegate to them such of the powers vested in the corporation as he may determine, and require that those he may designate be bonded.

Financing. The CCC has an authorized capital stock of $100 million held by the United States and authority to borrow up to $14.5 billion. Funds are borrowed from the U.S. Treasury and from private lending agencies.

Each year the CCC submits in the budget of the United States the programs it expects to carry out in the coming year. Upon approval of the budget by the Congress, this becomes the basic operating plan of the CCC for the fiscal year. Approval of the operating plan, however, does not limit CCC spending to any specified amount. Authority granted to the CCC permits it to spend whatever amount is needed to finance programs approved for each year. It can borrow to meet obligations. If the CCC realizes losses on its operations, those losses are covered by congressional appropriations, thus restoring CCC's borrowing power. This method of funding is sometimes called "backdoor financing" since no advance dollar limit is placed on program expenditures, and the Congress continuously restores the operating capital of CCC. The CCC thus has greater flexibility and freedom in spending federal moneys than most other agencies of the government.

Price support activities. Price support operations are handled primarily through loan, purchase, and payment programs. Proposals for price support usually are prepared by ASCS divisions in the form of a docket — a group of documents covering such matters as the economic and other factors upon which the proposal is based; total funds required; proposed method of support; the average level of support; conditions of eligibility; the geographic area and the period for which support will be available; basic operating provisions; and an authorization for ASCS to carry out the program under the general direction and supervision of the president or executive vice-president of CCC, in accordance with bylaws of CCC.

When the action or program contained in the docket is approved by the board of CCC and the secretary of agriculture, a public announcement is made, usually a press release, and detailed operating instructions are sent to personnel in charge of administering the program in Washington and the field. Regulations are also issued and published in the Federal Register for the guidance of those who wish to participate in the program.

Price support operations in the field involving direct dealings with farmers are a responsibility of state and county Agricultural Stabilization and Conservation committees. The state and county committees also are responsible for local administration of acreage allotments, marketing quotas, storage, agricultural conservation, Sugar Act, and related programs. The state committee consists of three to five farmer members appointed by the secretary of agriculture, plus the state director of the Agricultural Extension Service as an ex officio member. County committeemen are elected by the farmers in each county. Terms are for three years. One term expires each year. County committees function under the general supervision of the state committee.

County office personnel assist the farmer in the preparation of price support documents, check his eligibility for price support including the adequacy of farm storage facilities and compliance with cropland set-aside, acreage allotments, or quotas, and keep him informed of program details.

To extend the maturity of loans made to farmer participants the CCC has authorized reseal loan programs on certain commodities, primarily grains, in several years. Under these programs farmers may continue loans for on-farm stored commodities for additional periods and receive storage payments. The payments serve as a source of income to farmers and keep the commodity in position for consumption in producing areas.

In the case of tobacco, peanuts, gum naval stores, and cotton, cooperative marketing associations handle certain phases of price support programs. Dairy price support is handled through purchases of products from the commercial trade by the Minneapolis Commodity Office. Producer payments for price support, acreage diversion, and set-aside cropland are also made by the CCC.

Inventory operations. Commodities are acquired by the CCC as a consequence of its price support activities. The collateral products for price support loans are taken over by the CCC if loans to farmers are not repaid. Prices of some commodities are supported by product purchases (e.g., dairy products); these commodities are placed in the CCC inventory if there are no immediate noncommercial outlets.

The storage of commodities while they are in CCC ownership is a responsibility and function of ASCS. Commercial storage facilities are used to the fullest extent practicable, and the major part of CCC stocks is stored in these facilities. Grain and related commodities in inventory and under price support loan are stored under a uniform storage agreement with commercial warehouses throughout the United States. Cotton, tobacco, dairy products, and other commodities are also stored under uniform agreements in commercial facilities. These agreements provide for uniform storage, handling payments, and other requirements needed to keep the inventory safe.

In the past, the CCC has acquired supplemental bin storage in areas where storage was short, primarily in the corn-producing area. Such bin capacity declined in the late 1960's as unneeded bins were sold to farmers and private individuals, mostly for continued use in storing agricultural commodities. At the end of 1970, CCC-owned bin-type storage had a capacity of about 382 million bushels. At the peak, this capacity was 989 million bushels. To encourage storage of grain on farms, the CCC is directed to make loans available to grain producers to finance the construction or purchase of suitable storage.

Commodities acquired by the CCC through price support activities are disposed of by sales and donation programs. Domestic and foreign food aid programs and special export programs are covered in Chapter 7. Domestic sales of CCC stocks require an additional comment.

Domestic sales of storable CCC-owned commodities below the level of price support are prohibited by Section 407 of the Agricultural Act of 1949, a provision which directs the CCC to establish prices, terms, and conditions that will not discourage or deter manufacturers, processors, and dealers from acquiring and carrying normal inventories of the current crop. A more specific directive in Section 407 provided that the CCC should not in general sell any storable commodity in the domestic market at less than 5 percent above the support price for the commodity, plus reasonable carrying charges. A number of exemptions to this requirement have applied. In the case of cotton, the minimum selling price was raised to 15 percent above the support price, plus carrying charges, for the 1961, 1962, and 1963 crops; for the 1964 and 1965 crops the level reverted to 5 percent; then again in 1966 the minimum sales price was raised to 10 percent above support, plus carrying charges, where it has remained through 1973. However, the secretary of agriculture may and frequently has set a higher minimum level. For feed grains and wheat the minimum selling price was raised to 15 percent above support, plus carrying charges, for the 1971 through 1973 crops. The Section 407 minimum sales price limit does not apply to exports, or to domestic sales of commodity stocks which have deteriorated or are in danger of deterioration. There are several other limited exceptions to cover special situations, including unusual end-use needs. Sales of peanuts and oilseeds for oil extraction fall into the latter category.

The objective of this provision is obvious. If the CCC sold commodities owned by it at prices below price support levels, such sales would tend to drive down market prices. This, in turn, would result in more price support activity — with more commodities coming into the CCC's price support inventory. There would then need to be still more sales from inventory, and the program operation wheel would go around and around.

In summary, and in the words of Charles S. Murphy, president of the Commodity Credit Corporation in 1964:

> CCC operations are big business. CCC operations have a direct effect on the National economy. CCC inventories are so large that the manner in which they are handled or merchandized is of key importance both to domestic and international markets.
>
> Decisions by officers of CCC must give full recognition to their effects on market prices. Business operations of many thousands of warehouses, elevators, handlers, banks, processors, exporters, importers, carriers, and manufacturers are affected. International relationships are involved in many decisions. Individual trade customs with respect to many different commodities must be observed.
>
> Disposals of commodities by the Corporation also have values, meanings, impacts, and influences far beyond the immediacy of providing needed food and fiber for domestic and foreign markets.
>
> Careful evaluations and extremely balanced judgments are required at all times by officials of the Corporation to meet the mandates of the Congress, to fulfill the obligations and commitments of the U.S. Government and its agencies, and to enable American merchants and traders to continue, and to further their vital and traditional role in the U.S. private enterprise system.[12]

Part II.

The Historical Record

CHAPTER 5

Farm Price and Income Legislation

Objectives and provisions of the major farm legislation effective at the beginning of 1948 and enacted in the ensuing 25 years are summarized in this chapter. This compilation is intended to provide a compact, objective reference to laws directly affecting (1) the demand and supply of farm products, (2) commodity prices, and (3) the incomes of farmers in the post–World War II period. For readers who wish to examine the legislation, citations are included to the U.S. Code (U.S.C.) for laws applying in 1948 and to the U.S. Statutes at Large (Stat.) for acts passed since then.[1]

New legislation most often amends previous legislation in whole or in part instead of repealing and replacing existing statutes. As an example, the Agriculture and Consumer Protection Act of 1973 amends the following earlier acts: Soil Conservation and Domestic Allotment Act of 1936, Agricultural Marketing Agreement Act of 1937, Agricultural Adjustment Act of 1938, Agricultural Act of 1949, National Wool Act of 1954 (Title VII of the Agricultural Act of 1954), Agricultural Trade Development and Assistance Act of 1954 (P.L. 480), Food Stamp Act of 1964, Rural Development Act of 1972, and several lesser acts. This amending practice serves two purposes. First, new features can easily be discerned by observing what words or sections have been altered by an amendment, and second, legal interpretations and decisions related to the previous legislation remain binding. But the amending procedure is not without its disadvantages. It creates a maze of legal authorities for farm programs that is virtually impossible to make one's way through without specialized legal training.

This chapter provides a key to the maze built up over more than two decades of agricultural legislation, the acts are listed, and their important features stated, generally in the order the bills were enacted into law, thus

131

unfolding the legislative history of the era.[2] First let us turn the calendar back to January 1, 1948, and review the laws on the books at that time in order to understand the foundation for subsequent legal action.

Prewar Legislation Effective in 1948

Soil Conservation and Domestic Allotment Act of 1936, as amended (16 U.S.C. 590; 49 Stat. 163, April 27, 1935): "An act to provide for the protection of land resources against soil erosion, and for other purposes"*[3]

The dual goals of this act were to promote conservation of the nation's soil resources and to reestablish and maintain fair levels of farm income. To achieve these ends, government payments to farmers were authorized for soil-building practices and for planting soil-conserving crops. Section 12(a) of the act granted permissive authority to use funds "appropriated to carry out this Act for the expansion of domestic and foreign markets or for seeking new or additional markets for agricultural commodities or the products thereof or for the removal or disposition of surpluses of such commodities or the products thereof" (16 U.S.C. 590l).

Commodity Credit Corporation (CCC) (15 U.S.C. 713–714)

The CCC was created by Executive Order No. 6340, October 16, 1933, and continued by successive congressional acts. The corporation was authorized to buy, sell, and make loans to farmers on agricultural commodities for the purposes of increasing agricultural production, stabilizing prices, assuring adequate supplies, and facilitating the efficient distribution of agricultural commodities.[4]

Agricultural Marketing Agreement Act of 1937, as amended (7 U.S.C. 601, 602, 608a–608d, 610, 612, 614, 671–674; 50 Stat. 246, June 3, 1937): "An act to reenact and amend provisions of the Agricultural Adjustment Act, as amended, relating to marketing agreements and orders"

Because portions of the Agricultural Adjustment Act of 1933, as amended, had been declared unconstitutional in 1936, the Congress passed the Agricultural Marketing Agreement Act in 1937, to reenact certain other sections in order to affirm their validity. The stated congressional policy in this legislation was "to establish and maintain such orderly marketing conditions for agricultural commodities in interstate commerce as will establish prices to farmers at a level that will give agricultural commodities a purchasing power with respect to articles that farmers buy, equivalent to the purchasing power of agricultural commodities in the base period" (7 U.S.C. 602). The base period

---

* An asterisk in the pages that follow indicates fuller information about the bill is available. See footnote 2.

was August 1909 to July 1914 for all commodities except tobacco and potatoes. For these two commodities, August 1919 to July 1929 was set as the base period. Commodities covered by this legislation were milk and milk products, most fruits, vegetables, tree nuts, soybeans, hops, honeybees, tobacco, and naval stores.

The act permitted the secretary of agriculture to enter into agreements with processors, producers, and others engaged in marketing agricultural products (1) to establish minimum prices for marketing milk and (2) to prevent depressed prices of produce by limiting quantities marketed. Agreements could be voluntary (marketing agreements) or compulsory (marketing orders). Marketing orders required approval by producers, through a referendum, and were enforceable by court injunctions or fines.

Section 22, Limitation on Imports (7 U.S.C. 624; 49 Stat. 773, August 24, 1935)[5]

The 1937 act also reenacted Section 22 of the Agricultural Adjustment Act, as amended, which authorized the president to set quotas for or to levy fees on imports of agricultural commodities that threatened domestic price support programs.

Section 32 (7 U.S.C. 612c; 49 Stat. 750, 774, August 24, 1935)

This section was part of P.L. 320, passed by the 74th Congress on August 24, 1935, to amend the Agricultural Adjustment Act of 1933. It allocated 30 percent of all customs receipts to the secretary of agriculture for three purposes: (1) to encourage exports of agricultural commodities, (2) to encourage domestic consumption of agricultural commodities, and (3) to reestablish farmers' purchasing power. Provisions allowed the use of funds as export subsidies, as payments to farmers, and to cover costs of distributing agricultural products to charitable institutions and schools and directly to needy people.

Agricultural Adjustment Act of 1938, as amended (7 U.S.C. 1281–1407; 52 Stat. 31, February 16, 1938): "An act to provide for the conservation of national soil resources[6] and to provide an adequate and balanced flow of agricultural commodities in interstate and foreign commerce and for other purposes"

The objective concerning the marketing of agricultural commodities was enlarged upon in the act as follows: "It is hereby declared to be the policy of Congress . . . to assist in the marketing of agricultural commodities for domestic consumption and for export; and to regulate interstate and foreign commerce in cotton, wheat, corn, tobacco, [peanuts] and rice to the extent necessary to provide an orderly, adequate, and balanced flow of such commodities . . . through storage of reserve supplies, loans, marketing quotas, assisting farmers to obtain insofar as practicable, parity prices for such commodities and parity of income, and assisting consumers to obtain an adequate and steady supply of such commodities at fair prices'' (7 U.S.C. 1282). A parity price was defined in the act as ''that price for the commodity which will give to the commodity a purchasing power with respect to articles that farmers buy equivalent to the purchasing power of such commodity in the base period.'' For most commodities the base period was August 1909 to July 1914.

The act provided measures for controlling production of farm output and for supporting farm income by means of price supports and direct payments. To control production of surplus crops, the government was authorized to undertake voluntary and mandatory acreage reduction programs. Planting goals under voluntary programs were called acreage allotments, and under mandatory programs the planting restriction was called a marketing quota. Marketing quotas required approval by producers, voting in a referendum, and were enforced by penalties. Prices were to be supported through commodity purchases by the government and through nonrecourse loans to farmers. Cash loans alleviated price-depressing effects of surpluses by making farmers financially able to hold surplus commodities off the market. Loans were contingent upon compliance with planting restrictions when they applied.

Production control and price support provisions were mandatory for the six ''basic'' crops named above; price supports were permissive for other commodities. Loans were made available to farmers from the CCC at the support rate if crops were stored in approved facilities. If a farmer chose not to redeem his loan, the CCC assumed title to the commodity.

This act also authorized direct payments to farmers, called parity payments, when the Congress appropriated funds.

Reciprocal Trade Agreements Act of 1934 (19 U.S.C. 1351–1352; 48 Stat. 943, June 12, 1934)

This act gave the president authority to raise or lower existing tariffs as much as 50 percent in return for similar concessions from trading partners of the United States. Under the authority of this act the president committed the United States to the General Agreement of Tariffs and Trade (GATT) in 1947. The objective of GATT was to establish rules for international trade policy and for trade negotiations in the postwar period.

Wartime and Postwar Legislation Applicable in 1948

Act of July 1, 1941, and Act of October 2, 1942 (15 U.S.C. 713a-8; 55 Stat. 498, 56 Stat. 767, 768)

Section 4 of the act of July 1, 1941, the Steagall Amendment, required that prices be supported for all commodities for which production expansion had been requested during World War II. These commodities became known as the "Steagall" commodities. The act of October 2, 1942, set the level of supports at 90 percent of parity both for Steagall commodities and for the six basic commodities (later legislation raised the minimum support for cotton to 92½ percent of parity) until two years after the war was officially declared ended. This stipulation resulted in coverage until December 31, 1948. The secretary of agriculture was to support prices by loans, purchases, or other operations.

National School Lunch Act (42 U.S.C. 1751–1760; 60 Stat. 230, June 4, 1946): "An act to provide assistance to the States in the establishment, maintenance, operation, and expansion of school-lunch programs, and for other purposes"

The Congress expanded upon the objective by declaring it to be congressional policy "to safeguard the health and well-being of the Nation's children and to encourage the domestic consumption of nutritious agricultural commodities and other food, by assisting the States, through grants-in-aid and other means, in providing an adequate supply of foods and other facilities for the establishment, maintenance, operation, and expansion of nonprofit school-lunch programs" (42 U.S.C. 1751).

This act authorized regular federal appropriations for cash grants to the states to support nonprofit school lunch programs for public and private schools. Previously, funds acquired under Section 32 had been the sole source of financing for school lunch programs. Funding was approved for equipment as well as for food. At least 75 percent of appropriations for food had to be paid to the states; the USDA was allowed to purchase food for direct distribution from the remainder. States were allocated funds on the basis of the number of schoolchildren and per capita income in the state, with more than a proportionate share provided to low-income states. Participating states and state agencies were required to comply with certain specifications; among these were the following: (1) to match funds, increasing from one-to-one to three-to-one over a ten-year period; lower matching requirements were established for low-income states; (2) to meet specified nutritional standards; and (3) to provide meals at no or low cost to poor children.

Sugar Act of 1948 (7 U.S.C. 1100–1160; 61 Stat. 922, August 8, 1947): "An act to regulate commerce among the several States, with the Territories and possessions of the United States, and with foreign countries; to protect the welfare of consumers of sugars and of those engaged in the domestic sugar-producing industry; to promote the export trade of the United States; and for other purposes" *

The Sugar Act of 1948 reenacted the quota system for regulating supplies of sugar in the U.S. market, due to expire under the Sugar Act of 1937, as amended. This legislation required an annual estimate of U.S. sugar consumption, to be allocated among domestic and foreign suppliers through a quota system. Quotas for domestic cane and beet producers and for Philippine suppliers were stated in tons. For other nations, quotas were stated as a percentage of the U.S. requirements above the domestic and Philippine quotas. Cuba received 98.64 percent of this residual. No duty was levied on sugar from the Philippines, Cuban sugar entered at a partial duty rate, and full duty was charged other nations. If the Philippines could not meet its quota, 95 percent of the deficit went to Cuba. Government payments to supplement incomes of domestic producers were also authorized under this legislation. The act applied for five years, until December 31, 1952.

Legislation Passed since January 1948

80th Congress

Foreign Assistance Act of 1948 (P.L. 472, 62 Stat. 137, 146, April 3,1948): "An act to promote world peace and the general welfare, national interest, and foreign policy of the United States through economic, financial, and other measures necessary to the maintenance of conditions abroad in which free institutions may survive and consistent with the maintenance of the strength and stability of the United States"[7]

Title I of this act, entitled the "Economic Cooperation Act of 1948" but more commonly called the Marshall Plan, provided economic aid to help rebuild war-ravaged Europe. The act declared that the purpose of the title was to furnish

. . . material and financial assistance to the participating countries in such a manner as to aid them, through their own individual and concerted efforts, to become independent of extraordinary outside economic assistance within the period of operation under this title, by

(1) promoting industrial and agricultural production in the participating countries;
(2) furthering the restoration or maintenance of the soundness of European currencies, budgets, and finances; and
(3) facilitating and stimulating the growth of international trade of participating countries with one another and with other countries by appropriate measures including reduction of barriers which may hamper such trade.

Participating European nations were required to prepare a regional recovery plan. The United States agreed to supply loans and grants to supplement European resources, which were inadequate for executing the plan. The program was to operate for four years. The act specified that agricultural products for the program must be purchased in the United States to the extent possible. Use of Section 32 funds was authorized to subsidize exports of surplus agricultural commodities destined for participating nations or for occupied areas.

Commodity Credit Corporation Charter Act (P.L. 806, 62 Stat. 1070, June 29, 1948): "An act to provide a Federal charter for the Commodity Credit Corporation"*

Section 2 states that the Commodity Credit Corporation was created "For the purpose of stabilizing, supporting, and protecting farm income and prices, of assisting in the maintenance of balanced and adequate supplies of agricultural commodities, products thereof, foods, feeds, and fibers . . . and of facilitating the orderly distribution of agricultural commodities . . ." and that the CCC was established as "an agency and instrumentality of the United States, within the Department of Agriculture, subject to the general direction and control of its Board of Directors."

Specific powers of the corporation were spelled out in Section 5. These powers are to

(a) Support the prices of agricultural commodities through loans, purchases, payments, and other operations.
(b) Make available materials and facilities required in connection with the production and marketing of agricultural commodities.
(c) Procure agricultural commodities for sale to other Government agencies, foreign governments, and domestic, foreign or international relief or rehabilitation agencies, and to meet domestic requirements.
(d) Remove and dispose of or aid in the removal or disposition of surplus agricultural commodities.
(e) Increase the domestic consumption of agricultural commodities by expanding or aiding in the expansion of domestic markets or by developing or aiding in the development of new and additional markets, marketing facilities, and uses for such commodities.
(f) Export or cause to be exported, or aid in the development of foreign markets for agricultural commodities.
(g) Carry out such other operations as the Congress may specifically authorize or provide for.

Agricultural Act of 1948 (P.L. 897, 62 Stat. 1247, July 3, 1948): "An act to authorize the Secretary of Agriculture to stabilize prices of agricultural commodities; to amend Section 22 of the Agricultural Adjustment Act, reenacted by the Agricultural Marketing Agreement Act of 1937; and for other purposes"*

Title I of this act, entitled "1949 Price Stabilization," continued high price supports for the 1949 marketing year; among the main provisions of Title II, which amended the Agricultural Adjustment Act of 1938, were a permanent, flexible price support schedule, effective as of January 1, 1950, and a new formula for calculating parity, the basis for determining price support levels.

Under Title I, 1949 price supports were required for the six basic commodities, the "Steagall" commodities, and wool. Supports were continued at 90 percent of parity for cotton, corn, wheat, rice, tobacco, peanuts, hogs, chickens, eggs, and milk. Minimum price supports for other so-called Steagall commodities were lowered to 60 percent of parity. Support of the price of wool was continued at the 1946 level until June 30, 1950. Authority was granted the secretary to support other crops if funds permitted.

Section 22 of the Agricultural Adjustment Act was amended to prohibit import-restricting actions contrary to international agreements.

Title II gave the secretary of agriculture general authority to support prices through loans, purchases, payments, and other operations beginning January 1, 1950. The minimum support level for the basic commodities would vary between 60 and 90 percent of parity depending upon estimated supply, except that tobacco supports would remain at 90 percent of parity whenever marketing quotas were in effect. For the basic commodities, supports for non-cooperators would be discretionary; the support level would drop to 50 percent of parity if marketing quotas were allowed but were not approved by producers.

The formula for computing parity was also revised by Title II and a transitional schedule adopted for implementing the new parity prices. Under the new formula, supports would be lower for wheat, cotton, peanuts, and the feed grains.

81st Congress

Commodity Credit Corporation Charter Act Amendments (P.L. 85, 63 Stat. 154, June 7, 1949): "An act to amend the CCC Charter Act of 1948, and for other purposes"

Under the provisions of this act, the CCC was permitted to own real property for the first time. Specifically, storage facilities could be acquired for storing agricultural surpluses if private facilities were unavailable. Cold storage facilities were excepted. Also, the CCC was authorized to loan farmers money to build their own storage facilities.

Other provisions granted authority to the CCC to barter surplus U.S. farm commodities for strategic and critical materials acquired abroad, and designated the secretary of agriculture to supervise and direct CCC activities. Formerly this power had been vested in the CCC board of directors.

Marketing Quota Amendments (P.L. 272, 63 Stat. 670, August 29, 1949): "An act to amend the cotton and wheat marketing quota provisions of the Agricultural Adjustment Act of 1938, as amended"[8]

This act revised cotton, peanut, and wheat quotas for the 1950 crop. Under the new provisions for cotton, the 1950 acreage allotment was about 20 percent lower than it would have been under the old formula but it was still above that needed to meet expected requirements. Likewise, a minimum acreage allotment for the 1950 crop of peanuts was set about 8.6 percent higher than the acreage needed to meet estimated needs. Other provisions changed the basis for allocating national wheat and peanut allotments among states and farms in order to prevent discrimination against areas brought into production of these two commodities during the war.

International Wheat Agreement (IWA) Act of 1949 (P.L. 421, 63 Stat. 945, October 27, 1949): "An act to give effect to the International Wheat Agreement signed by the United States and other countries relating to the stabilization of supplies and prices in the international wheat market"*

This act authorized the president, acting through the CCC, to carry out the provisions of the IWA governing quantities and prices for U.S. wheat exports. Objectives of the IWA were to assure markets for wheat to exporting countries and supplies of wheat to importing countries at equitable and stable prices. This agreement among major importers and exporters of wheat specified annual minimum and maximum levels for prices and quantities moving in international commerce from July 31, 1949, to July 31, 1953.[9] If agreement prices were lower than those prevailing in the United States, the CCC was permitted to pay subsidies to exporters or to absorb losses when selling its own stocks.

Agricultural Act of 1949 (P.L. 439, 63 Stat. 1051, October 31, 1949): "An act to stabilize prices of agricultural commodities"*

This legislation repealed price support provisions of the 1948 Agricultural Act and of the Agriculture Adjustment Act of 1938, as amended. Other features of these and earlier bills were amended and new price support provisions were enacted.

Price support levels were frozen at 90 percent of parity in 1950 for the basic crops if acreage allotments or marketing quotas were in effect. Minimum support levels for 1951 were lowered to 80 percent of parity and beginning in 1952 the minimum level, except for tobacco, would fall to 75 percent. Tobacco price supports were retained at 90 percent of parity whenever marketing quotas were in effect. If marketing quotas were not approved by producers, price supports would be maintained at 50 percent of parity for all basic commodities except tobacco. In such a case no supports would apply for tobacco prices.

Mandatory supports were also established for dairy products, tung nuts, honey, potatoes, and wool, at levels ranging from 60 to 90 percent of parity. For other commodities supports were permissive up to 90 percent of parity at the secretary's discretion.

Section 32 was amended so that customs receipts allocated to the secretary of agriculture "shall be devoted principally to perishable nonbasic agricultural commodities . . . and their products."

Three other key provisions were contained in the act: (1) The parity price formula for the basic commodities was modified to cushion the impact of the revision specified in the 1948 act. The change added direct farm labor costs and wartime subsidy payments to the computations and installed a dual parity system whereby the old formula was allowed to apply through 1954 if it meant higher prices than the revised formula. (2) The CCC was prohibited from selling farm commodities, except for export, at less than 105 percent of the support price plus carrying charges. (3) Donations of surplus U.S. agricultural products to needy persons at home and abroad were authorized under Section 416.

Marketing Quota and Price Support Amendments (P.L. 471, 64 Stat. 42, March 31, 1950): "An act relating to cotton and peanut acreage allotments and marketing quotas under the Agricultural Adjustment Act of 1938, as amended, and to price support for potatoes"

This act revised provisions of the 1949 amendment (P.L. 272) dealing with cotton and peanut acreage allotments for 1950. The revision offered cotton producers the opportunity to contest allotments assigned under P.L. 272 (Marketing Quota Amendments above) and added a provision for establishing minimum allotments for individual farms. These features raised the 1950 national cotton acreage allotment by about 2.5 percent. For peanuts, 1950 acreage allotments were adjusted upward about 4.8 percent by placing a limit on the planting reduction for each state. The section dealing with potato price supports in effect terminated price support authority after 1950. It linked future price supports to approval of marketing quotas by producers, but no authority was granted to establish marketing quotas.

Rice Quota Amendment (P.L. 561, 64 Stat. 232, June 16, 1950): "An act to amend the rice marketing quota provisions of the Agricultural Adjustment Act of 1938, as amended"

The formula for allocating the national allotment among states was changed to accommodate new production areas whose allotments would have been curtailed under the previous legislation to a greater extent than older production areas.

Section 22 and CCC Amendments (P.L. 579, 64 Stat. 261, June 28, 1950)

Although the main purpose of this act was "to increase the borrowing power of the Commodity Credit Corporation," it also contained a provision to amend import restrictions under Section 22. The use of Section 22 import restrictions had been curtailed by the Agriculture Act of 1948. This 1950 amendment weakened the 1948 proviso by directing that future treaties allow import restrictions under certain conditions.

Defense Production Act of 1950 (P.L. 774, 64 Stat. 798, September 8, 1950)

The purpose of this act was to provide emergency measures during the Korean War; it applied until June 30, 1951. For agricultural commodities, relatively high minimum price ceilings were authorized — 100 percent of parity or the highest price during a specified recent period, whichever was higher.

82nd Congress

Peanut Quota Amendment (P.L. 17, 65 Stat. 29, April 12, 1951)

This act eased peanut allotments and marketing quotas beginning in 1951 by adjusting the basis for computing state quotas. The effect for 1951 was to increase the national acreage allotment by 6.7 percent. Other provisions permitted the secretary of agriculture to differentiate among peanut varieties in order to encourage production of types in short supply (peanuts for crushing) while curtailing output of types in excess supply (varieties for eating as nuts).

The India Emergency Food Act of 1951 (P.L. 48, 65 Stat. 69, June 15, 1951)

The purpose of this act was "to furnish food aid to India." It authorized $19 million of credit for a one-year period. Funds were for the purchase of two million tons of U.S. grain to avert a famine. Interest from the loan was to be used in part for cultural and educational exchanges with India.

Section 22 Amendment (P.L. 50, 65 Stat. 72, 75, June 16, 1951)

One provision of the Trade Agreements Extension Act of 1951 further amended import restrictions under Section 22. This 1951 amendment provided that "no trade agreement or other international agreement heretofore or hereafter entered by the United States shall be applied in a manner inconsistent with the requirements of this section." In effect this repealed the restrictions on the use of Section 22 introduced in the Agriculture Act of 1948 and modified in 1950 (P.L. 579).

Defense Production Act Amendments of 1951 (P.L. 96, 65 Stat. 131, July 31, 1951)

This act extended emergency authorities of the 1950 act until June 30, 1952, and amended some features. Of most importance for agriculture was a new minimum price ceiling, higher than in the original act. Other features concerning agriculture prohibited quotas on livestock production and processing, extended a ban on imports of food fats and oils and rice, and imposed stringent import restrictions on certain dairy products (Section 104).

An Act to Extend and Amend the Sugar Act of 1948 (P.L. 140, 65 Stat. 318, September 1, 1951)

The Sugar Act was extended for four years, until December 31, 1956. Quotas for Puerto Rico and the Virgin Islands were raised and the Cuban share of the foreign market was reduced from 98.64 percent to 96 percent.

Defense Production Act Amendments of 1952 (P.L. 429, 66 Stat. 298, June 30, 1952)

Two provisions of this act were especially important for agriculture. First, 1953 price support loans for the six basic crops, wheat, corn, cotton, peanuts, rice, and tobacco, were set at 90 percent of parity, which was higher than they would have been under existing law. Second, price ceilings were removed from fresh and processed fruits and vegetables, allowing prices to rise.

Tobacco Quotas (P.L. 528, 66 Stat. 597, July 12, 1952)

This act set a minimum farm allotment for burley tobacco at 7/10 acre and limited yearly reductions in allotments to 1/10 acre for farms with allotments of one acre or less.

Price Supports (P.L. 585, 66 Stat. 758, July 17, 1952): "An act to continue the existing method of computing parity prices for basic agricultural commodities, and for other purposes"

For the six basic crops, supports at 90 percent of parity were continued for one more year, through 1954, maintaining prices at a higher level than under existing legislation. The dual parity system introduced in the Agricultural Act of 1949 was continued through 1955. It required that the higher of the new or the old parity formula would apply in computations of price support levels for the basic crops.

83rd Congress

Wheat for Pakistan (P.L. 77, 67 Stat. 80, June 25, 1953)

This measure was enacted "to provide for the transfer of price-support wheat to Pakistan." It authorized the president to give to Pakistan one million tons of surplus wheat from CCC stocks because Pakistan was threatened with a famine.

Defense Production Act Amendments of 1953 (P.L. 95, 67 Stat. 129, June 30, 1953)

Section 104, enacted in 1951 to restrict imports of cheese and other farm products, was allowed to expire on June 30, 1953. Freer imports of dairy products would have been possible, except that restrictions were subsequently imposed under Section 22 according to the emergency powers granted to the president by P.L. 215, the Trade Agreements Extension Act of 1953.

Wheat Acreage Allotments (P.L. 117, 67 Stat. 151, July 14, 1953): "An act to amend the wheat marketing quota provisions of the Agricultural Adjustment Act of 1938, as amended, and for other purposes"

The minimum national acreage allotment was raised from 55 million acres to 62 million acres for 1954.

Mutual Security Act of 1953 (P.L. 118, 67 Stat. 152, July 16, 1953)

This act amended and extended foreign economic and military aid programs for one year, until June 30, 1954. It contained one new provision affecting agriculture, Section 550. This provision stipulated that some MSA funds must be used to finance the sale of U.S. surplus agricultural products in developing nations and in new market areas.[10] In recipient countries, the products were to be sold for domestic currencies which were then made available for aid purposes in those nations. Interference with commercial international trade was to be avoided and, whenever possible, private trade channels were to be utilized.

Trade Agreements Extension Act of 1953 (P.L. 215, 67 Stat. 472, August 7, 1953)

One provision of this act amended Section 22. It granted the president power, in an emergency, to restrict imports of agricultural commodities that threatened price support programs without obtaining prior recommendations from the Tariff Commission. Previously, restrictions could not be imposed until the Tariff Commission had investigated the situation and recommended such action as necessary for the protection of domestic producers.

Famine Relief (P.L. 216, 67 Stat. 476, August 7, 1953): "An act to enable the President, during the period ending March 15, 1954, to furnish to peoples friendly to the United States emergency assistance in meeting famine or other urgent relief requirements"

This act appropriated $100 million for donating surplus agricultural commodities, owned by the government, to foreign nations. Peoples of any nation facing a famine or other emergency could qualify if the people were "friendly" even though "friendly" diplomatic relations were not maintained with the United States.

Cotton Acreage Allotments (P.L. 290, 68 Stat. 4, January 30, 1954): "An act to amend certain provisions of the Agricultural Adjustment Act of 1938, as amended"

This act raised the minimum national acreage allotment for 1954 so that the allotment would be about 22 percent higher than under existing legislation. Also, the method of allocating the allotment among states was altered to provide southwestern states a greater share than the old formula provided.

(Production had expanded in the Southwest during the previous three years when no planting restrictions applied.)

Tobacco Quotas (P.L. 425, 68 Stat. 270, June 22, 1954)

This act amended the Agricultural Adjustment Act of 1938, as amended, by raising the penalty 10 percent for marketing tobacco in excess of the quota.

Agricultural Trade Development and Assistance Act of 1954 (commonly known as P.L. 480) (68 Stat. 454, July 10, 1954): "An act to increase the consumption of United States agricultural commodities in foreign countries, to improve the foreign relations of the United States, and for other purposes" *

In section 2 of the bill the Congress expanded upon the purposes of this act by declaring it to be congressional policy to

. . . expand international trade among the United States and friendly nations, to facilitate the convertibility of currency, to promote the economic stability of American agriculture and the national welfare, to make maximum efficient use of surplus agricultural commodities in furtherance of the foreign policy of the United States, and to stimulate and facilitate the expansion of foreign trade in agricultural commodities produced in the United States by providing a means whereby surplus agricultural commodities in excess of the usual marketings of such commodities may be sold through private trade channels, and foreign currencies accepted in payment therefor. It is further the policy to use foreign currencies which accrue to the United States under this Act to expand international trade, to encourage economic development, to purchase strategic materials, to pay United States obligations abroad, to promote collective strength, and to foster in other ways the foreign policy of the United States.

This act combined and extended several existing authorities for utilizing surplus agricultural products in the furtherance of foreign policy goals. It applied for three years, ending June 30, 1957. Under Title I — "Sales for Foreign Currency" — "The President is authorized to negotiate and carry out agreements with friendly nations . . . for the sale of surplus agricultural commodities for foreign currencies." Programs operated under this authority continued those begun in 1953 under the Mutual Security Act, though financing was somewhat changed. Provisions were retained to avoid interference with commercial transactions and to utilize private trade channels.

Foreign currencies acquired under this program could be used (1) to develop new markets for U.S. farm goods, (2) to purchase strategic materials, (3) to buy military supplies, (4) for financing the purchase of goods or services for other friendly countries, (5) for promoting economic development and trade, (6) to pay U.S. obligations abroad, (7) for loans to promote trade and economic development, and (8) for financing international educational exchange activities.

Title II — "Famine Relief and Other Assistance" — extended for three years the Famine Relief Bill (P.L. 216) passed in 1953, authorizing donations of surplus agricultural commodities to "friendly populations" in any nation experiencing an emergency.

Title III consisted of two main parts: (1) Section 416 of the Agricultural Act of 1949 was amended to expand donations of CCC surplus commodities for domestic and foreign relief projects; (2) Section 4 of the Commodity Credit Corporation Charter Act was amended to broaden authority dealing with barter of surplus commodities for strategic materials.

Agricultural Act of 1954 (P.L. 690, 68 Stat. 897, August 28, 1954): "An act to provide for greater stability in agriculture; to augment the marketing and disposal of agricultural products; and for other purposes"*

Price supports. For the basic commodities, except tobacco, supports were authorized at between 82½ and 90 percent of parity for 1955; the minimum was lowered to 75 percent of parity beginning in 1956. Price support provisions for tobacco were retained at 90 percent of parity whenever marketing quotas were in effect; tobacco prices would not be supported if marketing quotas were disapproved by producers. Likewise no changes were made in existing provisions for dairy products or for honey and tung nuts. The range of supports for the former was continued at 75 to 90 percent of parity and for the latter two commodities at 60 to 90 percent of parity. Price supports for all of these commodities were mandatory. For other commodities price supports continued to be optional. The only change was to eliminate approval of marketing quotas as a qualification to obtain price supports for potatoes.

Parity. The "new" formula for calculating parity, contained in the Agricultural Act of 1948, was scheduled to become effective on January 1, 1956. To avoid too sharp a decline, a transitional adoption schedule was framed, limiting annual reductions to 5 percent for each commodity.

Production controls. Marketing quota provisions for corn were repealed, eliminating penalties for producers who did not plant within allotments. No change was made in provisions authorizing corn acreage allotments.

Commodity set-asides (reserves). The CCC was authorized to treat $2.5 billion of its stocks as reserves, removing such inventories from marketable supplies and excluding them from computations of carryovers for the purpose of determining marketing quotas. Reserves of wheat and cotton were mandatory and reserves of cottonseed oil, butter, nonfat dry milk solids, and cheese were optional.

The reserves were to be disposed of (a) for foreign relief purposes, (b) by developing new or expanding markets, (c) by donation to school lunch programs, (d) through transfers to the national stockpile, (e) for research, experimental, or educational purposes, (f) for disaster relief purposes in the United States, (g) through sales to meet the need for increased supplies, in which case the sales price was to be not less than 105 percent of parity.

Special dairy program (also referred to as the special milk program). Funding up to $50 million annually was authorized for two years for increasing utilization of milk in schools and for donations of surplus dairy products to the armed forces and to veterans' hospitals.[11]

National Wool Act. Title VII of the Agricultural Act of 1954, entitled the "National Wool Act of 1954," directed that the secretary of agriculture "support the prices of wool and mohair . . . by means of loans, purchases, payments, or other operations." If the payments method was chosen, the government would pay producers the difference between the market price and the support price. The support price could be set between 60 and 110 percent of parity depending upon the quantity of production desired. These provisions applied for four years.

84th Congress

Durum Wheat Allotments (P.L. 8, 69 Stat. 9, February 19, 1955)

This act, "to amend the wheat marketing quota provisions of the Agricultural Adjustment Act of 1938, as amended," increased durum wheat allotments for 1955 in Minnesota, North Dakota, South Dakota, and Montana.[12]

Tobacco Quotas (P.L. 21, 69 Stat. 23, March 31, 1955): "An act directing redetermination of the national marketing quota for burley tobacco for the 1955–56 marketing year, and for other purposes"

This act revised the method of determining the national minimum acreage allotment for burley tobacco in order to lower the minimum. For 1955 the allotment was about 22 percent smaller than the 1954 allotment.

Rice Allotments (P.L. 29, 69 Stat. 45, May 5, 1955)

This act, "to amend rice marketing quota provisions of Agricultural Adjustment Act of 1938, as amended," increased 1955 rice acreage allotments for each state by 2 percent.

Conservation Payments (P.L. 42, 69 Stat. 65, May 23, 1955)

This act repealed section 348 of the Agricultural Adjustment Act of 1938, added by the Agricultural Act of 1954. The 1954 amendment denied agricultural conservation payments to farmers who did not comply with acreage allotments assigned under commodity programs.

Rice Allotments (P.L. 288, 69 Stat. 576, August 9, 1955): "An act to amend the Agricultural Adjustment Act of 1938, as amended"

This act provided that the 1956 national acreage allotment be at least 85 percent of the 1955 allotment. It also established an annual minimum national acreage allotment amounting to 85 percent of the allotment in the previous year. This limited the amount of annual reduction in the national acreage allotment to 15 percent. Previously no minimum was specified.

Tobacco Quotas (P.L. 351, 69 Stat. 670, August 11, 1955)

This act, "to amend section 313 of the Agricultural Adjustment Act of 1938, with respect to tobacco allotments," limited the allowable reduction in allotments for 1956, 1957, and 1958.

P.L. 480 Amendment (P.L. 387, 69 Stat. 721, August 12, 1955): "An act to reemphasize trade and development as the primary purpose of Title I of the Agricultural Trade Development and Assistance Act of 1954"

This amendment to P.L. 480 more than doubled the funding authorized for financing programs under Title I, "Sales for Foreign Currency."

Tobacco Quotas (P.L. 425, 426, 427, 70 Stat. 34, 35, March 2, 1956)

These three laws readjusted allotments for burley, fire-cured, dark air-cured, and Maryland tobacco to eliminate cuts scheduled for 1956.

Agricultural Act of 1956 (P.L. 540, 70 Stat. 188, May 28, 1956)*

This omnibus bill comprised a variety of provisions, including amendments to price support, production control, and surplus disposal authorities for several commodities; Title I of the act instituted a major new feature, the Soil Bank.

The Soil Bank. Programs authorized under this title aimed at reducing production of surplus farm commodities through a withdrawal of land from production on short-term and long-term bases. As stated in the law, the purposes are "to protect and increase farm income, to protect the national soil, water, and forest and wildlife resources from waste and depletion, to protect interstate and foreign commerce from the burdens and obstructions which result from the . . . production of excessive supplies of agricultural commodities, and to provide for the conservation of such resources and an adequate, balanced, and orderly flow of such agricultural commodities in interstate and foreign commerce."

To achieve these purposes, "programs are herein authorized to assist farmers to divert a portion of the cropland from the production of excessive supplies of agricultural commodities, and to carry out a program of soil, water, forest and wildlife conservation." Two programs were authorized: an acreage reserve program, allowing an annual land-rental program for producers of the six basic crops; and a conservation reserve program, providing for long-term conversion of land to conservation uses in return for annual payments from the government.

Surplus disposal. No new measures were introduced but funding authorizations under several existing programs were expanded. Among these were (1) authorizations to supplement customs receipts for operation of surplus disposal programs under Section 32, and (2) authorizations for the CCC to finance ocean freight costs for shipping surplus agricultural commodities as foreign relief donations under Title II of P.L. 480 and Section 416 of the Agricultural Act of 1949. Also, authority for the CCC to sell surplus cotton at world prices (and absorb losses) was changed from permissive to mandatory.

Acreage allotments. For cotton and rice, minimum acreage allotments for 1957 and 1958 were frozen at the 1956 level, preventing cuts authorized by existing legislation.

Price supports. The minimum price support levels for oats, rye, barley, and sorghum were raised from 70 to 76 percent of parity for 1956. A two-year two-price system was instituted for rice, whereby rice for export could move at a lower price than rice for domestic consumption. Price supports for cotton-seed and soybeans were linked to assure a fair competitive relationship between the two oilseeds.

Several price support options were offered corn producers in commercial areas for 1956. One option tied price supports to participation in the Soil Bank; another offered a smaller allotment with no Soil Bank requirement; and finally, a lower support rate (about 13 percent lower) was offered to corn producers who did not comply with acreage allotments. For crops after 1956 a referendum was required to offer corn producers a choice between a continuation of the existing program of price supports coupled with acreage allotments and a program without acreage restrictions but with no legislated minimum price support rate.

Parity. Transition to the "new" parity formula was prohibited for 1957 for peanuts, corn, and wheat. This prevented a scheduled drop in the support rate for these commodities.

Sugar Act of 1948 Extension and Amendments (P.L. 545, 70 Stat. 217, May 29, 1956): "An act to amend and extend the act of 1948, as amended, and for other purposes"

The extension was for four years, until December 31, 1960. Quotas were revised to allocate a share of future growth in U.S. requirements to domestic producers and to reduce the Cuban share of the foreign supply. Whenever consumption needs expanded beyond 1956 levels, domestic producers were to receive 55 percent and foreign suppliers 45 percent of the annual additional requirement. The allocation of this additional requirement among foreign suppliers was also changed by reducing the Cuban share from 96 to 66 percent.

P.L. 480 Amendments (P.L. 962, 70 Stat. 988, August 3, 1956): "An act to amend the Agricultural Trade Development and Assistance Act of 1954, as amended, so as to increase the amount authorized to be appropriated for purposes of title I of the act, and for other purposes"

This amendment to P.L. 480 doubled the funding authorized for financing

Title I programs, making the authorization authority more than four times the amount specified in the original act. Other provisions added American schools in recipient countries to the list of approved uses of foreign currencies and loosened qualifications for Title II foreign relief donations.

Great Plains Conservation Program (P.L. 1021, 70 Stat. 1115, August 7, 1956): "An act to amend the Soil Conservation and Domestic Allotment Act and the Agricultural Adjustment Act of 1938 to provide for a Great Plains conservation program"

This act authorized a special land conservation program, designed to stimulate a permanent shift in land use, for the ten great plains states. Government payments are authorized "to assist farm and ranch operators to make . . . changes in their cropping systems and land uses which are needed to conserve the soil and water conservation measures needed under such changed systems and uses." Contracts could be negotiated for up to ten years, to terminate no later than December 31, 1971.

85th Congress

P.L. 480 Extension and Amendments (P.L. 128, 71 Stat. 345, August 13, 1957): "An act to extend Agricultural Trade Development and Assistance Act of 1954, and for other purposes"

This act extended Titles I and II for one year, until June 30, 1958, and raised expenditure authorizations under both titles. In addition, East European nations were made eligible for certain donations and for barter transactions.

Wheat Acreage Allotments (P.L. 203, 71 Stat. 477, August 28, 1957): "An act to amend Agricultural Adjustment Act of 1938, as amended, to exempt certain wheat producers from liability under the act where all [the] wheat crop is fed or used for seed or feed on the farm, and for other purposes"

This act exempted from penalties farms producing a maximum of 30 acres of wheat for on-farm use even if that acreage exceeded the allotment of the farm. Previously all farms planting more than 15 acres of wheat were subject to allotments and were penalized if they exceeded their allotments whenever marketing quotas were in force.

Soil Bank Amendments (P.L. 369, 72 Stat. 81, April 7, 1958): "An act to amend section 114 of the Soil Bank Act with respect to compliance with corn acreage allotments"

A provision tying compliance with corn acreage allotments to payments under the Acreage Reserve Program of the Soil Bank was eliminated by this amendment.

Agricultural Act of 1958 (P.L. 835, 72 Stat. 988, August 28, 1958): "An act to provide more effective price, production adjustment, and marketing programs for various agricultural commodities''*

The main provisions of the act revised price support levels for cotton, corn, other feed grains, and rice and extended the programs for wool and milk. Representative Cooley prepared a summary of the provisions and inserted it in the *Congressional Record*. Excerpts from his statement are as follows:

Cotton. — With respect to cotton the bill prevents a reduction in the national cotton acreage allotment from 17,500,000 acres in 1958 to approximately 14 million acres in 1959. The bill provides a minimum national allotment of 16 million acres in 1959 and subsequent years. It stipulates that no individual grower who had an allotment of 10 acres or less in 1958 shall have his allotment reduced and provides 310,000 additional acres for this purpose.

The Secretary of Agriculture is authorized to give each cotton farmer a choice in 1959 and 1960 between:

(a) Remaining within his acreage allotment and receiving price supports in 1959 at no less than 80 percent of parity, and in 1960 at no less than 75 percent of parity.

(b) Planting up to 40 percent above his allotment and receiving price support on all the cotton he produces at . . . no lower than 65 percent of parity [in 1959] and in 1960 no less than 60 percent of parity.

Price supports for choice (a) farmers (those planting within their original allotments) would be through a Government purchase program, and [CCC] cotton . . . could be made available for sale, through July 31, 1961, for unrestricted use at not less than 110 percent of the then current level of support for choice (b) farmers. . . .

The (a) and (b) choice programs would be discontinued after the 1960 crop, and price supports would be set at the discretion of the Secretary for all cotton producers at not less than 70 percent of parity in 1961 and not less than 65 percent of parity for 1962 and subsequent years. . . .

Feed grains. — The bill provides for a referendum, by December 15, 1958, in which farmers of the commercial corn area would choose between:

(1) The present program of acreage allotments and price supports at between 75 and 90 percent of parity; and

(2) A new program which would abandon the commercial area designation, abolish all corn acreage allotments and set price supports at 90 percent of the average market price for the preceding 3 years, or at 65 percent of parity (around $1.14 a bushel), whichever is higher. The support would apply to corn produced throughout the Nation, not to any designated commercial producing area. [For other feed grains, this act provided that beginning with the 1959 crop, price supports for oats, barley, rye, and grain sorghums were required at a level determined to be fair and reasonable in relation to the level of support for corn. This effectively shifted these grains from the permissive to the mandatory category of price supports.]

Rice. — The bill establishes a national minimum allotment of 1,652,000 acres, with price supports to be set by the Secretary in 1959 and 1960 at between 75 and 90 percent of parity, at not less than 70 percent of parity in 1961 and not less than 65 percent of parity in 1962 and subsequent years. The bill forestalls a cut in rice acreage from 1,652,000 in 1958 down to about 1 million in 1959.

Wool. — The National Wool Act is extended for 3 years, from March 31, 1957 to March 31, 1960.

Dairy. — The veterans and armed services milk program is extended for 3 years.[13]

86th Congress

P.L. 480 Extension and Amendments (P.L. 341, 73 Stat. 606, September 21, 1959): "An act to extend Agricultural Trade Development and Assistance Act of 1954, and for other purposes"

This act extended Titles I and II for two years, until December 31, 1961, and raised expenditure authorizations for both titles. Also, a major new feature was added, Title IV, providing long-term credit at low interest rates for the purchase of surplus agricultural commodities by underdeveloped nations.

Some features added to this bill did not relate to exports of surplus farm goods. Noteworthy among these was authority for the secretary of agriculture to establish a pilot food stamp program for the needy in the United States within the next two years. Food owned by the CCC would be eligible for purchase with the stamps.

Tobacco Price Supports (P.L. 389, 74 Stat. 6, February 20, 1960): "An act to stabilize support levels for tobacco against disruptive fluctuations and to provide for adjustment in such levels in relation to farm costs"

This act terminated the use of parity as the basis for computing tobacco price support levels. Instead, supports for 1960 were fixed at 1959 levels; subsequently they would be tied to costs of production. To obtain the price support level for a given year, the 1959 price support would be multiplied by a ratio of average prices paid by farmers in the three preceding calendar years to average prices paid by farmers in 1959. For example: 1961 price support rate = (1959 price support rate) × (average prices paid by farmers in 1958–60 ÷ average prices paid by farmers in 1959).

Sugar Act Extension and Amendments (P.L. 592, 74 Stat. 330, July 6, 1960)

This act, "to amend the Sugar Act of 1948, as amended," extended the Sugar Act for three months, from December 31, 1960, to March 31, 1961. It authorized the president to set the Cuban quota at whatever level was in the national interest. If this meant a cut, the deficit would be redistributed among domestic and other foreign suppliers according to a fixed formula.

87th Congress

Feed Grain Program for 1961 (P.L. 5, 75 Stat. 6, March 22, 1961): "An act to provide a special program for feed grains for 1961"*

This bill provided voluntary price support and supply control programs for growers of corn and grain sorghum in 1961. Prices were to be supported by loans, contingent upon compliance with a land retirement program. Government payments for land retirement were allowed in cash and/or in kind. Participants would be required to divert 20 percent of corn and grain sorghum acreage (based on normal 1959–60 production); diversion of an additional 20 percent of corn and sorghum acreage for payment in kind was optional. Instead of receiving grain as payment in kind, producers could obtain cash from the government. The government was then authorized to sell stocks it owned represented by such transactions.

The payment rate for the additional 20 percent diversion was higher than for the required diversion. Corn-sorghum farmers who planted 25 acres or less in 1959–60 were allowed to divert their entire acreage for payment. Weed, insect, and rodent control would be required on the retired acreage, and the diverted land had to constitute a net addition to soil-conserving acreage. In lieu of payments, the secretary could allow planting safflower, sunflower, sesame, and castor beans on diverted acreage.[14]

Agricultural Act of 1961 (P.L. 128, 75 Stat. 294, August 8, 1961): "An act to improve and protect farm prices and farm income, to increase farmer participation in development of farm programs, or adjust supplies of agricultural commodities in line with requirements therefor, to improve distribution and expand exports of agricultural commodities, to liberalize and extend farm credit services, to protect interest of consumers and for other purposes"*

A comprehensive declaration of policy in the act elaborated on the purposes of this piece of legislation:

In order more fully and effectively to improve, maintain, and protect the prices and incomes of farmers, to enlarge rural purchasing power, to achieve a better balance between supplies of agricultural commodities and the requirements of consumers therefor, to preserve and strengthen the structure of agriculture, and to revitalize and stabilize the overall economy at reasonable costs to the Government, it is hereby declared to be the policy of Congress to —

(a) afford farmers the opportunity to achieve parity of income with other economic groups by providing them with the means to develop and strengthen their bargaining power in the Nation's economy;

(b) encourage a commodity-by-commodity approach in the solution of farm problems and provide the means for meeting varied and changing conditions peculiar to each commodity;

(c) expand foreign trade in agricultural commodities with friendly nations, and in no manner either subsidize the export, sell, or make available any subsidized agricultural commodity to any nations other than such friendly nations and thus make full use of our agricultural abundance;

(d) utilize more effectively our agricultural productive capacity to improve the diets of the Nation's needy persons;

(e) recognize the importance of the family farm as an efficient unit of production and as an economic base for towns and cities in rural areas and encourage, promote, and strengthen this form of farm enterprise;

(f) facilitate and improve credit services to farmers by revising, expanding, and clarifying the laws relating to agricultural credit;

(g) assure consumers of a continuous, adequate, and stable supply of food and fiber at fair and reasonable prices;

(h) reduce the cost of farm programs, by preventing the accumulation of surpluses; and

(i) use surplus farm commodities on hand as fully as practicable as an incentive to reduce production as may be necessary to bring supplies on hand and firm demand in balance.

This act contained provisions for wheat and feed grain programs for 1962, extended the National Wool Act for four years until March 31, 1966, extended authority until December 31, 1971, to enter into new contracts under the Great Plains Conservation Act, extended and amended some features of P.L. 480, amended marketing order legislation, and extended the special milk programs.

Wheat program. The minimum price support level for wheat was continued at 75 percent of parity but supports were tied to reduction of planting 10 percent below the allotment instead of planting up to the allotment as in the past. Additional optional reduction of planted acreage was allowed and the government was authorized to pay farmers for the land withdrawn from production. Penalties for overproduction were retained and were made more severe. Farms with wheat acreage of 13.5 acres or less were exempted from planting restrictions and penalties.

Feed grain program. Corn and sorghum provisions of the feed grain program for 1961 (P.L. 5) were continued for 1962; barley was added to the program.

P.L. 480 amendments. Titles I and II were extended for three years from January 1, 1962, until December 31, 1964. A reduction was made in the annual authorization under Title I from $3.5 to $2.5 million and the three-year total was set at $4.5 million.

Special milk programs. The school milk program was extended for five years, until June 30, 1967; the military and veterans' programs were extended for three years through December 31, 1964.

Marketing orders. Peanuts, turkeys, cherries, cranberries, and apples were added to the list of commodities approved for marketing orders; soybeans were removed.

Sugar Act Amendments (P.L. 15, 75 Stat. 40, March 31, 1961)

This act "to extend and amend the Sugar Act of 1948, as amended," extended the act for 15 months, until June 30, 1962. The key amendment, directed toward Cuba, permitted suspension of quotas for countries with which the United States had broken diplomatic relations.

P.L. 480 Amendments (P.L. 28, 75 Stat. 64, May 4, 1961)

This act, "to amend title I of the Agricultural Trade Development and

Assistance Act of 1954,'' raised the level of authorized funding for Title I from $1.5 to $3.5 billion for 1961.

P.L. 480 Amendments (P.L. 92, 75 Stat. 211, July 20, 1961): "An act to continue the authority of the President under title II of the Agricultural Trade Development and Assistance Act of 1954, as amended, to utilize surplus agricultural commodities to assist needy peoples and to promote economic development in underdeveloped areas of the world"

Under this act, previous temporary authority under Title II to use food grants for economic development was made permanent.

Foreign Assistance Act of 1961 (P.L. 195, 75 Stat. 424, September 4, 1961)

This act replaced the Mutual Security Act as the authorization for foreign aid appropriations. The provision was retained that required expenditure of a share of foreign aid funds for financing the export and sale of surplus agricultural commodities.

Planting on Diverted Acres (P.L. 451, 76 Stat. 70, May 15, 1962): "An act to amend the Agricultural Act of 1961 to permit planting of additional nonsurplus crops on diverted acreage"

This act authorized the secretary of agriculture to permit planting of nonsurplus crops on diverted acres, with a reduction in diversion payments.

Sugar Act Amendments of 1962 (P.L. 535, 76 Stat. 156, July 13, 1962): "An act to amend and extend the provisions of the ·Sugar Act of 1948, as amended''*

The basic act was extended for four and one-half years, until December 31, 1966, and other major changes were made to apply until December 31, 1964. One change increased tonnage quotas for domestic producing areas and the Philippines and raised the domestic share in future demand growth from 55 to 65 percent. Another change authorized the president to suspend a nation's quota for diplomatic reasons; if diplomatic relations were severed, the quota would be suspended automatically. The latter provision affected the Cuban quota. The suspended Cuban quota became a "global quota," a quota not designated to a particular country. No fixed method was set for reassigning the "global quota" except that priorities were to be given to Western Hemisphere nations and to nations importing U.S. farm products.

Import fees, a new feature, were imposed on this reassigned sugar. Foreign suppliers meeting regular quotas were subject to a smaller import fee, scheduled to increase in steps for 1962, 1963, and 1964. The Philippines was exempted from the import fee.

Sugar Act Amendments (P.L. 539, 76 Stat. 169, July 19, 1962): "An act . . . to amend certain provisions of the Sugar Act of 1948, as amended"

Additional changes were made in quota assignments and import fees. A portion of the suspended Cuban quota reassigned to other nations was exempted from the full import fee and made subject to a lower, variable fee schedule. Also, reassignment of unmet foreign quotas was restricted to Western Hemisphere nations or to nations importing U.S. farm products.

Food and Agriculture Act of 1962 (P.L. 703, 76 Stat. 605, September 27, 1962): "An act to improve and protect farm income, to reduce costs of farm programs to Federal Government, to reduce Federal Government's excessive stocks of agricultural commodities, to maintain reasonable and stable prices of agricultural commodities and products to consumers, to provide adequate supplies of agricultural commodities for domestic and foreign needs, to conserve natural resources, and for other purposes"*

This law deals with three broad areas of concern: Titles I and IV provide authority and resources for rural land use adjustments; Title II amends P.L. 480; and Title III authorizes production management programs for feed grains and wheat.

Land use adjustment. Under Title I new authority and resources were provided for putting land to optimum economic and social uses. It expanded the Rural Areas Development Program, offered alternatives to the use of land for surplus crop production, broadened possibilities for outdoor recreational facilities on locally owned lands, and stimulated conservation of land and water resources, flood prevention, and development of local water supply.

Title IV authorized loans for recreational development and facilities to individual farmers and to associations serving farmers and other rural people. It also increased the authorization ceiling for Farmers Home Administration loans for recreational development from $10 million to $25 million.

P.L. 480 amendments. These amendments inaugurated several new authorities designed to promote the consumption of U.S. agricultural commodities in recipient countries. Food donations to nonprofit school lunch programs were specifically mentioned. Other measures eased payment requirements for foreign governments under P.L. 480 contracts.

Commodity programs. Title III provided the secretary of agriculture with new authority to work with farmers to bring agricultural production in line with domestic and export needs, improve and stabilize farm income, reduce surplus stocks, and reduce the costs of farm programs.

Wheat and feed grain programs were provided for 1963 similar to 1962 programs but with one key change. Loan rates were lowered and producers' returns from production were supported by a commodity loan and a price support payment. Cooperating producers were eligible for loans and price support payments on all of their production in addition to payments for diverting land from production of these crops. By considering part of government payments as price support payments, instead of classifying all payments as acreage diversion payments, statutory requirements that set price supports at a given level were met. The distinction had no import for producers.

For 1964 a new supply management program for wheat was authorized, pending approval in a referendum by growers. If approved, a mandatory production control program for wheat would be inaugurated. The new program eliminated the minimum 55-million-acre allotment. Instead, it provided for annual quotas based on estimated domestic and foreign needs and on the level of government stocks. Farm allotments were to be derived from the national quota; farmers who exceeded allotments would be subject to severe penalties. Farmers would be issued certificates from the USDA for the amount of wheat they were allowed to sell for domestic use and export. The price of this wheat would be supported between 65 and 90 percent of parity. Any remaining wheat from a farmer's allotment could be fed or marketed at a price related to the feed value and the world price of wheat. Payments for reductions in farm allotments below the 55-million-acre level were allowed for 1964 and 1965. The previous exemption from program features for producers of 15 or fewer acres of wheat was discontinued.[15]

Trade Expansion Act of 1962 (P.L. 794, 76 Stat. 872, October 11, 1962): "An act to promote the general welfare, foreign policy, and security of the United States through international trade agreements and through adjustment assistance to domestic industry, agriculture, and labor, and for other purposes"

The act included a provision of especial importance to agricultural trade. It granted the president authority to impose quotas or other import restrictions on nations restricting U.S. agricultural imports.

15-Acre Wheat Exemption (P.L. 801, 76 Stat. 909, October 11, 1962)

This act, "to amend section 309 of the Food and Agriculture Act of 1962," continued for the 1963 crop exemptions from marketing quotas for farms planting 15 or fewer acres of wheat.

School Lunch Act Amendments (P.L. 823, 76 Stat. 944, October 15, 1962): "An act to revise the formula for apportioning cash assistance funds among the states under the National School Lunch Act, and for other purposes"

This act changed the basis for allocating funds among states from the number of school-age children to the number participating in the program in each state. Previously, states with a low rate of participation received a high per pupil payment. Apportionment according to state need was not changed, continuing the practice of paying low-income states at a higher rate than high-income states. Also, a special appropriation for free lunches in very poor areas was authorized.

Feed Grain Act of 1963 (P.L. 26, 77 Stat. 44, May 20, 1963): ''An act to extend the feed grain program''*

The bill provided feed grain programs for 1964 and 1965 similar to the 1963 program. Price supports for corn were authorized at 65 to 90 percent of parity (with comparable levels for grain sorghums, barley, oats, and rye) if a feed grain diversion program was in effect. A diversion program required shifting land from feed grain production to conservation uses. Eligibility for price support was conditioned on participation in an acreage diversion program, or, at the secretary's discretion, on keeping within the farm base acreage if there were no diversion program.

Payments to producers were authorized. Payments consisted of price support payments computed on allowable production and acreage diversion payments computed on land withheld from feed grain production under the program. (See the discussion under the 1962 act for the meaning of the distinction between price support and acreage diversion payments.) While the bill did not contain any limit on the amount of price support payments, the secretary of agriculture on the basis of then current information and estimates indicated to the Senate Agriculture Committee that price support payments would not exceed the 18 cents per bushel for corn provided by law under the 1963 program. Acreage diversion payments could be made at rates up to 50 percent of the support price multiplied by the normal production of the acreage diverted. Maximum allowable diversion for payment was set at 50 percent of the farm feed grain base, or 25 acres if greater.

Provision was made for adjusting base acreages in any state or county and for up to 1 percent state reserve for farms with no base period history. Farms receiving apportionments from such reserve would not be entitled to diversion payments for the first year in which feed grain bases were established for them.[16]

P.L. 480 Amendments (P.L. 205, 77 Stat. 379, December 16, 1963): ''An act to amend further the Foreign Assistance Act of 1961, as amended, and for other purposes''

This act, the Foreign Assistance Act of 1963, contained several amendments to P.L. 480. Of most importance was the barring of concessional sales in 1964 (1) to any country engaging in or preparing for aggressive military efforts against the United States or against countries receiving U.S. aid, and (2) to any country transporting cargo to Cuba. These provisions prevented future Title I shipments to Poland and Yugoslavia.

Russian Wheat Sales (P.L. 258, 77 Stat. 857, January 6, 1964)

One feature of the Foreign Aid Appropriations Act made possible wheat sales to the U.S.S.R. It provided that credit could not be extended to any Communist country *except* when the president determined that such guarantees would be in the national interest and reported to the House and Senate within 30 days after each such determination was made.

Agricultural Act of 1964 (P.L. 297, 78 Stat. 173, April 11, 1964): "An act to encourage increased consumption of cotton, to maintain income of cotton and wheat producers, to provide voluntary marketing certificate program for 1964 and 1965 crop of wheat, and for other purposes"

Wheat program.[17] A voluntary two-year program was authorized, providing supplemental payments to farmers who curtailed their wheat planting. Payments were of three types: domestic marketing certificates, export marketing certificates, and diversion payments. The certificate payments covered wheat destined for domestic food use or for export and were in addition to the market or loan price received by farmers. Diversion payments were in essence rental payments for land held out of wheat production. Instead of receiving certificates for later redemption, farmers could elect to receive payment from the government by a check covering all three types of payments.

For 1964, producers who voluntarily diverted at least 10 percent of their allotments would receive price support loans at a level based upon the feed value of wheat and the world price — about $1.30. In addition they would receive domestic marketing certificates valued at 70 cents per bushel on their proportion of the wheat crop used domestically for food. Export marketing certificates, valued at 25 cents per bushel, would be issued on that portion of the wheat crop to be exported. Diversion up to 20 percent of the allotment was allowed; the payment rate would be at the discretion of the secretary.

For 1965, the support level and certificate values would be close to those set for 1964. There also would be the right of substitution of wheat and feed grain acres subject to voluntary participation in each program. This provision could not be put into effect for the 1964 crop owing to the late passage of this act.

For both years nonparticipating farmers were allowed to plant as much wheat as they desired. For them there were no restrictions, no penalties, no marketing quotas, no price support, no diversion payments, no certificates, and no restrictions on marketings.

The cost of domestic marketing certificates was to be passed along to millers by requiring that they purchase certificates from the government for all wheat processed for domestic food use. However, this entailed no appreciable change in the cost of wheat to millers because the added cost of the certificates would be offset by a lower market price of wheat.[18]

Cotton program. Two new features covering cotton crops of 1964 and 1965 were introduced in this legislation: (1) a subsidy for domestic mills so that they could buy U.S. cotton at the same price as foreign buyers, and (2) a higher price support available to producers who restricted production to their domestic allotment, about two-thirds of the base allotment. The mill subsidy, called a domestic equalization payment, was a payment in kind to mills from government stocks of cotton. This provision had the effect of reducing the price of cotton to domestic mills without lowering the price received by farmers. Likewise, payments in kind were one way that the difference between the basic loan rate and the higher price support was paid to qualifying farmers. If a farmer preferred, however, he could turn his cotton over to the government and obtain the higher support rate (the basic loan rate plus the supplement) as a loan instead of taking the payment in kind. Small farmers were exempted from the requirement of reducing acreage below their base allotment; they qualified for the higher loan rate if they planted their entire allotment.

Other important provisions in the act were (1) a reduction in the resale price of CCC-owned cotton from 115 percent to 105 percent of the basic loan rate, and (2) authorization for farmers to exceed basic allotments if the excess was sold for export without governmental assistance.

Meat Import Quotas (P.L. 482, 78 Stat. 594, August 22, 1964): "An act to provide for the free importation of certain wild animals, and to provide for the imposition of quotas on certain meat and meat products"

One provision of this act directed the president to impose quotas on imports of beef, veal, mutton, and goat meat whenever imports were expected to exceed a specified share of domestic supply. The limitation was based on actual imports and domestic production in 1959–63. For future years, the allowable quantity of imports was to be adjusted upward or downward to correspond with percentage changes in domestic production, thus maintaining a fairly fixed share of the U.S. market for domestic producers. Imports could rise to 110 percent of the quantity set by the formula above before quotas were imposed; and quotas would be removed whenever imports fell below the 110 percent figure. Quotas were to be allocated among importing nations according to market shares in the 1959–63 base period. The president was granted authority to suspend or increase quotas in the interest of national security or to assure an adequate supply at reasonable consumer prices.

Food Stamp Act of 1964 (P.L. 525, 78 Stat. 703, August 31, 1964): "An act to strengthen the agricultural economy; to help to achieve a fuller and more effective use of food abundances; to provide for improved levels of nutrition among low-income households through a cooperative Federal-State program of food assistance to be operated through normal channels of trade; and for other purposes" *

The major provisions of the act were summarized in a Senate report, as follows:

This bill authorizes the Secretary of Agriculture to formulate and administer a food stamp program in areas of the various States when such a program is requested by an appropriate agency of the State.

Under the program authorized by the bill —

(1) The State agency responsible for the administration of federally aided public assistance programs would submit to the Secretary for approval a plan of operation for the program in its State, specifying the various political subdivisions in which the program would be effective, the standards to be used in determining the eligibility of applicant households, and other details to insure compliance with the provisions of the act.

(2) Each State agency would develop eligibility standards which would limit participation to those households whose income is a substantial limiting factor in the attainment of a nutritionally adequate diet. Eligible households would receive coupons having a face value sufficient to provide an opportunity more nearly to obtain a low-cost nutritionally adequate diet. For its coupons, each household would pay an amount equivalent to its normal expenditure for food. Coupons would be redeemable at retail stores for any food or food product for human consumption, except alcoholic beverages, tobacco, those foods which are identified on the package as being imported, and meat and meat products which are identified as being from foreign sources when they arrive at the retail food store. The State agency shall insure that there is no discrimination in the certification of applicant households because of race, religious creed, national origin, or political beliefs.

(3) Retail food stores could redeem coupons through wholesale food concerns or banks. Retailers and wholesalers wishing to accept or redeem food coupons would be approved by the Department of Agriculture and would have administrative and judicial appeals from denial or withdrawal of approval.

(4) The State welfare agency would be responsible for the certification of applicant households, including those households which were not receiving any form of welfare assistance. That agency would also be responsible for the sale and issuance of the food coupons but it could, under its plan of operation, delegate overall operating issuance responsibility to another agency of the State government, if permitted by State law.

(5) Appropriations are authorized as follows: Not to exceed $75 million for the fiscal year ending June 30, 1965; not to exceed $100 million for the fiscal year ending June 30, 1966; and not to exceed $200 million for the fiscal year ending June 30, 1967. Appropriations for fiscal years after June 30, 1967, would be limited to amounts hereafter authorized by Congress. So much of each such appropriation as is required to make up the difference between the face value of coupons issued and the amounts paid by the recipients is to be put into an account maintained in the Treasury where, with the amounts paid by recipients, it will be available without fiscal year limitation for the redemption of coupons.[19]

P.L. 480 Extension and Amendments (P.L. 638, 78 Stat. 1035, October 8, 1964): "An act to extend the Agricultural Trade Development and Assistance Act of 1954, and for other purposes"

According to a summary prepared for the House Committee on Agriculture, this act

(1) Extends Titles I and II of *Public Law 480*, 83rd Congress, for two years, through December 31, 1966.

(2) Authorizes $2,700,000,000 plus carryovers and reimbursements to Commodity Credit Corporation from sales of foreign currencies for dollars to cover the extended period for Title I.

(3) Provides an annual authorization of $400,000,000 plus carryover for Title II.

(4) Prohibits sales under Title I to any Communist country or any country whose ships or aircraft are permitted to carry goods to Cuba, but provides that such countries shall be eligible for sales under Title IV.

(5) Limits financing on ocean freight charges on Title I shipments to U.S. flag vessel differentials.

(6) Requires exchange rates to be no less favorable than those obtainable by any other nation.

(7) Establishes an advisory committee to review the status and usage of foreign currencies, the maximum return from sales under Title I, and to make recommendations to the President, including recommendations for improving the act and its administration.

(8) Authorizes the use of CCC funds up to $7.5 million a year under Title II to purchase Title I foreign currencies for use on self-help activities designed to alleviate the causes of need for assistance.

(9) Requires that foreign currencies obtained from sales under Title I be converted to dollars to the extent consistent with the purposes of the act.

(10) Requires that expenditures be classified for purposes of budget presentation as expenditures for international affairs and finance.

(11) Removes the ceiling on foreign currencies reserved for loans to private business and provides that such currency shall be made available to the maximum usable extent.

(12) Provides that foreign currency nonmilitary grants and use of loan repayments be submitted to the Senate Agriculture Committee and prohibits them from being made if either Committee disapproves.

(13) Requires that Title I loans bear interest at not less than the cost of funds to the United States [and] makes the minimum interest rate provided by law for Development Loan Fund loans the minimum rate for interest on sales of surplus commodities for dollar credit under Title IV.

(14) Directs the Commodity Credit Corporation to sell extra long staple cotton determined by the Secretary of Agriculture to be surplus at competitive world prices.[20]

89th Congress

Tobacco Quotas (P.L. 12, 79 Stat. 66, April 16, 1965): "An act to amend Agricultural Act of 1938, as amended, to provide for acreage-poundage marketing quotas for tobacco, to amend tobacco price support provisions of Agricultural Act of 1949, as amended, and for other pruposes"

This act introduced a significant change in the manner of controlling tobacco production. For the first time in recent years quotas were stated in terms of quantities marketed instead of solely on an acreage basis. Previously all production from an allotment constituted the allowable quota. Now a poundage quota was authorized. A national poundage requirement would be determined and then apportioned to states. Each state quota would be converted to acreage and assigned to farms in acres and pounds. If marketings from a farm were less than the poundage quota, the difference was added to the farm's quota (in acres and pounds) for the following year.

Acreage-poundage quotas were to be placed on flue-cured tobacco for three years, if at least two-thirds of the growers voting in a referendum approved the new controls. If the new controls were not approved, the previously proclaimed acreage controls were to be in effect.

Beginning in 1966 the secretary could conduct referendums among growers of other kinds of tobacco to see whether they wanted acreage-poundage controls for the next three years. A two-thirds majority of farmers voting was necessary for approval.

Growers of all kinds of tobacco were to be permitted to market up to 10 percent more than their poundage quotas without penalty, but any excess marketings were to be deducted from a farm's quotas in subsequent years. Price supports were to be provided on all tobacco marketed without penalty.[21]

Food and Agriculture Act of 1965 (P.L. 321, 79 Stat. 1187, November 3, 1965): "An act to maintain farm income, to stabilize prices and assure adequate supplies of agricultural commodities, to reduce surpluses, lower Government costs and promote foreign trade, to afford greater economic opportunity in rural areas, and for other purposes"*

Major provisions of the act are as follows:

Title I — Dairy. — This title provides for a class I base plan in Federal milk market order areas. Its purpose is to reduce production of milk in excess of the market needs and to stabilize the income of dairy producers in market order areas. . . . It includes provisions for individual voting in farmer referenda on the class I base plan; for leaving the legal status of producer handlers unchanged; for authorizing marketing orders for manufacturing milk; and sets up conditions for the entry of new producers into these markets.

Title II — Wool. — This title extends the National Wool Act of 1954 through December 31, 1969. The support price for shorn wool would be tied to the average of the parity index for the 3 calendar years immediately preceding the calendar year for which the support price is determined. This modification is intended to increase the production of wool in the United States by increasing the support price if cost of production increases.

Title III — Feed Grains. — This title would extend the feed grain program for 4 years, with some modification. It provides for price support loans and payments-in-kind to program participants. [Producers could elect to receive cash instead of grains as payments.] Cooperators would be required to divert acreage from production of feed grains to conserving uses. The total price support (both loan and payment) could be set at between 65 and 90 percent of parity. The Secretary is authorized to lower the loan value gradually in order to increase the effectiveness of the program.

Title IV — Cotton. — The market price of cotton is to be supported at 90 percent of estimated world price levels, thus making payments to mills and export subsidies unnecessary. Incomes of cotton farmers are to be maintained through payments based on the extent of their participation in the allotment program, with special provisions for protecting the income of farmers with small cotton acreages. Participation is to be voluntary (although price support eligibility generally depends on participation) with a minimum acreage reduction of 12.5 percent from effective farm allotments required for participation on all but small farms.

Title V — Wheat. — This title continues the voluntary wheat certificate program for 4 years with slight modifications. ["Certificate" was a term used in the wheat program for authorized payments to farmers by the government and for payments to the government by processors.] In order to increase producer income, wheat used domestically as food would be supported at 100 percent of parity and support for wheat not accompanied by marketing certificates would be not less than $1.25 per bushel in 1966. For subsequent years producers are assured of returns from price support and other payments equal to not less than the total support provided for 1966 unless the acreage allotment is increased above 50 million acres exclusive of small farms. Costs of certificates to domestic processors for all 4 years would not be more than the difference between the loan value and $2 per bushel. The bill does not contain the so-called escalator clause whereby the Secretary could increase the costs of certificates to processors if the price of bread increased.

Title VI — Cropland Adjustment. — This title authorizes the secretary to enter into 5- to 10-year contracts with farmers calling for conversion of cropland into vegetative cover, water storage facilities, or other soil, water, wildlife or forest conserving uses. Payments would be at a rate of not more than 40 percent of the annual market value of the crop that would have been produced on the land. The Secretary is authorized to obligate not more than $225 million per year in new contracts signed during each of the next 4 years.

Title VIII — Rice. — This title provides for a 4-year rice diversion program effective only when the national allotment is reduced below the 1.8 million-acre national allotment in effect in 1965. In no event could the national allotment be reduced below the 1.6-million-acre minimum now in the law. This title also provides that for 1966 and 1967 rice value factors may not be reduced and differentials between value factors for the various varieties could not be increased.[22]

Sugar Act Amendments of 1965 (P.L. 331, 79 Stat. 1271, November 8, 1965)

This act "to amend and extend provisions of Sugar Act of 1948, as amended," extended the Sugar Act for five years, until December 31, 1971. New domestic and foreign quotas were established, enlarging the domestic share of the market. Cuba's permanent quota was reduced from 55.77 percent to 50 percent of the foreign quota. The "global quota" method of reassigning the suspended Cuban quota was not renewed. Instead, the suspended Cuban quota was assigned by law to specific countries. Also abandoned were import fees imposed by the expiring 1962 amendments.

Food Aid to India (P.L. 406, 80 Stat. 131, April 19, 1966): "An act to support United States participation in relieving victims of hunger in India and to enhance India's capacity to meet the nutritional needs of its people"

This joint resolution "endorses U.S. participation in an international program to relieve India's food crisis. [It] supports the use of U.S. agricultural commodities available under P.L. 480 to assist in meeting India's normal import needs as well as its emergency food shortage, [and] endorses assistance in expansion of India's agricultural production."[23]

Food for Peace Act of 1966 (P.L. 808, 80 Stat. 1526, November 11, 1966): "An act to promote international trade in agricultural commodities, to combat hunger and malnutrition, to further economic development and for other purposes"*

This act extended and amended the Agricultural Trade Development and Assistance Act of 1954, as amended (P.L. 480). The thrust of the amendments was to shift the focus of the act from disposal of U.S. surpluses to economic development in the developing nations. This new policy is spelled out in Section 2 of the act, which states:

The Congress hereby declares it to be the policy of the United States to expand international trade; to develop and expand export markets for United States agricultural commodities; to use the abundant agricultural productivity of the United States to combat hunger and malnutrition and to encourage economic development in the developing countries, with particular emphasis on assistance to those countries that are determined to improve their own agricultural production; and to promote in other ways the foreign policy of the United States.

The following provisions were included in the new act:

Emphasis on self-help. To qualify for U.S. food aid, developing countries must try to provide more of their own food requirements from their own resources and their own efforts.

The U.S. would reinforce self-help efforts to improve food production with technical and scientific support from the Department of Agriculture, land-grant universities, and private agricultural resources.

Removal of "surplus" requirement. U.S. food aid shipments would be made up of "available" commodities rather than those that were "surplus." Additional stress would be placed, especially in donation programs, on foods for children that met their requirements of proteins, minerals, and vitamins.

Transition to dollar sales. It was the goal of the new program to have countries then buying U.S. farm products with their local currencies shift to buying such products for dollars, or with dollar credits, by the end of 1971.

Friendly countries. The policy was continued of making concessional sales of U.S. farm products only to friendly countries. Excluded were countries controlled or dominated by the world Communist movement, or countries that did business with Cuba or North Vietnam. An exception might be made for countries exporting food, medicines, and nonstrategic agricultural supplies to Cuba.

Family planning. The new program authorized the use of foreign currencies from export sales to support programs of family planning only when requested by the recipient country.

Assistance from other countries. It supported the expansion of international food and agricultural assistance programs, including the U.N. World Food Program, since the world food problem was too immense for just one nation to solve.[24]

Child Nutrition Act of 1966 (P.L. 642, 80 Stat. 885, October 11, 1966): "An act to strengthen and expand food service programs for children"*

Provisions of this act included a three-year extension of the special milk program and a two-year program to provide breakfasts in schools. A permanent program was authorized for purchasing equipment for food service in schools serving children of low-income families. Authority was provided for funding state educational agencies to assist them in the administration of programs for poor children. All federally aided food programs for children were extended to preschool children enrolled in activities administered through the school system.

90th Congress

Emergency Food Aid to India (P.L. 7, 81 Stat. 7, April 1, 1967)

This was a joint congressional resolution "to support emergency food assistance to India." It was recommended in the resolution:

. . . that the United States provide an additional 3 million tons of food grain for calendar year 1967 at an estimated cost of $190 million toward meeting the India food deficit, [and] . . . that the President provide an additional $25 million of emergency food relief for distribution by CARE and other American voluntary agencies.

The resolution further expresses the sense of Congress that to avoid price-depressing uncertainty, the administration, in carrying out the program under Public Law 480 should make announcements of intention, purchases, and shipments on schedules and under circumstances designed to strengthen farm market prices to the maximum extent possible. The need for massive additional aid to India resulted from severe drought suffered by that country in the 1965–66 and 1966–67 crop years.[25]

P.L. 480 Amendments (P.L. 137, 81 Stat. 445, November 14, 1967)

These amendments to P.L. 480 were contained in the Foreign Assistance Act of 1967, and thereby coordinated P.L. 480 activities with other foreign aid programs to some extent. This act prohibited assistance under P.L. 480 to any country which made war-related materials available to North Vietnam or to a country which severed diplomatic relations with the United States.

And it required that the president suspend aid when development assistance was being diverted to unneeded military purposes which hampered a country's development.

School Lunch Act Amendments (P.L. 302, 82 Stat. 117, May 8, 1968): "An act to amend the National School Lunch Act to strengthen and expand food service programs for children, and for other purposes"

Eligibility for funds under the National School Lunch Act was expanded to include children in private nonprofit institutions or public institutions, such as child day-care centers, settlement houses, or recreation centers, that provided day care. Residential institutions were excluded. Both year-round and summer programs qualified.

Funds appropriated under these provisions were to be used by the states in reimbursing the institutions for meals served at a rate established by the secretary of agriculture. In cases of extreme need, the secretary could authorize payment up to 80 percent of the cost of operation of a program, including food and labor. Institutions were required to justify the need for assistance.

A state could use up to 25 percent of the funds received to reimburse institutions for equipment purchased or rented for the program, but the institution would be required to pay at least 25 percent of the cost or rental of the equipment.

Section 4 of the Child Nutrition Act was amended to extend the breakfast program through fiscal year 1971.

Appropriations under this act were to be considered functions of the Department of Health, Education, and Welfare rather than of the Department of Agriculture.[26]

International Grains Arrangement, 1967 (19 U.S.T. 5501, T.I.A.S. No. 6537, June 15, 1968) * [27]

The International Grains Arrangement (IGA) replaced the expired International Wheat Agreement (IWA). It comprised two legal instruments: the Wheat Trade Convention and the Food Aid Convention. The duration of both measures was set at three years,.beginning July 1, 1968.

Wheat Trade Convention. As stated in the arrangement, the objectives of this convention were

To assure supplies of wheat and wheat flour to importing countries and markets for wheat and wheat flour to exporting countries at equitable and stable prices;

To promote the expansion of the international trade in wheat and wheat flour and to secure the freest possible flow of this trade in the interests of both exporting and importing countries, and thus contribute to the development of countries, the economies of which depend on commercial sales of wheat; and

In general to further international co-operation in connection with world wheat problems, recognizing the relationship of the trade in wheat to the economic stability of markets for other agricultural products.

The convention resembled the earlier IWAs although the price ranges and mechanism were changed. Previously the minimum and maximum prices were specified only for one grade of wheat for shipment between two designated ports. The new IGA specified price ranges for several wheats between one origin and several destinations. The new ranges were higher than in the most recent IWA.

Food Aid Convention. The objective of this convention was to "carry out a food aid programme with the help of contributions for the benefit of developing countries." Participating nations agreed to contribute grain suitable for food use or cash to needy developing countries. The annual total contribution was set at 4.5 million metric tons.

P.L. 480 Amendments (P.L. 436, 82 Stat. 450, July 29, 1968): "An act to extend the Agricultural Trade Development and Assistance Act of 1954, as amended, and for other purposes"

The extension was for two years, through December 31, 1970. Other amendments aimed at (1) easing the nation's balance-of-payments problem, (2) preventing economic benefits from P.L. 480 operations for firms trading with North Vietnam, (3) encouraging population control in recipient countries, and (4) assisting cultural and educational exchanges between the United States and recipient nations. Measures to improve U.S. international finances included requiring estimates of U.S. expenditures in recipient nations in order to gear P.L. 480 payments to U.S. needs, requiring the president to take steps assuring that the United States shared in whatever growth took place in commercial agricultural markets in recipient nations, and permitting the United States to exchange some foreign currency for dollars.

Food Stamp Act Amendments (P.L. 552, 82 Stat. 958, October 8, 1968)

This act, "To amend the Food Stamp Act of 1964, as amended," increased the level of funding for 1969 from $225 million to $315 million and set the 1970 level at $340 million.

Extension of Food and Agriculture Act of 1965 (P.L. 559, 82 Stat. 996, October 11, 1968)

No change in provisions was made by this act which extended the 1965 act for one year, through December 31, 1970.

91st Congress

Food Stamp Act Amendment (P.L. 116, 83 Stat. 191, November 13, 1969)

This act, "To increase the appropriation authorization for the food stamp program for fiscal year 1970," increased the authorization from $340 million to $610 million.

School Lunch and Child Nutrition Act Amendments (P.L. 248, 84 Stat. 207, May 14, 1970): "An act to amend the National School Lunch Act and the Child Nutrition Act of 1966 to clarify responsibilities related to providing free and reduced-price meals and preventing discrimination against children, to revise program matching requirements, to strengthen the nutrition training and education benefits of the programs, and otherwise to strengthen the food service programs for children in schools and service institutions''

This act expanded and improved programs of free and reduced-price lunches for poor schoolchildren. For some needy children, the maximum price charged could not exceed 20 cents per meal; for others, free meals were authorized. Funding authorization for the school breakfast program was doubled for fiscal 1971.

Agricultural Act of 1970 (P.L. 524, 84 Stat. 1358, November 30, 1970): ''An act to establish improved programs for the benefit of producers and consumers of dairy products, wool, wheat, feed grains, cotton, and other commodities, to extend the Agricultural Trade Development and Assistance Act of 1954, as amended, and for other purposes''*

This comprehensive bill dealt chiefly with commodity programs. Other provisions extended P.L. 480 programs and authorized long-term land retirement on a pilot basis. Coverage was for three years, through crop year 1973. It included one new element and two major modifications. New was a limitation on payments to producers of upland cotton, wheat, and feed grains. Total payments to a producer for price support, set-aside acreage, diversion, public access, and marketing certificates for any one of these commodities were limited to $55,000. One major modification relaxed planting restrictions. The act did not require that a limit be placed on acreage of any particular crop. The provision for annual supply control, called set-aside, required reduction in total acreage devoted to crops. (Acreage controls on individual crops were not prohibited; they were permissive.) The second modification eliminated special provisions for small grain farms — those with a base acreage or an allotment of 25 or fewer acres.

Wheat program. Marketing quotas and acreage allotments were suspended for the 1971–73 crop years. A set-aside program was established under which wheat farmers, to be eligible for loans and payments under the program, were required to set aside or divert from the production of wheat or other crops an acreage determined by the secretary. The 1971 set-aside could not be more than 13.3 million acres and the 1972 and 1973 set-asides could not exceed 15 million acres. Payments were authorized for set-aside acres; additional payments were allowed if set-aside acres were opened for public recreation.

The act provided domestic wheat-marketing certificates (i.e., price support payments) for farmers participating in the set-aside program in an amount equal to U.S. food consumption, but not less than 535 million bushels annually. The face value of the domestic certificates was set at the difference between the wheat parity price and the average price received by farmers during the first five months of the wheat-marketing year (beginning July 1).

Farmers could elect to receive the value of certificates as a cash payment. The cost of certificates to wheat processors was continued at 75 cents per bushel. Processors' payments partially reimbursed the government for certificate payments to farmers.

The secretary was authorized to set nonrecourse loans to participating farmers from $1.25 per bushel to 100 percent of the parity price for wheat.

Feed grains program. A voluntary feed grain program (corn, grain sorghum, and barley, if designated by the secretary) was established for the 1971–73 crop years: a set-aside program under which participating farmers would be required to set aside or divert feed grain acres or other cropland in order to become eligible for loans and payments.

The act provided that price support payments to participating farmers on one-half of their feed grain base would be the difference between either (a) $1.35 per bushel or (b) 70 percent (68 percent under certain circumstances) of the parity price for corn, whichever was higher, and the average market price for the first five months of the marketing year (beginning on October 1 for corn and grain sorghum and July 1 for barley). In no event, however, would these payments be less than 32 cents per bushel for corn — with corresponding rates for grain sorghum and barley.

The secretary was authorized to set the nonrecourse loan level from $1.00 per bushel to 90 percent of parity.

Cotton program. A voluntary program was established under which marketing quotas and penalties would be suspended for three years. A cropland set-aside program, not to exceed 28 percent of the cotton allotment, was specified as a condition of eligibility for benefits under the program.

The act provided for payments on the estimated production from 11.5 million acres for the 1971 crop. In 1972 and 1973, the base acreage allotment would be set by the secretary, and total payments would be adjusted accordingly.

The payment to participating cotton farmers would be the difference between either (a) 65 percent of parity or (b) 35 cents, whichever was higher, and the average market price for the first five months following the beginning (August 1) of the marketing year, but in no event would the payment be less than 15 cents per pound. No refunds by farmers would be required. Small farms would be eligible for 30 percent bonus payments.

The price support loan rate was established for the 1971–73 crop years at 90 percent of the average world price for the two previous years.

Dairy program. Authority for the Class I Base Plan in milk market order areas provided that any area covered by the program during the 1971–73 period could continue to have it in effect up to December 31, 1976. Dairy indemnity payments were continued, the secretary's authority was extended for donation to the armed forces and veterans hospitals of dairy products owned by CCC, and the act suspended the operation of the mandatory butterfat price support program for farm-separated cream and permitted the secretary to secretary to set lower support prices for butter.

Wool program. The National Wool Act of 1954, as amended, was extended through December 31, 1973, and continued the 1970 incentive price of 72 cents per pound for shorn wool and 80.2 cents per pound for mohair for each year of the extension.[28]

Food Stamp Act Amendments (P.L. 454, 84 Stat. 969, October 15, 1970; and P.L. 671, 84 Stat. 2048, January 11, 1971)

These amendments expanded and liberalized the program. They raised the authorized level of funding the program substantially (from an annual maximum of $600 million to $1,750 million for fiscal 1971 and no limits for the following two years), eased requirements and lowered costs for low-income people, and added a work requirement provision. The liberalized requirements limited the charge for stamps to 30 percent of income and eliminated charges entirely for the extremely poor. The work provision required that recipients register for and accept employment under certain conditions. Other new provisions established uniform national eligibility standards, directed participating states to enhance information efforts advising low-income households about the program, permitted the elderly to use food stamps for prepared meals under some circumstances, and authorized both food stamp and commodities programs in localities requesting both programs.

92nd Congress

Tobacco Quotas (P.L. 10, 85 Stat. 23, April 14, 1971)

This act, "to amend the tobacco marketing quota provisions of the Agricultural Adjustment Act of 1938, as amended," established the use of pounds instead of acres for burley tobacco marketing quotas. Although poundage quotas were allowed previously, they had not been adopted for the burley tobacco program. Before implementation, the system required approval by two-thirds of the producers voting in a referendum. If approved, quotas would apply for three years; if they were not approved, another referendum was required after one year.

Food Programs for Children (P.L. 32, 85 Stat. 85, June 30, 1971)

This act, "to extend the school breakfast and special food programs," authorized use of Section 32 funds to supplement appropriations for the school lunch and breakfast programs. Additional funds were necessary because current appropriations were inadequate to cover costs of programs expanded by P.L. 671, 91st Congress.

International Wheat Agreement, 1971 (22 U.S.T. 821, T.I.A.S. No. 7144, July 24, 1971)

This agreement replaced the IGA which expired on July 1, 1971. The new IWA retained the two IGA conventions — the Wheat Trade Convention and the Food Aid Convention. The latter was continued in essentially the same form as in the IGA. But important changes were made in the Wheat Trade Convention. Of paramount importance was the omission of provisions to regulate prices. Instead, in the new agreement one objective was "to provide a framework . . . for the negotiation of provisions relating to the prices of wheat and to the rights and obligations of members in respect of international trade in wheat."

Sugar Act Amendments (P.L. 138, 85 Stat. 379, October 14, 1971)

This act, "to amend and extend the provisions of the Sugar Act of 1948," extended the act for three years, until December 31, 1974, and made some changes in quota assignments. No change was made in the total domestic tonnage quota, but the share allocated to Puerto Rico was reduced and the mainland cane share raised. New mainland cane areas were authorized for the future, to come out of the domestic suppliers' share of growth in the sugar market. Three new foreign nations were granted quotas. The suspended Cuban share was reduced from 50 percent to 23.74 percent of the foreign quota. Another provision of the act limited imports of confections.

Food Programs for Children (P.L. 153, 85 Stat. 418, November 5, 1971): "An act to assure that every needy school child will receive a free or reduced price lunch as required by Section 9 of the National School Lunch Act"

This act directed the secretary of agriculture to use Section 32 funds to supplement appropriated funds for school lunch and school breakfast programs to prevent cutbacks in the programs. (P.L. 32, passed in June, had authorized but not directed use of such funds.) Other provisions raised the level of federal contributions for each meal served to poor children and prohibited the secretary from changing eligibility requirements for the current year.

School Lunch Act and Child Nutrition Act Amendments (P.L. 433, 86 Stat. 724, September 26, 1972): "An act to expand and strengthen child nutrition programs"

The school lunch program was made permanent by this act and the school breakfast program and non-school food programs for children were extended for three years, until June 30, 1975. Standards for free and reduced-rate lunches were set as follows: lunches were free for all children from families below the poverty level; free lunches were allowed for all children from families with incomes up to 25 percent above the poverty level; and reduced-rate lunches were allowed for all children from families with incomes up to 50 percent above the poverty level. The requirement that states match federal funds for purchasing equipment was waived for schools in rural and low-income areas.

This act also authorized a new pilot program to provide supplemental feeding for new and expectant mothers and their infants.

93rd Congress

Food Programs for Children (P.L. 13, 87 Stat. 9, March 30, 1973)

Under this law the secretary of agriculture was required to spend moneys allocated to child nutrition programs in fiscal year 1973. If commodity distributions were less than the budgeted amount, the federal government had to make up the difference by paying states in cash.

Agriculture and Consumer Protection Act of 1973 (P.L. 86, 87 Stat. 221, August 10, 1973): "An act to extend and amend the Agricultural Act of 1970 for the purpose of assuring consumers of plentiful supplies of food and fiber at reasonable prices" *

This comprehensive bill contains provisions encompassing commodity programs, P.L. 480, rural development, conservation, and food programs. Most provisions applied for four years, until the end of the 1977 crop year.

Target prices and deficiency payments. The programs for wheat, feed grains, and cotton introduced two new concepts — target prices and deficiency payments. These concepts entailed a government guarantee of the target prices to producers through deficiency payments if the average market price fell below the target price. The target prices were set by the Congress for 1974 and 1975. They would be adjusted for 1976 and 1977 according to changes in production costs and changes in yields. Deficiency payments would be made only if the average market price received by farmers during the first five months of the marketing year (or, for cotton, during the calendar year in which the crop was planted) fell below the target price. Payments would be made on a farmer's allotment for the crop. Allotments were based on acreage estimated to meet domestic and export needs and desired stock adjustments for each crop year. Nonrecourse loans lower than target prices were continued for these commodities. They applied to all production.

Production control. Standby set-aside authority was retained for wheat, feed grain, and cotton programs, similar to provisions of the 1970 act. If the authority was imposed, a producer was required to remove a specified amount of his cropland from production to qualify for program benefits — loans and deficiency payments. Planting limitations on specified crops was permissive as under the 1970 act.

Payment limitations. A ceiling of $20,000 was placed on payments to an individual under wheat, cotton, and feed grain programs. This was lower than the previous limit. It did not include payments for set-aside acres, public access, loans, and purchases.

Other provisions for wheat, feed grains, and cotton. (1) Annual studies of production costs were required. (2) Shortfalls in production because of a natural disaster qualified producers of these crops for special payments. (3) The requirement that domestic wheat processors purchase wheat certificates was repealed. (4) A minimum allotment of 11 million acres was established for cotton.

Dairy. The minimum price support level for manufacturing milk was raised to 80 percent of parity for two years. After March 31, 1975, it would revert to 75 percent of parity. This act permanently suspended the requirement to support the price of butterfat, temporarily suspended under the 1970 act. Amendments to milk-marketing orders included continuation of authority to establish base plans for marketing milk for fluid use and a provision to require a hearing if applied for by one-third or more of the producers. Two studies of the dairy industry were required by this act — one related to dairy imports and the other to production costs. The special milk program for military and veterans' agencies was extended.

Wool. The National Wool Act of 1954 was extended; payment rates were continued at the same level as in 1971–73.

Exports. P.L. 480 was extended, authorizing shipments of U.S. agricultural products to developing countries to help meet their food needs and to promote their economic development. To facilitate and guide commercial trade the USDA was required to provide technical assistance to exporters and importers and to compile weekly reports on exports of key commodities.

Other provisions. Title X of the act contained provisions for converting cropland into soil-, water-, wildlife-, or forest-conserving uses. The Food Stamp Act of 1964 was extended and eligibility for food stamps was expanded.

School Lunch Act and Child Nutrition Act Amendments (P.L. 150, 87 Stat. 560, November 7, 1973)

These amendments provided increased federal aid for school nutrition programs to offset rising food costs. Future adjustments to rising costs were made automatic by linking federal payment rates to the consumer price index. Other provisions liberalized family income limits to qualify more children for reduced-price lunches in the current year, revised the formula for allocating funds for free and reduced-price lunches, and extended indefinitely the provisions of P.L. 13 (above) requiring cash payments to states if commodity deliveries were below programmed amounts.

Amendments to other programs (1) doubled the authorization for and extended the pilot program to provide supplemental feeding for new and expectant mothers and their infants; and (2) required that the special milk program be provided to any school requesting it and that eligibility for free milk be the same as for free lunches.

CHAPTER 6

Program Operations: Major Commodities

Legislation authorizing government programs to support farm prices and incomes or to curtail planted acreage usually provides some range within which annual programs are formulated. Actual program provisions are framed for one year at a time depending upon the expected supply and demand situations and other considerations. This chapter relates chronologically the key features of annual commodity programs for the major crops, dairy products, and wool; conservation and land retirement programs, food programs, and foreign food aid and export programs are surveyed in the next chapter. For the purpose of exposition, each of these groups of programs is described separately. Yet many are interrelated. For example, the linkage between land retirement programs and price support programs for wheat or cotton was considered when the programs were formulated and when they were administered. However, the understanding of how one program affected another was not entirely satisfactory. Inadequacies in one set of programs often led to new problems and new programs, as discussed in the section on program evolution in chapter 3. The consequences of the interrelations among programs are presented in chapter 8.

This review of program operations is intended to provide the reader with a broad perspective on the scope of the programs — the number of farmers directly involved, the amount of land affected, the volume of commodities covered, the level of price supports and government subsidies paid, and the like. The narrative traces the key operations of the programs through time. Only those program features are noted that have had a substantial impact on the program or that constitute a marked departure from previous programs.

The discussions of feed grain, wheat, cotton, and dairy programs are more detailed than discussions of other commodity programs because of the large

175

number of farmers affected and the high level of costs incurred for operating these programs. Tables and figures supplement prose descriptions. The material in the tables is more comprehensive than in the text; it provides a historical record of pertinent data for programs treated here. This chapter relies upon the Glossary, at the front of the book, for descriptions of terms that have specific meanings in the context of commodity programs.

The material in the text, tables, and figures draws heavily upon a variety of USDA documents. Many of these are out of print and can be found only by a time-consuming search in the recesses of an agricultural library or in private files. Citations to original documents are included only if an item is likely to be readily accessible.

Feed Grains

1948–58. From 1948 through 1958 there were two main components of feed grain programs: price supports and acreage allotments.[1] Prices of corn, grain sorghum, barley, and oats were supported principally by loans and purchase agreements. As described in the Glossary, both of these procedures buoyed prices by withdrawing supplies from the market. The national average loan rates offered are shown in figure 6-1 together with market prices for each grain. The closeness of the two lines for all commodities indicates the dependence of market prices on loan rates for most years. Purchase agreements were utilized extensively during this period. About one-sixth of the corn acquired by the CCC in this period was through purchase agreements; the remainder came from loan operations.

Acreage allotments, a means of controlling output, were authorized only for corn. They were required each year except when suspended because of an emergency. Allotments applied only to the commercial corn-growing area where three-fourths or more of the nation's corn was produced.[2] No restrictions were placed on land withdrawn from corn in compliance with the corn acreage allotments. The boundary of the commercial corn-producing area shifted slightly from year to year as cropping patterns in fringe counties changed. When acreage allotments were proclaimed, compliance was a requisite for obtaining a price support loan for corn in the commercial area. (This feature was revised in 1956.) In the rest of the nation, a lower loan without planting restrictions was offered to all corn growers.

In 1948 price support loans were the only operative feature of feed grain programs. Acreage allotments were not implemented, nor had they been implemented in recent years because strong postwar demand for feed grains absorbed all that U.S. farmers produced. Thus stocks had been sustained at low levels and market prices had moved above loan rates. But in 1948 a bumper crop was produced from record yields, creating a surplus of feed

dollars per bushel

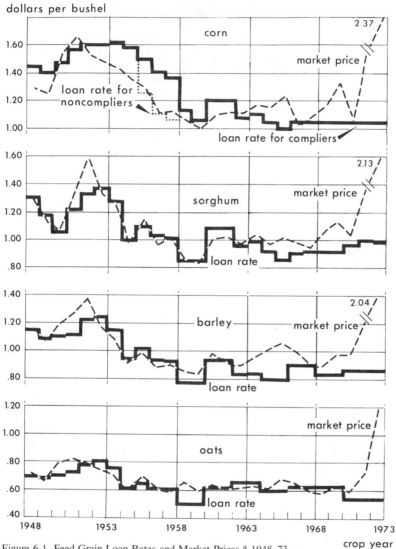

Figure 6-1. Feed Grain Loan Rates and Market Prices,[a] 1948–73
    [a] Average prices received by farmers.

grains (see table 6-1). Corn and sorghum prices fell sharply so that yearly averages were below loan rates. (See figure 6-1 and tables 6-2 and 6-3.) Stocks swelled. At the end of the year, 813,000 bushels of corn were carried over. This was 700,000 bushels greater than carry-in stocks and more than one-fourth of annual requirements.

The Historical Record

Table 6-1. Feed Grain Production, Utilization, and Stocks (in Million Tons), 1948–73[a]

Year (Oct.–Sept.)	Production[b]	Utilization Total[c]	Exports	Stocks: End of Year Carryover[d]
1948	127.1	105.1	5.5	30.4
1949	111.9	112.6	4.8	30.5
1950	113.1	115.8	6.4	28.6
1951	104.8	114.6	4.8	20.1
1952	111.0	105.8	5.3	27.0
1953	108.3	105.8	3.8	31.7
1954	114.1	107.6	5.5	39.1
1955	120.8	117.5	8.1	43.2
1956	119.3	114.6	7.7	48.8
1957	132.4	123.2	9.8	59.0
1958	144.1	136.0	12.6	67.5
1959	149.5	142.9	12.8	74.6
1960	155.5	145.5	12.7	85.0
1961	139.8	153.1	17.3	72.2
1962	141.7	149.7	16.8	64.4
1963	153.8	149.3	18.8	69.3
1964	134.2	149.1	21.6	54.8
1965	157.4	170.4	29.1	42.1
1966	157.6	162.9	22.0	37.1
1967	176.0	165.1	23.3	48.3
1968	168.9	167.5	18.4	50.2
1969	177.4	179.4	21.1	48.6
1970	160.1	175.9	20.7	33.2
1971	207.7	193.0	27.3	48.4
1972	199.9	216.3	43.1	32.4
1973	205.0	215.4	44.4	22.2

[a]Feed grains consist of corn, grain sorghums, oats, and barley.
[b]Production year: October 1–September 30 for corn and sorghum; July 1–June 30 for oats and barley.
[c]Including exports.
[d]Total, in all positions; corn and sorghum as of September 30, oats and barley as of June 30.

Loan rates for all feed grains were reduced slightly for 1949, but no acreage restrictions were imposed. There was a slight reduction in feed grain acreage planted (see figure 6-2) and, since yields returned to more normal levels, production was down about 12 percent from 1948. Utilization nearly equaled output, leaving the level of year-end stocks virtually unchanged. Notice in figure 6-3 the dominance of corn in the level of and changes in feed grain output and stocks.

Market prices slipped further but not as sharply as from 1947 to 1948. Many farmers who obtained government price support loans on corn in 1948

Crop Year (Oct.-Sept.)	National Average Loan Rate (per Bushel)	Average Price Received by Farmers (per Bushel)	Acreage (in Millions) Planted	Acreage (in Millions) Diverted under Programs[a]	Production (in Million Bushels)	Stocks: End of Year Carryover (in Million Bushels) Total[b]	Stocks: End of Year Carryover (in Million Bushels) Government Owned
1948	$1.44	$1.28	85.5		3,307	813	68
1949	1.40	1.24	86.7		2,946	844	335
1950	1.47[c]	1.52	82.8		2,764	740	403
1951	1.57	1.66	83.3		2,629	487	291
1952	1.60	1.52	82.2		2,981	769	236
1953	1.60	1.48	81.5		2,882	920	353
1954	1.62	1.43	82.2		2,708	1,035	681
1955	1.58	1.35	80.9		2,873	1,165	818
1956	1.50[c]	1.29	77.8	5.3	3,075	1,419	932
1957	1.25[d] 1.40[c]	1.11	73.2	5.2	3,045	1,469	1,101
1958	1.10[d] 1.36[c]	1.12	73.3	6.7	3,356	1,524	1,153
1959	1.06[d] 1.12	1.05	82.7		3,825	1,787	1,286
1960	1.06	1.00	81.4		3,907	2,016	1,327
1961	1.20	1.10	65.9	19.1	3,598	1,653	888
1962	1.20	1.12	65.0	20.3	3,606	1,365	810
1963	1.07	1.11	68.8	17.2	4,019	1,537	828
1964	1.10	1.17	65.8	22.2	3,484	1,147	540
1965	1.05	1.16	65.1	24.0	4,103	840	148
1966	1.00	1.24	66.3	23.7	4,168	823	139
1967	1.05	1.03	71.1	16.2	4,860	1,162	182
1968	1.05	1.08	65.1	25.4	4,450	1,118	295
1969	1.05	1.16	64.3	27.2	4,687	1,007	197
1970	1.05	1.53	66.8	26.1	4,152	667	97
1971	1.05	1.08	74.1	14.1	5,641	1,126	156
1972	1.05	1.57	67.0	24.4	5,573	709	4
1973	1.05	2.55	71.9	6.0	5,647	483	1

[a] There were no diversion programs in 1948–55 and 1959–60. Acres listed here as diverted were devoted to approved conserving uses or planted to approved nonsurplus crops.

[b] Total in all positions, including government owned and under loan to the government.

[c] Rate in commercial area for producers complying with acreage allotments. In noncommercial area, rates were $1.10 in 1950; $1.22 in 1954; $1.18 in 1955; $1.24 in 1956; $1.27 in 1957; $1.02 in 1958.

[d] Rate for noncompliers in commercial area.

179

Table 6-3. Sorghum Prices, Acreage, Production, and Stocks, 1948–73

Crop Year (Oct.–Sept.)	National Average Loan Rate (per Bushel)	Average Price Received by Farmers (per Bushel)	Acreage (in Millions) Planted	Acreage (in Millions) Diverted under Programs[a]	Production (in Million Bushels)	Stocks: End of Year Carryover (in Million Bushels) Total[b]	Stocks: End of Year Carryover (in Million Bushels) Government Owned
1948	$1.29	$1.28	13.2		131	19	15[c]
1949	1.17	1.13	11.1		149	60	60
1950	1.05	1.05	16.1		234	38	17
1951	1.22	1.32	15.0		163	10	1
1952	1.33	1.58	12.3		91	7	[d]
1953	1.36	1.32	14.6		116	22	22
1954	1.28	1.26	20.1		236	75	68
1955	1.00	.98	23.9		243	81	76
1956	1.10	1.15	21.4		205	79	75
1957	1.04	.97	26.9		568	309	295
1958	1.02	1.00	20.7		581	570	491
1959	.85	.86	19.5		555	581	562
1960	.85	.84	19.6		620	702	674
1961	1.08	1.01	14.3	6.1	480	661	648
1962	1.08	1.02	15.1	5.5	510	655	612
1963	.96	.98	17.8	4.6	585	649	615
1964	.99	1.05	16.8	6.5	490	566	540
1965	.92	.98	17.1	7.0	673	391	326
1966	.85	1.02	16.3	7.3	715	244	193
1967	.90	.99	19.0	4.1	755	289	193
1968	.91	.95	17.9	7.0	731	287	202
1969	.91	1.07	17.2	7.5	730	244	157
1970	.91	1.14	17.0	7.4	684	90	63
1971	.97	1.04	20.8	4.1	876	142	35
1972	1.00	1.37	17.3	7.3	809	73	5
1973	1.00	2.13	19.2	2.0	930	61	0

[a]There were no acreage diversion programs in 1948–60. Acres listed here as diverted were devoted to approved conserving uses or planted to approved nonsurplus crops.

[b]Total in all positions, including government owned and under loan to the government.

million acres

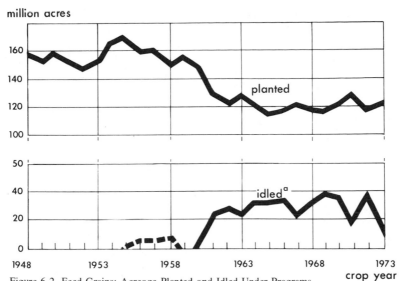

Figure 6-2. Feed Grains: Acreage Planted and Idled Under Programs

[a] Idled acreage in 1956–58 is withdrawn from corn only. Corn and sorghum lands are included in all remaining years; barley land is included in 1962–66, 1969–70, 1972–73. The 1956 land-retirement program was announced after planting so some acreage planted but not harvested was also reported as idled.

million tons

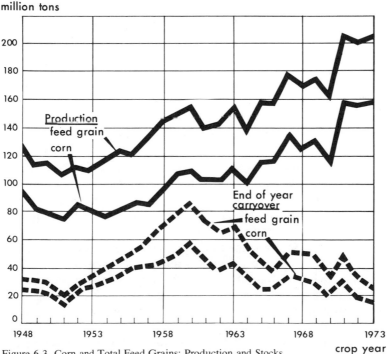

Figure 6-3. Corn and Total Feed Grains: Production and Stocks

181

and 1949 chose not to redeem their loans. Thus the government acquired ownership of a large share of corn stocks during 1949. At the beginning of the next crop year, about 40 percent of the corn carryover was owned by the government.

Production controls on corn were proclaimed in 1950 for the first time since before World War II. The allotment was 19.7 percent less than 1949 corn acreage in the commercial area. Compliance with the allotment was required to obtain a price support loan, which was 7 cents a bushel higher than the previous year. The corn loan rate for the rest of the nation was 75 percent of the commercial area rate. Producers in the commercial area who did not comply with acreage allotments were not eligible for price support loans but they were not subject to any penalties. They could sell their corn at the market price which was supported by the government loan program.

Loan rates for oats and barley were changed only slightly but the sorghum loan rate was lowered about 20 percent. No planting restrictions were authorized for these three grains. (See tables 6-4 and 6-5 for loan rates and other data pertaining to production of barley and oats respectively, and table 6-6 for corn allotment data.)

Farmers cut corn plantings 4 million acres from the previous year while they increased the combined acreage of sorghum, oats, and barley 9 million acres. Yet the reduction in corn output offset increases in the other grains so total feed grain production dropped 2.7 million tons below utilization, drawing down stocks of corn and sorghum. Market prices rose for corn, oats, and barley and fell for sorghum.

Because of the Korean War emergency, acreage allotments for corn were not continued in 1951. Loan rates for corn and sorghum were raised. Despite these incentives to expand output, total acreage planted to feed grains and feed grain production contracted in 1951. Market prices increased and stocks decreased.

Loan rates for all of the feed grains were raised for 1952. Acreage dropped again, but high yields for corn and barley led to larger total feed grain production than in 1951. A large corn carryover offset reductions in stocks of the other grains, enlarging feed grain stocks. Market prices for corn and oats dropped while prices for the other two feed grains advanced.

Loan rates for 1953 were maintained close to 1952 levels. Planted acreage climbed a little because of increased seeding of sorghum and oats, but total feed grain production was off from 1952. Despite lower production, output exceeded use for corn, sorghum, and barley because of a contraction in exports, resulting in net increases in stocks. All prices were lower than in 1952.

Acreage allotments on corn were imposed once more in 1954 as carryover

Crop Year (July–June)	National Average Loan Rate (per Bushel)	Average Price Received by Farmers (per Bushel)	Acreage (in Millions) Planted	Acreage (in Millions) Diverted under Programs[a]	Production (in Million Bushels)	Total[b]	Government Owned
1948	$1.15	$1.16	13.1		316	101	30[c]
1949	1.09	1.06	11.1		237	80	32
1950	1.10	1.19	13.0		304	94	20
1951	1.11	1.26	10.8		257	73	9
1952	1.22	1.37	9.2		228	51	2
1953	1.24	1.17	9.6		247	71	14
1954	1.15	1.09	14.7		379	131	74
1955	0.95	0.92	16.3		403	117	61
1956	1.02	0.99	14.7		377	127	68
1957	0.94	0.89	16.4		443	169	86
1958	0.93	0.90	16.1		477	196	99
1959	0.77	0.86	16.8		420	167	71
1960	0.77	0.84	15.5		429	152	54
1961	0.93	0.98	15.6		392	123	34
1962	0.93	0.92	14.4	2.4	428	146	47
1963	0.82	0.90	13.4	2.7	393	132	28
1964	0.84	0.95	11.7	3.7	386	100	20
1965	0.80	1.02	10.1	3.7	393	105	11
1966	0.80	1.06	11.1	3.7	392	122	6
1967	0.90	1.01	10.0		374	138	6
1968	0.90	0.92	10.5		426	201	27
1969	0.83	0.89	10.3	4.4	427	236	18
1970	0.83	0.97	10.5	3.9	416	155	29
1971	0.86	0.99	11.1		464	175	1
1972	0.86	1.21	10.6	4.9	423	163	1
1973	0.86	2.03	11.2	1.4	422	119	d

[a]There were no acreage diversion programs in 1948–61, 1967–68, and 1971. Acres listed here as diverted were devoted to approved conserving uses or planted to approved nonsurplus crops.

[b]Total in all positions, including government owned and under loan to the government.

[c]Estimated.

[d]Less than 500,000 bushels.

183

Table 6-5. Oats Prices, Acreage, Production, and Stocks, 1948–73

Crop Year (July–June)	National Average Loan Rate (per Bushel)	Average Price Received by Farmers (per Bushel)	Millions of Acres Planted	Production (in Million Bushels)	Stocks: End of Year Carryover (in Million Bushels) Total[a]	Government Owned
1948	$0.70	$0.72	43.8	1,450	290	10[b]
1949	0.69	0.66	43.1	1,220	208	12
1950	0.71	0.79	45.0	1,369	286	9
1951	0.72	0.82	41.0	1,278	277	5
1952	0.78	0.79	42.3	1,217	249	13
1953	0.80	0.74	43.2	1,153	227	16
1954	0.75	0.71	46.9	1,410	303	41
1955	0.61	0.60	47.5	1,496	346	57
1956	0.65	0.69	44.2	1,151	240	27
1957	0.61	0.61	41.8	1,290	324	30
1958	0.61	0.58	37.7	1,401	366	47
1959	0.50	0.65	35.1	1,050	267	15
1960	0.50	0.60	31.4	1,153	324	10
1961	0.62	0.64	32.3	1,010	276	17
1962	0.62	0.62	29.5	1,012	273	19
1963	0.65	0.62	28.0	966	312	33
1964	0.65	0.63	25.6	852	277	42
1965	0.60	0.62	24.0	927	316	51
1966	0.60	0.67	23.3	801	270	48
1967	0.63	0.66	20.6	789	273	45
1968	0.63	0.60	23.2	951	379	61
1969	0.63	0.58	23.6	966	499	104
1970	0.63	0.62	24.5	917	517	169
1971	0.54	0.60	22.0	881	541	178
1972	0.54	0.72	20.2	692	410	105
1973	0.54	1.17	19.1	667	255	24

[a]Total in all positions, including government owned and under loan to the government.
[b]Estimated.

Table 6-6. Corn Program Allotments and Compliance, 1948–58

Crop Year[a]	Total Acres Allotted (in Millions)	Number of States	Number of Counties	Number of Allotments (in Thousands)	Compliance with Allotments	
					Acreage	Farms
1950........	46.2	22	837	1,728	[b]	[b]
1954........	47.0	22	834	1,668	30%	40%
1955........	49.8	21	805	1,616	41	51
1956........	43.3	23	840	1,687	24	44
1957........	37.3	24	894	1,767	14	39
1958........	38.8	26	932	1,832	12	[b]

[a]In 1948–49 and 1951–53 no allotments were proclaimed.
[b]Figures are not available.

stocks of feed grains were nearly one-third of annual usage. Corn price supports in the commercial area were maintained at about the 1953 level, but were subject to compliance with planting restrictions. The corn acreage allotments were 17.6 percent below 1953 plantings in the designated commercial area. As before, price support loans for corn in noncommercial areas were set at an average of 75 percent of the commercial area rate. Loan rates for sorghum, barley, and oats were lowered from their 1953 levels, as allowed by existing legislation.

In the states where corn allotments applied, 56.5 million acres were planted in 1954 compared with 57.3 million in 1953 — a cut of 0.8 million acres. Two of every five eligible farms, containing 30 percent of the corn acreage in the commercial area, complied with allotments (see table 6-6). Other feed grain planting increased above 1953 levels; acreage increases were 1.5 million for corn in the noncommercial area, 5.5 million for sorghum, 5.1 million for barley, and 1.6 million for oats. Stocks mounted as production exceeded use and prices continued to slide.

Loan rates were lowered for all four feed grains for 1955. Acreage allotments for corn were enlarged 8 percent from the 1954 level. Corn planting in the commercial area was about the same as in 1954 but compliance with allotments was higher. In the rest of the nation, farmers cut corn plantings 1.3 million acres while they increased acreage of the other feed grains 6 million. Prices dropped again in the face of mounting stocks.

Loan rates were raised in 1956 for sorghum, barley, and oats and for corn produced in the noncommercial area. In the commercial corn area, the loan rate for those who complied with acreage allotments was reduced 8 cents a bushel. A new corn program feature was added in 1956. For the first time, corn producers in the commercial area could obtain price support loans without complying with acreage allotments. The rate was 25 cents a bushel lower than the rate for compliers. Corn acreage allotments for 1956 were cut about 15 percent from the previous year. Compliance with corn acreage allotments sagged.

A new land retirement program, the Soil Bank, was introduced in 1956 to augment the production adjustment features of the commodity programs. It consisted of an annual program for producers of the allotment crops, including corn, and a long-term program designed to shift land out of crop production into grass, trees, or water storage. Since these programs cut across commodity lines, they are discussed in more detail in the next chapter. The amount of land taken out of corn production under the annual program of the Soil Bank is listed in table 6-2 and shown in figure 6-2.

Planted acreage dropped for each of the four feed grains, reducing total feed grain plantings 10 million acres below the level of 1955. Fewer acres were planted to corn than since the turn of the century. Yet production rose because of record corn yields. Production of the other grains was down, offsetting the increase of corn, so total feed grain output in 1956 about equaled that of 1955. Stocks continued to build up. Corn prices fell, while prices of sorghum, oats, and barley rose.

In 1957 loan rates were lowered and corn acreage allotments were cut. Under these stringent conditions, corn-planting restrictions were followed by 39 percent of farms with allotments. These farms contained only 14 percent of allotted acres. Loans on corn produced by noncompliers were continued as well as the land retirement programs of the Soil Bank. Acreages planted to corn and oats were down 4.6 and 2.4 million respectively, while sorghum and barley acreages were up 5.5 and 1.7 million respectively. Total feed grain production rose 10 percent above 1956, further boosting stocks. Prices of all feed grains dropped.

Loan rates for 1958 were reduced slightly for corn, sorghum, and barley; the oats loan rate was not changed. Corn acreage allotments were left at approximately the same level as in 1957. Other program features were unchanged, i.e., a lower loan rate was allowed for corn grown by those who did not comply with acreage allotments and Soil Bank programs were continued.

Corn and barley plantings were at about the same levels as in the previous year. However, farmers cut acreages of sorghum and oats sharply. The trend of less compliance with acreage allotments continued. This had begun in 1956 when loans were first offered to noncomplying producers in the commercial corn area.

A new production high was reached in 1958 as yields continued their upward trend. The carryover of feed grains increased so that at the end of the crop year a six months' supply remained. Prices moved up 1 or 2 cents a bushel for corn, sorghum, and barley. The price of oats fell nearly 3 cents.

1959–60. Government programs affecting feed grain production were changed for 1959 and 1960. Under new legislation, the authorization for corn acreage allotments was terminated. Also discontinued was the annual land retirement program of the Soil Bank, the Acreage Reserve. As shown in figure 6-1, loan rates were lowered substantially. In 1959 corn farmers boosted acreage nearly 10 million acres. Feed grain production and carryover stocks reached new highs. Market prices dropped for all grains except oats.

The same feed grain programs applied in 1960 as in 1959 except that the loan rate for corn was reduced another 6 cents a bushel. Farmers cut combined acreage of the four feed grains about 6 million acres but continually rising yields lifted total output above the level of 1959. More than 10 million tons were added to the nation's stockpile of feed grains. Prices fell.

1961–70. Several new features were introduced in feed grain programs beginning in 1961. A new program was instituted to reduce output of corn and sorghum. Under this program cooperating producers were required to divert land from these two feed grains to conserving uses as a qualification for obtaining price support loans. To induce compliance, a payment from the government was made for idling this land; it was called an acreage diversion payment. Farmers had the option of diverting additional corn and/or sorghum land to conserving uses for an additional government payment. Producers with 25 or fewer corn or sorghum acres could divert their entire acreage for payment if they wished. (This was called the small farm provision.)

Farmers could elect to receive their payments in kind, that is, grain from the stocks owned by the government, or in cash. The cash option was chosen almost exclusively. The CCC was authorized to sell grain at the market price represented by the cash payments made to producers.

A fuller description of program features is provided in table 6-8. Details of program results appear in table 6-7. Figure 6-2 shows the amount of acreage diverted under feed grain programs along with total feed grain acreage planted.

For 1961, loan rates were raised for all four feed grains and payments were offered to corn and sorghum producers for idling land. Farmers cut corn and sorghum acreages substantially. Feed grain output fell below utilization for the first time in a decade and, as shown in figure 6-3, stocks were drawn down 13 million tons. Market prices rose.

Table 6-7. Feed Grain Program Participation and Payments, 1961–73

	Number of Farms (in Thousands)		Base Acreage[a] (in Millions)		
Crop Year	Eligible	Participating	Total	On Participating Farms	Payments[b] (in Millions)
1961[c]	2,861	1,146	107.8	63.6	$ 782
1962	3,259	1,250	123.4	68.1	844
1963	3,200	1,195	132.3	72.6	846
1964	3,191	1,243	132.5	73.5	1,171
1965	3,182	1,427	132.8	82.7	1,382
1966	3,171	1,404	133.1	79.0	1,295
1967[c]	3,027	1,308	115.1	66.4	867
1968[c]	3,022	1,427	115.1	72.1	1,369
1969	3,182	1,588	133.0	88.5	1,644
1970	3,131	1,538	133.0	87.3	1,510
1971[c]	2,831	1,691	112.1	91.2	1,060
1972	2,925	1,713	129.8	105.6	1,865
1973	2,925	1,871	130.1	114.1	1,171

[a] As established for corn and sorghum for all years, and for barley when in program.

[b] Total government payments to producers for price support, acreage diversion, and set-aside acres under feed grain programs.

[c] Barley was not included in the program.

Table 6-8. Summary of Provisions for Feed Grain Programs, 1961–73

Item	1961 Program		1962 Program	
	Price Support Loan		*Price Support Loan*	
Price support				
Corn (per bu.)	$1.20		$1.20	
Oats (per bu.)	.62		.62	
Barley (per bu.)	.93		.93	
Grain sorghum (per cwt.)	1.93		1.93	
Production eligible for price support	Normal production on acreage grown		Normal production on acreage grown	
Yield used for determination of payments	1959 and 1960 average		1959 and 1960 average	
Acreage diversion				
Grains included	Corn, grain sorghum		Corn, grain sorghum, and barley	
Base period	1959 and 1960		1959 and 1960	
Acreage to be diverted				
Minimum[3]	20% of base		20% of base	
Maximum[4]	40% of base (or 25 acres if larger)		40% of base (or 25 acres if larger)	
Payment rates for acreage diversion	*county support rate times:*		*county support rate times:*	
First 20% diverted	50% of normal production		50% of normal production	
Diversion of 20% to 40%	60% of normal production		60% of normal production	
Diversion of 40% to 50%	Not applicable		Not applicable	
Small producer: 25 acres of feed grains or less (may divert entire acreage)	Payment based on 50% of production on first 20% diverted; 60% for 20%–40%; 50% for diversion over 40%		Payment based on 50% of production on first 20% diverted; 60% for 20%–40%; 50% for diversion over 40%	

189

Table 6-8. Summary of Provisions for Feed Grain Programs, 1961–73 (Cont.)

Item	1963 Program			1964 Program		
	Price Support Loan	Price Support Payment	Total Support	Price Support Loan	Price Support Payment	Total Support
Price support						
Corn (per bu.)	$1.07	$0.18	$1.25	$1.10	$0.15	$1.25
Oats (per bu.)	.65	.00	.65	.65	.00	.65
Barley (per bu.)	.82	.14	.96	.84	.12	.96
Grain sorghum (per cwt.)	1.71	.29	2.00	1.77	.23	2.00
Production eligible for price support	Price support loan on total production; price support payment on normal production			Price support loan on total production; price support payment on normal production		
Yield used for determination of payments	1959 and 1960 average			1959–62 average		
Acreage diversion						
Grains included	Corn, grain sorghum, and barley			Corn, grain sorghum, and barley		
Base period	1959 and 1960			1959 and 1960		
Acreage to be diverted						
Minimum[3]	20% of base			20% of base		
Maximum[4]	40% of base (or 25 acres if larger)			50% of base (or 25 acres if larger)		
Payment rates for acreage diversion	county total support rate times:			county total support rate times:		
First 20% diverted	20% of normal production			20% of normal production		
Diversion of 20% to 40%	50% of normal production			50% of normal production		
Diversion of 40% to 50%	Not applicable			50% of normal proudction on all acreage diverted		
Small producer: 25 acres of feed grains or less (may divert entire acreage)	Payment for entire acreage based on 50% of normal production			Payment for entire acreage based on 50% of normal production		

Item	1965 Program			1966 Program		
	Price Support Loan	*Price Support Payment*	*Total Support*	*Price Support Loan*	*Price Support Payment*	*Total Support*
Price support						
Corn (per bu.)	$1.05	$0.20	$1.25	$1.00	$0.30	$1.30
Oats (per bu.)	.60	.00	.60	.60	.00	.60
Barley (per bu.)	.80	.16	.96[1]	.80[5]	.20	1.00
Grain sorghum (per cwt.)	1.65	.35	2.00	1.52	.53	2.05
Production eligible for price support	Price support loan on total production; price support payment on normal production			Price support loan on total production; price support payment on projected production of smaller of planted acreage or 50% of base		
Yield used for determination of payments	1959–63 average			Projected for 1966 (based on 1960–64 average adjusted for trend)		
Acreage diversion						
Grains included	Corn, grain sorghum, barley, wheat, oats, and rye[2]			Corn, grain sorghum, barley, wheat, oats, and rye[2]		
Base period	1959 and 1960 (but not in excess of 1964 acreage for oats and rye)			1959 and 1960 (but not in excess of 1964 acreage for oats and rye)		
Acreage to be diverted						
Minimum[3]	20% of base			20% of base		
Maximum[4]	50% of base (or 25 acres if larger)			50% of base (or 25 acres if larger)		
Payment rates for acreage diversion	*county total support rate times:*			*county total support rate times:*		
First 20% diverted	20% of normal production			No payment (except small farms)		
Diversion of 20% to 40%	50% of normal production			50% of projected production		
Diversion of 40% to 50%	50% of normal production on all acreage diverted			50% of projected production		
Small producer: 25 acres of feed grains or less (may divert entire acreage)	Payment for entire acreage based on 50% of normal production			Payment on first 20% based on 20% of projected production; additional diversion based on 50% of projected production		

Table 6-8. Summary of Provisions for Feed Grain Programs, 1961–73 (Cont.)

Item	1967 Program			1968 Program		
	Price Support Loan	Price Support Payment	Total Support	Price Support Loan	Price Support Payment	Total Support
Price support						
Corn (per bu.)	$1.05	$0.30	$1.35	$1.05	$0.30	$1.35
Oats (per bu.)	.63	.00	.63	.63	.00	.63
Barley (per bu.)	.90	.00	.90	.90	.00	.90
Grain sorghum (per cwt.)	1.61	.53	2.14	1.62	.53	2.15
Production eligible for price support	Price support loan on total production; price support payment on projected production of smaller of planted acreage or 50% of base			Price support loan on total production; price support payment on projected production of smaller acreage or 50% of base		
Yield used for determination of payments	Projected for 1967 (based on 1961–65 average adjusted for trend)			Projected for 1968 (based on 1962–66 average adjusted for trend)		
Acreage diversion						
Grains included	Corn and grain sorghum, substitution permitted[6] 1959 and 1960 (but not in excess of 1964 acreage for oats and rye)			Corn and grain sorghum, substitution permitted[6] 1959 and 1960		
Base period						
Acreage to be diverted						
Minimum[3]	20% of base			20% of base		
Maximum[4]	No additional diversion (except for small farms)[7]			50% of base (or 25 acres if larger)		
Payment rates for acreage diversion				county total support rate times:		
First 20% diverted	No payment (except small farms)			No payment (except small farms)		
Diversion of 20%–40%	No payment (except small farms)			45% of projected production		
Diversion of 40%–50%	No payment (except small farms)			45% of projected production		
Small producer: 25 acres of feed grains or less (may divert entire acreage)	Payment on first 20% based on 20% of projected production; additional diversion based on 50% of projected production[8]			Payment on first 20% based on 20% of projected production; additional diversion based on 55% of projected production[8]		

Item	1969 Program			1970 Program		
	Price Support Loan	Price Support Payment	Total Support	Price Support Loan	Price Support Payment	Total Support
Price support						
Corn (per bu.)	$1.05	$0.30	$1.35	$1.05	$0.30	$1.35
Oats (per bu.)	.63	.00	.63	.63	.00	.63
Barley (per bu.)	.83	.20	1.03	.83	.20	1.03
Grain sorghum (per cwt.)	1.61	.53	2.14	1.61	.53	2.14
Production eligible for price support	Price support loan on total production; price support payment on projected production of smaller of acreage planted to feed grains or 50% of base			Price support loan on total production; price support payment on projected production of smaller of acreage planted to feed grains or 50% of base		
Yield used for determination of payments	Projected for 1969 (based on 1963–67 average adjusted for trend)			Projected for 1970 (based on 1964–68 average adjusted for trend)		
Acreage diversion Grains included Base period	Corn, grain sorghum, and barley 1959 and 1960			Corn, grain sorghum, and barley 1959 and 1960		
Acreage to be diverted Minimum[3] Maximum[4]	20% of base 50% of base (or 25 acres if larger)			20% of base 50% of base (or 25 acres if larger)		
Payment rates for acreage diversion First 20% diverted	county total support rate times: No payment (except small farms)			county total support rate times: No payment (except small farms)		
Diversion of 20%–40%	45% of projected production			40% of projected production		
Diversion of 40%–50%	45% of projected production			40% of projected production		
Small producer: 25 acres of feed grains or less (may divert entire acreage)	Payment on first 20% based on 20% of projected production; additional diversion based on 45% of projected production[8]			Payment on first 20% based on 20% of projected production; additional diversion based on 40% of projected production[8]		

Table 6-8 Summary of Provisions for Feed Grain Programs, 1961–73 (Cont.)

Item	1971 Program		
	Price Support Loan	*Set-Aside Payment*	*Guaranteed Return (on Half of Base)*
Price support			
Corn (per bu.)	$1.05	Corn and sorghums: difference between Oct.–Feb. average price received and guaranteed return	$1.35
Grain sorghum (per cwt.)	1.73		2.21
Oats (per bu.)	.54		.00
Barley (per bu.)	.81		.00
Production eligible for loan and payment	Loan on total production; set-aside payment on production from 50% of the base—payment made if planted to feed grains, some other crop, or left idle		
Set-aside payments[10]	Payment applies to farm's yield on half of the base		
		Minimum Set-Aside 20% of Base	
Corn (per bu.)		32¢	
Grain sorghum (per bu.)		29¢	
Barley (per bu.)	Not in set-aside program		
Yield used for determination of payments	Based on yield established for the farm for the preceding year with necessary adjustment to be fair and equitable		
Acreage set aside			
Grains included	Corn and grain sorghum		
Base period	1959 and 1960		
Acreage to be set aside			
Minimum	Set aside 20% of base		
Maximum	No additional set-aside for payment		
Limitation on acreage planted	None after meeting set-aside requirement and maintaining conserving base		

194

meet requirements of both programs and maintain the farm's conserving base; producers participating in program must plant 45% or more of their base or their following year's base will be reduced by the amount of underplanting, up to 20% of the base. If no feed grains or permitted substitute crops are planted for three consecutive years, the farm's entire base is removed.

Cropping of set-aside acreage	Guar, sunflower, sesame, castor beans, mustard seed, safflower, crambe, plantago, and ovata may be grown after $10 per acre reduction in set-aside payment; sweet sorghum may be sown for grazing except in five-month restricted period with no reduction in payment
Small farms: producers with 25 acres or less of feed grains	No special provision

Table 6-8. Summary of Provisions for Feed Grain Programs, 1961–73 (Cont.)

Item	1972 Program[9]		
	Price Support Loan	Set-Aside Payment	Guaranteed Return (on Half of Base)
Price support			
Corn (per bu.)	$1.05	Difference between Oct.–Feb. average price received and guaranteed return	$1.35
Grain sorghum (per cwt.)	1.79		2.29
Oats (per bu.)	.54		.00
Barley (per bu.)	.86		1.10
Production eligible for loan and payment	Loan on total production; set-aside payment on production from 50% of the base—payment made if planted to feed grains, some other crop, or left idle		
Set-aside payments[10]	Option 1: Payment applies to farm's production on half of the base. Options 2 and 3: Payment applies to farm's production on acreage set aside.		
	Option 1: Minimum Set-Aside of 25% of Base	Option 2: Additional Set-Aside of up to 10% of Base	Option 3:[11] Additional Set-Aside of up to 5%–10% of Base
Corn (per bu.)	40¢	52¢	52¢
Grain sorghum (per bu.)	38¢	49¢	49¢
Barley (per bu.)	32¢	42¢[12]	

195

Table 6-8. Summary of Provisions for Feed Grain Programs, 1961–73 (Cont.)

Item	1972 Program[9]
Yield used for determination of payments	Based on yield established for the farm for the preceding year with necessary adjustment to be fair and equitable
Acreage set aside Grains included Base period	Corn, grain sorghum, and barley 1959 and 1960
Acreage to be set aside Minimum Maximum	Set aside 25% of base Two additional voluntary set-aside options *Option 1:* *Up to 10% of base for corn and sorghum; up to 20% of base for barley* *Option 2:* *Another 5% or 10% of base for corn and sorghum*[11]
Limited on acreage planted	None after meeting set-aside requirement and maintaining conserving base
Crop substitution and maintenance of base history	Same as in 1971 except soybeans are added to the list of crops which can be planted without loss of feed grain base or wheat allotment
Cropping of set-aside acreage	Castor beans, crambe, guar, mustard seed, plantago, ovata, safflower, sesame, and sunflower may be grown; set-aside payment will be reduced; grazing and haying also permitted with payment reductions
Small farms: producers with 25 acres or less of feed grains	No special provision

Table 6-8. Summary of Provisions for Feed Grain Programs, 1961–73 (Cont.)

Item	1973 Program		
	Price Support Loan	Set-Aside Payment	Guaranteed Return (on Half of Base)
Price support			
Corn (per bu.)	$1.05	Difference between Oct.–Feb. average price received and guaranteed return	$1.64
Grain sorghum (per cwt.)	1.79		2.76
Oats (per bu.)	.54		.00
Barley (per bu.)	.86		1.27
Production eligible for loan and payment	Loan on total production; set-aside payment on production from 50% of the base—payment made if planted to feed grains, some other crop, or left idle		
Set-aside payments[10]	Payment applies to farm's production on half of the base		
	Option 1: 10% Set-Aside		Option 2: 0 Set-Aside
Corn (per bu.)	32¢		15¢
Grain sorghum (per bu.)	30¢		14¢
Barley (per bu.)	26¢		12¢
Yield used for determination of payments	National average yields for program set at 87 bu. per acre for corn, 57 for sorghum, 44 for barley (compared with 1972 program yields of 81 for corn, 56 for sorghum, and 42 for barley)		
Acreage set aside			
Grains included	Corn, grain sorghum, and barley		
Base period	1959 and 1960 (bases were updated on request)		
Acreage to be set aside	Option 1:		Option 2:
Minimum	Set-aside 10% of base		No set-aside
Maximum	No additional set-aside for payment		
Limitation on acreage planted	Option 1: None		Option 2: Could not exceed 1972 feed grain plantings

Table 6-8. Summary of Provisions for Feed Grain Programs, 1961–73 (Cont.)

Item	1973 Program
Crop substitution and maintenance of base history	Same as in 1971, except soybeans are added to the list of crops which can be planted without loss of feed grain base or wheat allotment
Cropping of set-aside acreage	Castor beans, crambe, guar, mustard seed, plantago, ovata, safflower, sesame, and sunflower may be grown; set-aside payment will be reduced; grazing and haying also permitted with payment reductions
Small farms: producers with 25 acres or less of feed grains	No special provision

[1] Malting barley on exempted farms offered price support loan of 96¢, no price support payment.

[2] Farmers signing up for the wheat and feed grain programs could substitute acreages of these grains. Farmers could request an oats-rye base to substitute wheat for oats and rye.

[3] Minimum diversion to be eligible for diversion payments and price support.

[4] Maximum acreage that could be diverted for payment.

[5] Malting barley producers electing the exemption would receive no price support payments but an additional 12.5¢ per bushel loan rate.

[6] Barley excluded from the diversion program. Farms signing up for the wheat and feed grain programs could substitute acreages of wheat and corn or sorghums. Farmers requesting a barley, oats, or rye base could substitute wheat for barley, oats, and rye (unlike 1966, no diversion was required).

[7] Producers could divert for payment up to 25 acres if no feed grains were planted.

[8] Producers with bases of 26 through 125 acres could elect to have the base temporarily reduced to 25 acres and be paid as a small producer, provided no feed grains were planted.

[9] An additional option was added to the 1972 program close to planting time. It offered farmers 80¢ a bushel for corn to set aside an additional 10 percent (and possibly a further 5 percent) over the required 25 percent to participate in the program. For sorghum the payment was increased to 76¢ a bushel. These set-aside payment rates applied to the farm's established yield per acre. To qualify for this new option participants had to reduce their corn and sorghum plantings two acres below their 1971 acreage for each additional acre set aside under the 10 percent provision. Thus, one acre would be set aside and taken out of production and additional acreage would be free for planting to other crops, not subject to quota restrictions. In addition, producers could offer an additional 5 percent of their corn-sorghum base, at the same rate, which could be accepted at the option of the secretary. There was no extra option for barley producers. Their program was unchanged from that originally announced.

[10] Payments made soon after July 1. Payments for minimum set-aside preliminary; if final set-aside payment less than the preliminary payment, producers not asked for a refund. Payments made on additional set-aside acreage final at the time made.

[11] The government was to decide in mid-March whether to accept or reject this option. (It was accepted.)

[12] Barley producers could make an additional set-aside of up to 20 percent of the base after meeting minimum acreage set-aside requirements.

The basic features of the 1962 feed grain program were identical to those in 1961, except that barley was added to the production control program in which farmers were paid to idle land. Hence, in 1962, producers of corn, sorghum, and barley were required to curtail plantings of these crops to qualify for price support loans. Planted acreage was reduced slightly; production increased but remained below use. Another 8 million tons of feed grains were withdrawn from stocks. Market prices changed little.

A new feature was added to feed grain programs for 1963. Loan rates were lowered to world price levels and payments were offered to producers to make up for the loss in income this reduction would cause. To be eligible for loans and payments, producers were required to limit corn, sorghum, and barley plantings and devote the land taken out of these grains to conserving uses, as under the 1961 and 1962 programs. Although participating farmers received only one check from the government, the government payment was computed in two parts: one part, called the price support payment, was computed on a per bushel rate for estimated production from all land planted to corn, sorghum, and barley; the second part, called the acreage diversion payment, was computed on a per bushel rate for estimated production on the land idled under the program. The complex computational procedure permitted the government to claim a higher level of price support. For example, the 1963 loan rate for corn was $1.07, the price support payment $0.18, giving a "total support rate" of $1.25 per bushel, 79 percent of parity; the $1.07 loan rate was 56 percent of parity (the legal minimum was 65 percent of parity).

Loan rates for corn, sorghum, and barley were reduced 11 percent from 1962, but the level of total support — loan plus support payment — was slightly higher than in 1962. Payment rates for optional acreage diversion were lowered from the previous year. Acreage planted to corn and sorghums rose.

Total feed grain production increased and exceeded usage, so stocks grew about 5 million tons. Market prices changed little.

For 1964 two changes were made in the programs: (1) a few cents a bushel were shifted from payment rates to loan rates, leaving the level of total support for grains produced in compliance with the program unchanged, and (2) the maximum amount of land eligible for diversion payments per farm was raised from 40 to 50 percent of base acreage. Planted acreage and production fell. Utilization exceeded output, drawing down stocks nearly 15 million tons. Market prices rose a few cents a bushel for each grain.

In 1965, changes in program features entailed another shift between the loan rate and the direct payments without affecting the level of total support. Government payments were raised and the loan rates lowered. Also, substitution was permitted between feed grains and wheat without sacrifice of program benefits. Farmers cut total feed grain acreage yet higher yields boosted production above the 1964 level. Nonetheless, use still exceeded output so stocks were reduced another 13 million tons. Market prices were mixed, changing little.

A simplifying change was made in the method of computing government payments in 1966. The portion of the payment computed on production (the price support payment) was limited to projected production on 50 percent of base acreage instead of applying to all acreage planted by program compliers. This became the sole payment for those who diverted only the required 20 percent of base acreage. Under the programs for 1963, 1964, and 1965, in a producer's decision to idle more than the required 20 percent of his base acreage (up to 50 percent), he had to weigh the loss of price support payments (earned if he produced grain) versus the acreage diversion payment (earned if he idled the additional land). This partially offsetting feature was eliminated by the 1966 change. Loan rates for corn and sorghum were lowered. There was little change in acreage, production, or stocks. Market prices rose somewhat.

Some changes were made in acreage diversion features in 1967 to relax production restrictions as stock levels had been reduced to an adequate reserve level. For the first time since the acreage diversion program was begun in 1961, no government payments were offered for diversion above the required level. Also no acreage diversion from barley was required for obtaining the price support loan. Loan rates for all feed grains were raised a few cents a bushel.

Corn and sorghum acreages increased. Feed grain production rose sharply, exceeding use. Stocks rose 11 million tons. Corn prices fell 21 cents a bushel while price decreases for sorghum and barley were smaller.

Optional acreage diversion above the required level of 20 percent of base acreage was reinstated in 1968 for corn and sorghum. All other program features were unchanged from 1967. Corn and sorghum acreages were reduced, total production of feed grains also contracted, and stocks remained virtually unchanged. Prices dipped a few cents for sorghum, barley, and oats but rose for corn.

No program changes were made for 1969, except that barley was restored to the acreage diversion program. There were only small changes in acreage, production, stocks, and prices.

Major features of the 1970 program were identical to those in 1969. Acreage changed very little, but production was off sharply because corn blight substantially reduced yields. Corn prices jumped 18 cents a bushel and stocks were drained.

1971–73. New legislation brought about some major changes in the feed grain program beginning in 1971. As before, a government payment was authorized for cropland diverted to conserving use, but the diversion did not require a reduction on acreage planted to any particular crop. The diverted acreage was called "set-aside." Optional set-aside for additional payments was also allowed. Special land retirement provisions for farms with 25 or fewer acres of feed grains were discontinued. Price support loans were no longer contingent upon compliance with planting restrictions for a given crop. In order to retain eligibility for program benefits, producers were required to plant feed grains or an allowable alternate crop. And last, the amount of feed grain payments authorized for any one producer was limited to $55,000.

Loan rates for 1971 were realigned slightly; the corn rate was unchanged, but the rates for oats and barley were lowered and the sorghum rate was raised. Set-aside equivalent to 20 percent of base acreage was required of corn and sorghum growers. Payments were made for this. No payments were offered for additional, optional set-aside. Barley had no set-aside provisions. Acreage, output, and stocks advanced; prices fell.

For 1972 several variations of optional set-aside were offered participating corn, sorghum, and barley farmers. One rate was paid for set-aside with no restrictions on planting; another, a higher rate, was paid if 1972 feed grain plantings were reduced below the level of the previous year. (The latter feature was added in February 1972, before planting but a few months after the original provisions were announced.) Various levels of set-aside were permitted. Loan rates were about the same as in 1971. Acreage and production were cut back. Exceptionally strong export demand cut deeply into stocks. Prices rose.

Planting restrictions were eased for 1973 as export strength continued. Original provisions were announced in the autumn of 1972, modified in January 1973, and further relaxed in March 1973. Final provisions offered two options. One option required no set-aside but offered a government payment if 1973 feed grain acreage did not exceed 1972 acreage. The other option required a set-aside equivalent to 10 percent of base acreage, offered a higher payment, but placed no restrictions on planting. Corn, sorghum, and barley were included.

Acreage and production turned up again. Continuing strength in the export market drained stocks and prices soared to unprecedented highs.

Wheat

1948–61. Wheat programs during these 14 years had some similarities to and some differences from corn programs. For both crops, nonrecourse loans and purchase agreements were the primary means employed to support prices. In most years loan rates were set at the minimum legal level. For wheat the minimum was 90 percent of parity until 1955, 82 1/2 percent in 1955, and 75 percent through 1961. The national average loan rates for wheat are shown in figure 6-4 together with market prices. These and other data pertaining to wheat production and use are given in table 6-9.

Wheat differed from corn in that exports absorbed a substantial share of U.S. production. During most of this period, wheat exports depended largely upon special programs. Export programs provided subsidies and special terms to permit U.S. wheat to move in international markets when domestic prices

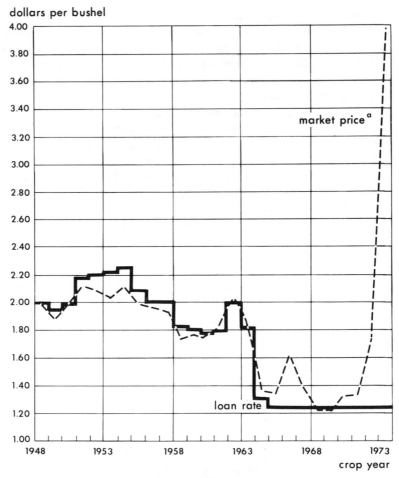

Figure 6-4. Wheat: National Average Loan Rates and Market Prices, 1948–73
[a] Average price received by farmers.

Crop Year (July–June)	National Average Loan Rate (per Bushel)	Average Price Received by Farmers (per Bushel)	Acreage (in Millions)		Production (in Million Bushels)	Utilization (in Million Bushels)		Stocks: End of Year Carryover (in Million Bushels)	
			Planted	Diverted under Programs[a]		Total[b]	Export	Total[c]	Government Owned
1948	$2.00	$1.98	78.3		1,294.9	1,185.0	503.6	307.3	227.2
1949	1.95	1.88	83.9		1,098.4	983.2	302.9	424.7	327.7
1950	1.99	2.00	71.3		1,019.3	1,055.7	365.9	399.9	196.4
1951	2.18	2.11	78.5		998.2	1,163.6	475.0	256.0	143.3
1952	2.20	2.09	78.6		1,306.4	978.5	317.5	605.5	470.0
1953	2.21	2.04	78.9		1,173.1	850.6	216.7	933.5	774.6
1954	2.24	2.12	62.5		983.9	885.4	274.0	1,036.2	975.9
1955	2.08	1.98	58.2		937.1	949.7	346.0	1,033.5	950.7
1956	2.00	1.97	60.6	5.7	1,005.4	1,137.8	549.1	908.8	823.9
1957	2.00	1.93	49.8	12.8	955.7	993.9	402.3	881.4	834.9
1958	1.82	1.73	56.0	5.3	1,457.4	1,051.4	442.8	1,295.1	1,146.6
1959	1.81	1.76	56.7		1,117.7	1,106.7	509.8	1,313.4	1,195.4
1960	1.78	1.74	54.9		1,354.7	1,264.9	661.5	1,411.3	1,242.5
1961	1.79	1.83	55.7		1,232.4	1,327.4	719.4	1,322.0	1,096.6
1962	2.00	2.04	49.3	10.7	1,092.0	1,224.2	643.8	1,195.2	1,082.5
1963	1.82	1.85	53.4	7.2	1,146.8	1,444.5	856.1	901.4	828.9
1964	1.30	1.37	55.7	5.1	1,283.4	1,368.6	725.0	817.3	646.0
1965	1.25	1.35	57.4	7.2	1,315.6	1,598.6	867.4	535.2	340.0
1966	1.25	1.63	54.4	8.3	1,311.7	1,423.6	744.3	425.0	124.0
1967	1.25	1.39	67.8		1,522.4	1,408.9	761.1	539.4	102.0
1968	1.25	1.24	62.5		1,570.4	1,298.1	544.2	818.6	162.7
1969	1.25	1.24	54.3	11.1	1,460.2	1,378.0	606.1	884.7	301.2
1970	1.25	1.33	49.5	15.7	1,378.5	1,506.0	738.0	730.2	369.9
1971	1.25	1.34	53.8	13.5	1,639.5	1,487.0	632.0	865.3	366.5
1972	1.25	1.76	54.9	20.1	1,544.8	1,970.9	1,186.3	438.4	209.2
1973	1.25	3.96	59.0	7.2	1,705.2	1,900.0	1,148.7	247.4	18.9

[a]There were no acreage diversion programs in 1948–55, 1959–61, and 1967–68. Acres listed here as diverted were devoted to approved conserving uses or planted to approved nonsurplus crops.

[b]Including exports.

[c]Including government owned and under loan to the government.

were maintained above the level of world prices. These programs are common to several commodities. They are discussed in the next chapter.

Production control measures also differed between wheat and corn. The control features for wheat were more stringent. When surpluses were anticipated, acreage allotments were proclaimed for both crops. But for wheat, marketing quotas were also required if the anticipated surplus was sufficiently large and if the program was approved by growers, voting in a referendum. When marketing quotas applied, producers who exceeded their allotments were penalized with fines and a reduction in future allotments. (Penalties could be avoided by storing excess wheat under seal and marketing it in later years when low yields produced below normal crops.) A legal minimum was placed on the size of the national acreage allotment; thus the allotment-marketing quota method could only be used to adjust supplies down to the minimum level. The size of the national allotments, the number of individual allotments established, and the number of farmers voting in referendums when marketing quotas were proclaimed appear in table 6-10.

Farmers who planted not more than 15 acres of wheat were exempt from marketing quota penalties. If they exceeded their allotments, however, their production did not qualify for price supports. But the loss of price supports was not a serious deterrent because market prices were close to loan levels in most years. Because of the exemption from penalties, these small producers were not eligible to vote in marketing-quota referendums. Growers with small wheat acreage accounted for a sizable number of allotments. In 1959, for

Table 6-10. Wheat Acreage Allotments and Number
Voting in Referendums, 1950–61

Crop Year[a]	Total Acres Allotted (in Millions)	Number of Allotments (in Thousands)	Number Voting in Referendums (in Thousands)
1950	72.8	2,025	[c]
1951	72.8[b]	[b]	[c]
1954	62.8[d]	1,496	448
1955	55.8[d]	1,525	285
1956	55.0[d]	1,554	348
1957	55.0[d]	1,570	280
1958	55.0[d]	1,710	235
1959	55.0[d]	1,707	230
1960	55.0[d]	1,710	210
1961	55.0[d]	1,670	179

[a] No allotments were proclaimed or referendums held in 1948–49 and 1952–53.
[b] Acreage allotments were proclaimed but terminated after winter wheat was planted.
[c] No referendum was held.
[d] Marketing quotas were in effect.

instance, 1,060,000 wheat producers had allotments of less than 15 acres. This is a large share of the 1,707,000 allotments established that year. This factor is largely responsible for the apparent discrepancy in table 6-10 between the number of allotments and the number of voters in referendums.

Another feature allowed farmers to earn new allotments by planting 15 or fewer acres of wheat each year for three years. This provision enlarged the wheat-producing area and reduced the share of the national allotment held in the older production areas. Production from farms with allotments of 15 or fewer acres was estimated to be one-fourth of total wheat production in the late 1950s.

Price support loans were offered in 1948 but no acreage control measures were employed. Strong export demand for wheat during and after World War II had precluded the need for production control in the United States for several years. The loan rate was raised from $1.83 in 1947 to $2.00 in 1948. This was 90 percent of parity, the lowest loan rate permitted by law. Production was greater than domestic and foreign demand, resulting in an increase in carryover stocks. The average price received by farmers dropped 30 cents a bushel, averaging near the loan rate for the year.

Price support loans with no acreage restrictions were continued for 1949. The loan rate was lowered 5 cents a bushel. Acreage expanded more than 5 million acres to an all-time peak of 84 million acres. Yet below normal yields produced a smaller crop than in 1948. Nonetheless production still outstripped demand, further boosting stocks. Prices slipped once more.

In 1949 distress loan privileges were allowed. This meant that farmers could store wheat on the ground temporarily where weather conditions permitted. Normally storage in approved facilities was a requisite for obtaining price support loans.

Acreage allotments, not accompanied by marketing quotas, were imposed in 1950 for the first time since before the war. The national allotment was about 17 percent less than planted acreage in 1949. The loan rate was raised a few cents. Farmers cut planted acreage sharply (see figure 6-5). Total use was greater than production, reducing stocks. Prices rose.

Acreage allotments announced for 1951 were suspended after winter wheat was sown because of food needs anticipated during the Korean War. The loan rate was increased 19 cents a bushel, to $2.18, in accordance with existing legislation. Seeded acreage increased substantially, but more acreage than usual was not harvested because of poor growing weather. Production dropped below the 1950 level. A high level of demand did materialize requiring withdrawals from stocks. Market prices advanced.

There were no acreage allotments or marketing quotas on 1952 wheat. A 2-cent increase was made in the loan rate. Planted acreage was about the same

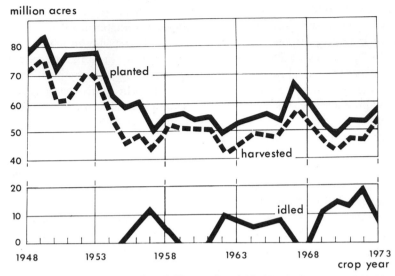

Figure 6-5. Wheat: Acreage Planted, Harvested, and Idled Under Programs, 1948–73

as in 1951 but harvested acreage and yields were up. The result was an increase in output of more than 300,000 bushels. Utilization fell nearly 200,000 bushels; year-end stocks more than doubled with 78 percent in government hands. Carryover stocks approached domestic needs for one year.

The only change in the wheat program for 1953 was a 1-cent increase in the loan rate. Planted acreage changed little. Harvested acreage and yields were down some from the previous year, reducing output. Exports fell to the lowest level in a decade contributing to an excess supply of wheat. Stocks mounted; prices slipped a few cents a bushel.

Acreage allotments accompanied by marketing quotas were reinstated for 1954. The national allotment was 20 percent below 1953 plantings. This was the minimum permitted by a special law enacted to cover the 1954 crop. It was higher than was necessary to meet anticipated needs. Actual plantings were cut 21 percent and production fell almost 200,000 bushels. This was still about 100,000 bushels more than domestic and export utilization. The market price rose 8 cents a bushel but remained below the loan rate as had been the case since 1951.

Acreage controls (allotments and marketing quotas) were continued for 1955. The allotment was lowered 7 million acres to the new legal minimum. Allotments, however, were now figured for harvested instead of planted acres, permitting overplanting as a hedge against partial crop failure. New legislation also permitted a 16-cent reduction of the loan rate. An even lower rate was authorized for noncommercial wheat-producing states.

Despite cutbacks in planted and harvested acreage, production was close to the 1954 level owing to record high yields. Stocks changed little. Because of the heavy surpluses, market prices were determined largely by the loan rate; thus the lowered loan rate allowed the market price to fall.

Acreage allotments and loan rates at the legal minimum were declared again in 1956. This meant no change in acreage allotments but a lower loan rate. Acreage and yields, and hence production, rose. Strong export demand led to a greater increase in usage, drawing down stocks.[3]

New land retirement programs were instituted in 1956, under the Soil Bank Act, providing farmers income for land withdrawn from crop production. Soil Bank programs are discussed in the next chapter. They had little effect on wheat acreage in 1956 because most wheat was planted before program provisions were announced.

No changes were made in wheat programs for 1957, except that the Soil Bank programs were known by wheat farmers in advance of planting. Harvested wheat acreage fell to the lowest level since 1934. Production, however, did not fall as sharply because of a new yield record. Stocks were cut very little.

Beginning in 1958 an exemption from acreage restrictions was made for wheat producers who fed all of their wheat. These producers were allowd to grow up to 30 acres of wheat without penalties. An 18-cent-per-bushel reduction was made in the loan rate. This lower rate was the legal minimum for 1958. A change in the Soil Bank program made participation less attractive to wheat producers. Increases in acreage and especially in yields produced a bumper crop — 50 percent higher than in 1957. Stocks shot up; prices dropped.

No changes were made in wheat allotments, marketing quotas, or price support loans for 1959, but the acreage reserve part of the Soil Bank was discontinued. There was little change in wheat acreage, yet production fell considerably as yields returned to a more normal level. The stock level and prices varied only slightly.

The loan rate for 1960 was lowered a few cents; allotments were not changed. Without much change in acreage, output surged once again because of exceptionally high yields. Stocks reached a new all-time high despite record exports. Nearly nine of every ten bushels in the carryover were owned by the government.

The same wheat program was continued in 1961. Output declined slightly as a consequence of smaller yields. Utilization was pushed over production by large exports. The stock buildup of the past decade was reversed (see figure 6-6). Prices rose above the loan rate for the first time since 1950.

1962–63. For these two years payments for idling a portion of the wheat allotment were added to the price support and planting restriction features of previous programs. Marketing quotas were announced and approved in referendums for both years, continuing the mandatory nature of the program. Penalties assessed for noncompliance were made more stringent to discourage overplanting. The program to idle part of the wheat allotment required that land withdrawn from wheat be devoted to approved conservation uses and that it constitute a new addition to normal conservation land use. Besides the required amount, a farmer could voluntarily divert more land to conserving uses for payment. Farmers with small allotments were eligible to participate in the program to idle wheat land if they wished to do so. If not, they could still plant 15 acres of wheat and be exempt from marketing quota penalties.

A more complete description of program features appears in table 6-12. Table 6-11 indicates the rate of participation in wheat programs for 1962–73. The difference between the number of farms eligible and the number participating comprises farms exempt from acreage allotments when compliance was mandatory, as well as farms not observing planting restrictions.

The loan rate was raised 21 cents a bushel to $2.00 in 1962. To obtain

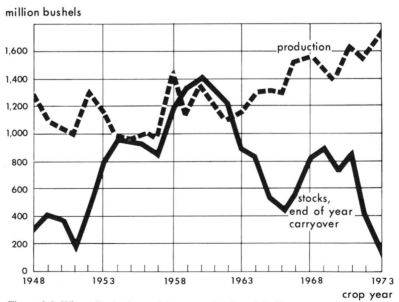

Figure 6-6. Wheat: Production and Carryover Stocks, 1948–73

Table 6-11. Wheat Program Participation, and Payments, 1962–73

Crop Year	Number of Farms (in Thousands)		Acreage Allotments (in Million Acres)		Payments (in Millions)[a]
	Eligible	Participating	Total	On Partici-pating Farms	
1962	1,804	778	55.0	41.2	$286
1963	1,728	410[b]	55.0	25.0[b]	243
1964	1,729	585	53.3	40.8	443
1965	1,715	820	53.3	44.8	509
1966	1,703	809	51.5	42.1	681
1967	1,692	769	68.2	56.9	727
1968	1,692	803	59.3	50.1	746
1969	1,692	953	51.6	45.2	856
1970	1,651	923	45.5	39.9	871
1971	1,331	1,012	19.7[c]	18.2	886
1972	1,295	976	19.7[c]	18.3	859
1973	1,300	1,053	18.4[c]	17.8	478

[a]Total government payments to producers for price support, acreage diversion, marketing certificates, and set-aside acres under wheat programs. Includes funds obtained by the government from the sale of certificates to processors.

[b]Farms participating in the voluntary diversion part of the wheat program. Additional farms complied with wheat allotments.

[c]Allotment for domestic food use.

loans, farmers were required to divert 11.11 percent of their allotments to conserving uses. Payments for this acreage diversion were based on an estimate of production from the land withdrawn from wheat. The rate per bushel was 45 percent of the loan rate. A higher rate was offered for diverting more than the required amount of acreage from wheat to conserving uses. Such additional idling of land was voluntary. Farmers cut wheat acreage 6.4 million acres. Output fell 11 percent below use, drawing down stocks. Market prices strengthened.

Participation in the program to idle a part of the wheat allotment for payment was completely voluntary under the 1963 program; however, payment and loan provisions made participation extremely attractive. The loan rate was lowered 18 cents a bushel; loans were available only to those who complied with acreage allotments. Payments for participants who voluntarily diverted part of their allotments to conserving uses were computed in two parts. One, called an acreage division payment, was computed on the amount of land idled — the same as the payment in 1962, except the rate was slightly higher. The second part, called the price support payment, was computed on the amount of land planted to wheat in compliance with the program. The price support payment was 18 cents a bushel for normal production on the designated acreage. The price support payment was a new feature. It compensated

Table 6-12. Summary of Provisions for Wheat Programs, 1962–73

Item	1962 Program	1963 Program	1964 Program
Price support (per bu.)			
Loan	$2.00	$1.82	$1.30
Price support payment	.00	.18	.00
Domestic certificates[1]	.00	.00	.70
Export certificates	.00	.00	.25
Total or blend	$2.00	$2.00	$1.73
National acreage allotment (in million acres)	55.0 (49.5[2])	55.0	49.5[3]
Marketing quotas			
In effect	Yes	Yes	No[4]
Farm exemption	High 1959, 1960, or 1961 wheat acres, not to exceed 15.0 acres	15.0 acres	None
Program farm yield	1959–60 adjusted average	1959–60 adjusted average	1958–62 adjusted average
Acreage diversion to conserving use from wheat production			
Minimum	Comply with allotment or 10% of high 1959, 1960, or 1961 wheat acres[5]	Larger of 20% of allotment or 1959–61 average wheat acres[6]	Comply with allotment (diversion of 10% already deducted)

210

Additional	Up to 33.33% of allotment or enough with minimum to total 10 acres	Up to 30% of allotment or enough with minimum to total 10 acres	Up to 20% of allotment or enough with minimum to total 15.0 acres, whichever is larger
Payment rates for diversion			
Minimum	*county loan rate times:* 45% of normal production	*county support rate times:* 50% of normal production	*county loan rate times:* 20% of normal production on such acreage
Additional	60% of normal production	50% of normal production	20% of normal production on such acreage
Substitution	Not applicable	Not applicable	Not applicable
Excess wheat	Not applicable	Not applicable	Not applicable
Production eligible for price support			
Loan[8]	Total production in commercial areas	Total production in commercial areas	Total production of allotment
Price support payment	. . .	Normal production of wheat acreage[9]	. . .
Domestic certificates	. . .	. . .	45% of farm's *normal* production of its allotment[10]
Export certificates	. . .	. . .	45% of farm's *normal* production of its allotment[11]

211

Table 6-12. Summary of Provisions for Wheat Programs, 1962–73 (Cont.)

Item	1965 Program	1966 Program	1967 Program
Price support (per bu.)			
Loan	$1.25	$1.25	$1.25
Price support payment	.00	.00	.00
Domestic certificates[1]	.75	1.32	1.36
Export certificates	.30	.00	.00
Total or blend	$1.69	$1.84	$1.73
National acreage allotment (in million acres)	49.5[3]	47.8[3]	63.3[3]
Marketing quotas			
In effect	No	No	No
Farm exemption	None	None	None
Program farm yield	1959–63 adjusted average	1960–64 average adjusted for abnormal weather, with trend projected forward to reflect expected yield	1961–65 average adjusted for abnormal weather, with trend projected forward to reflect expected yield
Acreage diversion to conserving use from wheat production			
Minimum	Comply with allotment (diversion of 10% already deducted)	Comply with allotment (diversion of 13% already deducted)	None
Additional	At least 10% of allotment up to 20% of allotment or enough with minimum to total 15.0 acres, whichever is larger	Up to 50% of allotment or enough with minimum to total 25 acres, whichever is larger	None

212

	county loan rate times:	county loan rate times:	Not applicable
Payment rates for diversion			
Minimum	No payment	No payment	
Additional	50% of normal production on such acreage	40% of projected production on such acreage	
Substitution	Producer who participates in both wheat and feed grain programs may grow wheat on feed grain base acres or feed grain on wheat al otment acres.	Same as for 1965	Same as for 1965 except that barley is excluded from the feed grain diversion program and producer may elect to grow wheat on entire barley base
Excess wheat	Producer may overplant allot-ment up to 50%, store excess wheat secured by bond or ware-house receipt and be eligible for domestic certificates.[7]	Same as for 1965	Same as for 1965
Production eligible for price support			
Loan[8]	Total production cf allotment, excluding excess wheat[12]	Same as for 1965	Same as for 1965
Price support payment			
Domestic certificates	... Same as for 1964	... 45% of farm's *projected* production of its allotment[10]	... 35% of farm's *projected* production of its allotment[10]
Export certificates	35% of farm's *normal* pro-duction of its allotment[11]	None	None

Table 6-12. Summary of Provisions for Wheat Programs, 1962–73 (Cont.)

Item	1968 Program	1969 Program	1970 Program
Price support (per bu.)			
Loan	$1.25	$1.25	$1.25
Price support payment	.00	.00	.00
Domestic certificates[1]	1.38	1.52	1.57
Export certificates	.00	.00	.00
Total or blend	$1.80	$1.90	$1.85
National acreage allotment (in million acres)	59.3	51.6	45.5
Marketing quotas			
In effect	No	No	No
Farm exemption	None	None	None
Program farm yield	1962–66 average adjusted for abnormal weather, with trend projected forward to 1968	1963–67 average adjusted for abnormal weather, with trend projected forward to 1969	Projected from 1966–68 average
Acreage diversion to conserving use from wheat production			
Minimum	None	15% of farm wheat allotment	30.3% of farm wheat allotment
Additional	None	Larger of 25 acres or 50% of farm wheat allotment	Same as for 1969

Payment rates for diversion			
Minimum	Not applicable	No payment	No payment
Additional		50% of county loan rate times farm yield	50% of county loan rate times farm yield
Substitution	Producer who participates in both wheat and feed grain programs may grow wheat on feed grain base acres or feed grain on wheat allotment acres. Producer may also elect to grow wheat on oats and rye base (adjusted for feed unit relationship to wheat). Barley is excluded from the feed grain diversion program, and producer may elect to grow wheat on entire barley base.	Same as for 1968 except that producer electing to grow wheat on feed unit adjusted oats/rye base must divert 15% of such base to conserving use. Barley is included in the feed grain program, and required diversion from barley is 20%, the same as for corn and grain sorghum.	Producer with wheat allotment and feed grain base who makes the required diversion and maintains his conserving base may plant the total of his wheat allotment and 80% of his feed grain base to wheat or feed grains without loss of base or allotment. However, he may only receive feed grain payments and wheat certificates by planting 90% of his certified acreage to wheat and 45% of his feed grain base to corn, sorghum, or barley.
Excess wheat	Same as for 1965	Same as for 1965	Same as for 1965
Production eligible for price support			
Loan[8]	...	...	...
Price support payment			
Domestic certificates	Production of 40% of farm wheat allotment	Production of 43% of farm wheat allotment	Production of 48% of farm wheat allotment
Export certificates	None	None	None

215

Table 6-12. Summary of Provisions for Wheat Programs, 1962–73 (Cont.)

Item	1971 Program	1972 Program	1973 Program
National wheat allotment	Not applicable	Not applicable	Not applicable
National domestic wheat allotment	19.7 million acres	19.7 million acres	18.7 million acres
Loan	$1.25 per bushel	$1.25 per bushel	$1.25 per bushel
Domestic certificate	Difference between average price received by farmers in July–Nov. 1971 and 100% of wheat parity on July 1, 1971	Difference between average price received by farmers in July–Nov. 1972 and 100% of wheat parity on July 1, 1972	Difference between average price received by farmers in July–Nov. 1973 and 100% of wheat parity on July 1, 1973.
Total support or guarantee to program participants for certified production	100% of parity ($2.93)	100% of parity ($3.02)	100% of parity ($3.39)
Production eligible for domestic certificates	Production on 100% of farm domestic wheat allotment	Same as for 1971	Same as for 1971
Production eligible for loan	Total production on participating farms	Same as for 1971	Same as for 1971
Timing of payments	75% of estimated value of certificates soon after July 1, 1971. Final payments made after Dec. 1. If preliminary payment is larger than final value of certificates, no refund will be required.	Same as for 1971. In addition, for 1972 producers electing voluntary set-aside received the entire payment for such acreage soon after July 1.	Same as for 1972
Payment limitations	Maximum value of 1971 wheat certificates to any person, $55,000	Maximum value of 1972 wheat certificates plus voluntary set-aside payments to any person, $55,000	Same as for 1972

	1971	1972	1973
Limitation on acreage planted to wheat	Participant who sets aside cropland equal to the required percentage of his domestic wheat allotment and maintains his conserving base may plant his remaining cropland to wheat or any other crop, except to the extent limited by other quota programs, without loss of certificates	Same as for 1971 except producers electing voluntary set-aside are required to limit plantings	Same as for 1971 except for the voluntary set-aside requirement limiting total wheat acreage planted for harvest
Required diversion or set-aside	75% of farm's domestic wheat allotment	83% of farm's domestic wheat allotment	86% of farm's domestic wheat allotment
Compensation for required diversion or set-aside	Value of wheat certificates and loan eligibility	Same as for 1971	Same as for 1971
Additional diversion or voluntary set-aside for payment	None	Up to 75% of farm's domestic allotment. Spring wheat producer's planted acreage plus voluntary set-aside cannot exceed his total planted acreage in 1971. Winter wheat producers are required to reduce 1972 plantings by the amount of voluntary set-aside.	Up to 150% of farm's domestic allotment. Producers electing voluntary set-aside must limit 1973 wheat acreage to 1972 wheat program acreage plus 1972 voluntary set-aside less 1973 voluntary set-aside. Some adjustments are permitted if 1972 program acreage is not representative for the farm.
Payment for additional diversion or voluntary set-aside	None	94¢ per bushel times farm yield times acre voluntary set-aside	88¢ per bushel times farm yield times acre voluntary set-aside

Table 6-12. Summary of Provisions for Wheat Programs, 1962–73 (Cont.)

Item	1971 Program	1972 Program	1973 Program
Planting requirement to prevent loss of allotment	Producer who fails to plant 90% of his domestic allotment to wheat in 1971 will have his 1972 allotment reduced by the amount of the underplanting—up to 20%. Acreage planted to corn or sorghum is considered planted to wheat. Acreage not planted due to national disaster or conditions beyond producer's control will be considered planted. Producer who makes a set-aside but elects to receive no payment will not suffer an allotment loss.	Same as for 1971 with the inclusion of barley and soybeans	Same as for 1971 with the inclusion of barley and soybeans
Substitution	Producer who sets aside cropland equal to the required percentages of his base and allotment and maintains his conserving base can plant his entire acreage to wheat, corn, or sorghum without loss of payments, certificates, base acreage, or allotment. Producer with only a base or only an allot-	Same as for 1971 with the inclusion of barley and soybeans	Same as for 1971 with the inclusion of barley and soybeans

ment can participate in one program and plant all wheat or all feed grains without loss of benefits, base, or allotment.

Conserving base	Same as for 1970	Same as for 1970	Same as for 1970
Farm program yield (used to calculate benefits)	Projected from 1967–69 average	Projected from 1968–70 average	Projected from 1969–71 average

Source: U.S.D.A.

[1] Domestic certificate value is difference between loan and 100% of parity for wheat on July 1 of each year for 1966, 1967, 1968, 1969, and 1970.

[2] All farm allotments reduced 10% to a total of about 49.5 million acres. Farm allotments in Minnesota, North Dakota, South Dakota, Montana, and two counties in California increased at request of producer by 40% of 1960–61 average farm durum acreage.

[3] Allotments on small farms were increased to 90% of 1959–61 average wheat acreage, if this was larger. Total of effective farm allotments was about 53.3 million acres in 1964 and 1965, 51.6 in 1966, and 68.2 in 1967. 1968–70 includes small farm increase.

[4] Quotas proclaimed but voted out.

[5] Compliance with the larger of allotment or exemption acreage required to avoid marketing quota penalty. Participants required to divert 10% of the farm allotment, based on a 55-million-acre national allotment.

[6] The 1959–61 average is an average of 1959, 1960, and 1961 including any zero acreages.

[7] Excess wheat produced under the excess wheat option not eligible for loan.

[8] Eligibility requirements: in 1962, compliance with allotment and participation in wheat stabilization program; in 1963 and 1964, compliance with allotment; in 1965–70, compliance with program requirements.

[9] Compliance with 1963 wheat acreage diversion program required.

[10] Domestic certificates based on portion of allotment planted: up to 45% for 1964–66 and up to 35% for 1967.

[11] Export certificates based on portion of allotment planted: from 46% to 90% for 1964 and from 46% to 80% for 1965.

[12] Loan also available on wheat grown on feed grain acres under the substitution provision.

219

compliers for the lower loan rate, which allowed the market price to fall, and it induced compliance with the acreage diversion features of the program.

Planted acreage and production rose above the levels of 1962, but remained below use, reducing stocks further. Market prices averaged 19 cents lower than in 1962.

1964–65. Several significant changes were made in wheat programs beginning in 1964: (1) All mandatory features of programs were discontinued. Compliance with program provisions would no longer be enforced by fines and by reductions in future acreage allotments. Referendums were discontinued. (2) The total national minimum allotment was cut 10 percent from 55.0 to 49.5 million acres, but special adjustments for small farms raised the effective minimum to 53.3 million acres. A portion of the acreage allotment was designated the domestic allotment for the purpose of supporting farmers' returns from wheat destined for domestic food use at a higher rate than other wheat. (3) The loan rate was dropped close to the world price of wheat. This made wheat competitive with feed grains. All producers who planted within their allotments were eligible for price support loans. (4) Incomes of cooperating producers were maintained by government payments. These payments were contingent upon diversion to conserving uses of the amount of land cut from the allotment. All diverted acreage was to be in addition to normal conserving practices and to acreage diverted under other government programs. Another stipulation was that allotments for other crops could not be exceeded. This was the first time that cross compliance among programs for various crops was made effective.

Farmers received payments computed in three categories. One, called the domestic certificate payment, applied to a producer's domestic allotment. That was 45 percent of the total allotment in 1964 and 1965. The government financed this payment by assessing wheat processors for the value of the certificates on all wheat purchased for domestic food use. This became known as the "bread tax." The second part of the government payment was called the export certificate payment. It applied to 45 percent of a producer's allotment in 1964 and 35 percent in 1965. The per bushel payment made for this portion of a farmer's payment was less than for the domestic certificate payment. The third part of the payment was called the acreage diversion payment. It was computed the same as such payments in 1962 and 1963. The full cost of the export certificate payments and the diversion payments was borne by the government.

Program provisions for 1964 were not known for certain until April when the new program became effective with the enactment of the Agricultural Act of 1964. This was many months after the winter wheat crop was sown. Under the new program, the loan rate was dropped from $1.82 to $1.30 a bushel, and, as described above, government payments were provided to protect farmers' incomes.

Acreage was up some from 1963, but for the fourth consecutive year output remained below use, and withdrawals from wheat stockpiles continued. Market prices fell nearly 50 cents a bushel, but remained above the new, lower loan rate.

A few changes were made in the program for 1965. Loans could no longer be obtained merely by planting within the allotment. Compliance with diversion features of the program was now required to qualify for all program benefits. Three new features were introduced which allowed more flexibility for producers who complied with the program: (1) Substitution between wheat and feed grains was allowed for producers who signed up for both programs. (2) A producer could request an oats-rye base for the purpose of planting wheat under the wheat–feed grain substitution provision. If this provision was adopted, part of the oats-rye base had to be diverted to conserving uses.[4] (3) The excess-wheat provision employed before 1962 was reinstated. Under this exemption wheat grown in excess of allotments could be stored under bond so that the remaining wheat would qualify for program benefits. Excess planting could not exceed 50 percent of the allotment.

The loan rate was reduced 5 cents to $1.25 a bushel; acreage allotments were not changed from 1964. Acreage rose slightly. U.S. stocks were drawn down nearly 300,000 bushels to meet exceptionally strong export demand for wheat. At the end of the crop year, stocks were at their lowest level since 1952. (The impact of the unusual demand for wheat was not felt until late in the 1965 crop year, after the 1966 program provisions were announced and after winter wheat was planted.)

1966–70. Programs for these five years were basically similar to those of the previous two years. The only major changes involved the payment computations. The export certificate part of the payment package was discontinued and the value of the domestic certificate payment was raised. The new value was the difference between the loan rate and 100 percent of parity on July 1 of each year. Processors continued to be charged 75 cents a bushel to help finance the cost of the domestic certificate payment; the remainder was paid from appropriated funds.

The size of the allotment was cut slightly in 1966 and the amount of land required to be diverted to conserving uses was raised. The reduction in the national allotment was from 49.5 to 47.8 million acres. Required diversion to conserving use was increased from 11.11 percent to 15 percent of the allotment. Also, maximum voluntary diversion was increased from 20 percent of the allotment or 15 acres to 50 percent of the allotment or 25 acres, whichever was larger. The loan rate was unchanged. As mentioned, these provisions to discourage planting were announced before exports began to rise early in 1966.

Acreage was cut, stocks further diminished as exports surged, and prices rose sharply. By June of 1967 government-owned wheat was at the lowest level since 1948.

Program features were changed in 1967 to stimulate output of wheat. The allotment was raised to 63.3 million acres and there was no requirement to idle part of the allotment as had been true since 1962. No payments were offered for voluntary diversion of wheat land to conservation uses. Planted acreage increased more than 12 million acres. Production outstripped domestic and export needs, causing a net addition to stocks for the first year since 1960. Prices fell.

Incentives for planting were reduced some for 1968 by lowering the allotment to 59.3 million acres. But there was no requirement to idle part of the allotment and no payments for voluntary idling of allotment land. Acreage was reduced some from the high level of 1967 but good yields led to a larger crop. Exports contracted more than 200 million bushels; carryover stocks increased nearly 300 million bushels. Prices slipped further.

In 1969 the allotment was lowered back to the level of 1966 and diversion provisions were reinstated. As in 1965 and 1966 the only payment to participants who idled the minimum amount of acreage was that called the domestic-certificate payment. The acreage diversion payment was offered for additional, voluntary diversion. Acreage and output were cut but not enough to prevent another increase in stocks. Prices remained low.

The national acreage allotment in 1970 was reduced 12 percent from 1969. All other program features were the same as in 1969. Cutbacks in acreage and production occurred. Use exceeded production, reducing stocks. Prices strengthened.

1971–73. Several changes were made in the wheat program by new legislation covering 1971, 1972, and 1973. An allotment was specified only for domestic food use instead of for total wheat needs as in previous years. No limit was placed on wheat planting. Designating allotments was only for the purpose of computing set-aside acreage requirements and marketing certificate payments. Land diverted to conserving uses was now called set-aside. If 55 percent or more of a farm's cropland was in fallow, set-aside requirements were considered to be fulfilled. A change was also made in computing the value of the marketing-certificate payment. The certificate value was changed from the difference between the loan rate and 100 percent of parity to the difference between the market price and 100 percent of parity. Marketing certificate payments were made only for the domestic food allotment. A maximum payment limitation of $55,000 per crop was introduced. This was the maximum a producer could receive from wheat set-aside and marketing certificate payments. Loans and direct purchases by the government were excluded from the payment limit.

The required set-aside for 1971 was put at 75 percent of the domestic allotment. No payments were offered for additional set-aside and there were no limits placed on wheat plantings. Acreage was increased. Production rose above use, adding to stocks. Prices were stable.

The required set-aside in 1972 was raised to 83 percent of the domestic allotment. Optional set-aside for payment was allowed up to another 75 percent of the domestic allotment. Acreage changed little but production was down some because of smaller yields than in 1971. The Russian wheat sale caused export demand to soar, more than doubling the previous year's level. Prices likewise soared.

Program provisions for 1973 were announced in July 1972 before the upsurge in prices of the 1972 crop. The provisions continued incentives to divert land from wheat. Required set-aside acreage was increased to 86 percent of the domestic allotment and an additional voluntary set-aside for payment was allowed up to 150 percent of a farm's allotment.

In the face of unprecedented high market prices when wheat was planted, 1973 acreage exceeded 1972 acreage and set-aside acreage dropped sharply. More than two-thirds of the crop was exported. Stocks were drained.

Cotton

1948–63. Cotton programs during these 16 years were similar to wheat programs in most of the same years.[5] The principal features were price supports and acreage controls. Cotton prices were supported principally by nonrecourse loans; purchase programs were infrequently used. Loans were made to farmers and to their marketing associations. With the exception of the Korean War period, the loan rate determined the market price for this period. The national average loan rates for upland cotton, middling 1-inch, and season average prices received by farmers for upland cotton of all grades are shown in figure 6-7. These and other data pertaining to cotton production and use are summarized in table 6-13.

Acreage control was achieved by acreage allotments and marketing quotas. The size of the national allotments and the number of individual allotments established appear in table 6-14. Marketing quotas, enforced by penalties, applied in all years that acreage allotments were in force. A lower limit was by law placed on the size of acreage allotments to protect producers' incomes. In many years this prevented curtailing production enough to avoid surpluses.

Price support loans were the only feature of government cotton programs in 1948. Supply and demand were in reasonable balance, forestalling the need for production controls. The loan rate was raised from 28.2 cents per pound in 1947 to 31.5 cents per pound in 1948. This was 92.5 percent of parity, the minimum rate allowed by law. Planted and harvested acreages were only slightly higher than in the previous year but record yields produced a bumper crop — 26 percent larger than the 1947 crop. The price for the season averaged slightly below the loan rate; carryover stocks rose.

cents per pound

Figure 6-7. Cotton (Upland): Loan Rates and Market Prices, 1948–73
[a] Season's average price received by farmers.
[b] Loan rate on gross weight basis 1948–70, net weight basis 1971–73. For 1959–60 the solid line is the loan rate offered for choice B; the dotted line is the purchase price offered for choice A.

Stocks:
End of Year
Carryover[b]
(in Thousand Bales)

Crop Year (August–July)	National Average Loan Rate (per Pound Gross Weight)	Average Price Received by Farmers (per Pound)	Acreage (in Millions) Planted	Acreage (in Millions) Diverted under Programs[a]	Production[b] (in Thousand Bales)	Utilization[b] (in Thousand Bales) Total[c]	Utilization[b] (in Thousand Bales) Export	End of Year Carryover[b] Total[d]	End of Year Carryover[b] Government Owned
1948	31.49¢	30.38¢	23.6		14,577	12,349	4,746	5,241	e
1949	30.03	28.57	28.3		15,905	14,376	5,771	6,781	3,137
1950	30.25	39.90	18.8		9,848	14,447	4,108	2,196	76
1951	32.36	37.69	29.3		15,030	14,461	5,515	2,741	2
1952	32.41	34.17	28.0		14,861	12,089	3,048	5,511	236
1953	33.50	32.10	26.8		16,253	12,181	3,760	9,570	129
1954	34.03	33.52	20.0		13,578	12,128	3,445	11,028	1,661
1955	34.55	32.27	17.9		14,501	11,118	2,194	14,399	5,952
1956	32.74	31.63	17.0	1.1	13,102	16,233	7,540	11,269	4,829
1957	32.31	29.46	14.2	3.0	10,801	13,459	5,707	8,615	937
1958	35.08	39.09	12.3	4.9	11,353	11,228	2,766	8,733	984
1959	34.10[f] / 28.40[g]	31.56	15.8		14,446	15,774	7,178	7,404	4,967
1960	32.42[f] / 26.63[g]	30.08	16.0		14,199	14,512	6,625	7,090	1,678
1961	33.04	32.80	16.5		14,263	13,616	4,906	7,741	1,449
1962	32.47	31.74	16.2		14,754	11,474	3,348	11,016	3,750
1963	32.02	32.02	14.7	0.5	15,129	14,023	5,661	12,125	4,303
1964	30.00	29.62	14.7	1.0	15,031	13,124	4,038	14,033	6,557
1965	29.00	28.03	14.1	4.6	14,850	12,300	2,936	16,574	9,715
1966	21.00	20.64	10.3	4.8	9,491	13,786	4,656	12,280	6,677
1967	20.25	25.39	9.4		7,370	13,394	4,161	6,258	552
1968	20.25	22.02	10.8	3.3	10,838	10,738	2,723	6,366	24
1969	20.25	20.94	11.8		9,860	10,572	2,753	5,653	1,890
1970	20.25	21.86	11.9		10,055	11,507	3,726	4,189	262
1971	19.50[h]	28.07	12.3	2.1	10,379	11,461	3,378	3,238	1
1972	19.50[h]	27.20	13.9	2.0	13,608	12,989	5,303	3,999	e
1973	19.50[h]	44.60	12.4		12,880	13,200	5,700	3,700	e

[a] There were no acreage diversion programs in 1948–55, 1959–63, 1969–70, and 1973. Acres listed here as diverted were devoted to approved conserving uses or planted to approved nonsurplus crops.

[b] Running bales through 1970, 480-pound net weight bales in 1971–73.

[c] Includes exports.

[d] Includes government owned and under loan to the government.

[e] Less than 500 bales.

[f] Government purchase price for program choice A.

[g] Loan rate for program choice B.

[h] Net weight basis; gross weight would be approximately 18.7¢ per pound.

Table 6-14. Cotton (Upland) Acreage Allotments and
Number Voting in Referendums, 1950–63

Crop Year[a]	Total Acres Allotted[b] (in Millions)	Number of Allotments (in Thousands)	Number Voting in Referendums (in Thousands)
1950	21.6	1,218	644
1954	21.4	1,003	487
1955	18.1	981	347
1956	17.4	963	292
1957	17.6	953	232
1958	17.6	957	229
1959	16.3[c] 17.3[d]	950	275
1960	16.3[c] 17.5[d]	946	188
1961	18.5	931	193
1962	18.1	886	280
1963	16.3	775	217

[a]No allotments were proclaimed or referendums held in 1948–49 and 1951–53.

[b]Marketing quotas applied all years that allotments were proclaimed.

[c]National allotment used as basis for program choice A.

[d]National allotment used as basis for program choice B.

Expected supplies for 1949 were not large enough to require acreage allotments and marketing quotas so no production controls were proclaimed for 1949. The loan rate was lowered slightly, as allowed by new legislation. Planting was increased by nearly 5 million acres. Supplies exceeded use once more causing an addition to stocks. Prices slipped slightly.

Acreage allotments and marketing quotas were imposed in 1950 for the first time since 1943. The national allotment of 21.6 million acres was 24 percent below plantings in 1949, but about equal to average plantings in the previous five years.

Acreage was cut back sharply; see figure 6-8. And, as shown in figure 6-9, production and stocks also fell. Strong domestic demand, reflecting wartime needs during the Korean conflict, boosted utilization to nearly 4.5 million bales more than production. Prices climbed 10 cents above the loan rate.

Marketing quotas and acreage allotments were not declared for the 1951 crop. Price supports were continued at 90 percent of parity, which meant an increase in the loan rate of 2.1 cents per pound. Acreage shot up again. Most of the resulting large crop was utilized for domestic and export needs, changing stocks very little. Prices fell 2 cents from the peak of 1950 but remained above the loan rate.

Cotton programs were not changed for 1952. Acreage, production, and prices were down slightly; stocks grew as export demand contracted.

million acres

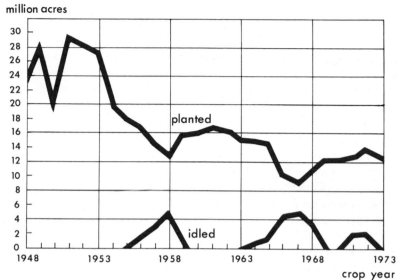

Figure 6-8. Cotton (Upland): Acreage Planted and Idled under Programs, 1948–73

million bales

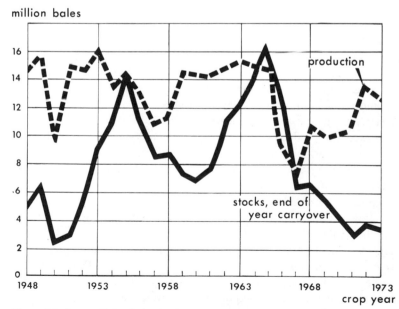

Figure 6-9. Cotton (Upland): Production and Carryover Stocks, 1948–73

In 1953 again no acreage allotments or marketing quotas were proclaimed. Acreage was cut back about 1 million acres but high yields pushed production over 16 million bales. Combined domestic and export use was 12 million bales, causing a sharp increase in stocks. Prices slipped below loan rates for the first time since 1949.

The surplus situation required acreage allotments and marketing quotas for 1954. The allotment was set at 21.4 million acres, the smallest permissible under existing legislation. The loan rate was advanced 0.5 cents per pound to meet the legal minimum requirement. Acreage and production contracted but remained above use. Stocks climbed further; about 15 percent of the carryover was owned by the government at the end of the crop year.

A lower minimum allotment was permitted and proclaimed for 1955. Acreage was reduced but record yields resulted in higher production than in the previous year. At the end of the crop year the carryover about equaled one year's production (see figure 6-9).

New legislation in 1956 created two programs affecting cotton production and use. First, under Soil Bank land retirement programs, cotton producers received income for land withdrawn from production. Late enactment of the law minimized the effect on cotton acreage in 1956. The amount of the cotton land placed in the acreage reserve part of the Soil Bank is listed in table 6-13 under ''diverted under programs'' and shown in figure 6-8 as ''acreage idled.''

The second new program encouraged cotton exports by making U.S. cotton available to foreign countries at competitive prices. The CCC was directed to sell its stocks at the world price and absorb losses. Previously, U.S. price support programs held the U.S. price above world cotton prices, deterring commercial exports. This export program was in addition to concessional sales under P.L. 480, which began in 1954.

Sharply higher exports, together with curtailed output, resulted in utilization in excess of production. Stocks were drawn down about 3 million bales, but remained high relative to use.

Soil Bank programs had their first substantial impact in 1957. About 3 million acres of cotton land were diverted to conservation use under the acreage reserve part of the Soil Bank. Planted acreage was reduced accordingly. Production was down and use remained high, cutting stocks by about 3.5 million bales.

The loan rate for 1958 was raised nearly 3 cents a pound; no other changes were made in cotton programs for 1958. Acreage was cut. Despite the lowest harvested acreage since 1878, extremely high yields pushed production over that of the previous year. Output and use were nearly in balance; stocks changed little. The higher loan rate pulled market prices up.

New agricultural legislation added several variations to cotton programs for 1959 and 1960. For both years producers were offered a choice between a fairly high price support with a relatively small allotment (Choice A) and a lower price support with a larger allotment (Choice B). Both price support rates are shown in table 6-13 and figure 6-7. The government agreed to purchase cotton at the higher rate from complying producers. Price support loans were offered only at the lower rate. Acreage allotments to correspond with the two choices appear in table 6-14. Acreage and production rose. Because of heavy export demand, use was greater than production so stocks were drawn down.

Only slight changes were made in program provisions in 1960. Similarly, there was little change in acreage, output, or prices.

The cotton program for 1961 reverted to the type of program in existence before 1959 — only one level of price supports and allotments was offered. Both the acreage allotment and the price support loan rates were raised. New legislation instituted a minimum per farm allotment. This meant that most of the increase in the national allotment went to small farms. There was little change in acreage, production, or stocks; prices rose 2.7 cents per pound.

For 1962 the allotment and the loan rate were lowered slightly. Acreage and production changed little but stocks rose sharply as exports declined.

The national acreage allotment was cut nearly 2 million acres for 1963; the price support loan rate was unchanged. Acreage contracted but production increased because of high yields. (Yields had risen more than 68 percent from 1948–50 to 1961–63). Despite some recovery in the volume of exports, the large production was not totally utilized in 1963. Stocks mounted. Yearly prices continued to average close to the loan rate.

1964–65. The Agricultural Act of 1964 provided a new two-year program for cotton. For 1964 and 1965 a dual set of acreage allotments and price supports were offered: (1) a high support with a small allotment, based on acreage estimated to produce adequate cotton for domestic consumption (about two-thirds of the total allotment); and (2) a lower support rate linked to compliance with the total allotment. An exception was made for producers with allotments of 15 acres or less; these small farmers were eligible for the higher price support without reducing their cotton acreage below their total allotment. A third option was authorized for cotton farmers who produced for the export market. These farmers could exceed their total allotment by a specified amount if they sold the production from the additional acreage for export without benefit of government subsidies. Penalties for noncompliance with one of the program choices were retained.

To stimulate domestic demand, a subsidy (payment in kind) was provided to U.S. raw cotton users. It was called the cotton equalization program because it equalized the cost of raw cotton to domestic and foreign mills. Previously, export subsidies made U.S. cotton more costly for domestic mills than for foreign users. Under this mechanism subsidies were paid for both domestic and export utilization. It permitted U.S. cotton to be competitive with cotton from other suppliers without lowering the price received by U.S. farmers. (Lowering the price and making a direct payment to farmers would have had the same effects; this latter method was adopted beginning with the 1966 crop year.)

The total national acreage allotment remained unchanged for 1964; a domestic allotment was set at two-thirds of the total allotment. The price support loan rate was lowered 2.5 cents per pound. This was the only price support available to producers who planted within their total allotment if their allotments exceeded 15 acres. Producers who planted only their domestic allotments, or those who had regular allotments of 15 acres or less, were eligible for a 2.5 cents per pound payment from the government in addition to the loan. Producers who wished to exceed their regular allotment for export were allowed to plant 105 percent of their allotment. Under the cotton equalization program, domestic mills received a subsidy of 6.5 cents per pound, paid with cotton from government stocks.

Acreage and production changed little from the previous year. Higher domestic use was more than offset by reduced exports resulting in an increase in carryover stocks. (Late enactment of the act limited the impact of the new provisions for 1964. Participation in the domestic allotment option of the program was highest among small producers. As may be seen in table 6-15, more than half of the allotments were in compliance, but these accounted for less than one-fourth of allotment acreage.)

Changes in cotton programs for 1965 increased the payment for compliance with the domestic allotment to 4.3 cents per pound, lowered the loan rate by 1 cent per pound, and discontinued the export acreage provision. Acreage and production were cut back modestly but not enough to offset sharply reduced exports. Cotton stocks rose to an all-time high, exceeding annual production. The government owned nearly 10 million bales of cotton at the end of the crop year.

1966–70. Comprehensive new legislation covering five years provided a coordinated program for cotton production and marketing. It continued the national minimum allotment at 16 million acres and retained the domestic allotment concept. However, producers who wished to receive program benefits were required to divert part of their allotments to conserving uses. Government payments, called diversion payments, were made for this diversion. In addition to the required diversion farmers could choose to divert more acreage from cotton to conserving uses for an additional payment. An excep-

Table 6-15. Cotton (Upland) Program, Participation, and Payments, 1964–73

Crop Year	Number of Farms (in Thousands)		Number Voting in Referendums (in Thousands)	Acreage Allotments (in Millions of Acres)		Payments[a] (in Millions)
	Eligible	Participating		Total	On Participating Farms	
1964	605	311[b]	235	16.2	3.6[b]	$ 39.3
1965	594	334[b]	305	16.2	4.9[b]	69.3
1966	557	512	212	16.2	15.1	774.0
1967	555	483	301	16.2	14.9	935.0
1968	555	460	276	16.2	14.9	783.5
1969	524	475	288	16.2	15.0	823.2
1970	514	476	267	17.1	16.0	914.8
1971	335	295	c	11.5	10.3	818.3
1972	297	268	c	11.5	10.2	807.3
1973	262	226	c	10.0	8.7	714.0

[a]Total government payments to producers for price support, acreage diversion, and set-aside under cotton programs.
[b]Participation in voluntary domestic allotment part of program.
[c]Referendums were not held in 1971–73.

231

tion was made to aid small farmers, those with allotments of 10 acres or less. These small producers qualified for the diversion payments without any reduction in cotton plantings.

The price support loan rate was reduced substantially. It was now linked to the world market price instead of parity as in the past. This lower loan rate permitted the domestic price to fall, thus eliminating the need for the domestic mill subsidy and for the export subsidy. Producers' incomes were protected by the payments from the government. Total payments from the government were divided into two categories: a diversion payment, based on the amount of land idled (described above), and a price support payment, based on the amount of production from the domestic allotment. Authority for the export-acreage exception was continued.

The price support loan rate in 1966 was lowered 8 cents a pound to 21 cents. Cotton farmers who planted only their domestic allotment (two-thirds of their regular allotments) and farmers with small allotments earned a price support payment of 9.42 cents per pound on their estimated production. Required diversion was 12.5 percent of the regular allotment; additional voluntary diversion up to 35 percent of the allotment was allowed for payment. The payment rate was 10.5 cents per pound for estimated production from all diverted acres.

Acreage, production, stocks, and prices fell. Diversion for payment under the cotton program was 4.6 million acres. A reduction in the cotton carryover reversed a five-year buildup in stocks.

The price support loan rate was lowered slightly for 1967 and the payment rates for acreage diversion and price support were raised. No other changes were made in acreage diversion features or in the allotments. Acreage, production, and stocks dropped further, while acreage diversion rose slightly. Large withdrawals from stocks virtually depleted the amount of cotton in government ownership. Market prices moved above the loan rate for the first time since the Korean War period.

Program provisions for 1968 increased incentives to plant cotton by loosening land diversion requirements, lowering the payment rate for voluntary diversion, and raising the price support payment for cotton grown on the domestic portion of an allotment. Required diversion was lowered from 12.5 percent to 5.0 percent of the allotment. The drop in the payment rate was from 10.78 cents to 6.00 cents per pound for voluntary diversion, up to 35 percent of the allotment. The payment rate for required diversion remained at 10.78 cents per pound. The price support payment was raised from 11.53 to 12.24 cents per pound.

Cotton acreage and production did rise. The new supply of cotton was nearly in balance with demand so stocks changed little. Prices dropped some but remained above the loan rate.

Program provisions for 1969 were modified to further strengthen incentives for planting. No payments were made for diverting acreage from cotton and no land was required to be diverted from the acreage allotment to obtain other program benefits. The price support loan rate was unchanged but the price support payment was raised. Planted acreage was increased by 1 million acres yet production was down because of lower yields than in 1968.[6] The carryover was down slightly.

The national acreage allotment in 1970 was increased about 1 million acres. No change was made in the loan rate; the price support payment was increased about 2 cents per pound. Acreage diversion was not required and no payment was offered for voluntary diversion. There was little change in acreage, production, or domestic use. Exports were up about 1 million bales. Stocks fell, prices strengthened.

1971–73. Some substantial changes were made in cotton programs for 1971, 1972, and 1973. Two key departures from previous programs were the suspension of marketing quotas and penalties, making participation in the cotton program voluntary for the first time, and the removal of planting restrictions as a condition for obtaining program benefits. Other changes modified features of earlier programs.

To obtain government price support loans and payments some diversion of cropland to conserving uses — set-aside — could be required if surpluses were anticipated. Government payments were authorized for the set-aside acreage; a bonus payment was authorized for farms with allotments of 10 acres or less.

Allotments were established only for the purposes of computing payments and of determining the amount of land to be set aside. The size of the national allotment was reduced from 16.2 and 11.5 million acres, the acreage estimated to meet domestic needs. The price support loan rate was lowered. Price support payments on production from the allotment were continued to support producers' incomes. Other new provisions limited government payments to $55,000 to any one cotton producer, required planting of cotton if payments were to be received, and reduced future allotments if no cotton was planted.

In 1971 the price support loan rate was reduced about 2 cents per pound from the comparable 1970 level. (The basis for computing the loan rate was changed from a gross weight to a net weight basis.) The national base acreage allotment was set at 11.5 million acres, about the same size as the domestic allotment in 1970. Program participants were required to set aside acreage equivalent to 20 percent of their farm base acreage allotment. A price-support or set-aside payment of at least 15 cents per pound was guaranteed for production on the allotment.

Modest increases in acreage and yield produced a larger crop in 1971 than in 1970. Usage fell slightly below the previous year's level but still outstripped production, drawing down stocks about 1 million bales. Government-owned stocks were depleted. Prices rose sharply.

The cotton program for 1972 was essentially the same as in 1971. Acreage and yields were up, producing a substantially larger crop. An upturn in the export market prevented a large buildup in stocks and held prices to a small decline.

All acreage diversion provisions were removed for 1973. The allotment was cut from 11.5 to 10.0 million acres. This is the acreage used to compute price support payments. The price support payment rate and the loan rate were continued at the same levels as in 1971 and 1972.

Planting and production declined. Utilization increased because of strong export demand. Prices reached their highest level since the Civil War.

Dairy Products

Government programs to support prices and incomes of dairy producers fall into five categories: the price support program, the marketing order program, several domestic food programs, export programs, and import quotas.[7] Dairy imports have been limited under authority of Section 22, which allows restrictions when necessary to prevent imports from interfering with U.S. agricultural price support programs (see chapter 5). Imports (on a milk equivalent, fat solids basis) were less than 1 percent of U.S. milk production until 1966. From 1966 to 1973 imports ranged from 1.1 to 3.4 percent of domestic production. To a large extent domestic food programs and export programs serve as outlets for surplus foods acquired under price support activities, although in recent years acquisitions for food programs have been based on program requirements rather than on the availability of surpluses. Discussions of domestic and foreign food programs for dairy products appear in the next chapter, which treats food and export programs for all commodities. Key features of the price support and marketing order programs are summarized here.

The price support program and the marketing order programs provide a two-tiered price support operation for milk. The price support program deals with manufactured milk products while marketing order programs directly affect fluid milk supplies and prices. These two programs are not linked together by law but the operation of one program affects the other.

Through marketing orders, milk for fluid use is supported at a higher rate than milk for manufactured dairy products, commonly called manufacturing milk. Marketing orders serve to divert any excess supply of milk into the manufacturing market. Thus, any surplus of milk ends up as a surplus of manufactured dairy products, not as fluid milk. The price support program provides a floor under the price of manufacturing milk, and, during most of the post–World War II period, a floor was likewise provided under the price of butterfat.

The price support program. Prices have been supported by purchases of the products of milk and butterfat, principally butter, cheddar cheese, and nonfat dry milk. Purchases are made from manufacturers and handlers. This, in turn, buoys the prices of milk and cream at the farm level. Government purchases of milk for food programs were not a formal part of the dairy price support program.

Before the beginning of each marketing year (April 1–March 31) the secretary of agriculture is required to announce support prices for manufacturing milk and butterfat (the requirement to set a support for butterfat was suspended for 1971–73 and terminated beginning in 1974); he also announces the prices at which the CCC will buy butter, cheddar cheese, and nonfat dry milk for the ensuing 12 months. Support levels may be raised during the year but not lowered. Permissible ranges to set support levels are linked to parity prices by law. The main elements of the price support program have remained the same throughout the postwar period, though the level of supports has been adjusted frequently — sometimes by legislative action but usually through administrative decisions.

The marketing order program. Federal milk orders are designed to aid in stabilizing marketing conditions in the sale of milk to handlers by dairy farmers who meet standards for selling milk for fluid use. Legislation authorizes the fixing of minimum milk prices to producers after public hearings. In 1968 about 70 percent of the milk eligible in quality for fluid use in the United States was covered by federal marketing orders. (A large share of the remaining 30 percent was covered by state laws regulating milk prices.)

Fluid milk marketing orders classify milk and set minimum prices by use. Usually two classifications are established — Class I for fluid milk use and Class II for milk used in the manufacture of dairy products. In most areas farmers are paid a "blend" price computed monthly according to the quantities of milk marketed in each class. Many milk orders set the Class I price on the basis of the manufacturing milk price plus a differential that more than covers the higher costs of producing milk for fluid use. Therefore, changes in the price support level for manufacturing milk generally have been accompanied by changes in Class I prices. Some marketing orders have considered economic factors such as the cost of living and production costs when setting marketing order prices; in these areas the correlation between the price support level and Class I prices has been less pronounced.

Dairy program highlights. Total milk production trended upward during the 1950s and early 1960s while commercial markets leveled off between 1956 and 1965 despite population and income growth. Supplies substantially exceeded demand, leading to sizable purchases by the government to maintain market prices at the support level. Unwieldly stock accumulations were avoided by channeling the excess production into domestic food programs and exports, mainly under P.L. 480. Figure 6-10 and table 6-16 show milk supply, use, and carryover.

For 1948 and 1949 support of manufacturing milk was required at 90 percent of parity. Beginning in 1950 the secretary was authorized to set the level between 75 and 90 percent of parity as needed to assure an adequate supply. During and immediately after the Korean War, supports were maintained at or near 90 percent of parity. To maintain this high support level, large government purchases were required in 1953. Supports were reduced to 75 percent of parity in 1954 and held near the legal minimum until 1960. In September 1960 the Congress raised the minimum support level to 80 percent of parity for the remainder of the marketing year. This higher support level was continued by the secretary of agriculture until March 31, 1962. Parity percentages along with other information about dairy price support operations are given in table 6-17. Notice that government removals from the market

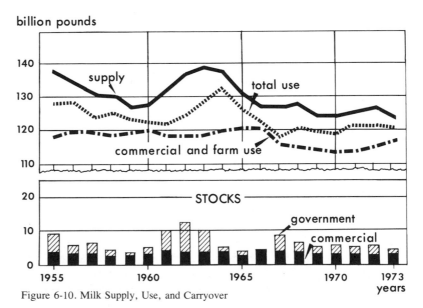

Figure 6-10. Milk Supply, Use, and Carryover

	Supply			Use				Stocks on December 31	
Year	Produc-tion	Imports	Total[a]	Commercial and Farm	Domestic Donations[b]	Government Exports[c]	Total	Commer-cial	Govern-ment
1948	112.7	0.2	115.5	112.5	0.1	0.3	112.9	3.6	d
1949	116.1	0.3	120.0	115.1	0.3	0.1	115.5	3.0	2.4
1950	116.6	0.5	122.5	116.1	1.3	1.0	118.4	3.1	1.6
1951	114.7	0.5	119.9	115.7	0.2	0.9	116.8	3.6	0.1
1952	114.7	0.7	119.1	114.2	0.1	d	114.2	4.9	0.2
1953	120.2	0.5	125.8	113.2	1.3	0.7	115.2	3.3	7.5
1954	122.0	0.4	133.2	115.8	2.5	1.4	119.7	3.2	10.5
1955	122.9	0.5	137.1	118.6	3.8	5.8	128.2	3.6	5.5
1956	124.9	0.5	134.5	120.1	3.8	4.9	128.8	3.6	2.0
1957	124.6	0.7	130.9	120.0	2.7	1.7	124.4	3.7	2.8
1958	123.2	0.5	130.2	118.8	4.5	2.2	125.5	3.8	1.0
1959	122.0	0.6	127.4	119.3	3.4	0.6	123.3	3.7	0.4
1960	123.1	0.6	127.8	120.0	2.3	0.1	122.4	4.2	1.2
1961	125.7	0.8	131.9	118.2	3.7	d	121.9	5.0	4.9
1962	126.3	0.8	137.0	118.4	5.5	0.9	124.8	4.3	7.8
1963	125.2	0.9	138.2	118.5	5.5	4.6	128.6	4.1	5.6
1964	127.0	0.8	137.5	119.9	5.7	6.7	132.3	4.3	1.0
1965	124.2	0.9	130.4	120.4	4.0	1.6	126.0	3.9	0.5
1966	119.9	2.8	127.1	121.1	1.1	0.1	122.3	4.8	d
1967	118.8	2.9	126.5	115.0	3.1	0.1	118.2	4.3	4.0
1968	117.2	1.8	127.3	114.5	5.2	0.9	120.6	4.0	2.7
1969	116.1	1.6	124.6	113.7	5.2	0.5	119.4	3.8	1.4
1970	117.0	1.9	124.2	113.5	4.9	d	118.4	3.7	2.1
1971	118.5	1.3	125.7	113.6	4.9	2.0	120.5	3.6	1.5
1972	119.9	1.7	126.7	115.9	4.4	0.9	121.2	3.5	2.0
1973	115.6	3.9	125.0	116.6	3.1	0.1	119.8	3.3	0.8

[a]Includes beginning commercial and government stocks.
[b]Includes donations and transfers to the military.
[c]Includes shipments to territories and exports under the Food for Peace Program.
[d]Less than 50 million pounds.

Table 6-17. Price Support Operations with Dairy Products, 1949–73

Year April-March	Manufacturing Milk			Butterfat			Product Purchase Price per Pound[b]			Product Purchases[f]				Net Government Expenditures on Price Support and Related Programs (in Million Dollars)[g]
	Support Level per Cwt.	Support Level as Percentage of Parity[a]	Average Price Received per Cwt.	Support Level per Pound	Support Level as Percentage of Parity[a]	Average Price Received per Pound	Butter[c]	Cheddar Cheese[d]	Nonfat Dry Milk, Spray Milk Processes[e]	Quantity (in Million Pounds)		Percentage of Milk and Cream Marketed by Farmers		
										Milkfat Content	Nonfat Solids Content	Milkfat Content	Nonfat Content	
1949[h]	$3.14	90%[i]	$3.14	58.5¢	90%	62.1¢	59.0¢[j]	31.75¢[k]	12.25¢[l]	102	321	2.7%	4.6%	$188
							62.0[k]		12.75[m]					
1950[n]	3.07	81	3.35	60.0	87	64.0	60.0	31.0	12.5	140	379	3.0	4.4	50
1951	3.60	86	3.97	67.6	89	74.1	66.0	36.0	15.0	1	69	...	1.0	9
1952	3.85	90	4.00	69.2	90	71.6	67.75	38.25	17.0	146	237	3.8	3.3	300
1953	3.74	89	3.46	67.3	90	65.7	65.75	37.0	16.0	431	775	10.6	9.8	474
1954	3.15	75	3.15	56.2	75	57.3	57.5	32.25	15.0	222	554	5.5	6.9	257
								33.25[o]	16.0[p]					
1955	3.15	80	3.19	56.2	76	57.7	57.5	33.25	15.15	198	630	4.7	7.5	284
1956	3.15	82	3.31	56.2	78	60.0	57.5	34.0	15.15	193	768	4.6	8.9	331
	3.25[q]	84		58.6[q]	81		59.5[q]	35.0[q]						
1957	3.25	82	3.28	58.6	79	60.3	59.5	35.0	15.15	260	949	6.1	10.8	360
1958	3.06	75	3.16	56.6	75	59.1	57.75	32.75	13.4	138	804	3.3	9.0	231
1959	3.06	77	3.22	56.6	77	60.7	57.854	32.75	13.4	131	839	3.1	9.3	218
							57.974[r]							
1960	3.06	76	3.30	56.6	76	61.1	57.974	32.75	13.4	130	805	3.0	8.7	281
	3.22[s]	80		59.6[s]	80		60.474[s]	34.25[s]	13.9[s]					
	3.40[t]	85		60.4[t]	82		60.466[u]	36.1[t]	15.9[t]					
1961	3.40	83	3.38	60.4	81	61.7	60.466	36.1	15.9	421	1,286	9.5	13.3	612
								36.5[v]	16.4[v]					
1962	3.11	75	3.19	57.2	75	59.1	57.966	34.6	14.4	333	1,272	7.5	13.1	486
1963	3.14	75	3.24	58.1	75	59.6	57.966	35.6	14.4	280	925	6.3	9.4	379
1964	3.15	75	3.29	58.0	75	60.4	57.966	35.6	14.4	239	775	5.4	7.7	334
1965	3.24	75	3.45	59.4	75	62.1	58.966	36.1	14.6	132	677	3.0	6.9	69
1966	3.50	78	4.11	61.6	75	68.6	60.966	39.3	16.6	102	418	2.5	4.3	317
	4.00[w]	89		68.0	83		66.466[w]	43.75[w]	19.6[w]					
1967	4.00	87	4.07	68.0	81	68.2	66.466	43.75	19.6	259	666	6.2	7.0	364
							66.413[x]		19.85[y]					

| | | | | | | | 69.71[dd] | | | | | |
							69.784[ee]					
1971	4.93	85	4.90	ff	69.5	67.784	54.75	31.7	252	489	6.0	5.0	338
1972	4.93	79	5.21	ff	68.2	67.708	54.75	31.7	208	283	4.9	2.9	153
1973	5.29	85	6.91	ff	67.2	60.900	62.0	37.5	28	53	0.7	0.6	71
	5.61[gg]	80										

[a] Percentage of the parity equivalent price for manufacturing milk and the parity price for butterfat as of the beginning of the marketing year.

[b] Announced purchase prices for products in bulk containers.

[c] U.S. Grade A or higher. Prices at all locations through March 31, 1953; at Chicago beginning April 1, 1953. Prices not announced for Chicago after March 31, 1959; thereafter, prices based on New York prices less 80 percent of the lowest rail freight rate from Chicago to New York.

[d] U.S. Grade A or higher, standard moisture basis.

[e] U.S. Extra Grade, not more than 3.5 percent moisture content. Prices quoted are for product in barrels and drums through November 3, 1954; 100-pound bags, November 4, 1955, through August 18, 1967; and 50-pound bags beginning August 19, 1967.

[f] Milkfat and nonfat solids content of butter, cheese, and nonfat dry milk purchased under price support and related programs. (Excludes purchases of fluid milk partly paid for by the CCC under the military and veterans' milk program. Includes purchases of butter and cheese in the 1966–67 marketing year and of cheese in the 1969–70, 1970–71, and 1971–72 marketing years for domestic school lunch and welfare programs under Section 709 of the Food and Agriculture Act of 1965. Beginning with the 1968–69 marketing year, includes evaporated milk, and beginning with the 1971–72 marketing year, dry whole milk purchased with Section 32 funds for distribution to needy persons.)

[g] Data are given on a fiscal year basis: Include net expenditures of the CCC, P.L. 480 and other export program costs, Section 32 expenditures, military milk program costs, and purchases to meet food program commitments in 1966–67 and 1969–70 through 1972–73.

[h] Calendar year.

[i] Based on parity equivalent published in March 1949.

[j] Effective February 8, 1949.

[k] Effective July 27, 1949.

[l] Effective April 18, 1949.

[m] Effective September 1, 1949.

[n] January 1, 1950, to March 31, 1951 (15 months).

[o] Effective July 12, 1954.

[p] Effective July 12, 1954; 15.15 cents effective for product in 100-pound bags beginning November 4, 1954.

[q] Effective April 18, 1956.

[r] Effective May 20, 1959.

[s] Effective September 17, 1960.

[t] Effective March 10, 1961.

[u] Effective October 24, 1960.

[v] Effective July 18, 1961.

[w] Effective June 30, 1966.

[x] Effective August 19, 1967.

[y] Effective for product in 50-pound bags beginning August 19, 1967.

[z] Effective June 24, 1968.

[aa] Effective November 28, 1968.

[bb] Effective November 19, 1969.

[cc] Effective June 9, 1970.

[dd] Effective November 20, 1970.

[ee] Effective January 10, 1971.

[ff] The requirement to support butterfat was suspended for three years by the Agricultural Act of 1970.

[gg] Effective August 10, 1973.

were largest from 1953 to 1965, peaking in 1961–62 when the equivalent of more than 10 percent of farmers' marketings was purchased by the government. Figure 6-11 shows the percentage of marketings purchased by the CCC in terms of milkfat and milk solids-not-fat.

Support levels for manufactured milk and butterfat were dropped to the legal minimum of 75 percent of parity in 1962 and held there for four years. Market prices fell accordingly as production continued to outstrip demand. Milk production reached an all-time high in 1964, then decreased sharply. Production of butter and nonfat dry milk declined markedly, resulting in decreased purchases of dairy products by the CCC in the 1965–66 marketing year.

The secretary of agriculture increased the support price for the 1966–67 marketing year. He also announced action to increase Class I prices for producers of fluid milk marketed under federal marketing orders. As a consequence of these actions, market prices rose. Commercial and farm use fell from 121.1 to 115.0 billion pounds from 1966 to 1967. The CCC stepped up purchases. For the rest of the decade, production and use leveled out, causing no notable changes in stocks or government purchases. (Since 1966, government purchases have been made to meet food program commitments when surpluses removed from the market under price support operations were inadequate.)

When, beginning in 1971, the requirement to support butterfat at a specific level was suspended, butter was made more competitive with vegetable fats. Since then butter purchases have been made as part of the price support program for manufactured milk or for food programs.

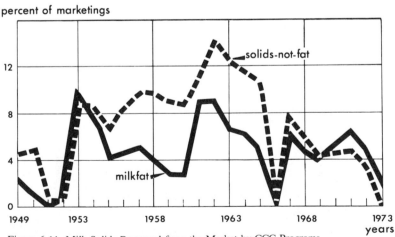

Figure 6-11. Milk Solids Removed from the Market by CCC Programs

Tobacco, Rice, Peanuts

Many features of government programs for these three commodity groups were similar to one another throughout the period from 1948 to 1973. All programs featured price support loans; various types of purchase programs were also used to support prices for rice and peanuts. Acreage allotments accompanied by marketing quotas were employed to control acreage for most years.

Tobacco. Production and marketing controls have kept tobacco supplies in line with demand at market prices above the loan rate during the 25-year period. Loan rates and market prices along with other data for burley and flue-cured tobacco are shown in tables 6-18 and 6-19 respectively. These two tobacco types account for about 90 percent of total tobacco production.[8]

From 1948 through 1964, production controls consisted of acreage allotments enforced by marketing quota penalties for both tobacco varieties. Because of the severity of penalties for noncompliance, virtually all tobacco growers in the U.S. participated in the tobacco program.

Since 1965 acreage-poundage quotas have applied to flue-cured tobacco. The national poundage requirement is determined and then apportioned to states. The state quota, in pounds, is converted to acreage and assigned to farms in acres and pounds. If marketings from a farm are less than its poundage quota, the difference is added to the farm's quota (both acres and pounds) for the following year.

The system of acreage allotments and marketing quotas was continued for burley tobacco until 1971 when legislation required poundage quotas for burley tobacco in lieu of acreage allotments. Acreage-poundage quotas had been authorized for burley since 1966 but had not been implemented because they were not approved in producer referendums.

The shift to poundage controls for both types of tobacco removed incentives to increase yields at the expense of tobacco quality. Yield increases encouraged by the acreage allotment means of controlling output were blamed for a deterioration in tobacco quality and a loss of export markets. In 1957, before the introduction of the poundage controls, low-quality flue-cured tobaccos were discounted; they were supported at one-half the level of better qualities. Discounts discouraged production of low-quality tobacco, but this method was recognized as only a stopgap solution to the quality problem.

Price support operations for tobacco are handled through producer associations. Tobacco farmers deal with their associations instead of directly with the government. The associations, under contract with the CCC, make payments to producers and process and store tobacco. These operations are financed by nonrecourse loans to the associations by the CCC through banks acting as servicing agents for the CCC. Over a period of time tobacco placed under loan

Table 6-18. Tobacco (Burley Type 31), Prices, Acreage, Production, Stocks, and Allotments, 1948–73

Crop Year (Oct.–Sept.)	National Average Loan Rate (per Pound)	Average Price to Growers (per Pound)	Acreage (in Thousands) Allotted	Acreage (in Thousands) Harvested	Production (in Million Pounds)	Stocks: End of Year Carryover (in Million Pounds)	Number (in Thousands) of Farms with Allotments
1948	42.4¢	46.0¢	463	432	603	974	281
1949	40.3	45.2	468	447	561	1,000	290
1950	45.7	49.0	418	408	499	980	298
1951	49.8	51.2	472	456	618	1,061	302
1952	49.5	50.3	475	464	650	1,163	308
1953	46.6	52.5	433	420	564	1,198	311
1954	46.4	49.8	399	421	668	1,347	317
1955	46.2	58.6	309	311	470	1,299	307
1956	48.1	63.6	309	310	506	1,295	301
1957	51.7	60.3	309	307	488	1,277	301
1958	55.4	66.1	309	297	466	1,224	302
1959	57.2	60.6	309	301	502	1,191	303
1960	57.2	64.3	309	296	485	1,127	302
1961	57.2	66.5	329	319	580	1,137	301
1962	57.8	58.6	349	339	645	1,228	301
1963	58.3	59.2	349	339	755	1,412	300
1964	58.9	60.3	316	307	620	1,416	299
1965	59.5	67.0	287	277	586	1,395	295
1966	60.6	66.9	250	241	587	1,382	295
1967	61.8	71.8	250	238	541	1,324	288
1968	63.5	73.7	250	238	563	1,316	285
1969	65.8	69.6	250	238	591	1,342	283
1970	68.6	72.2	231	216	561	1,346	282
1971	71.5	80.9	a	214	472	1,249	286
1972	74.9	79.2	a	236	601	1,229	289
1973	78.9	92.9	a	227	475	1,261	286

a No acreage allotments were specified for 1971–73; quotas were in pounds only.

Table 6-19. Tobacco (Flue-Cured Types 11–14), Prices, Acreage, Production, Stocks, and Allotments, 1948–73

Crop Year (July–June)	National Average Loan Rate (per Pound)	Average Price to Growers (per Pound)	Acreage (in Thousands) Allotted	Acreage (in Thousands) Harvested	Production (in Million Pounds)	Stocks: End of Year Carryover (in Million Pounds)	Number (in Thousands) of Farms with Allotments
1948	43.9¢	49.6¢	908	884	1,090	1,538	204
1949	42.5	47.2	959	935	1,114	1,484	207
1950	45.0	54.7	969	958	1,257	1,557	209
1951	50.7	52.4	1,119	1,110	1,453	1,731	212
1952	50.6	50.3	1,127	1,111	1,365	1,852	213
1953	47.9	52.8	1,045	1,022	1,272	1,915	214
1954	47.9	52.7	1,053	1,042	1,314	2,056	214
1955	48.9	52.7	1,007	991	1,483	2,258	213
1956	48.9	51.5	888	875	1,422	2,511	211
1957	50.8	55.4	711	663	975	2,308	211
1958	54.6	58.2	712	639	1,081	2,210	209
1959	55.5	58.3	713	693	1,081	2,106	207
1960	55.5	60.4	713	692	1,251	2,090	205
1961	55.5	64.3	714	699	1,258	2,081	203
1962	56.1	60.1	745	730	1,408	2,281	202
1963	56.6	58.0	708	695	1,371	2,386	201
1964	57.2	58.5	638	628	1,388	2,555	198
1965	57.7	64.6	607	562	1,059	2,439	193
1966	58.8	65.9	607	607	1,108	2,273	192
1967	59.9	64.2	607	610	1,250	2,302	194
1968	61.6	65.6	608	533	996	2,100	194
1969	63.8	72.4	608	577	1,053	1,973	194
1970	66.6	69.4	578	584	1,178	1,977	194
1971	69.4	77.2	578	526	1,077	1,910	193
1972	72.7	85.3	578	514	1,012	1,749	192
1973	76.6	87.0	636	575	1,157	1,607	193

by an association is marketed on the basis of prices proposed by the association and approved by the CCC.

Burley and flue-cured tobacco acreage allotments and harvested acreage trended downward throughout the study period. Production varied considerably from year to year, but the average level of output did not change. Support levels and farm prices are substantially higher at the end than at the beginning of the study period although prices have fluctuated considerably.

Rice. For 1948 and 1949 no acreage controls were imposed on rice production. Surpluses did not exist; market prices remained above loan rates. Loan rates and market prices along with other rice data appear in table 6-20.

Acreage allotments were declared for 1950 and 1951 as stocks began to mount. However, the surplus situation was short-lived because of the Korean War emergency. The 1951 allotment was terminated and no further acreage control measures were proclaimed until 1955. Since then acreage allotments accompanied by marketing quotas have been in effect each year. The national legal mimimum was set at 1,653,000 acres in 1956 and allotments were held at the legal minimum from 1956 through 1961.

Increasing market requirements allowed an increase in allotments later in the 1960s but a bumper crop from expanded acreage, in a year when exports contracted, led to a large carryover at the end of 1968. Allotments and plantings were reduced for 1969 and cut back further in 1970. Despite these acreage reductions, supplies outstripped demand resulting in small accretions to stocks each year.[9]

Market prices moved above the loan rate except in 1951 and 1954. A two-price plan for rice, authorized for the 1957 and 1958 crops, maintained high prices for domestic consumption but permitted rice to move into foreign markets at a lower price. Commercial exports were strengthened by this policy. Exports were further stimulated by export subsidies, which began in 1959, and by P.L. 480 programs. High world prices for rice precluded the need for export subsidies from mid-1967 until early in 1969. Because exports constitute a major market for U.S. rice production, the rice market is highly sensitive to export programs.

Peanuts. There have been no basic changes in peanut programs from 1948 through 1973. Price supports, acreage allotments, and marketing quotas have applied in all years except 1948. The size of the allotments was lowered during the first several years and has remained at the legal minimum since 1957. The price-support rate and the average farm price for peanuts have fluctuated within a narrow range throughout this time period. See table 6-21 for peanut data.

Prices are supported in two ways. One is through loans made to producer associations acting for farmers. Loans are also available to individuals but are used infrequently. The usual procedure is for growers to deliver peanuts to a

Crop Year (August–July)	National Average Loan Rate (per Cwt.)	Average Price Received by Farmers (per Cwt.)	Number of Allotments[a] (in Thousands)	Acreage (in Thousands) Allotted[a]	Acreage (in Thousands) Seeded	Production (in Million Cwt.)	Utilization (in Million Cwt.) Total[b]	Utilization (in Million Cwt.) Exports	Stocks: End of Year Carryover (in Million Cwt.) Total[c]	Stocks: End of Year Carryover (in Million Cwt.) Government Owned
1948	$4.08	$4.88			1,828	38.3	36.5	14.4	2.5	0.0
1949	3.96	4.10			1,885	40.8	39.7	16.2	3.5	0.5
1950	4.56	5.09	16	1,593	1,654	38.8	38.9	13.2	4.5	0.4
1951	5.00	4.82		1,868	2,033	46.1	48.2	24.1	2.0	0.2
1952	5.04	5.87			2,047	48.2	50.3	25.1	1.5	0.0
1953	4.84	5.19	18	1,928	2,210	52.8	48.0	22.7	7.5	0.9
1954	4.92	4.57			2,610	64.2	42.3	14.3	26.7	15.9
1955	4.66	4.81	17	1,928	1,851	55.9	47.8	18.7	35.5	27.1
1956	4.57	4.86	17	1,653	1,605	49.5	64.5	37.5	20.0	12.5
1957	4.72	5.11	17	1,653	1,372	42.9	44.6	18.3	18.2	12.0
1958	4.48	4.68	17	1,653	1,440	44.8	45.8	19.8	15.7	9.4
1959	4.38	4.59	17	1,653	1,608	53.6	57.2	29.2	12.1	6.8
1960	4.42	4.55	15	1,653	1,614	54.6	56.4	29.5	10.1	4.1
1961	4.71	5.14	15	1,653	1,618	54.2	58.7	29.1	5.3	0.3
1962	4.71	5.04	15	1,818	1,789	66.0	63.5	35.5	7.7	1.9
1963	4.71	5.01	14	1,818	1,785	70.3	70.6	41.8	7.5	1.4
1964	4.71	4.90	14	1,818	1,797	73.2	73.6	42.5	7.7	1.0
1965	4.50	4.93	14	1,819	1,804	76.2	74.2	43.3	8.2	0.6
1966	4.50	4.95	14	2,001	1,980	85.0	83.5	51.6	8.5	0.1
1967	4.50	4.97	13	2,001	1,982	89.4	90.5	56.9	6.8	0.1
1968	4.60	5.00	13	2,401	2,367	104.1	91.7	56.1	16.2	6.3
1969	4.72	4.95	13	2,161	2,141	91.9	90.0	56.9	16.4	8.3
1970	4.86	5.17	15	1,836	1,826	83.8	80.9	46.5	18.6	9.4
1971	5.07	5.34	14	1,836	1,826	85.8	92.3	56.9	11.4	2.7
1972	5.27	6.73	14	1,836	1,824	85.4	89.8	54.0	5.1	0
1973	6.07	14.10	14	2,020	2,181	92.8	86.4	49.7	7.8	[d]

[a] No acreage allotments were proclaimed in 1948–49, 1952–54; allotments were proclaimed but suspended in 1951.
[b] Includes exports.
[c] In all positions, includes government owned.
[d] Less than 50,000 cwt.

Table 6-21. Peanut Prices, Acreage, Production, and Stocks, 1948–73 (Farmers' Stock Basis)

| Crop Year | National Average Loan Rate (per Pound) | Average Price Received by Farmers (per Pound) | Number of Allotments (in Thousands) | Acreage (in thousands) | | Production (in Million Pounds) |
				Allotted	Harvested for Nuts	
1948	10.8¢	10.5¢	none	none	3,296	2,336
1949	10.5	10.4	170	2,629	2,308	1,865
1950	10.8	10.9	173	2,200	2,262	2,035
1951	11.5	10.4	160	1,889	1,982	1,659
1952	12.0	10.9	146	1,706	1,443	1,356
1953	11.9	11.1	138	1,679	1,515	1,574
1954	12.2	12.2	130	1,610	1,387	1,009
1955	12.2	11.7	119	1,731	1,669	1,548
1956	11.4	11.2	119	1,650	1,384	1,608
1957	11.1	10.4	116	1,611	1,481	1,436
1958	10.7	10.6	117	1,612	1,516	1,814
1959	9.7	9.6	118	1,612	1,435	1,523
1960	10.1	10.0	116	1,612	1,395	1,718
1961	11.1	10.9	111	1,612	1,398	1,657
1962	11.1	11.0	106	1,613	1,400	1,719
1963	11.2	11.2	98	1,612	1,396	1,942
1964	11.2	11.2	94	1,613	1,397	2,009
1965	11.2	11.4	92	1,613	1,435	2,384
1966	11.4	11.3	90	1,613	1,418	2,410
1967	11.4	11.4	89	1,613	1,402	2,473
1968	11.0	11.9	88	1,613	1,436	2,543
1969	12.4	12.3	87	1,612	1,451	2,588
1970	12.8	12.8	85	1,613	1,467	2,980
1971	13.4	13.6	84	1,613	1,454	3,005
1972	14.3	14.5	82	1,613	1,486	3,275
1973	16.4	16.2	81	1,613	1,496	3,474

Table 6-21. Peanut Prices, Acreage, Production, and Stocks, 1948–73 (Farmers' Stock Basis) (Cont.)

Crop Year	CCC Acquisitions[a] (in Million Pounds)	Utilization (in Million Pounds)			Stocks: End of Year Carryover (in Million Pounds)	
		Domestic Food Use	Crushing	Exports	Total[b]	CCC Owned
1948	1,167	961	473	725	84	0
1949	763	863	610	172	187	5
1950	835	981	629	69	332	7
1951	540	1,015	432	8	416	142
1952	106	1,008	195	3	422	92
1953	294	1,017	303	239	286	30
1954	. . .	1,019	107	9	209	c
1955	268	955	257	6	387	37
1956	334	1,029	260	102	456	151
1957	108	1,084	239	48	361	118
1958	383	1,096	335	62	514	196
1959	246	1,154	292	72	424	172
1960	299	1,244	362	81	368	103
1961	231	1,265	256	34	389	70
1962	331	1,293	302	43	397	105
1963	371	1,347	380	97	410	106
1964	512	1,411	473	179	373	64
1965	688	1,445	517	238	412	88
1966	701	1,420	587	222	372	114
1967	605	1,496	644	198	353	12
1968	581	1,539	654	105	357	c
1969	588	1,577	581	140	353	c
1970	1,062	1,583	799	290	453	11
1971	1,175	1,623	814	552	392	4
1972	1,178	1,694	850	521	429	24
1973	834	1,840	683	702	553	0

[a] From loan and purchase programs.
[b] In all positions, includes government owned.
[c] Less than 500,000 pounds.

247

warehouse having a storage contract with a grower cooperative association. The grower receives payment for his peanuts and the association is eligible for a CCC loan for the peanuts it holds.

In addition to loan operations, the CCC purchases peanuts and diverts them from food use as nuts to crushing into oil and meal or to exports. Prices in these markets have been about one-half the support price. The CCC absorbs the difference in a loss. The volume of CCC acquisitions is shown in table 6-21. In 1971 more than one-third of the crop was acquired by the CCC. Largely through the diversion program the CCC has prevented a buildup of peanut stocks.

The United States produces peanuts primarily for the domestic food market which commands higher prices than peanuts for crushing. The CCC price support rate is related to the value of peanuts for domestic food use. This maintains the U.S. price above the world price of peanuts. In other major producing countries peanuts are produced primarily for their oil and meal and hence prices average below those in the United States. For this reason the United States plays a relatively minor role in the international trade of peanuts for crushing into oil and meal.

Two alterations made in peanut programs had some impact on the peanut market. One was in 1950 and 1951 when producers were permitted to harvest peanuts from acreage in excess of their allotments without penalty if these peanuts were sold for crushing. Such production amounted to 65 and 194 million pounds respectively in 1950 and 1951. The other program change was quality regulations established in 1964 for peanuts marketed for food use. This was to increase the use of better grade peanuts for edible purposes. Under provisions of this program, the CCC offered to purchase peanuts not meeting specific quality standards and divert them to crushing. This program was terminated in 1973.

Other Commodities

Soybeans. Two government programs directly affect soybean production and marketing. One is price supports for soybeans; the other is P.L. 480 exports of soybean oil. Prices are supported by loans. The program is permissive. Beginning in 1956 the level of support for soybeans was linked to the cottonseed support rate so that both compete on equal terms in the market. Table 6-22 contains data on soybean prices, production, and stocks.

Soybeans differ from the previous commodities in that demand has matched supplies at or above the support rate in most years and the market has expanded steadily during the period under study. Over five times more soybeans were marketed in the 1970s than at the beginning of the 1950s. This contrasts with slower or almost no growth for markets of many other commodities. Much of the growth has come from demand for soybeans and soybean meal in

Crop Year[a]	National Average Loan Rate[b] (per Bushel)	Average Price Received by Farmers (per Bushel)	Millions of Acres Planted	Production (in Million Bushels)	Utilization[c] (in Million Bushels)		Stocks: End of Year Carryover (in Million Bushels)	
					Total	Exports	Total[d]	Government Owned
1948	$2.18	$2.27	12.6	227.2	226.7	23.0	3.2	0
1949	2.11	2.16	12.6	234.2	234.5	13.1	2.9	0
1950	2.06	2.47	15.6	299.2	298.0	27.8	4.2	0
1951	2.45	2.73	15.7	283.8	284.3	17.0	3.6	0
1952	2.56	2.72	16.4	298.8	292.3	31.9	10.2	2.0
1953	2.56	2.72	16.7	269.2	278.0	39.7	1.3	0
1954	2.22	2.46	18.9	341.1	332.5	60.6	9.9	6.6
1955	2.04	2.22	20.0	373.7	379.9	67.5	3.7	0
1956	2.15	2.18	22.0	449.3	443.1	85.4	9.9	5.2
1957	2.09	2.07	22.2	483.4	472.2	85.5	21.1	13.9
1958	2.09	2.00	25.3	580.3	539.2	110.1	62.1	44.2
1959	1.85	1.96	23.6	532.9	571.8	141.4	23.2	9.7
1960	1.85	2.13	24.6	555.1	572.0	130.1	6.0	0
1961	2.30	2.28	28.0	678.5	626.8	153.1	57.6	42.5
1962	2.25	2.34	28.6	669.2	711.9	180.3	15.1	1.6
1963	2.25	2.51	29.6	699.2	681.8	191.2	31.9	3.0
1964	2.25	2.62	31.8	700.9	735.5	205.9	29.7	0
1965	2.25	2.54	35.2	845.6	839.8	250.6	35.6	0
1966	2.50	2.75	37.3	928.5	874.0	261.6	90.1	7.3
1967	2.50	2.49	40.8	976.4	900.3	266.6	166.3	29.4
1968	2.50	2.43	42.3	1,107.0	946.5	286.8	326.8	171.4
1969	2.25	2.35	42.5	1,133.1	1,230.2	432.6	229.8	150.2
1970	2.25	2.85	43.1	1,127.1	1,258.1	433.8	98.8	2.5
1971	2.25	3.03	43.5	1,176.0	1,202.8	416.8	72.0	0
1972	2.25	4.37	46.9	1,270.6	1,283.0	479.4	59.6	0
1973	2.25	5.68	56.7	1,547.2	1,435.9	539.1	170.9	0

[a]October 1–September 30, 1948–64; September 1–August 31, 1965–73.
[b]Loan rate for no. 2 soybeans 1948–68, no. 1 soybeans 1969–73.
[c]Total includes exports; exports are beans only.
[d]Total, all positions, includes government owned.

foreign nations. In the 1970s, exports take one of every three bushels of soybeans produced and one of every four tons of soybean meal production.

The market price has remained above the loan level except in 1957, 1958, 1961, 1967, and 1968. Stocks accumulated in these years, with the government acquiring ownership of a substantial share of the carryover. These were years when production expansion exceeded growth in utilization.

Wool. Wool is a deficit commodity in the United States. We depend on imports to supplement domestic production. However, as may be seen in table 6-23, the share of the apparel wool market supplied by imports has declined from 1948 to 1973. For carpet wool we depend entirely on imports; all domestic wool is destined for apparel use.

Government programs protect domestic wool producers by supporting their incomes. From 1948 through 1954 incomes were supported by loan and purchase programs to support wool prices in the market. Since 1955 the government has given wool producers a direct payment to supplement incomes, permitting market prices to be determined by world supply and demand conditions (except that a duty is imposed on imports of foreign wool for apparel use).

The payment per pound is the difference between the market price received by wool producers and the support level; in 1972 these values were 35 cents and 72 cents respectively (see table 6-23). Because the market price was below the support level from 1955 to 1972, government payments were made each year. High market prices in 1973 obviated the need for payments.

Wool consumption has fallen off substantially since the early 1960s. The decline has been accompanied by downward trends in domestic production and imports. Only half the number of wool producers received payments in 1972 as in the 1950s.

Sugar. From 1948 through 1973 sugar was the most comprehensively controlled agricultural commodity in the United States. Close to one-half of the nation's supply was imported under strictly regulated import quotas and fixed prices. Likewise, domestic production was governed rigidly by production quotas and fixed prices. The domestic program also entailed income support payments to growers by the government.

From 1948 through 1973 the basic features of sugar programs remained the same.[10] These features are as follows:

1. *Setting U.S. sugar requirements.* The quantity of sugar needed to maintain adequate supplies for consumption and inventory needs at reasonable prices for U.S. consumers and to assure fair prices to U.S. producers was determined for each year.

2. *Establishing sugar quotas.* The yearly sugar requirement was divided

Year[a]	Support Level[b] (per Pound)	Average Price Received by Producers (per Pound)	Government Payments[c] (in Millions)	Number (in Thousands) of Producers Receiving Payments	Apparel Wool (in Million Pounds, Clean Content) Domestic Production	Imports
1948	42.3¢	49.2¢			136.9	246.2
1949	42.3	49.4			120.4	154.9
1950	45.2	62.1			119.8	250.1
1951	50.7	97.1			119.8	272.0
1952	54.2	54.1			127.9	248.4
1953	53.1	54.9			133.8	165.7
1954	53.2	53.2			136.4	103.9
1955	62.0	42.8	$57.6	d	137.4	112.8
1956	62.0	44.3	51.9	d	136.9	103.8
1957	62.0	53.7	16.1	d	130.4	78.2
1958	62.0	36.4	85.1	292.9	130.0	67.1
1959	62.0	43.3	53.9	275.2	140.2	100.5
1960	62.0	42.0	59.5	d	144.6	74.3
1961	62.0	42.9	56.9	d	142.5	90.3
1962	62.0	47.7	39.2	248.1	133.4	125.8
1963	62.0	48.5	27.2	d	126.2	109.2
1964	62.0	53.2	20.3	d	119.6	98.4
1965	62.0	47.1	34.2	d	113.1	162.6
1966	65.0	52.1	26.2	180.6	110.6	162.5
1967	66.0	39.8	57.7	177.4	106.4	109.1
1968	67.0	40.5	54.4	174.8	99.7	129.8
1969	69.0	41.8	50.6	163.9	91.5	93.5
1970	72.0	35.5	64.0	151.6	88.2	79.8
1971	72.0	19.4	102.3	143.6	85.1	42.7
1972	72.0	35.0	67.6	145.6	81.6	24.8
1973	72.0	82.7	0	0	74.7	19.2

[a] Calendar year for 1948–54 and 1964–73; marketing year (April 1–March 31) for 1955–63.
[b] Beginning in 1955 the support level was used only to compute payments; it did not support the market price as in earlier years.
[c] Includes payments for pulled wool which are made at a rate comparable to shorn wool. Less than 20 percent of the payments are for pulled wool.
[d] Figures are not available.

among specified domestic and foreign producing areas through quotas assigned to each.

3. *Providing marketing allotments.* Within domestic quotas, allotments were established for domestic processors when needed to prevent marketings in excess of quotas.

4. *Setting farm proportionate shares.* Domestic farm production was limited to the acreage required for meeting domestic quotas if the secretary of agriculture determined that without restrictions sugar production would have exceeded the area quota. Allotments were divided between beet- and cane-growing areas and then apportioned to individual growers. Domestic quotas were allocated on the basis of history and other factors.

5. *Making grower payments.* Payments were made to domestic growers to augment farm income and as a means of compensating them for adjusting their production, not employing child labor, paying fair wages, and paying fair prices for sugar crops bought from other growers. Payments to growers were financed from the general funds of the treasury. However, sugar taxes (an excise tax of one-half cent per pound, raw value basis, on all sugar marketed within the quota system) frequently exceeded total payments by $15 million to $20 million annually.

6. *Obtaining equitable division of sugar returns.* Provisions were included to assure an equitable division of returns from sugar among beet and cane growers, farm workers, and sugar processors in the domestic producing areas.

Import quotas have been revised from time to time to reflect changes in U.S. foreign policy. The most momentous change occurred in the early 1960s when the quota for Cuba was suspended. Previously Cuba had supplied almost three-fourths of U.S. import requirements. The Cuban quota is now reallocated to other foreign suppliers.

About one-third of the annual increase in sugar marketings since 1948 has come from imports and about two-thirds from domestic areas. See table 6-24 for the sources of sugar for the United States, 1948–73. The largest increase in tonnage has been supplied by the domestic beet sugar industry but the largest percentage increase has come from the mainland sugar cane area. Most of the increase in the mainland cane area has been in Florida.

Acreage expansion occurred in both cane and beet areas (see table 6-25), but the number of growers, as suggested by the number receiving Sugar Act payments, declined. Payments per ton were slightly lower in the 1970s than at the beginning of the period, while market prices advanced — especially prices received by cane growers. Growers' returns consisted of the market price plus the government payment.

One objective of the sugar program was to stabilize U.S. sugar prices.

Table 6-24. Sources of Sugar (in Thousand Tons, Raw Value) for the United States, 1948–73

Calendar Year	Mainland		Hawaii	Puerto Rico	Virgin Islands	Philippines	Cuba	Other Foreign Countries	Total
	Beet	Cane							
1948	1,656	456	714	1,013	4	252	2,927	62	7,084
1949	1,487	557	769	1,091	4	525	3,103	52	7,588
1950	1,749	522	1,145	1,053	11	474	3,264	61	8,279
1951	1,730	457	941	959	6	706	2,946	13	7,758
1952	1,560	579	972	983	6	860	2,980	51	7,991
1953	1,749	513	1,087	1,118	12	932	2,760	111	8,282
1954	1,802	501	1,040	1,082	10	974	2,718	113	8,240
1955	1,797	500	1,052	1,080	10	977	2,862	118	8,396
1956	1,955	601	1,091	1,135	13	982	3,089	126	8,992
1957	2,066	636	1,037	912	15	906	3,127	217	8,916
1958	2,240	680	630	823	6	980	3,438	279	9,076
1959	2,241	578	977	958	12	980	3,215	279	9,240
1960	2,165	619	845	896	7	1,155	2,390	1,445	9,522
1961	2,608	774	1,045	980	16	1,356	0	2,953	9,732
1962	2,415	780	1,084	904	11	1,257	0	3,341	9,792
1963	2,966	1,065	1,033	876	16	1,196	0	3,363	10,515
1964	2,699	911	1,110	792	16	1,174	0	2,407	9,109
1965	3,025	1,100	1,137	829	4	1,178	0	2,647	9,920
1966	3,024	1,100	1,202	712	5	1,190	0	3,122	10,355
1967	2,824	1,169	1,250	705	0	1,122	0	3,314	10,384
1968	3,085	1,204	1,192	504	0	1,124	0	3,842	10,951
1969	3,216	1,169	1,160	341	0	1,124	0	3,725	10,735
1970	3,569	1,308	1,145	352	0	1,298	0	3,879	11,551
1971	3,438	1,255	1,087	143	0	1,592	0	3,779	11,294
1972	3,511	1,630	1,113	148	0	1,432	0	4,006	11,840
1973	3,512	1,613	1,142	76	0	1,454	0	3,879	11,676

Table 6-25. Sugar Prices, Acreage, and Payments, 1948–73

| | Sugar Beets | | Sugar Cane | | Acres Harvested (in Thousands) | | Sugar Act Payments | | | |
| | | | | | | | Number of Payees (in Thousands) | | Total Payments (in Millions) | |
Year	Price Received by Farmers (per Ton)	Sugar Act Payment (per Ton)	Price Received by Farmers (per Ton)	Sugar Act Payment (per Ton)	Beets	Cane, for Sugar[a]	Beet	Cane[b]	Beet	Cane[b]
1948	$10.57	$2.41	$5.76	$1.11	694	409	45.8	27.1	$23.2	$32.6
1949	10.82	2.47	6.25	1.13	687	424	45.7	27.8	26.6	33.1
1950	11.18	2.41	7.80	1.20	925	420	55.0	27.9	33.7	33.6
1951	11.69	2.40	6.37	1.01	691	406	41.4	29.3	25.9	34.6
1952	11.99	2.35	6.96	1.11	665	426	36.4	30.2	24.7	34.5
1953	11.62	2.34	7.25	1.19	745	433	38.2	29.2	30.0	35.6
1954	10.80	2.31	6.95	1.17	876	393	43.5	28.6	33.2	34.3
1955	11.16	2.31	6.51	1.11	740	373	38.8	27.7	29.1	34.2
1956	11.94	2.34	8.04	1.22	785	341	38.4	26.5	31.3	32.4
1957	11.22	2.29	6.90	1.13	878	365	39.6	24.8	36.4	31.0
1958	11.74	2.31	7.48	1.19	891	338	40.6	23.2	36.2	29.8
1959	11.24	2.30	7.13	1.11	905	407	40.8	22.1	38.9	31.6
1960	11.58	2.31	7.41	1.13	957	408	39.1	21.0	39.3	32.0
1961	11.16	2.26	7.71	1.19	1,077	441	39.9	20.1	42.4	34.7
1962	12.78	2.25	8.40	1.11	1,103	477	38.0	19.1	43.2	34.9
1963	12.22	2.20	10.20	1.15	1,235	543	37.9	18.3	52.3	38.5
1964	11.79	2.20	6.93	1.01	1,395	656	40.0	17.6	53.9	37.8
1965	11.95	2.18	7.90	1.12	1,248	583	36.6	16.6	46.7	36.5
1966	12.80	2.16	8.49	1.11	1,161	590	32.4	15.2	45.5	36.2
1967	13.55	2.17	9.38	1.16	1,122	596	30.5	13.9	43.9	37.1
1968	13.81	2.16	9.29	1.16	1,410	577	31.9	12.5	56.8	32.5
1969	12.72	2.02	9.94	1.18	1,541	503	32.5	11.4	60.4	29.6
1970	14.84	2.07	10.50	1.17	1,413	551	29.0	9.9	54.2	29.6
1971	15.50	2.05	11.11	1.15	1,325	607	26.9	9.3	56.2	29.5
1972	16.00	2.03	11.70	1.04	1,335	664	25.8	9.3	57.9	31.8
1973	18.00	2.12	14.80	1.08	1,241	710	26.0	8.8	52.1	34.0

[a] Includes Hawaii.
[b] Includes Hawaii, Puerto Rico, and the Virgin Islands.

Table 6-26 indicates how well this objective has been attained, by comparing sugar prices in the United States and world sugar prices. World prices do display considerably more variability than prices in New York. Domestic prices were stabilized by holding them above world prices, thus creating an attractive market for foreign sugar suppliers who had access to the market.

Table 6-26. Trends in Raw Sugar Prices in the United States
and "World" Sugar Markets, 1948–73

Year	Price per Pound in New York[a]	Adjusted Price per Pound in "World" Market[b]
1948	5.54¢	5.13¢
1949	5.81	5.03
1950	5.93	5.82
1951	6.06	6.66
1952	6.26	5.08
1953	6.29	4.27
1954	6.09	4.14
1955	5.95	4.19
1956	6.09	4.47
1957	6.24	6.10
1958	6.27	4.36
1959	6.24	3.86
1960	6.30	4.09
1961	6.30	3.85
1962	6.45	3.87
1963	8.18	9.41
1964	6.90	6.79
1965	6.75	3.07
1966	6.99	2.81
1967	7.28	2.95
1968	7.52	2.96
1969	7.75	3.37
1970	8.07	3.75
1971	8.52	4.52
1972	9.09	7.43
1973	10.29	9.61

[a] Spot prices in New York.
[b] Spot prices in Cuba or, since 1961, greater Caribbean ports adjusted to New York delivery basis.

CHAPTER 7

Program Operations: Land Retirement, Exports, and Food

Some programs or price and income support cut across commodity lines. Among these are conservation and land retirement programs, intended to curtail aggregate farm output, and export, food, and Section 32 programs, designed to expand demand for food and other agricultural products. The impact of these programs on farm prices and income is less direct than that of commodity programs, but curtailing supply and expanding demand had indirect effects both real and important in 1948–73. Moreover, the costs of these programs were substantial, as the next chapter reveals.

Most of these programs had dual goals. Export and domestic food programs aided farmers while assisting needy consumers in the United States and in other parts of the world. Similarly, conservation and land retirement programs offered opportunities to improve the nation's land resources, preserving this resource for future generations, and to develop recreational and wildlife facilities on former farm land. As these programs evolved through time, often the initial primary goal, economic assistance to farmers, receded and the secondary goals emerged as prime justifications for continuing and expanding the programs. The discussion that follows treats the form and scope of these programs in the 1948–73 period.

Conservation and Land Retirement Programs

Programs described here are those authorized and operated in conjunction with commodity programs. Their primary purposes were to reduce agricultural surpluses by removing land from production for varying periods of time. Besides these, there are other government programs concerned with land and water use, such as the Soil Conservation Service administered by the

256

Department of Agriculture. Although such programs have an impact on agricultural output, they are beyond the scope of this work because their principal goals and operating guidelines do not deal with farm prices and incomes.

Agricultural Conservation Program

The Agricultural Conservation Program (ACP), operating until 1971, was designed to (1) restore and improve soil fertility, (2) minimize erosion caused by wind and water, and (3) conserve water on the land. The ACP was renamed the Rural Environmental Assistance Program (REAP) in 1971, when program goals and projects were redesigned to emphasize pollution prevention and environmental improvement. A further reorganization for 1974 transferred some features of REAP to the Rural Environmental Conservation Program (RECP)

Both ACP and REAP paid farmers for part of their costs in soil-building, soil- and water-conserving, and environmental improvement practices, including development of wildlife habitats, that would not have been carried out by farmers alone. About half the costs for approved activities were borne by ACP/REAP. The government share was in the form of cash, materials, and services. Technical advice was made available by arrangements with the Soil Conservation Service, U.S. Forest Service, state foresters, county agricultural agents, and others.

Funding ranged from $124 million to $252 million annually (see table 7-1). Funds for the 1973 program were withheld by the administration in December 1972; they were released in April 1974, following a court decision reversing the impounding action. The estimated number of acres served did not fluctuate greatly during the study period, though some reduction occurred in the 1970s corresponding to somewhat lower funding levels. The number of farms served fell sharply. The decline was even greater than the reduction in all farms. In 1948 ACP served 40 percent of all farms, compared with only 24 percent in 1972.[1]

Soil Bank Program

The Soil Bank program was instituted in 1956 to reduce agricultural production by shifting land from crop production to conservation uses. It consisted of two parts — the acreage reserve and the conservation reserve.

Acreage reserve. The acreage reserve was designed to reduce production of wheat, corn, cotton, rice, tobacco, and peanuts while maintaining producers' incomes. These were the "allotment crops," those subject to acreage restrictions at the time the Soil Bank program went into effect. The acreage reserve was an annual program applying for three years, from 1956 to 1958. It was authorized for 1959 but no funds were appropriated. It was not renewed when the authority terminated. Farmers who participated agreed to take land out of production in return for a land-rental payment from the government. The payments were at least equal to the net income farmers would have earned from production on the acres put into the reserve. The per-acre rate varied considerably among parts of the country because of differences in land productivity, methods of farming, and other conditions. The national average payment rates under the program, the number of acres and contracts involved, and the funds obligated are shown in table 7-2.

Under the acreage reserve, producers entered into formal contracts with the

Table 7-1. Agricultural Conservation Program, 1948–70,
and Rural Environmental Assistance Program, 1971–73

Year (Calendar)	Number of Participating Farms (in Thousands)	Gross Assistance (in Thousands)	Approximate Acres Served[a] (in Millions)
1948	2,296	$124,257	28.2
1949	2,587	223,573	50.8
1950	2,577	251,592	57.1
1951	2,357	245,623	55.8
1952	2,285	214,918	48.8
1953	2,013	184,986	42.0
1954	1,069	138,857	31.5
1955	1,119	186,811	42.4
1956	1,185	213,878	48.6
1957	1,160	214,635	48.7
1958	1,079	215,337	48.9
1959	1,004	208,566	47.3
1960	1,029	212,565	48.3
1961	1,205	229,072	48.9
1962	1,187	218,477	50.0
1963	1,128	213,622	51.0
1964	1,080	214,476	52.0
1965	1,099	216,488	52.1
1966	1,017	210,603	52.7
1967	987	221,684	45.5
1968	951	199,787	46.6
1969	871	185,577	40.7
1970	829	180,893	41.5
1971	611	146,329	33.7
1972	678	196,382	40.7
1973[b]	391	195,593	23.6

[a] Estimated by ASCS.

[b] The 1973 program operated during the calendar year 1974 concurrently. with the 1974 program because funds were withheld in 1973 (see the text).

Table 7-2. Acreage Reserve Program of the Soil Bank, 1956–58

Crop Year	Wheat	Corn	Cotton	Rice	Tobacco	Peanuts[a]	Total
	Acres Placed in the Program (in Thousands)						
1956..........	5,670	5,316	1,121	28	33	44	12,212
1957..........	12,783	5,233	3,016	242	80		21,354
1958..........	5,289	6,658	4,926	174	111		17,158
	Number of Contracts (in Thousands)						
1956..........	111	315	96	1	20	5	548
1957..........	233	324	301	5	52		914
1958..........	174	356	444	6	69		1,049
	National Average Payment Rates Offered[b]						
Per unit of output..........	$1.20 bu.	$0.90 bu.	$0.15 lb.	$2.25 cwt.	$0.18 lb.[c]	$0.03 lb.	
Per acre							
1956..........	$19.80	$40.05	$45.00	$59.22	$255.42	$27.00	
1957..........	20.04	42.66	54.15	63.18	255.42		
1958..........	20.88	44.46	d	d	d		
	Total Funds Obligated (in Millions)						
1956..........	$ 44.7	$179.7	$ 27.3	$ 1.4	$ 6.6	$0.6	$260.4
1957..........	230.9	196.4	153.3	15.5	17.8		613.8
1958..........	105.1	282.3	270.2	11.9	26.5		696.0

[a]Peanuts were not in the 1957 and 1958 programs.
[b]Actual payment rates paid differ slightly because of the quality of land placed in the program. Increases in acreage rates for 1957 and 1958 reflect increases in yield per acre.
[c]Rates for flue-cured tobacco.
[d]Not available.

259

government for reducing the acreage of allotment crops by a specified amount. Producers agreed neither to harvest nor to graze any other crops on the acreage withdrawn from the allotment crops; however, if emergency conditions prevailed, the secretary of agriculture was authorized to allow grazing. Contracts were for one year only. In 1956 and 1957 there were no restrictions on the use of the remaining land on farms if only part of the cropland was placed in the acreage reserve. Thus, acreages of other crops could be increased. But in 1958 farmers who took part were required to reduce their total acreage of harvested crops by the number of acres they placed in the program. This provision had the largest impact in the wheat-growing area where summer fallow land qualified for the acreage reserve in 1956 and 1957. Notice the reduction in wheat acreage participation for 1958 in table 7-2. Other changes made in 1958 set a payment limit at $3,000 per farm and permitted entire allotments to be placed in the reserve. Previously the farm limit was less than the total allotment for a crop. Under these provisions entire allotments on many small farms were placed in the reserve.

Conservation reserve. The conservation reserve was a long-term program designed to retire general cropland from production and to help conserve soil, water, trees, and wildlife. Producers of all crops were eligible to participate in the conservation reserve. Land retirement contracts were entered into between 1956 and 1960; they were issued for three to 10 years depending upon the land use, except that contracts for tree cover could extend for 15 years. The last contracts expired in 1972. If the land already had suitable cover, contracts could be for three years, otherwise longer contracts were required. When trees were planted for cover, the minimum contract was 10 years. All land used regularly for cultivated crops or tame hay was eligible for the conservation reserve.

Farmers received two kinds of payments: annual per-acre rental payments for each year of the contract and cost-sharing payments for carrying out conservation measures in the year such measures were undertaken. Payments were allowed (1) for establishing cover, (2) for planting trees, (3) for dam and pond construction to protect cover crops or to store water, and (4) for protecting wildlife through cover, shallow flooding of cropland, or marsh management.

The average per-acre payment rate was low; hence relatively productive land was not placed in the reserve. Payments, acreage, and the number of contracts involved are listed in table 7-3. Although up to $450 million was authorized annually for payments to farmers, actual payments were much less than this amount. The type of land placed in the reserve is shown in table 7-4. About one-third of the retired land was formerly planted to hay or minor crops.

Table 7-3. Conservation Reserve Program of the Soil Bank, 1956–72

Year (Calendar)	No. of Contracts in Effect	Acreage in Program (in Thousands)	Average Rental Rate Paid (per Acre)	Total Payments (in Millions)
1956	16,327	1,429	$ 8.68	$ 12.4
1957	79,791	6,427	8.84	56.8
1958	125,502	9,887	8.87	87.7
1959	245,937	22,464	11.48	257.8
1960	306,186	28,661	11.85	339.6
1961	303,413	28,512	11.85	338.0
1962	271,240	25,805	12.06	311.2
1963	251,572	24,256	12.19	295.7
1964	167,064	17,437	11.48	200.1
1965	125,511	13,980	11.00	153.8
1966	123,397	13,316	11.07	147.4
1967	107,395	10,980	11.49	126.1
1968	89,886	9,243	11.95	110.5
1969	35,658	3,397	11.82	40.1
1970	1,896	75	11.36	0.9
1971	195	8	10.83	0.1
1972	7	1	11.75	a

a$8,271.

Table 7-4. Estimated Composition of Cropland Placed under
Conservation Reserve Contracts of the Soil Bank, 1956–60

Crop	Acreage under Agreement (in Thousands)	Portion of Total
Food grains		
Wheat	3,183	11.1%
Rice	7	a
Rye	886	3.1
Feed grains		
Corn	3,662	12.8
Barley	1,368	4.8
Grain sorghum	3,964	13.8
Oats	3,956	13.8
Oilseeds		
Soybeans	1,078	3.8
Peanuts	132	.5
Other		
Cotton	683	2.4
Tobacco	11	a
Potatoes	35	.1
Hay and miscellaneous	9,696	33.8
Total	28,661	100.0%

aLess than .05 percent.

Payment limitations of $5,000 per farm were imposed in 1958. In 1959, when the acreage reserve program was discontinued, two major changes were made in program provisions for the conservation reserve in order to encourage placement of relatively high-yielding land in the conservation reserve and to make participation of whole farm units more attractive. These changes were an increase of 35 percent in the national basic rental rate and a bonus to farm owners who agreed to enroll all eligible land on their farms in the program for a minimum of five years. The impact of these changes is reflected by the data in table 7-3, showing higher levels of participation and payments.

About 70 percent of all the cropland in the conservation reserve was whole farm units. This type of contract removed the entire production potential of a farm and left no land for more intensive cultivation. Under this program the farmer could continue to live on the farm, plant a garden, and use permanent pasture and orchard land.

Estimated conservation achievements during the entire life of the conservation reserve are as shown in the accompanying tabulation.

	Acres
Permanent vegetation	18,439,000
Tree cover	2,155,000
Wildlife cover	311,000
Dams and ponds (6,603 structures)	14,000
Marsh management	10,000

Cropland Conversion Program

The Cropland Conversion Program (CCP) was a pilot program designed to shift land from surplus crops to conservation and recreation uses on a long-term basis. It was authorized in 1962, two years after the last land retirement contracts were extended under the conservation reserve. Farmers were offered agreements from 1963 to 1967; all agreements expired by 1975. Annual expenditures were limited to $10 million. As a pilot program, the CCP was to test the feasibility and effectiveness of various long-term transfers of land from farming to other uses.

In total there were 10,592 farms with CCP agreements, covering 608,000 acres. Funds obligated totaled $29.2 million.

Cropland Adjustment Program

On the basis of CCP and conservation reserve experience, the Cropland Adjustment Program (CAP) was developed. It included long-term land retirement under the regular CAP and a new approach, called the Greenspan Program. The latter program provided funds to federal agencies and local governments for purchasing cropland for permanent conservation or recreation use. Because the Greenspan Program established open space, it was advanced as a benefit for urban dwellers as well as for farmers.

The CAP was authorized in 1965. Farmers were offered agreements during 1966 and 1967 for periods up to 10 years, with the last agreements expiring in 1976. The regular CAP was aimed at land used for growing crops in surplus supply. The government paid farmers for each acre diverted from crops and for part of the cost of establishing protective conservation cover. Additional payments were offered if the land was opened for public use without charge for hunting, trapping, fishing, and hiking.

Under the CAP (excluding Greenspan) agreements were made with 67,000 farms applying to 4 million acres. These agreements obligated the government to pay $707 million. The Greenspan Program required another $1 million for 8,000 acres, committed under 139 agreements.

Although authority existed to offer long-term land retirement programs, no new agreements were entered into from 1967 to 1973.

Section 32

Under the authority known as Section 32, 30 percent of all U.S. customs receipts is allocated to the secretary of agriculture for three purposes: (1) encouragement of exports; (2) encouragement of domestic consumption of agricultural products; and (3) reestablishment of farmers' purchasing power. This broad authority has permitted a wide range of programs financed with Section 32 funds, including purchases of surplus commodities for donation to domestic food programs, payments to exporters to permit sales of designated commodities in certain markets at competitive world prices, financial assistance to federal and local government agencies for developing and carrying out domestic food programs, and payments to producers to divert products to new or different uses or to protect producers' incomes in certain emergency situations. These four types of programs were authorized throughout the 1948–73 period although not all programs were operated in every year. Annual programs were designed to fit the marketing conditions prevailing for the various commodities.

The chief usage of Section 32 funds has been to purchase commodities when heavy supplies depress or threaten to depress market prices. In most cases, purchases are limited to quantities which have immediate outlets; commodities are seldom stored and none can be resold. Legislation specified that funds were to be used principally for perishable commodities not covered by mandatory price support legislation. Hence most expenditures have been for fruits, vegetables, and livestock products (see table 7-5), with dairy products the main exception. Substantial amounts of Section 32 funds have been

Table 7-5. Section 32 Expenditures by Commodity Group, for Purchase, Diversion, and Export Programs, 1948–73 (in Millions)

Year (Fiscal)	Fruits	Vegetables	Nuts	Potatoes	Eggs	Poultry and Turkey	Meat	Lard	Dairy	Other[a]	Total
1948	$19.5	$0.2	$1.1	$20.9	$19.7	0	0	0	0	$11.9	$73.3
1949	10.1	0.2	10.2	11.0	13.9	0	0	0	$1.8	6.1	53.3
1950	28.5	0.3	7.8	5.0	9.6	$3.6	0	0	15.5	3.2	73.5
1951	22.8	b	0.9	0.1	2.6	2.5	0	0	0	8.6	37.5
1952	25.1	b	2.4	0	3.7	0	$12.2	0	4.2	3.6	51.2
1953	13.6	0	1.0	0	0	26.7	1.4	0	21.8	4.0	68.6
1954	9.4	1.2	0.4	1.8	0	0	83.9	0	87.1	15.9	199.7
1955	4.5	8.8	0.1	0.2	0	0	0.4	0	0.4	13.9	28.3
1956	4.3	5.1	0	4.3	0	0	95.3	$6.0	78.3	20.3	213.6
1957	1.5	2.3	0	5.0	16.0	10.3	29.4	4.0	54.7	12.4	135.6
1958	1.2	b	0.9	2.4	0.1	0	0	0	121.7	0	126.3
1959	0.1	0.1	1.4	7.5	6.4	0	0	0	101.1	0.1	116.7
1960	7.8	0	2.3	0.2	17.5	6.5	0	8.0	51.2	11.2	104.7
1961	1.1	1.9	12.6	1.2	37.4	0.2	61.6	16.6	116.3	4.0	252.9
1962	1.5	6.2	7.9	10.6	13.5	17.7	65.8	16.2	0.9	3.2	143.5
1963	3.7	0	3.0	2.7	9.9	14.5	53.3	5.7	0	3.3	96.1
1964	3.1	4.7	12.4	1.3	12.3	14.8	108.0	14.9	85.0	3.0	259.5
1965	4.3	2.2	12.6	0	5.2	0	157.0	13.9	25.0	7.0	227.2
1966	10.9	2.2	13.1	0.3	b	9.3	22.3	0.4	39.6	18.4	116.5
1967	38.0	5.3	6.4	0	b	4.3	93.9	18.8	0	7.6	174.3
1968	11.5	12.6	10.9	11.2	17.2	27.4	58.0	9.2	9.1	1.0	168.1
1969	17.4	23.4	14.9	6.8	18.0	37.8	82.3	13.7	120.9	1.0	336.2
1970	37.8	27.6	15.3	10.4	14.6	56.7	72.7	3.5	103.8	b	342.4
1971	33.5	21.5	15.9	7.6	12.1	43.5	99.1	2.7	63.8	0.7	300.4
1972	39.5	23.0	0.1	10.6	24.1	59.2	99.7	1.3	16.1	b	273.6
1973	24.6	25.1	16.4	4.3	1.8	77.9	14.2	1.8	16.0	b	182.1

[a] Includes honey, grains and flour, vegetable oil and oilseeds (except peanuts which are in the nut category), cotton, and tobacco.
[b] Less than $500,000.

264

spent for purchasing milk, cheese, and butter, though these purchases constitute only about 15 percent of total government purchases of dairy products. The remainder were made under regular price support authority for dairy products discussed in chapter 6.

Purchases under price support authority were often undertaken in conjunction with purchases under Section 32. For instance, if a commodity was subject to seasonal variation in production, as well as an overall surplus, price support purchases could be made to even out the seasonal variation by storing the commodity and returning it to the market when production was low, while Section 32 purchases would permanently remove a portion of the output from the market.

Section 32 purchases were distributed to children and needy families through the commodity distribution program and the school lunch and other child nutrition programs. In 1972, 36 percent of foods donated through the school lunch program were Section 32 commodities.

A second Section 32 program subsidized exports of surplus commodities. From 1948 through 1973 about $150 million was paid to exporters to permit sales of U.S. commodities abroad when U.S. prices were above world prices. Payments were authorized for designated commodities to specific destinations for a limited time period. In the late 1960s and early 1970s payments were made for lard and chickens exported to Western Europe to "recapture" traditional markets. In earlier years programs were instituted for tobacco, cotton, wheat, fruits, and other commodities when surpluses occurred. Export payments are included in the values in table 7-5.

Another program to expand demand for agricultural production channeled financial assistance into a variety of domestic food programs. During the early years of the school lunch program Section 32 funds were used to make cash grants to help finance local purchases of food. Similarly the food stamp program was inaugurated under this authority until a separate appropriation was authorized. And in the 1970s a pilot project was begun providing supplemental food to expectant mothers and infants paid for with Section 32 funds. Cash assistance for child nutrition programs from Section 32 swelled dramatically after 1969. In that year $45 million was spent compared with over $500 million in 1973. These expenditures are not included in table 7-5 because no breakdown by commodity is available.

Two different types of payments to producers have been made with Section 32 moneys. In the early 1960s payments were made to cranberry growers to offset losses entailed when sales were stopped after improper use of an agricultural chemical. This was the only example of a "payment to reestablish farmers' purchasing power" during the study period. Other programs were operated to compensate producers of surplus commodities who sold their output in secondary markets. These programs were called diversion programs because surplus commodities were diverted from normal markets to other uses. Large-scale diversion programs for potatoes were carried out in several years. Potatoes were sold for animal feed at a lower price than potatoes for food. The government paid the difference to producers to protect their incomes while preventing a glut in the potato market. Approximately $50 million was spent on all diversion programs from 1948 through 1973. These expenditures are shown in table 7-5.

Export Programs

The federal government engaged in several export programs to expand demand for U.S. agricultural output. These programs enhanced commercial sales by providing subsidies when the prices of supported commodities in the United States were above world levels, short- and long-term credit to facilitate financial arrangements between U.S. firms and foreign firms or governments, and barter agreements whereby foreign nations obtained U.S. goods without the outlay of money. Under other programs friendly foreign nations received food donations and purchased U.S. agricultural products with their own currencies. These latter were chiefly foreign food aid programs serving foreign policy goals as well as providing outlets for American farm products.

To consider government export programs, we divide the post–World War II years into two periods: the years before and after enactment of the Agricultural Trade Development and Assistance Act of 1954, commonly known as P.L. 480. This law expanded and consolidated under one authority an array of surplus disposal and foreign aid programs that had evolved to help meet food needs abroad and deal with food surpluses at home. There were very few new program features embodied in P.L. 480 but its enactment marked a turning point in government export policies and programs, especially those dealing with concessional or noncommercial shipments. Before P.L. 480, foreign food aid programs were viewed as emergency measures principally to ameliorate critical food shortages and to assist post–World War II reconstruction. This new legislation recognized both excess productive capacity in U.S. agriculture and the dollar shortage in many food-short nations, impeding commercial imports from the United States.

1948–54

During these seven years government programs played a crucial role in financing exports of agricultural products. In the first three years nearly three-fifths of U.S. farm exports were donations or were financed by grants or loans (see table 7-6). (The value of total U.S. farm exports appears in table 7-9.) Grants and donations became less important as postwar programs were

Table 7-6. Value (in Millions of Dollars) of U.S. Agricultural Exports under Various Forms of Governmental Assistance, 1948–54[a]

Year (Fiscal)	Food Donations and Grants			Loans and Credits			Foreign Currency Sales	Commercial with Export Subsidies
	Aid to Other Governments[b]	By the U.S. Military[c]	By Voluntary Agencies[d]	Export-Import Bank	Other	Barter		
1948.........	$ 739	$837	...[e]	$17	$306	...	...	[f]
1949.........	1,516	753	...	35	7	...	...	[f]
1950.........	1,262	461	$ 6	24	46	$ 8	...	[f]
1951.........	966	175	47	14	1	9	...	[f]
1952.........	511	68	2	89	184	43	...	[f]
1953.........	377	58	...	62	34	14	...	$600
1954.........	473	24	67	113	...	34	$116	400

[a]Some exports receive subsidies as well as another form of assistance; hence these categories are not mutually exclusive and cannot be summed to a total.

[b]Includes food shipments and financial aid spent for food purchased in the United States through government-to-government arrangements.

[c]Sometimes referred to as "civilian supplies" or GARIOA.

[d]Food donations handled by nongovernmental welfare agencies, under Section 416 of the Agricultural Act of 1949.

[e]... indicates none or negligible.

[f]Data are unavailable for 1948–52; subsidies were paid in these years under Section 32, IWA, and other authorities; see the text. Data for 1953–54 are ERS estimates.

phased out, yet a substantial share of exports continued to move under some form of aid program. Concurrently, many commercial exports were buoyed by subsidies to lower their prices so that U.S. products could compete in world markets. Each of these major types of government assistance for exports is briefly treated here.[2]

Grants and donations. Foreign food aid[3] first developed on a large scale as a result of the necessities of World War II and continued in the immediate postwar period as part of emergency programs to help rebuild war-torn nations. As mentioned, the early postwar programs were largely grants and loans to needy countries. The European Recovery Program (Marshall Plan), the largest such program, provided dollar grants allowing recipients to increase their imports — including food imports — and quicken the pace of reconstruction and development. Marshall Plan agreements required that agricultural commodities be procured from the United States if the commodities were considered to be in surplus. Other foreign food aid programs of especial importance in the immediate postwar years included U.S. contributions to United Nations Relief and Rehabilitation Administration and post-UNRRA operations and civilian feeding programs under U.S. military auspices.

In 1949 the CCC was authorized to donate food commodities in excess of domestic needs to private welfare organizations for the assistance of needy persons outside the United States (Section 416 of the Agricultural Act of 1949). Donations under this authority began in 1950 when agricultural commodities valued at $6 million were exported. These exports are identified as donations by voluntary agencies in table 7-6.

Two special laws were passed in 1953 permitting donations of U.S. agricultural commodities to foreign governments whose nations were threatened with famine. One act provided wheat for Pakistan; the other granted authority to the USDA to donate CCC stocks to any friendly needy nation. Both acts were for specific, short durations with modest funding authorizations.

Loans and credits. Under these programs the government assumed the risk of loss for exports that could not secure private financing. Between 1948 and 1954 the only continuous program was the Export-Import Bank, established in 1934 as an independent governmental agency to encourage foreign trade. In certain circumstances, the bank extended credit to foreign buyers when commercial credit could not be obtained. Credit for food purchases was a minor activity of the bank; major emphasis was on loans for economic development assistance.

Other loan and credit programs, providing financing for agricultural commodities, included USDA cotton credits, grain loans to India, and special loans to the United Kingdom, India, Spain, Pakistan, and Afghanistan.

Barter. Barter authority permitted the exchange of CCC stocks for an equivalent value of strategic or other materials produced abroad, with a specific emphasis on exchanging perishable goods for durable goods. Barter transactions were authorized in 1949; the first agricultural exports under the program were in 1950.

Foreign currency sales. A provision of the Mutual Security Act of 1953 mandated expenditures of mutual security funds on surplus U.S. agricultural commodities to be sold abroad for foreign currencies. Sales proceeds were then used for financing mutual security operations overseas. This technique permitted nations short of foreign exchange to obtain food from the United States. Participation, however, was necessarily limited to those countries that had aid programs.

Export subsidies. Cash subsidy payments were authorized as early as 1935 under Section 32 to encourage the export of agricultural commodities. Section 32 annual export payments ranged from $12 million to $27 million between 1948 and 1954, averaging $20 million yearly. More than two-thirds were for fruit exports; sorghum, wheat, peanuts, and eggs each accounted for about 6 percent of Section 32 export payments in this period.

Other subsidy programs were established by 1948 and 1949 laws, permitting additional commercial foreign sales when U.S. domestic prices were noncompetitive with other exporting nations. Subsidies were provided in two forms: (1) when exporters purchased commodities at the U.S. market price and sold at a lower, world price, a cash subsidy was paid; (2) when exporters purchased CCC commodities at the world price instead of the higher U.S. price, the subsidy was called an "export differential." The term "differential" refers to the difference between domestic and export prices — the price advantage, or subsidy, obtained by the exporter.

Wheat exports received the most assistance under subsidy programs during 1948–54. Most commercial wheat was exported under the International Wheat Agreement (IWA) in 1949 and subsequent extensions. The IWA set price ranges for wheat trade that were below the U.S. domestic price, thus implicitly sanctioning export subsidies and precluding the charge of "dumping" in the export market. The first subsidies under the IWA were paid in 1950. Annual payments ranged from $56 million to $178 million, averaging $120 million, for the first five years of the program.

1955–73

With the passage of P.L. 480 in 1954 many of the existing export programs were drawn together under one authority and extended. Food aid, which had often been a combination of *ad hoc* responses to famine or disaster abroad, became institutionalized under P.L. 480. In its earliest form P.L. 480 was essentially a surplus disposal program designed to relieve burdensome agricultural surpluses with a minimal disruption of normal trade flows. As conditions and policy goals changed, program features were altered in accord with the new situations. Several amendments were made during the first 12 years of the program, adding some new features and making minor changes in the original provisions. A major change was made in 1966 when the structure and goals were revised considerably. New in the Food for Peace Act of 1966 was an emphasis on self-help by recipient countries. They were required to take measures for increasing per capita food production and for improving food storage and distribution systems. Also, food aid was no longer limited to surplus commodities. The 1966 provisions supplanted the original stress on surplus disposal by foreign policy and trade objectives.[4]

Sales for foreign currency. The foreign currency sales provision, Title I of P.L. 480, in many respects was the core of the original program, and in most years more than 50 percent of P.L. 480 exports were made under this authority.[5] Title I authorized the sale of surplus agricultural commodities for foreign currencies to "friendly nations" with the stipulation that precautions be taken to protect normal U.S. marketings and to avoid disrupting world prices.[6] Also, private trade channels were to be employed as often as possible and special efforts made to develop new markets and expand old ones on a long-term basis.

Although Title I was patterned after the Mutual Security Act, the latter was a less flexible instrument. The requirement that mutual security sales proceeds be used for financing normal mutual security operations prevented sales to many countries where no aid program existed. Under Title I of P.L. 480, only certain Communist countries were excluded, so the number of potential customers increased greatly. Also mutual security sales had all the unpopular characteristics of "tied aid" while Title I sales agreements held out the prospect of increased aid through the use of the foreign currency proceeds.[7] Consequently foreign currency sales under the Mutual Security Act were phased out by 1962 and completely replaced by Title I (see table 7-7).

Title I foreign currencies became the property of the United States government and were allocated to specific categories of use by mutual agreement between the U.S. and the respective governments. Overall, more than 50 percent was allocated to economic development aid, about 25 percent to U.S. uses (most of which replaced dollar expenditures), and about 13 percent to military aid; there was considerable variation in this pattern across countries. In some countries, notably India, Pakistan, and the United Arab Republic, large surpluses of U.S.-owned foreign currencies accumulated. Partly for this reason, the Food for Peace Act of 1966 stipulated that foreign currency sales be phased out and replaced by credit sales for dollars and convertible currencies. As seen in table 7-7 and figure 7-1, this objective was nearly achieved by fiscal year 1973.

Table 7-7. Value (in Millions of Dollars) of U.S. Agricultural Exports under P.L. 480 and Other Forms of Governmental Assistance, 1955–73[a]

Year (Fiscal)	Foreign Currency Sales		P.L. 480 Donations			Barter		Loans and Credits			Export Subsidies[d]	
	P.L. 480	Mutual Security Act	To Other Governments	By Voluntary Agencies[b]	Foreign Aid Food Assistance[c]	P.L. 480	CCC Charter Act	P.L. 480 Credit	Export-Import Bank	CCC Credit Sales	Commercial	Non-commercial
1955	73	281	52	135	170	125	...[e]	...	69	...	400	[f]
1956	439	327	63	185	28	298	...	...	60	2	600	[f]
1957	908	386	52	165	8	400	...	...	69	4	1,100	[f]
1958	658	218	51	173	9	100	...	...	191	12	1,200	[f]
1959	724	210	30	131	...	132	...	...	54	39	800	[f]
1960	824	167	38	105	...	149	...	...	34	1	1,300	[f]
1961	951	186	75	146	...	144	...	...	43	18	1,300	[f]
1962	1,030	67	88	160	7	198	...	19	71	33	1,056	987
1963	1,088	...	89	174	14	47	13	57	85	77	721	975
1964	1,056	...	81	189	24	43	69	48	79	118	1,380	915
1965	1,142	...	55	183	26	32	98	158	72	95	1,060	1,155
1966	866	...	87	180	42	32	197	181	62	217	1,219	1,032
1967	803	...	110	157	37	22	273	178	103	335	1,341	770
1968	723	...	100	150	18	6	296	299	71	144	1,016	571
1969	345	...	110	154	6	1	268	428	51	116	550	129
1970	309	...	113	128	13	...	467	506	67	211	1,156	410
1971	204	...	138	142	57	...	870	539	97	391	1,602	36
1972	143	...	228	152	66	...	876	535	86	372	1,513	415
1973	6	...	159	128	84	...	1,088	653	66	1,029	2,496	254

[a]Some exports receive subsidies as well as another form of assistance; hence these categories are not mutually exclusive and cannot be summed to a total.
[b]Food donations handled by nongovernmental welfare agencies.
[c]Assistance consists of donations, grants, and loans under the Mutual Security Act and AID.
[d]Value of exports receiving a subsidy, not the amount of the subsidy. See the text for the amount of subsidy payments.
[e]. . . indicates none or negligible.
[f]Not available.

271

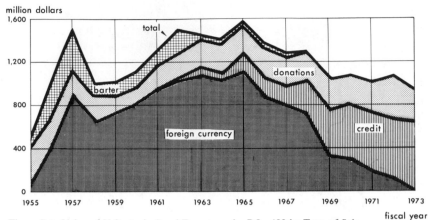

million dollars

Figure 7-1. Value of U.S. Agricultural Exports under P.L. 480 by Type of Sale

Donations. There were two types of foreign donations initially authorized by P.L. 480: government-to-government grants for emergency relief under Title II, and donations to needy persons through voluntary relief agencies under Title III.[8] In both cases, commodities were to come from CCC stocks of surplus agricultural commodities.

The evolution in emphasis of P.L. 480 from surplus disposal to economic aid had a significant effect on the donation programs. An amendment in 1960 added the promotion of economic development to the objectives of Title II and opened the way for Title II commodities to be utilized less for relief purposes and more for self-help and economic development activities. The same shift in emphasis for the voluntary agency donations was mandated in 1964 and accelerated the trend away from relief and toward the use of food in projects with longer range economic significance. By the 1970s more than 20 percent of Title II commodities were being used as wage goods in food-for-work programs, which were designed to create employment opportunities, or in projects like reforestation and infrastructure improvements, which contribute to economic and community development.

The Food for Peace Act of 1966 combined both types of donation under a revised Title II, increased the emphasis on the principle of self-help, and removed the requirement that commodities for donation come from CCC stocks. The latter change placed donations on a par with P.L. 480 sales programs in terms of commodities available for shipments.

Foreign aid food assistance. The importance of food shipments under foreign economic aid programs diminished rapidly between 1955 and 1962 as the P.L. 480 program became the primary instrument for foreign food aid.[9]

During this period International Cooperation Administration food assistance (in the categories listed in column 5, table 7-7) fell to negligible levels. After the Foreign Assistance Act of 1916 and the establishment of the Agency for International Development (AID), food assistance through loans and grants increased, but as mentioned earlier, AID discontinued foreign currency sales. In the 1971 to 1973 period there was a substantial rise in the level of AID food assistance. Rice and inedible tallow were the principal products, each accounting for 36 percent of these exports. Most of the rice shipments during this period were exports to Korea under long-term development loans, a widely used form of assistance under foreign economic aid programs.

Barter. As a part of the P.L. 480 program, Title III barter transactions had an erratic history. The barter authorization permitted the exchange of CCC stocks for an equivalent value of strategic or other materials produced abroad. A comparison of barter exports in tables 7-6 and 7-7 reveals that early P.L. 480 barter levels increased more than tenfold over pre-1954 levels. However, because of the nature of barter transactions, responsible officials in the USDA felt that private traders were using the program to undersell and thus displace normal exports. On May 28, 1957, the USDA issued an edict which made additionality certificates a prerequisite for all barter transactions.[10] Barter shipments plummeted. The Congress responded with an amendment in 1958 disallowing such blanket restrictions. This had the effect of increasing P.L. 480 barter shipments temporarily. But in 1963 P.L. 480 barter shipments dropped again.

Initially barter transactions were engaged in primarily to acquire foreign-produced strategic materials for government stockpiles. These needs were largely met by 1963 and the program was shifted to procurement of goods and services for overseas U.S. agencies, primarily the Department of Defense and AID. These barter activities were carried out under the CCC Charter Act instead of P.L. 480. By 1970 barter transactions had disappeared from the P.L. 480 program.

It is difficult to classify barter unequivocally as a commercial or a noncommercial form of export. And for our purposes here, it is not necessary to do so. For the user of government statistics, it is only necessary to know that these transactions are now considered a form of commercial exports by USDA and classified as such.

Long-term credit sales. A long-term dollar credit sales provision for government-to-government transactions was added to P.L. 480 by amendment in 1959 and was broadened in 1962 to authorize similar sales agreements between the United States and private traders in the U.S. or friendly countries.[11] Such agreements, whether with private traders or governments, specified not only the commodity delivery schedule and repayment terms but also how the importing government or private trade entity would use the revenues generated by the local sale of the commodities. The delivery schedule was allowed to span a maximum of ten years but generally spanned three years or less. There was a maximum grace period of two years between the last delivery in each calendar year and the first installment payment; the maximum repayment period was 20 years. Within these constraints, terms were negotiable.

One objective of the Food for Peace Act of 1966 was to shift recipient countries to dollar customers as much and as soon as possible. In order to facilitate the transition the act authorized government-to-government "convertible local currency credit" (CLCC) sales. CLCC sales were similar to dollar credit sales in that the importing governments were required to guarantee the convertibility (into dollars) of all local currency repayments, but the maximum leniency was increased under CLCC to a 10-year grace period and a 40-year repayment period. Both CLCC and dollar credit agreements were constrained by the minimum interest rates of the Foreign Assistance Act of 1961, as amended: 2 percent during the grade period and 3 percent thereafter.

Long-term credit sales expanded rapidly at the expense of foreign currency sales and after 1970 accounted for more than 50 percent of P.L. 480 shipments (figure 7-1). This shift in emphasis from foreign currency sales to dollar credit or CLCC sales was in essence a second stage in transforming aid recipients into commercial customers.

CCC credit sales. The CCC Export Credit Sales Program was inaugurated in 1956 to finance a limited amount of commercial exports from private stocks. The normal term of such credit is one year, although a maximum of three years may be granted in some cases. Interest rates are generally below market rates but are set to cover the costs incurred by the CCC. Exports financed in this way have included a broad range of commodities and importing countries, yet in 1973 nearly 45 percent of the total was accounted for by grain exports to the USSR.

Export-Import Bank. After 1955, as before, the Export-Import Bank extended credit to supplement private capital. The principal use of the Bank for agricultural exports was credits and guarantees for cotton sales to Japan. In 1963 a system of guarantees was initiated to protect commercial banks and other financial institutions against political and/or financial risk. Export-Import Bank assistance for agricultural exports has been relatively small and has declined as a share of total exports.

Export subsidies. Subsidies to aid the export of agricultural commodities were indispensable while U.S. commodity prices were supported above world prices. Several forms of payments were available, under a variety of administrative arrangements — all permitting commodities with domestic prices above world prices to be exported at world price levels. In the period 1955–66 an average of 30 percent of dollar exports received export payment assistance. During the same period, annual export subsidy payments ranged between $500 million and $600 million except for the year 1964 when payments reached $822 million. When levels of price support in domestic farm programs were dropped to near world prices in the mid-1960s, subsidy payments contracted. Annual payments from 1967 to 1972 were under $260 million; they dropped to $64 million in 1969. In fiscal 1973 they peaked again when large wheat subsidies raised the total to $405 million. Payment rates were set to reflect the difference between domestic and world prices; they were under frequent review by the USDA.

Subsidies were paid for noncommercial as well as commercial exports. For commodities shipped under various government programs the commodity was valued at the export, or world, price and that value used in foreign currency, barter, or credit sales agreements with other nations. The difference between the export value of the commodity and the domestic price was paid to exporters for commodities purchased in the market or absorbed as a loss by the CCC for commodities sold from CCC stocks. Payment methods were identical to methods employed for commercial exports. The value of noncommercial exports receiving such subsidy assistance is shown in table 7-7. Notice that the value of noncommercial exports receiving subsidies diminished, as it should, after domestic grain prices were lowered. Data for the value of commercial exports receiving subsidies did not reflect a similar decline either in relative or absolute terms. This suggests that the mix of commodities exported commercially differed from those exported under noncommercial arrangements.

Until 1956 export subsidies for wheat and flour, begun in 1949 under the IWA, were made in cash or by the CCC selling its stocks to exporters at an export price lower than the domestic price (called the "export differential"). Beginning in the fall of 1956 a payment in kind (PIK) was established under which certificates worth the applicable subsidy rate were issued to exporters on proof of export from private stocks. These certificates were redeemable in wheat from CCC stocks. Wheat thus obtained was restricted to export; it could not be sold in the higher priced domestic market. Cash subsidy payments were continued for flour. Payment rates for wheat and flour were announced daily.

Wheat subsidies constituted more than half of all export payments from 1960 to 1973. For each bushel exported, payments ranged from 11 cents in 1968 to 64 cents in 1963. Subsidies paid in 1969 were more than offset by receipts when world prices rose above the U.S. level. Under the International Grains Arrangement, which was in force for fiscal years 1969 and 1970, exporters were required to buy export certificates from the CCC during periods when world prices were higher than domestic prices — a kind of export tax to avoid windfall profits for exporters who bought specially priced CCC wheat but sold at a higher price in a strong world market. These payments to the government resulted in a reduction in net payments for wheat in both 1969 and 1970.

Before 1958 the CCC occasionally offered feed grains for export at world prices. In April 1958 the PIK program was extended to corn and in July 1958 to other feed grains including rye. Certificates earned by exporters of these grains were redeemable in any feed grain from CCC stocks. After domestic price support loan rates for feed grains were reduced to near world price levels in 1963, the need to assist commercial exports was diminished and assistance was only sporadic. Peak payments were in 1960, 1961, and 1966 when subsidies of $23 million, $24 million, and $23 million were paid.

The PIK program was extended to rice in December 1958. Export payments were announced weekly and certificates could be redeemed for either rice or feed grains. Rice export subsidies were substantial. From 1960 to 1973 payments ranged from $28 million to $64 million annually except in 1968 and 1969, when they fell to $2 million and $5 million respectively. In many years the subsidy payment per cwt. was greater than the export price.

Cotton was exported from CCC stocks at world prices after 1955; a PIK program for cotton began in May 1958. Payment rates were announced at the beginning of each marketing year and usually held for the remainder of the year. Upland cotton was second to wheat in the amount of export payment assistance received until 1965 legislation reduced the cotton loan rate to near world price levels. No export subsidies were paid for upland cotton from 1968 to 1973.

Nonfat dry milk began receiving PIK assistance in June 1962 and payment rates in this case were announced in advance for two-week periods. The most versatile of all certificates, these were redeemable for CCC wheat, rice, feed grains, or dairy products when available. Annual subsidies varied greatly; the largest payments were $55 million in 1965 and the lowest, $1 million, in 1973. Butter exports also received export payments. Per-pound payments ranged from 14 cents to 35 cents from 1959 to 1973.

Cash export payments for tobacco were offered under Section 32 funding in 1962 but they applied only to off-grade tobacco and were very limited. In July 1966 cash export payments of 5 cents a pound were extended to most kinds of tobacco, replacing Section 32 payments. From 1967 to 1973 payments were close to $30 million in each year.

Beginning in December 1964 export PIK certificates could be redeemed for a variety of CCC-owned commodities (including tobacco under loan). All such commodities, however, were required to be exported. The use of PIK certificates for all commodities was discontinued beginning in August 1966 and by April 1967 the CCC had reverted completely to cash export payments.

The proportion of exports assisted by export payments varied considerably from year to year depending upon changes in world prices relative to domestic prices. In the period after 1960 this proportion reached a maximum of 40 percent in 1962 and a minimum of 12 percent in 1969 when net payments for wheat were zero. Although total and average payments in the fiscal year 1973 were rather large, especially for wheat and rice, payment rates during the year decreased as world prices increased. By the end of the fiscal year 1973 no payments were made for wheat and rice; the export payment program was terminated for all tobacco harvested after the 1973 crop; and the payments for chicken and lard exports were terminated in January 1973.

The authority to provide export payment assistance remains and presumably could be exercised should world prices fall below domestic support levels. However, changes in farm programs have for the most part moved away from price supports to direct payment schemes, allowing the domestic and world market prices to move together, and have thus removed the principal basis for export payment programs.

Magnitude of Government Export Programs

Data in tables 7-8 and 7-9 indicate the importance of governmental assistance for exports of U.S. agricultural commodities. The total value of commodities exported under P.L. 480 from July 1, 1954, to June 30, 1973, was $22.3 billion, which represented about 20 percent of all U.S. agricultural exports during that period. This percentage was as high as 32 percent in 1957 but dropped to 7 percent in 1973. Exports under other government aid programs averaged only 2 percent of total U.S. agricultural exports over this period.

More than half of the P.L. 480 shipments were sales for foreign currencies. Among commodity groups, the importance of P.L. 480 exports varied considerably, as indicated in table 7-8. Exports of dairy products, cotton and soy oils, wheat, and rice depended largely upon these programs.

From 1948 to 1973 an increasing share of agricultural commodities was exported under commercial arrangements, including those assisted through subsidy and government financing programs (see figure 7-2). In 1948–50, 54 percent of U.S. agricultural exports were shipped under noncommercial, government programs; in the 1970–72 period the share dropped to 14 percent. When the extraordinarily heavy export year of 1973 is considered, only 8 percent of agricultural exports moved under noncommercial programs. Nevertheless, for some commodities, namely rice and soybean oil, P.L. 480 programs accounted for more than half of the value of 1973 exports.

Table 7-8. Value (in Millions of Dollars) of P.L. 480 Exports from July 1, 1954, through June 30, 1973, for Selected Commodities

Item	Feed Grains and Products	Wheat and Products	Cotton	Cotton- seed and Soy Oil	Tobacco	Rice	Dairy Products	Other	Total
Sales for foreign currency	$814	$6,796	$1,695	$1,069	$415	$1,019	$209	$274	$12,291
Long-term dollar credit	344	1,659	458	272	96	678	5	90	3,602
Government-to-government donations	219	923	15	146		86	250	80	1,719
Voluntary agency donations	207	831		273	126	54	1,332	241	2,938
Barter	569	633	322	4		15	20	43	1,732
Total P.L. 480	2,153	10,842	2,491	1,763	701	1,852	1,816	664	22,282
Total agricultural exports	16,474	21,437	11,444	3,380	8,335	4,079	2,863	43,848	111,860
P.L. 480 as a percentage of total agricultural exports	13%	51%	22%	52%	8%	45%	63%	2%	20%

What role government export programs will play in the future depends importantly upon the state of world commerce. This question is dealt with at some length in a later chapter.

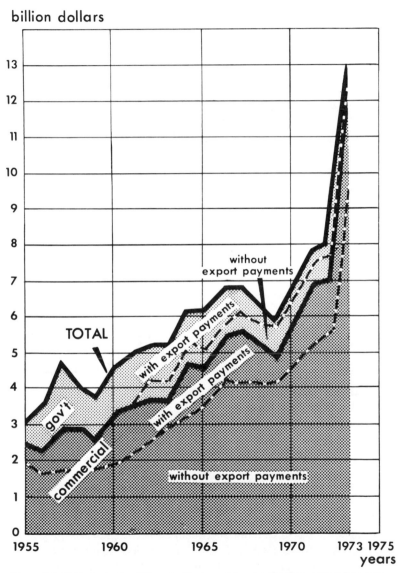

Figure 7-2. U.S. Agricultural Exports: Commercial and under Government Programs

Table 7-9. Value (in Millions of Dollars) of U.S. Agricultural Exports: Total, under Specified Government Programs, and Commercial 1948–73

Year (Fiscal)	Total	Under Specified Government Programs[a]	Commercial[b]
1948	$3,505	$1,576	$1,929
1949	3,830	2,269	1,561
1950	2,986	1,737	1,249
1951	3,411	623	2,214
1952	4,053	449	3,430
1953	2,819	598	2,370
1954	2,936	451	2,338
1955	3,144	835	2,309
1956	2,496	1,339	2,156
1957	4,728	1,919	2,809
1958	4,003	1,208	2,794
1959	3,719	1,227	2,492
1960	4,519	1,283	3,236
1961	4,946	1,502	3,443
1962	5,142	1,569	3,573
1963	5,078	1,470	3,608
1964	6,068	1,441	4,626
1965	6,097	1,596	4,501
1966	6,676	1,389	5,288
1967	6,771	1,308	5,463
1968	6,311	1,297	5,015
1969	5,741	1,050	4,691
1970	6,721	1,068	5,653
1971	7,758	1,079	6,679
1972	8,047	1,124	6,923
1973	12,894	1,030	11,864

[a]Includes exports under P.L. 480, AID, and similar predecessor programs.

[b]Includes commercial exports receiving assistance under short-term credit, subsidy, and loan programs. Barter transactions under the CCC Charter Act are included.

Domestic Food Programs

The federal government operates several food programs "to make effective use of American farm products in improving the nutrition of needy families and the nation's school children." Under these programs food is provided at no, or modest, cost to children and qualified needy persons. Such programs aid farmers by enlarging the market for farm products and benefit low-income consumers by providing them with more food at less cost than they would have otherwise.

In 1948 two programs were operative — the school lunch program and the commodity distribution program. Others added subsequently were the special milk program in 1954, the food stamp program in 1961, and additional child nutrition programs in 1966 and 1968. All programs have been modified from time to time, mainly to expand their scope — bringing in new areas of child nutrition and extending benefits to more needy people. Throughout the 1948–73 period food programs evolved from an adjunct to farm programs to a wide-ranging, comprehensive bundle of food aid services for low-income families and American children.[12]

Commodity Distribution Program

When the commodity distribution program was inaugurated, the main objective was to find constructive uses for a part of U.S. food production that could not move through commercial channels at prices fair to farmers. Through Section 32 purchases and as a result of price support loan and purchase operations the U.S. Department of Agriculture acquired foods that were then donated to school lunch programs, charitable and nonprofit institutions serving needy persons and children, and low-income families.

The USDA arranged for and financed necessary processing or packaging of surplus commodities and paid the cost of transporting them in carload lots to designated receiving points. From these points the foods were transferred to county warehouses maintained and paid for by county agencies. Local government then distributed the foods to individual families and schools, or qualified recipients called at the county warehouse for their allotments.

Before receiving commodities, recipients had to be certified by an appropriate state or local public welfare authority. Foods were distributed both to persons receiving public assistance and to others who met state-established standards of economic need. Qualified recipient institutions and persons included (1) hospitals, orphanages, homes for the aged, and similar types of institutions; (2) nonprofit summer camps for children and child care centers; (3) local public welfare agencies servicing needy persons; (4) needy Indians; (5) schools with lunch programs; and (6) victims of natural disasters such as hurricanes, tornadoes, floods, and drought.

The basic features of commodity distribution programs remained the same from 1948 through 1973, though legislative and administrative changes served to enlarge the scope of the programs. First, the list of eligible institutions was expanded in 1954. Next, beginning in 1956, the CCC was authorized to pay for processing wheat and corn into flour and meal before making donations. Then in 1958 it was authorized to buy flour and meal on the market instead of doing its own processing; the purchase of fats and oils on the market was also permitted. Six years later, in 1964, the CCC was authorized to buy any grain product on the market instead of processing grain itself. Additional new authority was provided in 1966 for purchases of dairy products (other than fluid milk) when CCC stocks were inadequate to meet program needs. And in the following year, 1967, the USDA offered assistance to poor counties that could not pay storage and distribution costs to operate a program. Finally, in the face of drastically reduced food availability in the early 1970s, authority was provided in 1973 for purchase of foods on the open market without regard to surplus removal and price support legislation; the original authority was for one year only, scheduled to expire June 30, 1974. The numbers of persons served and the quantity and cost of foods donated under commodity distribution programs for institutions and needy persons appear in table 7-10. (Annual values of food donations to child nutrition programs are shown in table 7-11.)

Table 7-10. Commodity Distribution Program: Number of Persons Served, Quantity and Cost of Food Donated to Individuals and Institutions[a]

Year (Fiscal)	Number of Needy Persons Served[b] (in Thousands)	Institutions: Number of Persons Participating (in Thousands)	Food Donations to Institutions and Needy Persons	
			Millions of Pounds	Millions of Dollars
1948	96	1,102	180	$13.7
1949	119	987	174	14.0
1950	248	1,077	255	24.5
1951	1,225	1,280	238	25.3
1952	169	1,301	41	7.3
1953	114	1,435	44	16.9
1954	1,089	1,334	172	60.9
1955	3,291	1,375	297	97.4
1956	3,248	1,396	524	134.6
1957	3,822	2,267	644	104.4
1958	4,735	2,329	620	109.5
1959	5,762	2,484	863	136.9
1960	4,381	2,447	654	75.2
1961	6,488	2,438	1,011	174.0
1962	7,943	2,581	1,557	252.8
1963	7,075	2,519	1,411	233.4
1964	6,156	2,550	1,322	234.6
1965	6,093	2,540	1,313	256.7
1966	5,169	2,526	1,000	151.0
1967	3,739	2,686	849	116.2
1968	4,136	2,694	871	147.3
1969	3,920	2,504	1,200	250.4
1970	4,798	2,747	1,330	311.9
1971	4,423	2,823	1,466	345.7
1972	3,965	2,675	1,362	337.3
1973	3,319	2,736	1,110	282.1

[a]Excluding schools; donations to schools appear in table 7-11.
[b]Needy persons are those on public assistance or with incomes below state standards.

The variety of foods donated under the direct distribution program initially was quite limited and varied from time to time since the supply depended upon foods available from price support and surplus removal Section 32 operations. In 1949, for example, foods donated were potatoes, sweet potatoes, honey, canned and dried fruits, citrus juice, fresh vegetables, and dried eggs. The list was even more limited in 1960 when only lard, flour, corn meal, nonfat dry milk, and rice were donated. Early in 1961 the quantity and variety of donated foods were expanded, with special emphasis upon assuring the continuing availability of protein items. The list of foods available in 1965 illustrates the impact of this change.

In addition to the items available in 1960, the 1965 list included dry beans, canned beef, bulgur, cheese, corn grits, margarine, chopped meat, split peas, peanut butter, and rolled wheat. Further steps were taken to improve the nutritional value and variety of foods offered under the donation program so that the 1969 program contained 22 foods. These foods would provide from 80 to 150 percent of the minimum daily requirement for all nutrients. By 1973 the list had been expanded still more to include butter, an egg mixture, canned fruits, fruit and vegetable juices, macaroni, evaporated milk, instant potatoes, dried fruit, shortening, corn syrup, and canned vegetables in addition to the items offered in 1965. Thus, by 1973 the commodity distribution program for needy families had shifted focus from a surplus disposal program to a program designed to meet the nutritional needs of recipients.

Beginning in the early 1960s a policy was implemented to phase out the commodity distribution program for families, replacing it with food stamps. A locality could have one program or the other, but not both. By December 1973 food donations served families in 530 counties and cities, of which 400 were in the process of shifting to food stamps. In accordance with provisions of 1973 farm legislation, the entire distribution program for families was scheduled to end by July 1, 1974; however, a few areas were granted extensions beyond that date pending initiation of the food stamp program.

In the early 1970s, because of changing agricultural and marketing conditions and farm programs, the Department of Agriculture encountered increasing difficulties in acquiring foods for distribution. Commodity distribution programs for schools and institutions continued through fiscal year 1974. After July 1, 1975, however, the department proposed to rely on all-cash assistance in conducting its food programs.

School Lunch and Other Child Nutrition Programs

When the National School Lunch Act was passed in 1946 its purpose, as declared in the act, was "to safeguard the health and well-being of the Nation's children and to encourage the domestic consumption of nutritious agricultural commodities and other food." Under the school lunch program the federal government provided cash, commodities, and technical assistance to schools operating the program. Federal funds were apportioned to the states to reimburse schools for part of the cost of foods utilized in the program. Originally it was required that at least 75 percent of appropriated funds for food be granted to the states in cash. These funds, called general assistance funds, had to be matched from sources within each state. Later, additional federal cash assistance for meals was provided for children who came from low-income families. The federal government also donated foods to the schools, supplementing local purchases. Both public and nonprofit private schools for grades up to and including high school were eligible to participate in the program.

Schools participating in the program were required (1) to serve lunches meeting minimum nutritional requirements, (2) to serve meals without cost or at reduced cost to poor children and not to segregate or discriminate against such children in any way, (3) to operate the program on a nonprofit basis, (4) to utilize surplus and donated commodities as far as practicable, and (5) to maintain proper records and submit reports to the state agency as required.

States were required to match federal general assistance funds with $1.00 for each $1.00 until 1950; $1.50 for each federal $1.00 from 1951 through 1955; and thereafter, $3.00 for each federal $1.00. The matching requirement was lower for states where per capita income was below per capita income for the United States as a whole. To meet matching requirements the states could include children's payments for lunches and money paid for equipment, as well as labor and foods donated to the program. However, under 1970 legislation, state revenue must constitute a certain portion of the matching requirement.

The share of the nation's schools participating in the program increased from less than one-fourth in 1948 to more than three-fourths in 1973 (see table 7-11 and figure 7-3). By 1959, programs were in operation in all 50 states, the District of Columbia, Puerto Rico, the Virgin Islands, and Guam. The number of children participating increased four times during our 25-year study period. About one-fourth of students enrolled in U.S. schools participated in 1948 while nearly one-half of a larger enrollment participated in the school lunch program by 1973. The percentage of free or reduced-rate lunches served varied between about 10 and 17 percent of total lunches served from 1948 through 1969. After that the share of free or reduced-rate lunches jumped to over one-third of all lunches.

Federal assistance to the school lunch program consisted of cash payments for local food purchases, federal donations of food, and cash for acquiring food service equipment. The national average cash payment per lunch dropped from 7.3 cents in 1948 to between 4.1 cents and 4.8 cents from 1954 through 1970 and then rose to 8.0 cents in 1973. Supplemental payments for

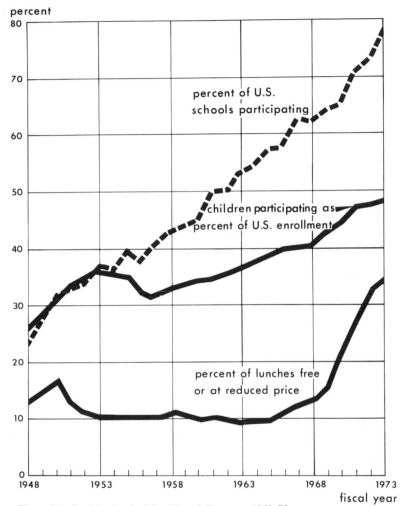

Figure 7-3. Participation in School Lunch Program, 1948–73

free and reduced lunches averaged 5.0 cents in 1967 and 39.7 cents in 1973. Under legislation applying in 1973, states earned federal funds at a guaranteed national average rate per lunch served. But within each state, the state school lunch agency could vary reimbursement payments to schools according to need.

Commodities donated to the schools came from stocks acquired by the federal government under its price support activities, purchases by the government of agricultural commodities in surplus supply, and special purchases

Table 7-11. Child Nutrition Program Participation and Federal Assistance, 1948–73

Year (Fiscal)	School Lunch Program					School Breakfast Program: Children Participating, Daily Average (in Thousands)
	Children Participating		Percentage of Lunches Free or at Reduced Price[a]	Schools Participating		
	Total No.[a] (in Millions)	Percentage of U.S. Enrollment		Total No. (in Thousands)	Percentage of U.S. Total	
1948	6.6	24.8%	12.7%	44.5	23.7%	...[e]
1949	7.6	28.3	14.8	47.8	28.3	...
1950	8.6	31.2	16.6	54.2	32.0	...
1951	9.5	33.7	12.8	54.4	33.2	...
1952	10.2	35.2	11.4	55.7	33.9	...
1953	10.7	36.2	10.6	56.9	36.7	...
1954	11.1	35.9	10.4	56.3	36.4	...
1955	12.0	35.4	10.5	58.5	39.1	...
1956	11.6	32.4	10.5	56.1	37.5	...
1957	11.7	31.9	10.5	57.3	40.6	...
1958	12.6	32.8	10.8	59.9	42.5	...
1959	13.3	33.7	10.5	60.9	44.3	...
1960	14.1	34.6	10.1	62.3	45.2	...
1961	14.8	35.0	10.1	64.0	49.7	...
1962	15.6	35.8	9.9	66.0	50.1	...
1963	16.4	36.3	9.6	67.7	53.1	...
1964	17.5	37.4	9.9	69.6	54.5	...
1965	18.7	38.8	9.9	70.1	57.4	...
1966	19.8	39.8	10.0	70.6	57.8	...
1967	20.2	40.1	12.2	72.9	62.5	80
1968	20.6	40.2	13.0	72.0	61.7	165
1969	22.1	42.7	15.1	74.9	64.4	243
1970	23.1	44.4	20.9	75.6	65.0	442
1971	24.6	47.4	26.1	79.9	70.5	796
1972	24.9	48.0	32.4	83.4	73.5	1,026
1973	25.1	48.9	34.7	86.4	79.0	1,175

286

Federal Assistance (in Millions of Dollars)

Year (Fiscal)	Nonschool Food Program: No. of Children Served (in Thousands)	Food Donations[b]	Cash Payments to States			
			School Lunch[c]	School Breakfast	Nonfood Assistance[d]	Nonschool Program
1948	...	32.8	53.9	...	...	...
1949	...	36.0	58.8	...	...	...
1950	...	55.2	64.6	...	...	...
1951	...	49.9	68.3	...	...	...
1952	...	32.2	66.3	...	...	...
1953	...	56.5	67.2	...	...	...
1954	...	109.0	67.2	...	...	...
1955	...	83.1	69.1	...	...	...
1956	...	114.7	67.1	...	...	...
1957	...	146.6	83.9	...	...	...
1958	...	90.8	83.8	...	...	...
1959	...	109.5	93.9	...	...	...
1960	...	122.0	93.8	...	...	...
1961	...	132.7	93.7	...	...	...
1962	...	182.1	98.8	...	...	...
1963	...	179.8	108.6	...	...	...
1964	...	194.9	120.8	...	...	...
1965	...	272.4	130.4	...	...	...
1966	...	174.9	141.1	...	...	...
1967	...	183.4	149.7	0.6	0.7	...
1968	...	276.0	159.8	2.0	0.7	...
1969	138	272.1	203.8	5.4	10.8	3.2
1970	320	265.8	300.3	10.8	17.4	7.3
1971	616	279.2	532.2	19.4	40.6	20.3
1972	1,162	315.2	738.8	24.9	20.0	40.9
1973	1,370	260.2	888.2	34.6	15.2	44.9

[a]Peak daily number, 1948–66; daily average, 1967–73.
[b]Includes donations to school breakfast program, beginning in 1967, and to nonschool programs, beginning in 1969.
[c]Includes special assistance for needy schools, beginning in 1966.
[d]Includes funds for state administrative expense, beginning in 1969.

[e]Not appropriate.

of food by the federal government to meet the needs of schools participating in the school lunch program. The value of foods donated and cash payments made to states are shown in table 7-11. The first donations from price support activities were in 1950 under Section 416. Through 1973 they had been made each year since 1950 except in 1953 and 1954. Other food for donations was acquired under Section 32 and purchased with funding authorized under Section 6 of the School Lunch Act. The total values of food donated under each of these three authorities were $1.2 billion, $1.6 billion, and $1.0 billion respectively from 1947 through 1972.

By the early 1960s it became apparent that many needy children were not being reached by the lunch program. Many older urban and rural schools had no lunchroom facilities and no money to build them. To assist such needy schools a special program was undertaken for the 1961–62 school year to provide them with commodities valued at $2.5 million. The program was for one year only.

The first major changes made in the school lunch program were in 1962. First, the formula for distributing funds to states was changed. Previously states with a low participation rate had received higher benefits per lunch than states with a high participation rate because assistance was determined by the number of students in the state, not the number in the program. Under the new provisions funds were apportioned on the basis of participation in each state. (The higher payment rate for low-income states was unchanged.) Second, this 1962 legislation authorized special reimbursement of federal funds to states for serving free or reduced-price lunches to needy children, but no funds were appropriated for this purpose until fiscal year 1966.

Several new facets were added to the school lunch program in 1967. For the first time cash was provided to purchase equipment to prepare and serve school lunches in low-income areas. Previously authority had existed but no appropriations were made. At least one-fourth of the purchase price of any equipment was required to be provided by state or local funds. Peak outlays were made in 1971 when $37.1 million was paid. The federal government was also authorized to provide financial assistance for state administrative expenses incurred for providing benefits to children of low-income families. The first such funds were allocated in 1969. In 1971 states received $3.5 million in such funds.

Starting in the late 1960s, steps were taken to expand the availability of free and reduced lunches. Federal contributions for this purpose jumped from $4.8 million to $42.0 million from 1968 to 1969, and further soared to $555.3 million in 1973. National minimum and maximum standards for determining eligibility for free and reduced price lunches were established. Schools were required to send applications for such lunches to parents of all schoolchildren and to establish and publicize local policies for providing free and reduced price lunches, including fair hearing procedures. Another new phenomenon that caused a major change in the program occurred in 1973 when there was an inadequate stockpile of foods for donations because of diminishing farm surpluses. This stimulated the Congress to authorize cash payments in place of food donations when shortages occurred.

Other changes enacted in 1966 and 1968 expanded the scope of food programs for children. These combined the special milk and the school lunch programs into a broader food program for schools, authorized a pilot school breakfast program, and inaugurated nonschool food programs. The entire collection of programs is now called the Child Nutrition Program.

Special milk program. A special program was begun in the 1954–55 school year to encourage the consumption of fluid whole milk by children. Until then milk purchases were part of the school lunch program, competing with other foods for available funds. The new program provided additional funds, earmarked specifically for lowering the price of milk sold to children. Schools were reimbursed by the federal government for milk served over and above the amounts normally used in the school lunch program. This was milk served as snacks, as a beverage with nonprogram lunches, or as an *extra* serving with the school lunch. (One serving of milk was required for each lunch.)

Milk was purchased by each participating institution at the local market price. The government payment allowed milk to be sold to children at a lower cost than was otherwise possible. Table 7-12 shows the number of outlets receiving aid under this program, the number of half pints of milk subsidized, and the total amount of federal payments made to participating institutions.

In 1956, the program was broadened to include child care centers, settlement houses, nursery schools, summer camps, and other nonprofit institutions devoted to the care and training of children. Although payments to such outlets rose from $0.4 million to $4.8 million from 1957 to 1973, this is a small share of the total. In the same two years payments to schools were $60.0 million and $85.7 million respectively.

A special feature was inaugurated in fiscal 1962 to provide extra assistance to schools in low-income areas so that they could serve milk without charge to needy children. Under this program the federal government paid the total cost of milk.

School breakfast program. A pilot breakfast program was authorized for the school years 1966–67 and 1967–68. An average of 80,000 children were served daily in the first year and 165,000 in the second year of the pilot program. Federal cash assistance for this program is listed separately in table 7-11; the value of food donations is included with donations to the school lunch program. Initially the program was available to schools that had many

Table 7-12. Special Milk Program Participation
and Federal Assistance, 1955–73

| Year (Fiscal) | Participation | | Federal Cash Assistance[a] (in Millions) |
	No. of Outlets (in Thousands)	No. of Half Pints Reimbursed (in Millions)	
1955	41.1	449.8	$17.2
1956	62.3	1,394.2	45.8
1957	71.2	1,752.7	60.4
1958	76.5	1,918.2	66.3
1959	81.6	2,176.2	74.2
1960	83.9	2,384.7	80.3
1961	86.5	2,476.7	84.0
1962	88.2	2,631.0	88.7
1963	90.5	2,765.6	93.3
1964	91.9	2,929.0	99.2
1965	92.0	2,966.8	97.2
1966	97.4	3,059.1	96.0
1967	95.1	3,027.2	98.8
1968	94.4	3,035.7	101.9
1969	98.4	2,944.4	101.9
1970	97.2	2,901.9	101.2
1971	97.6	2,570.0	91.1
1972	97.2	2,498.2	90.3
1973	98.0	2,533.8	90.5

[a] Excludes administrative expenses, which ranged from $0.2 million in 1955 to $0.7 million in 1973.

needy pupils or to which children traveled long distances. Students from needy families were eligible for free and reduced-price breakfasts under the same guidelines as were used for the school lunch program. The school breakfast program was broadened in 1972 to be available to all schools the same as the national school lunch program. By 1973, 1.2 million children received breakfast daily. This compares with 25.1 million children participating in the school lunch program daily.

Nonschool food programs. A special food service program was authorized in 1968 to assist nonresidential child care institutions in providing nutritious meals — breakfast, lunch, dinner, and between-meal snacks. The program was aimed at nonprofit institutions providing child care in low-income areas and areas with many working mothers. Previously, these institutions were eligible for the special milk and the commodity distribution program already discussed; this new program offered complete meal assistance. The program operated in a twofold manner: year-round in day care centers primarily for preschool children and during the summer as part of organized activities for school age children in parks, playgrounds, recreation centers, and the like. Federal assistance consisted of donated commodities, cash reimbursements, financial help to purchase or rent food preparation equipment, and technical assistance and guidance in establishing the program. Nearly 1.2 million children were involved in the summer program in 1973 with over 200,000 children served by the year-round program. During the first five years of the operation of this program federal cash assistance increased from $3.2 million to $45.2 million (see table 7-11).

Another nonschool program was one for expectant mothers and infants. Under a pilot project scheduled to run through September 30, 1975, participants were provided with selected foods to supplement their special needs. These foods included milk, baby cereal, and prepared baby formula.

Food Stamp Program

The purposes of the food stamp program, as stated in the 1964 act, were "to strengthen the agricultural economy; to help to achieve a fuller and more effective use of food abundances; [and] to provide for improved levels of nutrition among economically needy households." The program extended the purchasing power of low-income households to buy food by providing coupons, i.e., stamps, worth more than they cost the needy family. Eligible families paid a certain amount of cash, based on their size and income, for stamps of higher monetary value that were valid only for buying food. The extra stamps received were called bonus coupons. All coupons could then be spent to purchase food at prevailing prices from approved grocery stores. The retail food stores redeemed the coupons at local banks where the coupons flowed through regular banking channels for eventual payment by the USDA.

The USDA paid the entire cost of the stamps over and above the amount paid by food stamp recipients. In addition, the USDA paid all federal and part of states' administrative expenses.

The program's basic features had not changed between 1961, when the program was inaugurated as a pilot project, and 1974. Modifications that occurred expanded the program to new localities and made the program more attractive to low-income people. Specific changes were (1) to ease minimum income requirements and to permit deductions from income for certain medical expenses and excess shelter costs, (2) to reduce the cost of stamps to participants, and (3) to provide for coupon purchase more frequently than once a month. All these adjustments made more people potentially eligible for stamps and made participation more appealing.

The food stamp program was intended to replace the commodity distribution program for needy families. However, in the past in areas where the food stamp program was not operating, the commodity donation program was continued or, if none was in operation, a food program was encouraged. Compare the number of persons served by each program, tables 7-10 and 7-13. Notice that participation in the commodity distribution program increased during the early years of the food stamp program, then declined as it was replaced by food stamps.

Table 7-13. Food Stamp Program Participation and
Value of Stamps, 1961–73

Year (Fiscal)	Participation (in Thousands)		Value of Stamps (in Millions)		Average Value of Stamps Purchased with $1.00
	No. of Persons (Peak Month)	No. of Areas	Total	Bonus Coupons[a]	
1961	50	6	$ 1	[b]	$1.86
1962	151	8	35	$ 13	1.60
1963	359	42	50	19	1.60
1964	399	43	74	29	1.64
1965	633	110	86	33	1.61
1966	1,218	324	174	65	1.59
1967	1,832	838	296	106	1.55
1968	2,488	1,027	452	173	1.62
1969	3,222	1,489	603	229	1.61
1970	6,457	1,747	1,090	551	2.02
1971	10,549	2,027	2,713	1,523	2.28
1972	11,594	2,126	3,309	1,797	2.26
1973	12,647	2,227	3,893	2,134	2.22

[a] These constitute the federal government subsidy. The difference between the value of the bonus coupons and the total value of stamps was paid by recipients.
[b] Less than $500,000.

New communities were added to the food stamp program on the basis of priorities established within each state. Each state welfare agency assigned priorities among those areas for which participation was requested from county governments. State agencies were also responsible for issuance of food coupons and for informing low-income households about the program. Eligibility requirements were set by states for 1961–71; subsequently, uniform national standards applied. Public welfare recipients were eligible for the program without regard to income or resources.

The pilot program was begun in 1961 in eight project areas (a project area is a county, independent city, or welfare district); by 1964, the end of the pilot phase, programs were operating in 43 project areas. During these four years, monthly participation rose from 49,600 to 399,400 (see table 7-13). The program was made permanent in 1964, allowing extension to more areas on a gradual basis. The pace of expanding the program was limited by funding. More communities desired programs and more participants became eligible than could be served by annual appropriations during the 1960s. The steady, but moderate, increase in participation and in the value of bonus stamps (the federal subsidy) from 1961 to 1969 is apparent in figure 7-4.

In 1967 the minimum monthly purchase requirement was reduced from $2.00 per person, or $16.00 per family, to 50 cents per person, or $3.00 per family. Other changes eased certification procedures and purchase requirements for the first month of participation. These changes made it easier for low-income consumers to adjust to program criteria.

The price of stamps was further reduced in 1969 so that no family would pay more than 35 percent of its income for food stamps. In 1971 the total coupon allotment was set at a uniform level nationally and linked to the

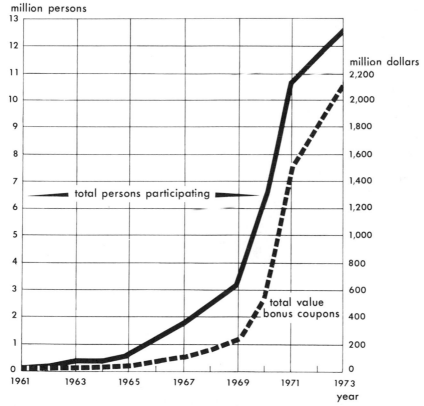

Figure 7-4. Growth of Food Stamp Program Participation and Value of Bonus Coupons, 1961–73

USDA economy food plan. The increase in the value of coupons received for each dollar paid by recipients (from about $1.60 in earlier years to over $2.00 after 1970) reflects this and subsequent revisions that increased the level of aid per household.

The sharp increase in participation and in the value of bonus coupons issued in 1971 resulted from several new regulations issued in accordance with amendments to the Food Stamp Act. Major among these were free food coupons for the poorest households and maximum payments of 30 percent of income for all others; establishment of uniform national standards of eligibility; periodic adjustments in the coupon allotments to reflect changes in the prices of food published by the Bureau of Labor Statistics; permission for the elderly and disabled to use coupons for meals-on-wheels and similar programs; and stepped-up activities to inform low-income persons of their potential eligibility. Some other new regulations were designed to curb abuses of the program.

Sufficient funds were available for fiscal 1972 and 1973 to serve all eligible families who could be reached. In earlier years funding had prevented the expansion of the program to all eligible persons. Beginning with 1973 the list of eligible foods was enlarged to include imported foods and seeds and plants for home gardens. Previously stamps were limited to purchases of domestically produced foods.

By the end of fiscal year 1973 the food stamp program was operating in 2,227 project areas. These were located in 47 states and the District of Columbia.

CHAPTER 8

Program Interrelations and Costs

The presentation of program operations treated the various commodity, export, food, and other programs individually. But to imply that one program was unrelated to the others belies the reality. In some cases programs were created and administered with full knowledge of their interaction; in other instances programs caused unforeseen consequences that required further attention. But whether the spillover effects among programs were anticipated and planned for or not, they were nonetheless real. It is these spillover effects — the interrelationships among programs — that are addressed first in this chapter. Then, and of paramount concern to all students of farm policy, we examine program costs.

Program Interrelationships

The problems that gave rise to farm programs usually emerged in the form of depressed prices and incomes for one or more groups of farmers — cotton farmers in the South, wheat farmers on the plains, dairy farmers in the Lake states, or corn farmers in the Corn Belt. But the problem of American agriculture in the 1950s and 1960s, as discussed in chapter 1, was one of general excess production capacity, not unique surplus situations for isolated groups of farmers. When programs were implemented to correct a specific commodity problem, such as a surplus situation in wheat, without consideration of the effects on other commodities, the problem was simply transferred from one commodity in agriculture to another. This follows from the fact that there are usually several technically feasible production possibilities for each parcel of land. If a farmer is restrained from planting one crop by a control program he simply shifts his productive resources to his next best alternative. Let us

295

consider, therefore, the substitution that took place among controlled and uncontrolled commodities as a result of the operation of commodity programs that failed to take into account the aggregate problem.

The production control programs of the 1950s consisted of acreage restrictions on corn, wheat, and cotton. These three crops together with the other feed grains and soybeans occupied three of every four acres of land planted to

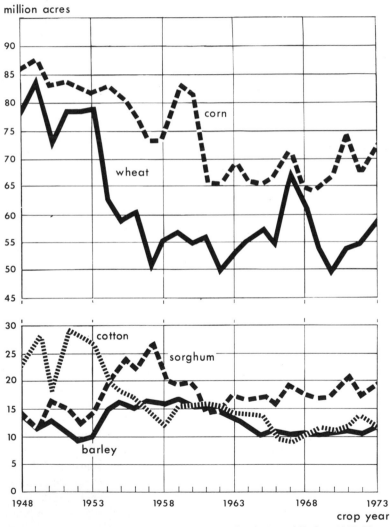

Figure 8-1. Acres Planted to Corn, Wheat, Cotton, Sorghum, and Barley, 1948–73

million acres

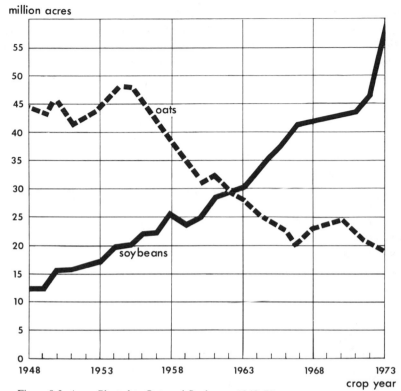

Figure 8-2. Acres Planted to Oats and Soybeans, 1948–73

crops in the United States. The supposition underlying the programs was that the crop sector of U.S. agriculture could be managed if these crops could be managed.

Production controls were in force in 1950 and after 1953 (except there were no acreage controls for corn in 1959 and 1960), and as shown in figure 8-1, acreage of these crops did decline in the years when acreage controls were imposed. What is also shown in figure 8-1 is that acreage of barley and sorghum expanded when planting of the three controlled crops was restricted. The opposite movements of sorghum and wheat acreage are especially notice-able. Another cropping shift occurred in the South where oats moved to some land withdrawn from cotton in the early 1950s; meanwhile, soybean acreage was expanding in all parts of the nation (see figure 8-2). Acreage was shifted to soybeans chiefly from cotton, corn, small grains, hay, and former pasture land. In this period there were no acreage controls on oats or soybeans so farmers were free to plant either one on land taken out of the controlled crops.

The net effect of these and all other cropping shifts is revealed in figure 8-3. We see that aggregate acreage in the United States changed very little from 1948 to 1955; acres removed from the production of one crop were simply replanted to another. Because of the substitution possibility among crops, the attempt to control production by restraining acreage of the three major crops did not work. This approach did not address itself to the essence of excess capacity problem — too many resources in agriculture *in the aggregate*.

Beginning in 1956, land retirement was added to the government's package of production control programs. This was the first effort to reduce the total resources employed in agriculture. As is evident in figure 8-3, these programs did reduce the aggregate amount of land sown to crops. Recall that under these programs the government paid farmers to idle land formerly planted to surplus crops. This gave farmers a new option: instead of planting all their cropland they could receive a government payment for withdrawing land from production; in essence, they could "rent" the land to the government. After this option became available, the shift to oats in the South ceased and oats

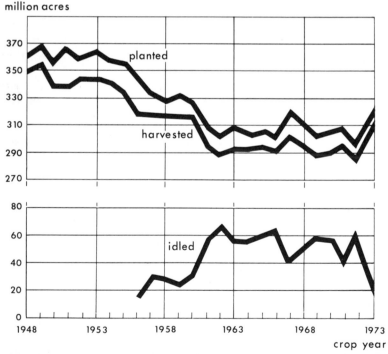

Figure 8-3. Acres Planted and Harvested for 59 Crops and Total Acres Idled under Government Programs, 1948–73

began to trend downward nationally. (This phenomenon was abetted by the increasing availability of herbicides that reduced the need to plant oats in rotation with corn or with corn and soybeans for weed control. This factor was especially important in the Corn Belt.)

In the 1960s production controls were added for sorghum and barley, thus curtailing shifts to these crops from other controlled crops. Also the retirement of land, in which the acres removed from the production of any crop must be held idle, was made a central feature of production control in the 1960s. The cumulative effect of these features was to hold some 50 million to 60 million acres of land out of production under government programs from 1961 through 1972, or more than was planted to any one of four major crops: barley, sorghum, cotton, and oats.

But year to year changes in acres planted and acres idled under commodity programs do not balance out neatly and exactly. For example, in 1960, when there was no acreage control program for corn, 81.4 million acres were planted to corn; in 1961 corn was planted on 65.9 million acres while 19.1 million acres were idled under the control program. This was a total of 85.0 million acres, 3.6 million more than was planted to corn in 1960. This phenomenon was called "slippage" by program administrators. However, this phenomenon is not so apparent when total acreage is examined. The sum of acres planted to 59 major crops and acres idled under government programs (depicted in figure 8-3) ranged from 340 million in 1973 to 365 million in 1962, compared with a range in acres planted from 353 to 365 million between 1948 and 1955 when there were no government programs to idle acres for payment.

Throughout the period 1948–73 oats and soybeans remained free of planting restrictions. Soybeans continued to move onto land previously planted to other crops and to new cropland, principally along the Mississippi Delta. Thus in 1973 the acres devoted to soybeans were almost five times that in 1948. Moving in the opposite direction, oats acreage contracted about 13 million acres in the period 1961–73.

Acreage controls in conjunction with land retirement programs did succeed in reducing the land resource in U.S. agriculture from the late 1950s to the early 1970s. But controlling output primarily through acreage restraints did not result in a production decline proportionate to the reduction in acreage. Technological advances were increasing farm productivity during this period — raising yields per acre. Farmers planted new and improved varieties, planted in narrower rows, and added purchased inputs — fertilizer, herbicides, and pesticides. Farmers employed more purchased inputs in part because they were embodied in the new and improved technologies that they were adopting, and in part because those purchased inputs were cheap relative to land. The net result was a substitution of purchased capital inputs for land under the programs. The consequences of substitution between land and other inputs is elaborated on in chapter 9.

To the extent that production control efforts do not reduce supplies to match demand at supported prices, physical surpluses are generated. Stocks are costly to carry and require careful handling to prevent or deter deterioration of the product. The stocks cannot be disposed of commercially without defeating the price support goals of the program. Hence means must be sought to expand demand through noncommercial domestic outlets and foreign markets. The scenario above is the one that took place in the 1950s and 1960s. It depicts the interaction among programs to control output and programs to handle and dispose of surpluses.

Weak production controls in the 1950s led to the accumulation of large stocks, especially stocks of feed grains, wheat, and cotton. The CCC became the manager of a huge and costly volume of these commodities through loan and purchase programs designed to maintain market prices at supported levels (see figure 8-4). Management of the stocks necessitated warehousing, transporting, processing, storing, and otherwise handling the commodities and providing the needed financial services.

The domestic and foreign food aid programs and the subsidies and credit assistance for commercial exports described in chapter 7 are the final link in the chain of inadequate production controls which led to surpluses which in turn stimulated disposal programs.[1]

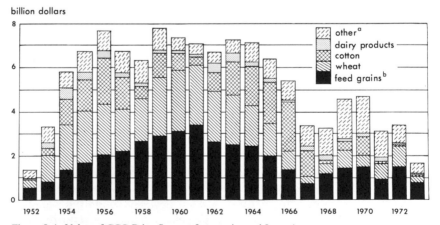

billion dollars

Figure 8-4. Value of CCC Price Support Inventories and Loans*
*Year ending June 30.
[a]Primarily soybeans and tobacco.
[b]Includes corn, barley, grain sorghums, oats, and rye.

The Cost of Farm Programs

To determine the cost of farm price and income support programs is not a simple matter. What constitutes such programs is one question. What definition of costs to employ is another. For our purposes throughout this book we have defined farm programs to be those directly affecting the demand for and supply of farm products, commodity prices, and the incomes of farmers. That practice is continued here. The concept of program costs employed here may then be defined as follows: all outlays by the federal government in each fiscal year made to influence the demand for and supply of farm products, commodity prices, and the incomes of farmers. Cost data are reported by fiscal year because government accounting procedures employ fiscal years. Although annual fiscal data do not permit exact comparison between annual costs and annual programs, the latter of which operate on crop or marketing year bases, the time periods are close enough to make approximate comparisons. For example, cost data for the fiscal year 1948 give a rough estimate of program costs for the crop year 1947.

Detailed annual expenditure and cost data by commodity group and type of program for the period 1948–73 are presented in tables 8-1 to 8-26 (at the end of this chapter). A study of the data presented in these tables permits one to analyze the broad components of program costs and how they changed through time. Two totals are presented for each year: line 10, total expenditures for all programs, and line 12, total farm program costs. The values of the two concepts, total expenditures for all programs and total farm program costs, are shown graphically by years in figure 8-5. The upper line in figure 8-5, total expenditures for all programs, is composed of (1) CCC costs in acquiring, handling, and disposing of commodities, less returns from sale of stocks or transfers to other governmental agencies in the same fiscal year (items 1 and 3 in tables 8-1 through 8-26); (2) administrative and other operating costs of price support programs (items 4 and 5 in the tables); (3) payments made to farmers (item 2 in the tables); (4) outlays for export subsidies and foreign and domestic food aid programs (items 6, 7, and 9 in the tables); and (5) expenditures of funds received under Section 32 (item 8 in the tables).

Estimates of total farm program costs are derived by reducing expenditures by one-half on the following four items: (1) CCC donations, (2) removal of surplus agricultural commodities (Section 32 expenditures), (3) school lunch and other food items, and (4) foreign aid and P.L. 480. This, we recognize, represents a somewhat arbitrary decision. But we could find no firmer basis for crediting the total farm expenditure account for benefits received by non-farm people from the operation of all farm programs. It is an estimate of these benefits and in our judgment a reasonable estimate. The amount credited, or

Figure 8-5. Government Costs of Farm and Related Programs, 1948–73

deducted, in this fashion averaged about one-fifth to one-fourth of total expenditures throughout most of the period, but varied considerably from year to year.

Total farm program costs are negative in 1951 since the credits in our accounting procedure exceed total expenditures on all programs in that year. This resulted from large sales from CCC stocks that had accumulated the two previous years; CCC inventory and loan transactions in 1951 obtained a net gain of $1.5 billion (table 8-4, line 1-e). Credits for nonfarm benefits peaked in 1957 and 1973 when food and foreign food aid programs were exceptionally large relative to farm program costs. In these two years about one-third of total expenditures was estimated to benefit people other than farmers. At the opposite extreme, only 8 percent of total expenditures was credited in 1953 and 1954 after the peak of post–World War II foreign aid programs and before the advent of P.L. 480. In figure 8-5 credits appear as the difference between the two lines.

Both total program expenditures and farm program costs trended upward over the period 1948–73: total program expenditures rising from a level of $1 billion in fiscal 1948 to a level of $8 billion in 1973; total farm program costs rising from a level of $1 billion in 1948 to a level of $6 billion in 1973. But the upward pace was exceedingly uneven. From 1952 to 1963 costs climbed in all but four scattered years. Then costs were reduced for four consecutive years, 1964–67, when once again they turned upward. The upward trend since 1968 is much more marked for the category total program expenditures, than for the category total farm program costs, reflecting the growth in food programs during these later years.

The changing structure of farm programs, from the early 1950s to the early 1970s, is portrayed in figure 8-6. In the period 1953–55, when product prices rode on the loan rate and were held at those levels by withdrawals of supplies from the market, two-thirds of expenditures occurred for CCC inventory and loan operations. The second largest category of expenditure was for foreign aid programs.

Foreign aid data for 1948–54 (tables 8-1 to 8-7) include only those outlays classified as foreign economic aid to other governments that were spent in the United States for agricultural products. During the late 1940s and early 1950s there were two other types of foreign food aid programs that might be included in this category. They were (1) food supplies for foreign civilians distributed through U.S. military auspices and (2) special loans to foreign

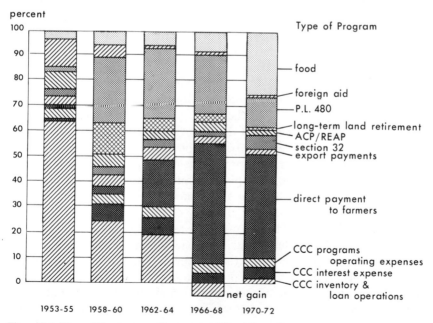

Figure 8-6. Type of Program as a Percentage of Total Expenditures

nations to help meet specific emergency needs. Expenditures for these two categories of foreign aid are given in table 8-27, along with adjustments that would occur in the totals in lines 10 and 12 in tables 8-1 to 8-7 if these programs were added. These additions would raise total expenditures for 1948, 1949, and 1950 by $1,143 million, $760 million, and $507 million respectively. Valid arguments can be offered for either the inclusion or the exclusion of these items from the cost data presented here for the purpose of evaluating farm program costs. But in our judgment, these programs were undertaken solely for foreign policy objectives at a time when surpluses did not exist at home and no consideration was given to farm price and income consequences; hence they are excluded from computations of farm program costs in tables 8-1 to 8-7.

By 1958–60, after P.L. 480 was operating in high gear, it took the largest share of expenditures for farm and related program activities (see figure 8-6). P.L. 480 and other foreign aid programs accounted for nearly one-third of total expenditures in 1958–60. CCC inventory and loan transactions dropped to less than one-fourth as stock accumulations were partially offset by stock liquidation. New in this period were the land retirement programs of the Soil Bank — the third largest category of costs.

New programs introduced in the early 1960s to support farmers' incomes by direct payments instead of through price-supporting action are reflected in the 1962–64 bar of figure 8-6. About one-fifth of expenditures were direct payments to farmers — the same share as CCC inventory and loan operations. The share devoted to land retirement programs dropped from 1958–60 to 1962–64, but some of these types of programs were picked up in the direct payment category in the 1962–64 period. Annual acreage diversion programs in the 1960s are classified as direct payments in these tables whereas the annual Soil Bank programs of the late 1950s are classified as short-term land retirement. If land retirement and direct payments are summed, their combined share of expenditures was 16 percent in 1958–60 and 24 percent in 1962–64. Together with the program efforts to reduce production of surplus commodities, strong impetus was given to foreign surplus disposal programs in the 1960s. Hence P.L. 480 programs continued to absorb the largest share of program costs in the early 1960s.

When price support for the major crops was lowered to world levels in the mid-1960s, and the surplus-producing capacity of agriculture was held in check by a system of voluntary acreage controls, the shift from government commodity operations to farm income support through direct payments became marked. Fifty percent of government outlays for farm and related programs in 1966–68 were direct payments to farmers (figure 8-6). Commodity operations by CCC resulted in a net gain to the government in this period, as stocks were sold in a buoyant export market. P.L. 480 continued to loom large, accounting for one-fourth of expenditures for all programs. Also during this period the expanding role of food programs began to emerge, but it was not until the 1970s that food program costs increased sharply.

In the 1970–72 period, food programs accounted for one-fourth of expenditures. Direct payments remained as the largest category, but slipped below one-half — not because the absolute level of payments was down but because total expenditures were up. The share accounted for by P.L. 480 was cut in half from the level of the previous decade. Though small, another category, export subsidies, is worth noting. Subsidies ran about 5 percent of total expenditures from the mid-1950s to the mid-1960s, when U.S. prices were supported above world levels for such important export commodities as cotton and wheat. After U.S. prices were lowered to world levels the need for subsidies was reduced and export payments decreased in importance.

The variation of program costs among commodity groups is presented in figure 8-7. Feed grains, wheat, and cotton were the three most costly commodity groups. The combined share of these three commodities for the five

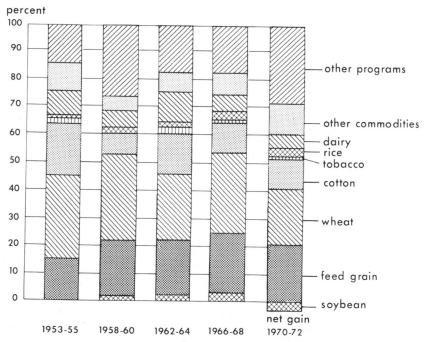

Figure 8-7. Expenditures by Commodity Groups and Other Programs as a Percentage of Total Expenditures

periods shown ranged from 54 to 64 percent of total expenditures. In all periods except the last, wheat was the most expensive, though in 1970–72 wheat and feed grain programs cost about the same.

The various program expenditures which sum into the category of total expenditures for all programs, in tables 8-1 to 8-26, represent for the most part transfer payments from taxpayers to some combination of farmers, middlemen, and consumers.[2] These transfers of moneys were made for a purpose — to support the incomes of farmers, to provide food aid to the poor and the needy, and to enable the agricultural industry to grow and restructure itself in an orderly fashion over time. But those program expenditures did not, as the direct result of productive activities, increase the national income. The total product available to society was not increased in any given year as the result of the transfer payment.. The government, through a set of revenue raising and expenditure programs, simply transferred moneys from taxpayers to farmers, middlemen, and consumers.

The category of total farm program costs (total expenditures for all programs *less* credits for nonfarm benefits) in tables 8-1 to 8-26 again is a measure of transfer payments. But in this latter case the category represents an attempt to measure the transfer payments made to assist in some way farm business enterprises. It is possible to argue that the estimates presented for each year from 1948 to 1973 under the heading of total farm program costs is not an accurate, or proper, measure of those transfer payments made to assist the farm sector of the economy. This is the case for two reasons. First, the credits indicated for nonfarm program benefits (item 11, tables 8-1 to 8-26) were, for lack of a rational basis, arbitrarily determined to be equal to one-half of the program expenditures for the programs included in item 11 of tables 8-1 through 8-26. It could be argued that we were either too generous or too niggardly in the credits employed. Second, it might be argued that we provided credits for nonfarm benefits in item 11 of table 8-1 through 8-26 for programs that should not have been included under item 11; or, contrariwise, it might be argued that credit for certain nonfarm benefits should have been included under item 11 which were not included. Two such possible nonfarm benefits come to mind: the assured food supply, and resulting price stability, that derived to consumers from that large stock of storable commodities acquired and held by government under the farm programs; and the increased efficiency in farm production, hence lower relative food prices to consumers in the long run, resulting from the elimination of price risk to farmers under the farm programs. If we had provided some measure of credit under item 11 of tables 8-1 through 8-26 for the possible nonfarm benefits noted above, the values indicated under the category of total farm program costs would have been somewhat smaller for most years in the period 1948–73.

But we did not include credits for the latter possible nonfarm benefits because the fact of the benefits is controversial and it is difficult if not impossible to measure those benefits quantitatively. Thus, given the data available, we present one estimate, one we believe is reasonable, of the transfer payments made to assist farm business enterprises under the category of total farm program costs in tables 8-1 through 8-26.

To summarize this discussion, the money costs to U.S. taxpayers of all government programs — production control, surplus disposal, storage, price support, and direct payments — aimed at supporting farm prices and incomes for the period 1948–73 were very great indeed. Gross government expenditures on all these programs for the 26-year period were $126.4 billion. A concept of total farm program costs, in which credit is given for nonfarm benefits, yields a total of $96.2 billion for the 26-year period. In other words, after credit is given for the nonfarm benefits of the many programs involved, U.S. taxpayers paid on the average $3.7 billion per year to support farm prices and incomes from 1948 to and including 1973.

In one year, 1951, taxpayers earned a profit of $340 million from the operation of farm price and income support programs (surplus stocks were sold at a profit during the Korean conflict); in 1969 and again in 1972 the cost of farm programs to the taxpayer reached a high of $6.6 billion. In general, the trend in farm program costs over the period was up — from a level approximating $1 billion per year in 1948 to a level approximating $6 billion per year in the early 1970s.

General Sources and Explanatory Notes
For Tables 8-1 to 8-26

The presentation of the data in tables 8-1 to 8-26 generally follows the accounting concepts and definitions used by G. E. Brandow to determine government costs of the 1968 farm program in Iowa State University Center for Agricultural and Economic Development, "Cost of Farm Programs," *Benefits and Burdens of Rural Development* (Ames: Iowa State University Press, 1970), pp. 77–88.

Primary Data Sources

The primary data sources are as follows:

Commodity Credit Corporation Report of Financial Condition and Operations as of June 30 . . . for the years 1948–73. *Commodity Credit Corporation Revised Comparative Financial Data Fiscal Years 1953–1961.* Unpublished Commodity Credit Corporation table "Realized Loss or Gain and CCC Costs," data for 1955–61, prepared February 1964. *Budget of the U.S. Gov-*

ernment for the years 1950–64. *Budget of the U.S. Government Appendix* for the years 1963–75. See the sections containing budgets for the U.S. Department of Agriculture. (Outlays for each fiscal year are given in the budget for two years later, e.g., 1948 outlays are in the 1950 budget.)

Additional sources that apply for specific years are noted on individual tables as appropriate.

Descriptions of Cost Items

Descriptions of cost items follow. Item numbers and letters below correspond with item identification in the tables. Some items do not appear for every year because of the introduction of new programs and the termination of others during the study period. For example, table 8-1 does not contain items 5a, 5b, 6b, 7a, 9a, 9c, 11a, 11c, 11e, and 11f because programs represented by those items did not operate in the fiscal year 1948. These descriptions are of necessity abbreviated. See chapters 6 and 7 for more thorough descriptions of the various programs.

   1. CCC inventory and loan transactions for price support programs.
      a. Sales plus loan repayments: This item represents loan redemptions and disposal of commodities acquired during price support operations of the CCC. It includes sales for dollars, barter, commodities paid for by other government agencies or by special congressional appropriations (e.g., P.L. 480). Donations by the CCC under Section 416 are not included. "Other costs and recoveries" by the CCC are included (Costs appear as negative items.)
      b. Purchases plus loans made: This item represents outlays for loans on farm products and the cost of acquiring inventories under purchase programs. Cost items called "other additions or deductions" by CCC are included. (Deductions appear as negative items.)
      c. Gross loss (gains) on stocks: The difference between lines 1a and 1b.
      d. Storage, handling, transportation, and reseal expense; sometimes called "inventory carrying charges."
   2. Direct commodity payments made to producers participating in commodity programs.
   3. CCC interest (net): Net interest income is not allocated to commodities for 1948 and 1949. For 1950–73, net interest cost is allocated to commodities on the basis of average value of inventories and loans, e.g., for 1950, values as of July 1, 1949, and June 30, 1950, are averaged for commodity groups.
   4. Operating expenses of price support programs — specific coverage varies by year; see the footnotes to the tables.

5. a. Long-term land retirement (1956–73).
   b. Short-term land retirement (1957–59): Contains costs of Soil Bank acreage reserve program. Annual land retirement under commodity programs for 1961–73 appear under item 2, Direct commodity payment.
   c. Agricultural conservation: Agricultural Conservation Program, ACP (1948–70); Rural Environmental Assistance Program, REAP (1971–73).
6. a. Commodity export program: Subsidies paid or losses incurred by the CCC for exports when domestic prices exceeded world prices. If the sale price is larger than the cost, net gain is shown as a negative item.
   b. International Wheat Agreement (1950–66): Includes differential payments for exportation of private and CCC stocks. Only differential payments are charged to IWA. The cost of and proceeds from CCC stocks exported under the IWA are in lines 1a and 1b; when commodity costs exceed proceeds, the difference is the differential payment, a form of export subsidy.
7. a. P.L. 480 (1955–73).
   Gross program costs: This item represents the total cost of the food aid program. It includes the total of P.L. 480 sales for foreign currencies, credit sales for dollars, and Title II donations. For 1955–66 it also includes the cost of ocean transportation on commodities donated through voluntary agencies and some costs of exporting CCC inventories but not the acquisition or storage costs of these inventories. (Donations through voluntary agencies and under CCC authority were not part of P.L. 480 in 1955–66).
   (i) Sale of foreign currencies: This item shows the proceeds to the CCC from the sale and use of foreign currencies.
   (ii) Dollar repayments: This item shows the recovery of costs through dollar repayments to the CCC by foreign governments and private trade entities.
   b. Foreign aid: Includes only expenditures specifically identified as made in the United States for agricultural products.
8. Removal of surplus agricultural commodities: Section 32. Data are not available to allocate expenditures by commodity groups, except dairy; hence most costs are recorded in ''Other'' column.
9. a. Special school milk (1955–73).
   b. School lunch/child nutrition (1948–73): School lunch costs exclude the value of foods obtained under Section 416 by the CCC and under Section 32 authority. The school lunch program was incorporated into the child nutrition program in 1967.

    c. Food stamp (1961–73).

10. Total expenditures for all farm and related programs: Sum of items le to 9.

11. Credit for nonfarm benefits: A credit of one-half of cost represents an arbitrary decision to take account of the positive benefits of these programs to individuals and groups other than farmers. Because of rounding, these lines do not exactly equal one-half of the lines above.

    a. CCC donations (1950–73): Commodities donated from CCC inventories under Sections 202 and 416 of the Agricultural Act of 1949. The costs of these inventories are included in line 1b and are not deducted in line 1a. The amounts shown here are one-half of the total cost of commodities donated.

    b. Removal of surplus agricultural commodities: one-half of item 8.

    c. Special school milk (1955–73): one-half of item 9a.

    d. School lunch/child nutrition: one-half of item 9b.

    e. Food stamp (1961–73): one-half of item 9c.

    f. P.L. 480 (1955–73): one-half of item 7a.

    g. Foreign aid: one-half of item 7b.

    h. Total of items 11a–11g above.

12. Total farm program costs: Line 10 minus line 11h. Totals for individual commodities do not include unallocated costs.

Definitions of Commodity Headings

Feed grains: corn, grain sorghum, barley, oats, and rye, and their products; for item 7b, foreign aid, 1948–54, rye is included with wheat

Wheat: wheat and wheat products

Cotton: cotton and cotton products

Soybeans: soybeans and soybean products; for item 7b, foreign aid, 1948–54, soybeans and products are included with "other"

Rice: rough and milled

Other: direct commodity payments consist of Sugar Act payments all years and Wool Act payments 1956–73

Miscellaneous Notes

. . . means zero or negligible.

Values in parentheses indicate negative items, i.e., gains or credits.

Cost Item[a]	Feed Grains	Wheat	Cotton	Soybeans	Tobacco	Rice	Dairy Products	Other	Total
1. CCC inventory and loan transactions for price support programs									
a. Sales plus loan repayments	$ 18.28	$ 56.73	$ 1.90	$ 7.18	$ 8.80	...	$ 19.62	$563.29	$ 675.80
b. Purchases plus loans made ...	2.13	63.76	36.85	7.25	123.97	...	8.33	390.93	633.22
c. Gross loss on stocks ...	(16.15)	7.03	34.95	.07	115.17	...	(11.29)	(172.36)	(42.58)
d. Storage, handling, transportation	...	...	.07	.01	.19	...	.90	23.52	24.69
e. Subtotal ...	(16.15)	7.03	35.02	.08	115.36	...	(10.39)	(148.84)	(17.89)
2. Direct commodity payments ...	...	...	...	...	...	...	...	60.29	60.29
3. CCC interest (net) ...	...	...	...	...	...	...	...	(7.31)	(7.31)
4. Operating expenses[b] ...	...	...	...	...	...	...	...	20.50	20.50
5. c. Agricultural conservation ...	...	...	...	...	...	...	...	211.77	211.77
6. a. Commodity export program ...	...	...	...	...	...	...	...	.01	.01
7. b. Foreign aid[c] ...	53.90	421.90	80.00	...	32.40	$ 8.20	21.90	143.20	761.50
8. Removal of surplus agricultural commodities ...	...	...	...	...	...	...	...	50.79	50.79
9. b. School lunch ...	...	...	...	...	...	...	...	...	68.31
10. Total expenditures for all programs ...	37.75	428.93	115.02	.08	147.76	8.20	11.51	105.44	1,147.97
11. Credit for nonfarm benefits (one-half of cost)									
b. Removal of surplus agricultural commodities ...	...	...	...	...	...	...	...	25.40	25.40
d. School lunch ...	...	...	...	...	...	...	...	...	34.16
g. Foreign aid ...	27.00	211.00	40.00	...	16.20	4.10	10.90	71.60	380.80
h. Total credits ...	27.00	211.00	40.00	...	16.20	4.10	10.90	97.00	440.36
12. Total farm program costs ...	10.75	217.93	75.02	.08	131.56	4.10	.61	8.44	707.61

[a]Items 5, 6, 7, 9, and 11 contain only those subitems appropriate for 1948. Programs represented by the missing letters did not operate in 1948. This practice is followed for tables 8-1 through 8-26. See Explanatory Notes.

[b]Includes operating and administrative expenses for Production and Market Administration, Sugar Act, Section 392 (National and State Administration) and Section 388 (Local Administration). Also includes net other program costs and adjustments of the CCC.

[c]Data adopted from *Foreign Aid Program, Compilation of Studies and Surveys*, Senate Document no. 52, 84th Congress, 1st session, 1957, pp. 833–836. Data recorded for fiscal 1948 are one-half of 1948 calendar year. This amount ($761.5 billion) compares reasonably well with the value of food donation and grant aid to other governments reported in table 7-6 ($739 billion).

Table 8-2. Government Cost (in Millions of Dollars) of Farm and Related Programs for Year ending June 30, 1949

Cost Item	Feed Grains	Wheat	Cotton	Soybeans	Tobacco	Rice	Dairy Products	Other	Total
1. CCC inventory and loan transactions for price support programs									
a. Sales plus loan repayments	$ 41.54	$148.34	$218.04	$ 1.60	$ 94.26	$ .63	$ 1.00	$392.28	$ 897.69
b. Purchases plus loans made	586.95	640.48	822.31	24.01	107.70	.68	14.36	860.86	3,057.35
c. Gross loss on stocks	545.41	492.14	604.27	22.41	13.44	.05	13.36	468.58	2,159.66
d. Storage, handling, transportation	18.76	67.25	.16	1.91	.01	...	.60	52.17	140.86
e. Subtotal	564.17	559.39	604.43	24.32	13.45	.05	13.96	520.75	2,300.52
2. Direct commodity payments	...	...	...	...	...	...	...	55.95	55.95
3. CCC interest (net)	...	...	...	...	...	...	...	2.59	2.59
4. Operating expenses[a]	...	...	...	...	...	...	...	47.66	47.66
5. c. Agricultural conservation	...	...	...	...	...	...	...	148.31	148.31
6. a. Commodity export program	...	...	.06	...	...	...	...	...	.06
7. b. Foreign aid[b]	138.80	617.00	318.80	...	109.20	11.20	52.00	245.20	1,492.20
8. Removal of surplus agricultural commodities	...	...	...	...	...	...	...	75.36	75.36
9. b. School lunch	...	...	...	...	...	...	...	74.90	74.90
10. Total expenditures for all programs	702.97	1,176.39	923.29	24.32	122.65	11.25	65.96	897.26	4,197.55
11. Credit for nonfarm benefits (one-half of cost)									
b. Removal of surplus agricultural commodities	...	...	...	...	...	...	...	37.68	37.68
d. School lunch	...	...	...	...	...	...	...	37.45	37.45
g. Foreign aid	69.40	308.50	159.40	...	54.60	5.60	26.00	122.60	746.10
h. Total credits	69.40	308.50	159.40	...	54.60	5.60	26.00	160.28	821.23
12. Total farm program costs	633.57	867.89	763.89	24.32	68.05	5.65	39.96	736.98	3,376.32

[a]See table 8-1 (1948), footnote b.

312

Cost Item	Feed Grains	Wheat	Cotton	Soybeans	Tobacco	Rice	Dairy Products	Other	Total
1. CCC inventory and loan transactions for price support programs									
a. Sales plus loan repayments	$227.25	$514.70	$407.13	$52.58	$78.23	$10.83	$30.30	$370.98	$1,692.00
b. Purchases plus loans made	826.30	703.75	459.32	20.57	68.91	15.83	193.32	541.09	2,829.09
c. Gross loss on stocks	599.05	189.05	52.19	(32.01)	(9.32)	5.00	163.02	170.11	1,137.09
d. Storage, handling, transportation	82.74	87.39	3.27	1.31	.01	.67	7.63	69.19	252.21
e. Subtotal	681.79	276.44	55.46	(30.70)	(9.31)	5.67	170.65	239.30	1,389.30
2. Direct commodity payments	...	...	...	...	...	...	...	59.54	59.54
3. CCC interest (net)	7.56	5.84	5.49	.12	1.10	.02	.75	3.76	24.64
4. Operating expenses[a]	...	...	...	...	...	...	...	...	86.28
5. Agricultural conservation	...	...	...	...	...	...	...	...	212.59
6. a. Commodity export program	...	...	...	...	...	...	...	...	...
b. International wheat agreement	...	75.51	...	...	...	...	...	...	75.51
7. b. Foreign aid[b]	149.60	321.60	480.40	...	153.50	9.20	41.60	170.40	1,326.30
8. Removal of surplus agricultural commodities	...	...	...	...	...	...	...	95.97	95.97
9. b. School lunch	...	...	...	...	...	...	...	...	83.07
10. Total expenditures for all programs	838.95	679.39	541.35	(30.58)	145.29	14.89	213.00	568.97	3,353.20
11. Credit for nonfarm benefits (one-half of cost)									
a. CCC donations	...	...	...	...	...	...	4.29	5.41	9.70
b. Removal of surplus agricultural commodities	...	...	...	...	...	...	...	47.99	47.99
d. School lunch	...	...	...	...	...	...	...	...	41.54
g. Foreign aid	74.80	160.80	240.20	...	76.80	4.60	20.80	85.20	663.20
h. Total credits	74.80	160.80	240.20	...	76.80	4.60	25.09	138.60	762.43
12. Total farm program costs	764.15	518.59	301.15	(30.58)	68.49	10.29	187.91	430.37	2,590.77

[a] See table 8-1 (1948), footnote b.

[b] For source, see table 8-1 (1948), footnote c. Data for fiscal 1950 are one-half calendar 1949 and one-half calendar 1950.

Table 8-4. Government Cost (in Millions of Dollars) of Farm and Related Programs for Year ending June 30, 1951

Cost Item	Feed Grains	Wheat	Cotton	Soybeans	Tobacco	Rice	Dairy Products	Other	Total
1. CCC inventory and loan transactions for price support programs									
a. Sales plus loan repayments	$599.59	$770.80	$786.10	$32.07	$91.30	$13.10	$121.10	$365.56	$2,779.62
b. Purchases plus loans made	202.92	379.31	3.85	31.16	80.08	11.06	49.39	322.20	1,079.97
c. Gross loss on stocks	(396.67)	(391.49)	(782.25)	(.91)	(11.22)	(2.04)	(71.71)	(43.36)	(1,699.65)
d. Storage, handling, transportation	66.39	88.06	2.67	.12	.01	.30	7.81	21.85	187.21
e. Subtotal	(330.28)	(303.43)	(779.58)	(.79)	(11.21)	(1.74)	(63.90)	(21.51)	(1,512.44)
2. Direct commodity payments	...	...	...	...	...	...	...	68.88	68.88
3. CCC interest (net)	7.82	4.84	2.61	.01	.88	.03	.61	2.47	19.27
4. Operating expenses[a]	...	...	...	...	...	...	...	...	82.29
5. c. Agricultural conservation	...	...	...	...	...	...	...	...	274.23
6. a. Commodity export program	...	...	...	...	...	...	...	...	...
b. International wheat agreement	...	178.18	...	...	...	...	...	...	178.18
7. b. Foreign aid[b]	118.60	305.60	411.80	...	113.40	8.80	22.60	103.70	1,084.50
8. Removal of surplus agricultural commodities	...	...	...	...	...	...	...	45.98	45.98
9. b. School lunch	...	...	...	...	...	...	...	...	82.76
10. Total expenditures for all programs	(203.86)	185.19	(365.17)	(.78)	103.07	7.09	(40.69)	199.52	323.65
11. Credit for nonfarm benefits (one-half of cost)									
a. CCC Donations	...	...	...	...	...	...	33.80	23.05	56.85
b. Removal of surplus agricultural commodities	...	...	...	...	...	...	...	22.99	22.99
d. School lunch	...	...	...	...	...	...	...	...	41.38
g. Foreign aid	59.30	152.80	205.90	...	56.70	4.40	11.30	51.90	542.30
h. Total credits	59.30	152.80	205.90	...	56.70	4.40	45.10	97.84	663.42
12. Total farm program costs	(263.16)	32.39	(571.07)	(.78)	46.37	2.69	(85.79)	101.68	(339.77)

[a] Includes operating and administrative expenses for Agriculture Production Programs, Production and Marketing Administration, Sugar Act, Section 392

Cost Item	Feed Grains	Wheat	Cotton	Soybeans	Tobacco	Rice	Dairy Products	Other	Total
1. CCC inventory and loan transactions for price support programs									
a. Sales plus loan repayments	$451.67	$610.55	$158.36	$25.49	$48.40	$22.48	$8.45	$176.31	$1,501.71
b. Purchases plus loans made	84.35	450.48	189.23	25.71	129.79	21.15	9.16	202.44	1,112.31
c. Gross loss on stocks	(367.32)	(160.07)	30.87	.22	81.39	(1.33)	.71	26.13	(389.40)
d. Storage, handling, transportation	40.03	68.02	.16	.01	.02	.06	.84	9.61	118.75
e. Subtotal	(327.29)	(92.05)	31.03	.23	81.41	(1.27)	1.55	35.74	(270.65)
2. Direct commodity payments	…	…	…	…	…	…	…	60.30	60.30
3. CCC interest (net)	7.46	4.59	.33	.01	1.55	.02	.05	2.03	16.04
4. Operating expenses[a]	…	…	…	…	…	…	…	…	58.59
5. c. Agricultural conservation	…	…	…	…	…	…	…	…	261.20
6. a. Commodity export program	…	…	…	…	…	…	…	…	…
b. International wheat agreement	…	166.93	…	…	…	…	…	…	166.93
7. b. Foreign aid[b]	71.60	247.60	234.20	…	48.00	2.80	11.40	48.60	664.20
8. Removal of surplus agricultural commodities	…	…	…	…	…	…	…	37.53	37.53
9. b. School lunch	…	…	…	…	…	…	…	…	83.57
10. Total expenditures for all programs	(248.23)	327.07	265.56	.24	130.96	1.53	13.00	184.20	1,077.71
11. Credit for nonfarm benefits (one-half of cost)									
a. CCC donations	…	…	…	…	…	…	.06	4.35	4.41
b. Removal of surplus agricultural commodities	…	…	…	…	…	…	…	18.77	18.77
d. School lunch	…	…	…	…	…	…	…	…	41.79
g. Foreign aid	35.80	123.80	117.10	…	24.00	1.40	5.70	24.30	332.10
h. Total credits	35.80	123.80	117.10	…	24.00	1.40	5.76	47.42	397.07
12. Total farm program costs	(284.03)	203.27	148.46	.24	106.96	.15	7.24	136.78	680.64

[a] See table 8-4 (1951), footnote a.

[b] For source, see table 8-1 (1948), footnote c. Data for fiscal 1952 are one-half calendar 1951 and one-half calendar 1952.

Table 8-6. Government Cost (in Millions of Dollars) of Farm and Related Programs for Year ending June 30, 1953

Cost Item	Feed Grains	Wheat	Cotton	Soybeans	Tobacco	Rice	Dairy Products	Other	Total
1. CCC inventory and loan transactions for price support programs									
a. Sales plus loan repayments	$243.74	$244.68	$119.05	$ 21.69	$134.43	$ 2.53	$22.54	$127.88	$ 916.54
b. Purchases plus loans made	517.37	990.18	390.74	30.96	161.89	1.15	290.58	429.96	2,812.83
c. Gross loss on stocks	273.63	745.50	271.69	9.27	27.46	(1.38)	268.04	302.08	1,896.29
d. Storage, handling, transportation	30.78	79.15	2.20	.70	.21	.22	1.78	22.20	137.24
e. Subtotal	304.41	824.65	273.89	9.97	27.67	(1.16)	269.82	324.28	2,033.53
2. Direct commodity payments	...	...	...	...	...	...	...	62.62	62.62
3. CCC interest (net)	9.51	11.13	2.44	.07	2.73	.01	1.84	4.54	32.27
4. Operating expenses[a]	...	...	...	...	...	...	...	...	61.30
5. c. Agricultural conservation	...	...	...	...	...	...	...	...	272.74
6. a. Commodity export program	...	...	...	...	...	...	...	...	...
b. International wheat agreement	...	125.87	...	...	...	...	...	...	125.87
7. b. Foreign aid[b]	43.70	103.40	151.40	...	11.60	...	8.00	27.60	345.70
8. Removal of surplus agricultural commodities	...	...	...	...	...	...	...	82.29	82.29
9. b. School lunch	...	...	...	...	...	...	...	...	82.84
10. Total expenditures for all programs	357.62	1,065.05	427.73	10.04	42.00	(1.15)	279.66	501.33	3,099.16
11. Credit for nonfarm benefits (one-half of cost)									
a. CCC donations	...	...	...	...	...	...	.97	.37	1.34
b. Removal of surplus agricultural commodities	...	...	...	...	...	...	...	41.15	...
d. School lunch	...	...	...	...	...	...	...	...	41.15
	...	...	...	...	...	...	...	...	41.42
g. Foreign aid	21.90	51.70	75.70	...	5.80	...	4.00	13.80	172.90
h. Total credits	21.90	51.70	75.70	...	5.80	...	4.97	55.32	256.81
12. Total farm program costs	335.72	1,013.35	352.03	10.04	36.20	(1.15)	274.69	446.01	2,842.35

[a]Includes operating and administrative expenses for Agriculture Adjustment Program, Commodity Stabilization Service, Sugar Act, Section 392 (National

Cost Item	Feed Grains	Wheat	Cotton	Soybeans	Tobacco	Rice	Dairy Products	Other	Total
1. CCC inventory and loan transactions for price support programs									
a. Sales plus loan repayments	$367.06	$399.95	$301.12	$ 86.49	$ 81.85	$ 7.92	$127.02	$291.89	$1,663.30
b. Purchases plus loans made	861.93	1,123.31	1,155.43	76.83	118.43	19.81	500.51	358.06	4,214.31
c. Gross loss on stocks	494.87	723.36	854.31	(9.66)	36.58	11.89	373.49	66.17	2,551.01
d. Storage, handling, transportation	60.20	144.03	12.94	.40	.21	.36	26.85	12.63	257.62
e. Subtotal	555.07	867.39	867.25	(9.26)	36.79	12.25	400.34	78.80	2,808.63
2. Direct commodity payments	17.55	...	...	...	...	...	...	66.45	66.45
3. CCC interest (net)	...	27.15	11.79	.09	3.74	.10	6.52	7.60	74.54
4. Operating expenses[a]	...	...	...	...	...	...	...	...	147.91
5. c. Agricultural conservation	...	...	...	...	...	...	...	...	171.34
6. a. Commodity export program	...	26.09	...	...	...	...	...	...	26.09
b. International wheat agreement	...	55.89	...	...	...	...	...	...	55.89
7. b. Foreign aid[b]	35.40	130.60	119.30	...	3.75	...	22.55	32.80	344.40
8. Removal of surplus agricultural commodities	...	...	...	...	...	...	...	177.56	177.56
9. b. School lunch	...	...	...	...	...	...	...	...	83.52
10. Total expenditures for all programs	608.02	1,107.12	998.34	(9.17)	44.28	12.35	429.41	363.21	3,956.33
11. Credit for nonfarm benefits (one-half of cost)									
a. CCC donations	...	...	...	...	...	...	24.94	...	24.94
b. Removal of surplus agricultural commodities	...	...	59.60	...	...	...	...	88.78	88.78
d. School lunch	17.70	65.30	...	...	...	...	11.30	...	41.76
g. Foreign aid	...	...	...	...	1.90	...	...	16.40	172.20
h. Total credits	17.70	65.30	59.60	...	1.90	...	36.24	105.18	327.68
12. Total farm program costs	590.32	1,041.82	938.74	(9.17)	42.38	12.35	393.17	258.03	3,628.65

[a]See table 8-6 (1953), footnote a.

[b]For source, see table 8-1 (1948), footnote c. Data for fiscal 1954 are one-half calendar 1953 and one-half calendar 1954, plus exports under P.L. 77 and P.L. 216, bills providing wheat for Pakistan and foreign famine relief.

317

Table 8-8. Government Cost (in Millions of Dollars) of Farm and Related Programs for Year ending June 30, 1955

Cost Item	Feed Grains	Wheat	Cotton	Soybeans	Tobacco	Rice	Dairy Products	Other	Total
1. CCC inventory and loan transactions for price support programs									
a. Sales plus loan repayments	$373.42	$684.09	$197.05	$ 52.34	$ 55.38	$128.94	$ 65.05	$256.99	$1,813.26
b. Purchases plus loans made	739.50	914.57	420.26	83.59	203.53	229.52	38.21	231.56	3,060.74
c. Gross loss on stocks	366.08	230.48	223.21	31.25	148.15	100.58	173.16	(25.43)	1,247.48
d. Storage, handling, transportation	108.16	210.48	16.54	.37	.20	5.32	32.30	19.69	393.06
e. Subtotal	474.24	440.96	239.75	31.62	148.35	105.90	205.46	(5.74)	1,640.54
2. Direct commodity payments	...	...	...	...	...	...	...	69.35	69.35
3. CCC interest (net)	11.49	17.39	9.51	.13	2.41	.55	3.32	3.09	47.89
4. Operating expenses[a]	...	...	...	...	...	...	...	...	169.47
5. Agricultural conservation	...	...	...	...	...	...	...	...	235.15
6. a. Commodity export program	...	49.58	...	...	...	...	...	...	49.58
b. International wheat agreement	...	98.48	...	...	...	...	...	...	98.48

Item									
7. a. P.L. 480									
Gross program costs	26.61	141.63	11.19	…	3.94	3.80	13.11	15.51	215.79
Less:									
(i) Sale of foreign currencies	…	…	…	…	…	…	…	…	…
(ii) Dollar repayments	…	…	…	…	…	…	…	…	…
Subtotal	…	…	…	…	…	…	…	…	215.79
b. Foreign aid[b]	26.06	129.36	210.13	17.69	11.37	.01	1.61	54.42	450.65
8. Removal of surplus agricultural commodities	…	…	…	…	…	…	…	58.91	58.91
9. a. Special school milk	…	…	…	…	…	…	22.23	…	22.23
b. School lunch	…	…	…	…	…	…	…	…	83.10
10. Total expenditure for all programs	538.40	877.40	470.58	49.44	166.07	110.26	245.73	195.54	3,141.14
11. Credit for nonfarm benefits (one-half of cost)									
a. CCC donations	30.59	…	…	…	…	1.87	168.96	7.65	209.07
b. Removal of surplus agricultural commodities	…	…	…	…	…	…	…	29.46	29.46
c. Special school milk	…	…	…	…	…	…	11.12	…	11.12
d. School lunch	…	…	…	…	…	…	…	…	41.55
f. P.L. 480	13.31	70.82	5.59	…	1.97	1.90	6.56	7.75	107.90
g. Foreign aid	13.03	64.68	105.07	8.84	5.69	.01	.81	27.20	225.33
h. Total credits	56.93	135.50	110.66	8.84	7.66	3.78	187.45	72.06	624.43
12. Total farm program costs	481.47	741.90	359.92	40.60	158.41	106.48	58.28	123.48	2,516.71

[a] See table 8-6 (1953), footnote a.
[b] Value of agricultural commodities exported under Mutual Security Act authority, data from unpublished ERS tables.

Table 8-9. Government Cost (in Millions of Dollars) of Farm and Related Programs for Year ending June 30, 1956

Cost Item	Feed Grains	Wheat	Cotton	Soybeans	Tobacco	Rice	Dairy Products	Other	Total
1. CCC inventory and loan transactions for price support programs									
a. Sales plus loan repayments	$412.22	$775.77	$389.25	$ 87.96	$122.91	$134.43	$ 94.06	$316.44	$2,333.04
b. Purchases plus loans made	855.73	646.28	1,186.56	55.98	249.13	201.94	275.16	265.28	3,736.06
c. Gross loss on stocks	443.51	(129.49)	797.31	(31.98)	126.22	67.51	181.10	(51.16)	1,403.02
d. Storage, handling, transportation	189.87	163.64	35.25	2.63	...	12.26	27.63	83.92	515.20
e. Subtotal	633.38	34.15	832.56	(29.35)	126.22	79.77	208.73	32.76	1,918.22
2. Direct commodity payments[a]	...	...	...	...	...	...	...	122.38	122.38
3. CCC interest (net)	40.74	53.79	37.85	.35	9.61	3.55	5.43	7.06	158.38
4. Operating expenses[b]	...	...	...	...	...	...	...	...	193.34
5. a. Long-term land retirement	...	...	...	...	...	...	...	...	3.76
c. Agricultural conservation	...	...	...	...	...	...	...	...	215.16
6. a. Commodity export program	...	69.58	...	...	...	...	...	...	69.58
b. International wheat agreement	...	89.68	...	...	...	...	...	...	89.68

7. a. P.L. 480

Gross program costs	44.53	356.69	93.24	27.14	35.71	47.69	26.92	76.32	708.24
Less:									
(i) Sale of foreign currencies	...	...	...	...	...	...	...	...	(9.53)
(ii) Dollar repayments	...	...	...	...	...	...	...	...	...
Subtotal	...	...	...	...	...	...	...	...	693.71
b. Foreign aid[c]	32.27	112.98	115.22	13.58	1.65	2.46	16.55	59.76	354.47
8. Removal of surplus agricultural commodities	...	...	...	...	...	...	78.50	100.57	179.07
9. a. Special school milk	...	...	...	...	...	...	45.30	...	45.30
b. School lunch	...	...	...	...	...	...	...	...	82.69
10. Total expenditures for all programs	750.92	716.87	1,078.87	11.72	173.19	133.47	381.43	398.85	4,130.74
11. Credit for nonfarm benefits (one-half of cost)									
a. CCC donations	11.30	5.54	...	...	...	2.43	179.75	3.69	203.21
b. Removal of surplus agricultural commodities	...	...	...	...	...	...	39.25	50.29	89.34
c. Special school milk	...	...	...	...	...	...	22.65	...	22.65
d. School lunch	...	...	...	...	...	...	...	...	41.55
f. P.L. 480	22.27	178.35	46.62	13.57	17.85	23.84	13.46	38.16	354.12
g. Foreign aid	16.13	56.49	57.61	6.79	.83	1.23	8.27	29.89	177.24
h. Total credits	50.20	240.38	104.23	20.36	18.68	27.50	263.38	122.03	888.11
12. Total farm program costs	700.72	476.49	974.64	(8.64)	154.51	105.97	118.05	276.82	3,242.63

[a] Data for Wool Act payments obtained by telephone from CCC fiscal division.

[b] Includes operating and administrative expenses for Acreage Allotments and Marketing Quotas, Sugar Act, Section 392 (National and State Administration) and Section 388 (Local Administration). Also includes net other program costs and adjustments.

[c] See table 8-8 (1955), footnote b.

321

Table 8-10. Government Cost (in Millions of Dollars) of Farm and Related Programs for Year ending June 30, 1957

Cost Item	Feed Grains	Wheat	Cotton	Soybeans	Tobacco	Rice	Dairy Products	Other	Total
1. CCC inventory and loan transactions for price support programs									
a. Sales plus loan repayments	$509.92	$895.01	$1,190.86	$78.15	$149.39	$303.07	$129.98	$376.95	$3,633.33
b. Purchases plus loans made	784.93	566.76	780.89	127.46	199.81	230.09	321.20	261.73	3,272.87
c. Gross loss on stocks	275.01	(328.25)	(409.97)	49.31	50.42	(72.98)	191.22	(115.22)	(360.46)
d. Storage, handling, transportation	243.55	214.53	20.75	.29	...	12.15	20.60	12.73	524.60
e. Subtotal	518.56	(113.72)	(389.22)	49.60	50.42	(60.83)	211.82	(102.49)	164.14
2. Direct commodity payments[a]	...	...	...	...	...	...	...	118.98	118.98
3. CCC interest (net)	80.98	86.73	65.45	.94	19.49	5.20	5.97	10.12	274.88
4. Operating expenses[b]	...	...	...	...	...	...	...	...	193.79
5. a. Long-term land retirement[c]	...	...	...	...	...	...	...	...	37.25
b. Short-term land retirement[d]	...	...	...	...	...	...	...	...	510.79
c. Agricultural conservation	...	...	...	...	...	...	...	...	262.03
6. a. Commodity export program	...	133.18	14.23	...	...	...	.01	...	147.42
b. International wheat agreement	...	86.37	...	...	...	...	...	...	86.37

7. a. P.L. 480

Gross program costs	75.31	599.77	299.68	100.44	54.17	198.76	43.60	110.67	1,432.40
Less: (i) Sale of foreign currencies	...	...	...	...	...	...	...	...	(72.65)
(ii) Dollar repayments	...	...	...	...	...	...	...	...	...
Subtotal	...	...	...	...	...	...	...	...	1,409.75
b. Foreign aid[e]	43.13	122.81	120.44	20.70	.65	1.26	27.18	58.16	394.33
8. Removal of surplus agricultural commodities	...	...	...	...	...	...	55.40	115.70	171.10
9. a. Special school milk	...	...	...	...	...	...	56.57	...	56.57
b. School lunch	...	...	...	...	...	...	...	...	99.19
10. Total expenditures for all programs	717.98	915.14	110.58	171.68	124.73	144.39	400.55	311.14	3,926.59
11. Credit for nonfarm benefits (one-half of cost)									
a. CCC donations	74.07	21.98	...	...	...	25.39	100.97	3.92	226.33
b. Removal of surplus agricultural commodities	...	...	...	...	...	...	27.70	57.85	85.55
c. Special school milk	...	...	...	...	...	...	28.29	...	28.29
d. School lunch	...	...	...	...	...	...	...	...	49.60
f. P.L. 480	37.66	299.89	149.84	50.22	27.08	99.38	21.80	55.33	741.20
g. Foreign aid	21.56	61.41	60.22	10.35	.32	.63	13.59	29.08	197.16
h. Total credits	133.29	383.28	210.06	60.57	27.40	125.40	192.35	146.18	1,328.13
12. Total farm program costs	584.69	531.86	(99.48)	111.11	97.33	18.99	208.20	164.96	2,598.46

[a] See table 8-9 (1956), footnote a.
[b] See table 8-9 (1956), footnote b.
[c] Conservation Reserve Program of the Soil Bank.
[d] Acreage Reserve Program of the Soil Bank.
[e] See table 8-8 (1955), footnote b.

Table 8-11. Government Cost (in Millions of Dollars) of Farm and Related Programs for Year ending June 30, 1958

Cost Item	Feed Grains	Wheat	Cotton	Soybeans	Tobacco	Rice	Dairy Products	Other	Total
1. CCC inventory and loan transactions for price support programs									
a. Sales plus loan repayments	$550.01	$520.48	$1,166.58	$116.33	$ 77.72	$166.48	$161.50	$204.43	$2,963.53
b. Purchases plus loans made	948.64	489.44	490.30	148.03	82.91	165.66	357.16	251.99	2,934.13
c. Gross loss on stocks	398.63	(31.04)	(676.28)	31.70	5.19	(.82)	195.66	47.56	(29.40)
d. Storage, handling, transportation	271.69	199.50	19.27	.70	.04	9.31	19.76	9.33	529.60
e. Subtotal	670.32	168.46	(657.01)	32.40	5.23	8.49	215.42	56.89	500.20
2. Direct commodity payments[a]	...	...	...	...	...	...	...	84.33	84.33
3. CCC interest (net)	120.37	104.84	45.07	3.26	25.96	3.78	6.97	12.63	322.88
4. Operating expenses[b]	...	...	...	...	...	...	...	...	213.05
5. a. Long-term land retirement[c]	...	...	...	...	...	...	...	...	132.72
b. Short-term retirement[d]	...	...	...	...	...	...	...	...	518.82
c. Agricultural Conservation	...	...	...	...	...	...	...	...	213.85
6. a. Commodity export program	.51	85.00	15.47	...	...	...	.04	...	101.02
b. International wheat agreement	...	79.80	...	...	...	...	...	...	79.80

324

7. a. P.L. 480

Gross program costs	116.81	637.51	194.77	62.87	28.02	58.76	40.98	65.29	1,205.01
Less:									
(i) Sale of foreign currencies	...	...	...	...	...	...	...	...	(97.36)
(ii) Dollar repayments	...	...	...	...	...	...	...	...	...
Subtotal	...	...	...	...	...	...	...	...	1,107.65
b. Foreign aid[e]	12.77	65.94	98.86	21.25	...	1.06	18.30	9.22	227.40
8. Removal of surplus agricultural commodities	...	...	...	...	...	...	...	125.45	125.45
9. a. Special school milk	...	...	...	...	...	...	66.14	...	66.14
b. School lunch	...	...	...	...	...	...	...	...	99.99
10. Total expenditures for all programs	920.78	1,141.55	(302.84)	119.78	59.21	72.09	347.85	353.81	3,793.30
11. Credit for nonfarm benefits (one-half of cost)									
a. CCC donations	18.64	43.00	...	...	...	6.50	113.13	1.23	182.50
b. Removal of surplus agricultural commodities	...	...	...	...	...	...	...	62.73	62.73
c. Special school milk	...	...	...	...	...	...	33.07	...	33.07
d. School lunch	...	...	...	...	...	...	...	...	50.00
f. P.L. 480	58.41	318.76	97.39	31.43	14.01	29.38	20.49	32.64	602.51
g. Foreign aid	6.38	32.97	49.43	10.63	...	.53	9.15	4.61	113.70
h. Total credits	83.43	394.73	146.82	42.06	14.01	36.41	175.84	101.21	1,044.51
12. Total farm program costs	837.35	746.82	(449.66)	77.72	45.20	35.68	172.01	252.60	2,748.79

[a] See table 8-9 (1956), footnote a.
[b] See table 8-9 (1956), footnote b.
[c] See table 8-10 (1957), footnote c.
[d] See table 8-10 (1957), footnote d.
[e] See table 8-8 (1955), footnote b.

Table 8-12. Government Cost (in Millions of Dollars) of Farm and Related Programs for Year ending June 30, 1959

Cost Item	Feed Grains	Wheat	Cotton	Soybeans	Tobacco	Rice	Dairy Products	Other	Total
1. CCC inventory and loan transactions for price support programs									
a. Sales plus loan repayments	$561.90	$553.98	$438.68	$195.94	$93.81	$89.69	$126.10	$422.15	$2,482.25
b. Purchases plus loans made	871.94	1,122.16	1,172.96	261.20	106.25	93.20	230.03	302.91	4,160.65
c. Gross loss on stocks	310.04	568.18	734.28	65.26	12.44	3.51	103.93	(119.24)	1,678.40
d. Storage, handling, transportation	304.71	221.64	12.84	1.17	.99	7.36	13.10	8.30	570.11
e. Subtotal	614.75	789.82	747.12	66.43	13.43	10.87	117.03	(110.94)	2,248.51
2. Direct commodity payments[a]	...	...	...	...	...	...	...	152.38	152.38
3. CCC interest (net)	58.49	51.12	16.46	2.40	10.92	1.34	2.04	4.18	146.95
4. Operating expenses[b]	...	...	...	...	...	...	...	...	196.76
5. a. Long-term land retirement[c]	...	...	...	...	...	...	...	...	170.73
b. Short-term land retirement[d]	...	...	...	...	...	...	...	...	608.82
c. Agricultural conservation	...	...	...	...	...	...	...	...	239.30
6. a. Commodity export program	42.12	63.87	21.92	...	...	4.52	...	...	132.43
b. International wheat agreement	...	46.71	...	...	...	...	...	...	46.71

7. a. P.L. 480

Gross program costs	119.46	687.50	153.89	90.68	29.32	35.50	20.71	47.52	1,184.58
Less:									
(i) Sale of foreign currencies	...	...	...	...	...	...	...	...	(95.97)
(ii) Dollar repayments	...	...	...	...	...	...	...	...	...
Subtotal	...	...	...	...	...	...	...	...	1,088.61
b. Foreign aid[e]	.92	43.06	115.34	20.08	2.80	...	12.20	15.45	209.85
8. Removal of surplus agricultural commodities	...	...	...	...	...	...	...	140.95	140.95
9. a. Special school milk	...	...	...	...	...	...	74.02	...	74.02
b. School lunch	...	...	...	...	...	...	...	...	143.79
10. Total expenditures for all programs	835.74	1,682.08	1,054.73	179.59	56.47	52.23	226.00	249.54	5,599.81
11. Credit for nonfarm benefits (one-half of cost)									
a. CCC donations	12.69	40.97	...	...	...	8.29	88.13	.23	150.31
b. Removal of surplus agricultural commodities	...	...	...	...	...	...	...	70.48	70.48
c. Special school milk	...	...	...	...	...	...	37.01	...	37.01
d. School lunch	...	...	...	...	...	...	...	...	71.90
f. P.L. 480	59.73	343.75	76.95	45.34	14.66	17.75	10.35	23.76	592.29
g. Foreign aid	7.17	11.32	26.49	14.25	9.20	.44	6.05	18.66	83.58
h. Total credits	79.59	396.04	103.44	59.59	23.86	26.48	141.54	103.13	1,005.57
12. Total farm program costs	756.15	1,286.04	951.29	120.00	32.61	25.75	84.46	146.41	4,594.24

[a] See table 8-9 (1956), footnote a.
[b] See table 8-9 (1956), footnote b.
[c] See table 8-10 (1957), footnote c.
[d] See table 8-10 (1957), footnote d.
[e] See table 8-8 (1955), footnote b.

Table 8-13. Government Cost (in Millions of Dollars) of Farm and Related Programs for Year ending June 30, 1960

Cost Item	Feed Grains	Wheat	Cotton	Soybeans	Tobacco	Rice	Dairy Products	Other	Total
1. CCC inventory and loan transactions for price support programs									
a. Sales plus loan repayments	$332.66	$641.08	$1,641.85	$193.59	$217.93	$ 55.15	$ 61.82	$416.96	$3,561.04
b. Purchases plus loans made	700.54	619.53	1,487.89	83.85	56.18	67.34	223.35	226.86	3,465.54
c. Gross loss on stocks	367.88	(21.55)	(153.96)	(109.74)	(161.75)	12.19	161.53	(190.10)	(95.50)
d. Storage, handling, transportation	308.34	238.65	32.72	7.46	.55	6.14	9.02	9.08	611.96
e. Subtotal	676.22	217.10	(121.24)	(102.28)	(161.20)	18.33	170.55	(181.02)	516.46
2. Direct commodity payments								127.85	127.85
3. CCC interest (net)	168.61	151.54	51.26	5.33	24.31	2.52	4.30	5.49	413.36
4. Operating expenses[a]									181.59
5. a. Long-term land retirement[b]									323.79
c. Agricultural conservation									236.97
6. a. Commodity export program	18.96	27.50	253.11			11.54			311.11
b. International wheat agreement		65.27							65.27

7. a. P.L. 480

Gross program costs	99.45	885.94	121.42	66.96	33.63	98.02	17.23	50.09	1,372.74
Less:									
(i) Sale of foreign currencies	...	...	...	...	...	...	...	...	(89.01)
(ii) Dollar repayments	...	...	...	...	...	...	...	...	...
Subtotal	...	...	...	...	...	...	...	...	1,283.73
b. Foreign aid[c]	14.34	22.64	52.98	28.49	18.40	.89	12.11	17.32	167.17
8. Removal of surplus agricultural commodities	...	...	...	...	...	...	...	89.66	89.66
9. a. Special school milk	...	...	...	...	...	...	80.56	...	80.56
b. School lunch	...	...	...	...	...	...	...	...	152.83
10. Total expenditures for all programs	977.58	1,369.99	357.53	(1.50)	(84.86)	131.30	284.75	109.39	3,950.35
11. Credit for nonfarm benefits (one-half of cost)									
a. CCC donations	9.95	38.66	...	...	...	13.78	59.27	.18	121.84
b. Removal of surplus agricultural commodities	...	...	...	...	...	...	...	44.83	44.83
c. Special school milk	...	...	...	...	...	...	40.28	...	40.28
d. School lunch	...	...	...	...	...	...	...	...	76.42
f. P.L. 480	49.72	442.97	60.71	33.48	16.81	49.01	8.62	25.05	686.37
g. Foreign aid	7.17	11.32	26.49	14.25	9.20	.44	6.05	8.66	83.58
h. Total credits	66.84	492.95	87.20	47.73	26.01	63.23	114.22	78.72	1,053.32
12. Total farm program costs	910.74	877.04	270.33	(49.23)	(110.87)	68.07	170.53	30.67	2,897.03

[a]See table 8-9 (1956), footnote b.
[b]See table 8-10 (1957), footnote c.
[c]See table 8-8 (1955), footnote b.

329

Table 8-14. Government Cost (in Millions of Dollars) of Farm and Related Programs for Year ending June 30, 1961

Cost Item	Feed Grains	Wheat	Cotton	Soybeans	Tobacco	Rice	Dairy Products	Other	Total
1. CCC inventory and loan transactions for price support programs									
a. Sales plus loan repayments	$531.33	$879.24	$1,828.07	$ 97.14	$ 79.60	$ 60.25	$105.36	$133.98	$3,714.97
b. Purchases plus loans made	859.27	868.06	1,290.99	46.22	50.98	67.00	286.28	207.26	3,676.06
c. Gross loss on stocks	327.94	(11.18)	(537.08)	(50.92)	(28.62)	6.75	180.92	73.28	(38.91)
d. Storage, handling, transportation	317.28	269.39	23.28	1.67	...	3.65	12.34	11.30	638.91
e. Subtotal	644.22	258.21	(513.80)	(49.25)	(28.62)	10.40	193.26	85.58	600.00
2. Direct commodity payments	333.22	...	...	...	18.34	1.42	...	131.08	464.30
3. CCC interest (net)	160.69	134.63	28.71	1.27	...	...	5.81	3.14	354.01
4. Operating expenses[a]	...	...	...	...	...	...	...	...	216.28
5. a. Long-term land retirement[b]	...	...	...	...	...	...	...	...	363.21
c. Agricultural conservation	...	...	...	...	...	...	...	...	249.74
6. a. Commodity export program	20.25	74.32	191.93	...	...	18.61	...	4.63	309.74
b. International wheat agreement	...	74.44	...	...	...	...	...	...	74.44
7. a. P.L. 480									
Gross program costs	146.55	1,082.58	224.81	67.65	29.57	109.27	9.09	40.06	1,709.58

Less									
(i) Sale of foreign currencies									(109.49)
(ii) Dollar repayments									1,600.09
Subtotal	20.61	58.98	42.53	20.08	16.52	.50	12.60	14.21	186.03
b. Foreign aid[c]									
8. Removal of surplus agricultural commodities[d]							117.10	85.53	202.63
9. a. Special school milk							85.04		85.04
b. School lunch									154.36
c. Food stamp									.66
10. Total expenditures for all programs	1,325.54	1,683.16	(25.82)	39.75	35.81	140.20	422.90	364.23	4,860.53
11. Credit for nonfarm benefits (one-half of cost)									
a. CCC donations	12.44	43.43				14.93	66.77	4.63	142.20
b. Removal of surplus agricultural commodities							58.55	42.77	101.32
c. Special school milk							42.52		42.52
d. School lunch									77.18
e. Food stamp									.33
f. P.L. 480	73.28	541.29	112.40	33.82	14.78	54.64	4.55	20.03	854.79
g. Foreign aid	10.31	29.49	21.26	10.04	8.26	.25	6.30	7.11	93.02
h. Total credits	96.03	614.21	133.66	43.86	23.04	69.82	178.69	74.54	1,311.36
12. Total farm program costs	1,229.51	1,068.95	(159.48)	(4.11)	12.77	70.38	244.21	289.69	3,549.17

[a]Includes operating and administrative expenses for Acreage Allotments and Marketing Quotas, Sugar Act, Section 392 (National and State Administration) and Section 388 (Local Administration). Also includes other costs and recoveries of the CCC.

[b]See table 8-10 (1957), footnote c.

[c]See table 8-8 (1955), footnote b.

[d]Excludes $660,000 of Section 32 funds for financing the food stamp program.

Table 8-15. Government Cost (in Millions of Dollars) of Farm and Related Programs for Year ending June 30, 1962

Cost Item	Feed Grains	Wheat	Cotton	Soybeans	Tobacco	Rice	Dairy Products	Other	Total
1. CCC inventory and loan transactions for price support programs									
a. Sales plus loan repayments	$1,430.55	$1,080.79	$312.88	$105.57	$144.76	$ 48.11	$ 75.22	$239.64	$3,437.52
b. Purchases plus loans made	1,000.82	572.80	804.99	263.27	70.19	42.28	607.56	300.84	3,662.75
c. Gross loss on stocks	(429.73)	(507.99)	492.11	157.70	(74.57)	(5.83)	532.34	61.20	225.23
d. Storage, handling, transportation	341.23	212.43	7.95	.95	...	3.38	15.28	16.53	597.75
e. Subtotal	(88.50)	(295.56)	500.06	158.65	(74.57)	2.45	547.62	77.73	822.98
2. Direct commodity payments	782.50	...	...	...	...	...	...	137.68	920.18
3. CCC interest (net)	126.55	106.09	25.29	3.49	14.71	.67	11.16	2.69	290.65
4. Operating expenses[a]	...	...	...	...	...	...	...	...	218.25
5. a. Long-term land retirement[b]	...	...	...	...	...	...	...	...	343.99
c. Agricultural conservation	...	...	...	...	...	...	...	...	248.20
6. a. Commodity export program	6.95	56.75	174.28	...	...	30.13	...	.01	268.12
b. International wheat agreement	...	89.96	...	...	...	...	...	...	89.96
7. a. P.L. 480	157.86	1,218.63	204.52	64.54	19.93	88.77	16.70	87.96	1,858.91
Gross program costs									
Less:									
(i) Sale of foreign currencies	...	...	...	...	...	...	...	...	(154.22)

332

									Total
(ii) Dollar repayments	...	...	...	...	...	...	...	...	...
Subtotal	3.10	4.67	14.97	15.63	1.78	3.55	10.40	19.56	1,704.69
b. Foreign aid[c]	...	...	...	...	...	...	...	...	73.66
8. Removal of surplus agricultural commodities[d]	...	...	...	...	...	...	...	200.54	200.54
9. a. Special school milk	...	...	...	...	...	...	81.18	...	81.18
b. School lunch	...	...	...	...	...	...	...	...	169.11
c. Food stamp	...	...	...	...	...	...	...	...	14.29
10. Total expenditures for all programs	988.46	1,180.54	919.12	242.31	(38.15)	120.67	667.06	526.17	5,445.80
11. Credit for nonfarm benefits (one-half of cost)									
a. CCC donations	11.46	55.96	...	...	...	7.36	139.04	26.05	239.87
b. Removal of surplus agricultural commodities	...	...	...	...	...	...	...	100.27	100.27
c. Special school milk	...	...	...	...	...	...	40.59	...	40.59
d. School lunch	...	...	...	...	...	...	...	...	84.56
e. Food stamp	...	...	...	...	...	...	...	...	7.15
f. P.L. 480	78.93	609.32	102.26	32.27	9.97	44.38	8.35	43.98	929.46
g. Foreign aid	1.55	2.33	7.49	7.82	.89	1.77	5.20	9.78	36.83
h. Total credits	91.94	667.61	109.75	40.09	10.86	53.51	193.18	180.08	1,438.73
12. Total farm program costs	896.52	512.93	809.37	202.22	(49.01)	67.16	473.88	346.09	4,007.07

[a] Includes "Other costs and recoveries" of the CCC and program operating costs of Agricultural Stabilization and Conservation Service. Additional moneys are expended by other USDA agencies to administer CCC programs. These include Foreign Agricultural Service or Agricultural Marketing Service costs for warehouse and export inspections. These costs are relatively small (usually $5 million to $6 million annually); they are excluded from these tables because of inadequate data.

[b] See table 8-10 (1957), footnote c.

[c] Value of agricultural commodities exported under Mutual Security Act authorization by Agency for International Development (AID); data from unpublished ERS tables.

[d] Excludes $14.29 million of Section 32 funds to finance the food stamp program.

Table 8-16. Government Cost (in Millions of Dollars) of Farm and Related Programs for Year ending June 30, 1963

Cost Item	Feed Grains	Wheat	Cotton	Soybeans	Tobacco	Rice	Dairy Products	Other	Total
1. CCC inventory and loan transactions for price support programs									
a. Sales plus loan repayments	$1,168.07	$834.53	$436.30	$250.03	$ 60.30	$21.35	$ 42.87	$159.22	$2,972.67
b. Purchases plus loans made	1,018.74	722.75	1,080.30	149.41	209.06	39.70	648.59	38.65	3,907.20
c. Gross loss on stocks	(149.33)	(111.78)	644.00	(100.62)	148.76	18.35	605.72	(120.57)	934.53
d. Storage, handling, transportation	329.27	202.03	23.95	4.85	...	1.02	33.62	26.36	621.10
e. Subtotal	179.94	90.25	667.95	(95.77)	148.76	19.37	639.34	(94.21)	1,555.63
2. Direct commodity payments	842.86	285.20	...	...	...	...	...	116.79	1,244.85
3. CCC interest (net)	137.04	125.40	62.68	6.31	20.13	.64	21.64	3.77	377.61
4. Operating expenses[a]	...	...	...	...	...	...	...	...	226.55
5. a. Long-term land retirement[b]	...	...	...	...	...	...	...	...	309.38
c. Agricultural conservation	...	...	...	...	...	...	...	...	210.79
6. a. Commodity export program	(.16)	26.29	121.13	...	...	24.06	6.68	2.14	180.14
b. International wheat agreement	...	73.82	...	...	...	...	...	...	73.82
7. a. P.L. 480									
Gross program costs	88.63	1,372.25	215.56	59.20	24.90	123.37	39.06	92.99	2,015.96

Less:									
(i) Sale of foreign currencies									(254.23)
(ii) Dollar repayments									(.14)
Subtotal									1,761.59
b. Foreign aid[c]	.77	3.06	1.48			2.23	1.08	4.80	13.42
8. Removal of surplus agricultural commodities[d]								111.54	111.54
9. a. Special school milk							95.37		95.37
b. School lunch									169.60
c. Food stamp									20.25
10. Total expenditures for all programs	1,249.08	1,976.27	1,067.32	193.79	(28.78)	169.67	803.17	237.82	6,350.54
11. Credit for nonfarm benefits (one-half of cost)									
a. CCC donations	11.56	57.68				5.75	178.92	22.65	276.56
b. Removal of surplus agricultural commodities								55.77	55.77
c. Special school milk							47.69		47.69
d. School lunch									84.80
e. Food stamp									10.13
f. P.L. 480	44.32	686.13	107.78	12.45	29.60	61.68	19.53	46.49	1,007.98
g. Foreign aid	.38	1.53			.74	1.12	.54	2.40	6.71
h. Total credits	56.76	745.34	107.78	12.45	30.34	68.55	246.68	127.31	1,489.64
12. Total farm program costs	1,192.82	1,230.93	959.54	181.34	(59.12)	101.12	556.49	110.51	4,860.90

[a] See table 8-15 (1962), footnote a.

[b] Includes conservation reserve and cropland conversion programs.

[c] Value of agricultural commodities exported by AID; data from unpublished ERS tables.

[d] Excludes $20.25 million of Section 32 funds to finance the food stamp program

Table 8-17. Government Cost (in Millions of Dollars) of Farm and Related Programs for Year ending June 30, 1964

Cost Item	Feed Grains	Wheat	Cotton	Soybeans	Tobacco	Rice	Dairy Products	Other	Total
1. CCC inventory and loan transactions for price support programs									
a. Sales plus loan re-payments	$650.35	$1,103.95	$856.44	$123.98	$63.44	$31.41	$89.17	$109.50	$3,028.24
b. Purchases plus loans made	623.88	303.81	1,297.10	154.60	304.86	43.33	382.49	314.86	3,424.93
c. Gross loss on stocks	(26.47)	(800.14)	440.66	30.62	241.42	11.92	293.32	205.36	396.69
d. Storage, handling, transportation	294.31	259.53	34.62	.18	...	1.51	24.92	7.61	622.68
e. Subtotal	267.84	(540.61)	475.28	30.80	241.42	13.43	318.24	212.97	1,019.37
2. Direct commodity payments[a]	844.30	242.33	62.61	...	...	...	...	113.30	1,262.54
3. CCC interest (net)	199.03	166.20	129.66	6.82	44.45	.75	23.88	7.29	578.08
4. Operating expenses[b]	...	...	...	...	...	...	...	...	223.16
5. a. Long-term land retirement[c]	...	...	...	...	...	...	...	...	297.02
c. Agricultural conservation	...	...	...	...	...	...	...	...	213.56
6. a. Commodity export program	...	96.62	40.01	...	...	38.83	36.56	.01	212.03
b. International wheat agreement	...	124.94	...	...	...	...	...	...	124.94
7. a. P.L. 480	95.80	1,276.31	171.93	58.91	27.29	125.78	47.67	107.54	1,911.23
Gross program costs									

Less:									
(i) Sale of foreign currencies	...	...	...	...	...	...	...	...	(222.23)
(ii) Dollar repayments	...	...	...	...	...	...	...	...	(4.67)
Subtotal	1.03	1.52	1.82	5.92	.70	2.52	1.86	...	1,684.33
b. Foreign aid[d]	...	...	...	...	...	...	...	8.09	23.46
8. Removal of surplus agricultural commodities[e]	...	...	...	...	...	...	85.00	154.61	239.61
9. a. Special school milk	...	...	...	...	...	...	97.48	...	97.48
b. School lunch	...	...	...	...	...	...	...	...	180.66
c. Food stamp	...	...	...	...	...	...	...	...	30.45
10. Total expenditures for all programs	1,408.00	1,367.31	881.31	102.45	313.86	181.31	610.69	603.81	6,186.69
11. Credit for nonfarm benefits (one-half of cost)									
a. CCC donations	11.88	62.09	...	...	...	6.93	232.68	4.69	318.27
b. Removal of surplus agricultural commodities	...	...	...	...	...	...	42.50	77.31	119.81
c. Special school milk	...	...	...	...	...	...	48.74	...	48.74
d. School lunch	...	...	...	...	...	...	...	...	90.33
e. Food stamp	...	...	...	...	...	...	...	...	15.23
f. P.L. 480	47.90	638.16	85.97	29.46	13.64	62.89	23.83	53.77	955.62
g. Foreign aid	.52	.76	.91	2.96	.35	1.26	.93	4.04	11.73
h. Total credits	60.30	701.01	86.88	32.42	13.99	71.08	348.68	139.81	1,559.73
12. Total farm program costs	1,347.70	666.30	794.43	70.03	299.87	110.23	262.01	464.00	4,626.96

[a] Cotton payments were made to mills under the cotton equalization program. See Chapter 6.

[b] See table 8-15 (1962), footnote a.

[c] See table 8-16 (1963), footnote b.

[d] See table 8-16 (1963), footnote c.

[e] Excludes $30.45 million of Section 32 funds to finance the food stamp program. "Other" includes $4.7 million of grains.

Table 8-18. Government Cost (in Millions of Dollars) of Farm and Related Programs for Year ending June 30, 1965

Cost Item	Feed Grains	Wheat	Cotton	Soybeans	Tobacco	Rice	Dairy Products	Other	Total
1. CCC inventory and loan transactions for price support programs									
a. Sales plus loan repayments	$922.91	$664.46	$863.05	$154.67	$102.52	$ 40.86	$162.18	$152.56	$3,063.21
b. Purchases plus loans made	376.52	396.42	1,064.38	64.06	262.38	51.08	326.60	212.67	2,754.11
c. Gross loss on stocks	(546.39)	(268.04)	201.33	(90.61)	159.86	10.22	164.42	60.11	(309.10)
d. Storage, handling, transportation	287.32	164.41	36.96	.84	...	1.18	14.57	8.30	513.58
e. Subtotal	(259.07)	(103.63)	238.29	(89.77)	159.86	11.40	178.99	68.41	204.48
2. Direct commodity payments[a]	1,168.59	442.30	486.18	...	...	...	...	112.35	2,209.42
3. CCC interest (net)	165.93	120.08	135.56	4.26	55.48	.55	11.58	7.72	501.16
4. Operating expenses[b]	...	...	...	...	...	...	...	...	211.37
5. a. Long-term land retirement[c]	...	...	...	...	...	...	...	203.37	203.37
c. Agricultural conservation	...	...	...	...	...	...	...	216.14	216.14
6. a. Commodity export program	...	11.08	4.40	...	...	38.35	44.70	.16	98.69
b. International wheat agreement	...	34.10	...	...	...	...	...	...	34.10
7. a. P.L. 480	...	...	...	...	...	...	...	...	...
Gross program costs	81.08	1,258.35	157.56	84.92	20.02	103.33	33.53	123.83	1,862.62

Less:									
(i) Sale of foreign currencies	...	...	...	...	...	...	...	...	(204.13)
(ii) Dollar repayments	...	...	...	...	...	...	...	...	(10.78)
Subtotal	...	...	...	...	...	...	...	...	1,647.71
b. Foreign aid[d]	.61	.26	2.01	4.83	2.80	.28	2.66	12.24	25.69
8. Removal of surplus agricultural commodities[e]	...	...	...	...	...	...	25.00	247.93	272.93
9. a. Special school milk	...	...	...	...	...	...	86.61	...	86.61
b. School lunch	...	...	...	...	...	...	...	...	178.58
c. Food stamp	...	...	...	...	...	...	...	...	34.40
10. Total expenditures for all programs	1,157.14	1,762.54	1,024.00	4.24	238.16	153.91	383.07	572.64	5,924.65
11. Credit for nonfarm benefits (one-half of cost)									
a. CCC donations	10.13	55.92	...	...	...	6.18	91.92	4.02	168.17
b. Removal of surplus agricultural commodities	...	...	...	...	...	...	12.50	123.97	136.47
c. Special school milk	...	...	...	...	...	...	43.31	...	43.31
d. School lunch	...	...	...	...	...	...	...	...	89.29
e. Food stamp	...	...	...	...	...	...	...	...	17.20
f. P.L. 480	40.54	629.16	78.78	42.46	10.01	51.67	16.77	61.92	931.31
g. Foreign aid	.30	.13	1.01	2.42	1.40	.14	1.33	6.12	12.85
h. Total credits	50.97	685.21	79.79	44.88	11.41	57.99	165.83	196.03	1,398.60
12. Total farm program costs	1,106.17	1,077.33	944.21	(40.64)	226.75	95.92	217.24	376.61	4,526.05

[a] Wheat payments include total value of certificates issued to producers, i.e., costs borne by processors as well as those borne by the CCC. Cotton payments include $434.97 million paid to mills under the cotton equalization program; see chapter 6.

[b] See table 8-15 (1962), footnote a.

[c] Includes conservation reserve, cropland adjustment, and cropland conversion programs.

[d] See table 8-16 (1963), footnote c.

[e] "Other" includes $2.2 million of grains.

Table 8-19. Government Cost (in Millions of Dollars) of Farm and Related Programs for Year ending June 30, 1966

Cost Item	Feed Grains	Wheat	Cotton	Soybeans	Tobacco	Rice	Dairy Products	Other	Total
1. CCC inventory and loan transactions for price support programs									
a. Sales plus loan repayments	$976.16	$961.06	$604.54	$189.62	$161.51	$53.60	$101.66	$89.26	$3,137.41
b. Purchases plus loans made	379.94	317.68	967.43	193.02	96.90	61.74	105.82	177.41	2,299.94
c. Gross loss on stocks	(596.22)	(643.38)	362.89	3.40	(64.61)	8.14	4.16	88.15	(837.47)
d. Storage, handling, transportation	240.62	169.33	48.93	...	...	1.16	7.99	4.82	472.85
e. Subtotal	(355.60)	(474.05)	411.82	3.40	(64.61)	9.30	12.15	92.97	(364.62)
2. Direct commodity payments[a]	1,377.07	979.56	506.18	...	...	...	...	123.82	2,986.63
3. CCC interest (net)	79.86	52.90	98.10	.72	37.75	.25	3.28	5.29	278.15
4. Operating expenses[b]	...	...	...	...	...	...	...	...	214.21
5. a. Long-term land retirement[c]	...	...	...	...	...	...	...	...	158.51
c. Agricultural conservation	...	...	...	...	...	...	...	...	209.52
6. a. Commodity export program	...	159.79	...	.39	...	42.39	3.82	34.05	240.44
b. International wheat agreement	...	10.17	...	...	...	...	...	...	10.17
7. a. P.L. 480									
Gross program costs	125.66	1,306.15	103.15	38.31	31.09	61.97	41.61	77.01	1,784.95

340

Less:

(i) Sale of foreign currencies									(149.17)
(ii) Dollar repayments									(41.12)
Subtotal									1,594.56
b. Foreign aid^d	.41	.34	.91	1.55	4.05	14.50	3.29	17.60	42.55
8. Removal of surplus agricultural commodities^e							39.60	78.15	117.75
9. a. Special school milk							97.00		97.00
b. School lunch									196.66
c. Food stamp									69.49
10. Total expenditures for all programs	1,277.40	2,034.86	1,120.16	44.37	8.28	128.41	200.75	428.89	5,851.22
11. Credit for nonfarm benefits (one-half of cost)									
a. CCC donations	9.90	53.59				5.94	65.10	22.97	157.50
b. Removal of surplus agricultural commodities							19.80	39.08	58.88
c. Special school milk							48.50		48.50
d. School lunch									98.33
e. Food stamp									34.75
f. P.L. 480	62.83	653.08	51.58	19.16	15.55	30.98	20.80	38.50	892.48
g. Foreign aid	.21	.17	.46	.77	2.02	7.25	1.65	8.80	21.33
h. Total credits	72.94	706.84	52.04	19.93	17.57	44.17	155.85	109.35	1,311.77
12. Total farm program costs	1,154.46	1,328.02	1,068.12	24.44	(9.29)	84.24	44.90	319.54	4,539.45

^a See table 8-18 (1965), footnote a, except that cotton equalization payments were $322.22 million.
^b See table 8-15 (1962), footnote a.
^c See table 8-18 (1965), footnote c.
^d See table 8-16 (1963), footnote c.
^e "Other" includes $2.1 million of grains.

Table 8-20. Government Cost (in Millions of Dollars) of Farm and Related Programs for Year ending June 30, 1967

Cost Item	Feed Grains	Wheat	Cotton	Soybeans	Tobacco	Rice	Dairy Products	Other	Total
1. CCC inventory and loan transactions for price support programs									
a. Sales plus loan repayments	$985.24	$673.33	$954.49	$220.90	$185.98	$ 72.76	$ 64.33	$131.15	$3,288.18
b. Purchases plus loans made[a]	293.14	220.11	296.56	372.64	111.28	79.79	296.24	160.89	1,830.65
c. Gross loss on stocks	(692.10)	(453.22)	(657.93)	151.74	(74.70)	7.03	231.91	29.74	(1,457.53)
d. Storage, handling, transportation	170.87	86.35	40.79	...	...	.47	6.37	5.84	310.69
e. Subtotal	(521.23)	(366.87)	(617.14)	151.74	(74.70)	7.50	238.28	35.58	(1,146.84)
2. Direct commodity payments[b]	1,291.62	679.00	813.02	...	...	...	...	114.25	2,897.89
3. CCC interest (net)	67.87	34.15	108.26	5.83	45.43	.14	4.43	7.54	273.65
4. Operating expenses[c]	...	...	...	...	...	...	...	...	215.50
5. a. Long-term land retirement[d]	...	...	...	...	...	...	...	...	195.97
c. Agricultural conservation	...	...	...	...	...	...	...	...	215.57
6. a. Commodity export program	(.18)	106.98	...	...	33.10	21.98	...	17.82	179.70
7. a. P.L. 480[e]									
Gross program costs	334.75	723.66	147.31	59.83	21.22	143.91	80.93	113.30	1,624.91
Less:									
(i) Sale of foreign currencies	...	...	...	...	...	...	...	...	(170.78)
(ii) Dollar repayments	...	...	...	...	...	...	...	...	(44.80)
Subtotal	...	...	...	...	...	...	...	...	1,409.33
b. Foreign aid[f]	.22	3.45	(.08)	.87	2.25	(.13)	1.87	28.88	37.33

342

8. Removal of surplus agricultural commodities								145.42	145.42
9. a. Special school milk						96.06			96.06
b. Child nutrition									208.30
c. Food stamp									114.10
10. Total expenditures for all programs	1,180.37	1,173.05	451.37	218.27	27.30	173.40	421.57	462.79	4,841.98
11. Credit for nonfarm benefits (one-half of cost)									
a. CCC donations[g]	26.82	5.37				4.85	41.53	.13	78.70
b. Removal of surplus agricultural commodities								72.71	72.71
c. Special school milk							48.03		48.03
d. Child nutrition									104.15
e. Food stamp									57.05
f. P.L. 480	361.83	167.38	73.66	29.92	10.61	71.95	40.46	56.65	812.46
g. Foreign aid	1.73	.11	(.04)	.43	1.13	(.07)	.94	14.44	18.67
h. Total credits	390.38	172.86	73.62	30.35	11.74	76.73	130.96	143.93	1,191.77
12. Total farm program costs	789.99	1,000.19	377.75	187.92	15.56	96.67	290.61	318.86	3,650.21

aIncludes purchases by CCC of butter and cheese for donation under Section 709 of the Food and Agriculture Act of 1965. (These donations are not included in line 1a).

bSee table 8-18 (1965), footnote a, except that cotton equalization payments were $20.40 million.

cSee table 8-15 (1962), footnote a.

dSee table 8-18 (1965), footnote c.

eBeginning January 1, 1967, two new CCC accounting procedures were instituted affecting P.L. 480 costs. Previously the cost of commodities plus CCC carrying charges were charged to P.L. 480 for shipments from CCC stocks. Under the new procedure P.L. 480 was charged only the sale price of the commodity; any difference between the sale price and CCC costs was absorbed as a loss by CCC. A second change shifted the acquisition and storage costs of commodities donated through voluntary agencies to P.L. 480. Previously these costs were absorbed as losses by CCC. The two changes had opposite effects on P.L. 480 costs, of indeterminant magnitude. Neither of these changes affects commodity totals or totals for all programs but does affect the incidence of costs among items 1a to 1e and 7a. No attempt has been made to adjust the data to account for these changes. Hence there is a definitional difference between tables 8-8 to 8-19 (based on original procedure), 8-20 (July–December based on original procedure and January–June on new procedure), and 8-21 to 8-26 (based on new procedure).

fSee table 8-16 (1963), footnote c.

gIncludes one-half of donations under Section 705 (see footnote a above) in addition to donations under authorities listed in explanatory notes.

Table 8-21. Government Cost (in Millions of Dollars) of Farm and Related Programs for Year ending June 30, 1968

Cost Item	Feed Grains	Wheat	Cotton	Soybeans	Tobacco	Rice	Dairy Products	Other	Total
1. CCC inventory and loan transactions for price support programs									
a. Sales plus loan repayments	$232.94	$196.04	$825.85	$266.59	$167.13	$81.09	$ 88.64	$111.79	$1,970.07
b. Purchases plus loans made	593.69	380.85	144.54	500.96	246.11	90.05	344.58	129.94	2,430.72
c. Gross loss on stocks	360.75	184.81	(681.31)	234.37	78.98	8.96	255.94	18.15	460.65
d. Storage, handling, transportation	78.33	36.72	10.83	3.75	...	.45	11.19	5.45	146.72
e. Subtotal	439.08	221.53	(670.48)	238.12	78.98	9.41	267.13	23.60	607.37
2. Direct commodity payments[a]	864.04	726.44	855.29	...	...	...	...	153.25	2,599.02
3. CCC interest (net)	66.25	27.21	50.38	21.08	52.89	.04	12.93	10.40	241.18
4. Operating expenses[b]	...	...	...	...	...	...	...	...	210.09
5. a. Long-term land retirement[c]	...	...	...	...	...	...	...	...	208.67
c. Agricultural conservation	...	...	...	...	...	...	...	...	219.36
6. a. Commodity export program	(.31)	40.77	...	...	28.36	1.89	...	(.60)	70.11
7. a. P.L. 480[d]	126.58	776.11	120.62	...	31.12	142.33	94.36	187.00	1,478.12
Gross program costs									
Less:									
(i) Sale of foreign currencies	...	...	...	...	...	...	...	...	(223.21)

344

	(1)	(2)	(3)	(4)	(5)	(6)	(7)	(8)	Total
(ii) Dollar repayments									(51.93)
Subtotal									1,202.98
b. Foreign aid[e]	.10	1.17	(.16)	1.33	.57	4.38	.85	9.21	17.45
8. Removal of surplus agricultural commodities[f]							9.10	165.63	174.73
9. a. Special school milk							103.73		103.73
b. Child nutrition									216.86
c. Food stamp									184.73
10. Total expenditures for all programs	1,495.74	1,793.23	355.65	260.53	191.92	158.05	488.10	548.49	6,056.28
11. Credit for nonfarm benefits (one-half of cost)									
a. CCC donations	3.52	13.08				4.66	94.46	2.60	118.32
b. Removal of surplus agricultural commodities							4.55	82.82	87.37
c. Special school milk							51.87		51.87
d. Child nutrition									108.43
e. Food stamp									92.37
f. P.L. 480	63.29	388.06	60.31		15.56	71.16	47.18	93.50	739.06
g. Foreign Aid	.05	.59	(.08)	.66	.29	2.19	.42	4.61	8.73
h. Total Credits	66.86	401.73	60.23	.66	15.85	78.01	198.48	183.53	1,206.15
12. Total farm program costs	1,428.88	1,391.50	295.42	259.87	176.07	80.04	289.62	364.96	4,850.13

[a] See table 8-18 (1965), footnote a, except that cotton equalization payments were $110.000.

[b] See table 8-15 (1962), footnote a.

[c] See table 8-18 (1965), footnote c.

[d] See table 8-20 (1967), footnote c.

[e] See table 8-16 (1963), footnote e.

[f] "Other" includes $10.6 million of grains.

Table 8-22. Government Cost (in Millions of Dollars) of Farm and Related Programs for Year ending June 30, 1969

Cost Item	Feed Grains	Wheat	Cotton	Soybeans	Tobacco	Rice	Dairy Products	Other	Total
1. CCC inventory and loan transactions for price support programs									
a. Sales plus loan re-payments	$398.38	$200.77	$234.91	$363.34	$127.66	$ 85.72	$147.90	$104.52	$1,654.20
b. Purchases plus loans made	717.65	583.18	453.53	848.90	137.76	126.74	296.29	183.03	3,347.08
c. Gross loss on stocks	328.27	382.41	218.62	485.56	10.10	41.02	148.39	78.51	1,692.88
d. Storage, handling, transportation	140.63	65.76	.60	22.56	…	1.00	13.30	3.33	247.18
e. Subtotal	468.90	448.17	219.22	508.12	10.10	42.02	161.69	81.84	1,940.06
2. Direct commodity payments[a]	1,364.85	746.50	731.09	…	…	…	…	152.21	2,994.65
3. CCC interest (net)	105.14	50.99	20.85	52.66	61.61	1.32	15.44	7.15	315.16
4. Operating expenses[b]	…	…	.	…	…	…	…	…	219.04
5. a. Long-term land re-tirement[c]	…	…	…	…	…	…	…	…	189.21
c. Agricultural con-servation	…	…	…	…	…	…	…	…	199.41
6. a. Commodity export program	(.21)	(.13)	…	…	27.87	3.19	…	(1.18)	29.54
7. a. P.L. 480[d]	60.92	528.60	123.93	.01	31.26	187.27	122.86	176.57	1,231.42
Gross program costs									
Less:									
(i) Sale of foreign currencies	…	…	…	…	…	…	…	…	(207.47)

346

(ii) Dollar repayments	...	...	...	...	...	...	...	(50.62)
Subtotal	.07	...	...	...	...	...	...	973.33
b. Foreign aid[e]	...	2.38	...	.09	1.10	.36	7.48	11.48
8. Removal of surplus agricultural commodities[f]	...	...	...	...	...	120.90	294.00	414.90
9. a. Special school milk	...	...	...	...	...	101.93	...	101.93
b. Child nutrition	...	...	...	...	...	...	...	237.01
c. Food stamp	...	...	...	...	...	...	...	247.77
10. Total expenditures for all programs	1,999.67	1,776.51	1,095.09	560.79	130.93	234.90	523.18	718.07	7,873.49
11. Credit for nonfarm benefits (one-half of cost)								
a. CCC donations	3.58	13.76	...	...	...	5.13	95.31	...	117.73
b. Removal of surplus agricultural commodities	...	...	...	...	...	...	60.45	147.00	207.45
c. Special school milk	...	...	...	...	...	50.97	50.97	...	50.97
d. Child nutrition	...	...	...	...	...	...	...	...	118.5_
e. Food stamp	...	...	...	...	...	...	...	...	123.89
f. P.L. 480	30.46	264.30	61.97	...	15.63	93.64	61.43	88.28	615.71
g. Foreign aid	.04	1.19	...	...	.04	.55	.18	3.74	5.74
h. Total credits	34.08	279.25	61.97	...	15.67	99.32	268.34	239.02	1,240.05
12. Total farm program costs	1,965.59	1,497.26	1,033.12	560.79	115.26	135.58	254.84	479.05	6,633.44

[a]Wheat payments include total value of certificates issued to producers, i.e., costs borne by processors as well as by CCC.

[b]See table 8-15 (1962), footnote a.

[c]See table 8-18 (1965), footnote c.

[d]See table 8-20 (1967), footnote e.

[e]See table 8-16 (1963), footnote c.

[f]"Other" includes $8.8 million of grains.

Table 8-23. Government Cost (in Millions of Dollars) of Farm and Related Programs for Year ending June 30, 1970

Cost Item	Feed Grains	Wheat	Cotton	Soybeans	Tobacco	Rice	Dairy Products	Other	Total
1. CCC inventory and loan transactions for price support programs									
a. Sales plus loan re-payments	$601.10	$368.90	$351.92	$635.96	$132.69	$111.21	$181.49	$126.43	$2,509.70
b. Purchases plus loans made[a]	599.52	552.61	390.06	420.76	217.53	130.51	265.60	169.55	2,746.14
c. Gross loss on stocks	(1.58)	183.71	38.14	(215.20)	84.84	19.30	84.11	43.12	236.44
d. Storage, handling, transportation	171.76	98.47	15.51	47.62	...	4.91	10.79	5.76	354.82
e. Subtotal	170.18	282.18	53.65	(167.58)	84.84	24.21	94.90	48.88	591.26
2. Direct commodity payments[b]	1,643.74	857.56	827.57	...	...	...	...	145.62	3,474.49
3. CCC interest (net)	169.77	103.88	43.30	91.57	93.18	4.28	17.56	11.67	535.21
4. Operating expenses[c]	...	...	...	...	...	...	...	...	236.56
5. a. Long-term land re-tirement[d]	...	...	...	...	...	...	...	...	118.27
c. Agricultural con-servation	...	...	...	...	...	...	...	...	182.62
6. a. Commodity export program	(.24)	55.85	...	...	29.52	13.70	...	(1.07)	97.76
7. a. P.L. 480[e]	89.83	537.87	142.94	...	22.54	182.25	93.18	175.66	1,244.27
Gross program costs									
Less:									
(i) Sale of foreign currencies	...	...	...	...	...	...	...	...	(231.88)

	C1	C2	C3	C4	C5	C6	C7	C8	C9
(ii) Dollar repayments	…	…	…	…	…	…	…	…	(77.11)
Subtotal	.02	…	…	…	…	…	…	…	935.23
b. Foreign aid[f]				.20		.49	1.85	9.86	12.42
8. Removal of surplus agricultural commodities[g]							103.60	345.94	449.54
9. a. Special school milk							83.80		83.83)
b. Child nutrition									299.13
c. Food stamp									576.81
10. Total expenditures for all programs	2,073.30	1,837.34	1,067.46	(75.81)	230.08	224.93	394.89	736.56	7,593.15
11. Credit for nonfarm benefits (one-half of cost)									
a. CCC donations[h]	3.55	15.08				5.22	58.44	6.28	88.57
b. Removal of surplus agricultural commodities							53.30	171.47	224.77
c. Special school milk							41.90		41.90
d. Child nutrition									149.57
e. Food stamp	44.92				11.27	91.13	46.59	87.83	288.41
f. P.L. 480		268.93	71.47		11.27	.25	.92	4.93	622.14
g. Foreign aid	.01			.10					6.21
h. Total credits	48.48	284.01	71.47	.10	11.27	96.60	201.15	270.51	1,421.57
12. Total farm program costs	2,024.82	1,553.33	995.99	(75.91)	218.81	128.33	193.74	466.05	6,171.58

a See table 8-20 (1967), footnote a.
b See table 8-22 (1969), footnote a.
c See table 8-15 (1962), footnote a.
d See table 8-18 (1965), footnote c.
e See table 8-20 (1967), footnote e.
f See table 8-16 (1963), footnote c.
g "Other" includes $15.5 million of grains.
h See table 8-20 (1967), footnote g.

Table 8-24. Government Cost (in Millions of Dollars) of Farm and Related Programs for Year ending June 30, 1971

Cost Item	Feed Grains	Wheat	Cotton	Soybeans	Tobacco	Rice	Dairy Products	Other	Total
1. CCC inventory and loan transactions for price support programs									
a. Sales plus loan repayments	$1,050.61	$579.66	$588.54	$951.03	$123.59	$ 93.75	$185.53	$111.88	$3,684.59
b. Purchases plus loans made[a]	466.03	316.82	252.26	318.68	163.07	111.86	389.96	209.42	2,228.10
c. Gross loss on stocks	(584.58)	(262.84)	(336.28)	(632.35)	39.48	18.11	204.43	97.54	(1,456.49)
d. Storage, handling, transportation	151.99	101.62	10.58	14.78	...	5.71	13.03	7.78	305.49
e. Subtotal	(432.59)	(161.22)	(325.70)	(617.57)	39.48	23.82	217.46	105.32	(1,151.00)
2. Direct commodity payments[b]	1,503.64	870.90	917.24	...	...	...	...	157.77	3,449.55
3. CCC interest (net)	131.38	93.56	25.88	42.18	94.32	4.87	16.68	11.26	420.13
4. Operating expenses[c]	...	...	...	...	...	...	...	...	254.39
5. a. Long-term land retirement[d]	...	...	...	...	...	...	...	...	76.79
c. Agricultural conservation (REAP)	...	...	...	...	...	...	...	...	167.12
6. a. Commodity export program	(.28)	127.78	(.01)	...	29.10	17.82	...	(1.36)	173.05
7. a. P.L. 480[e]	98.79	500.36	126.70	.03	25.92	175.76	118.36	198.68	1,244.60
Gross program costs									
Less:									
(i) Sale of foreign currencies	...	...	...	...	...	...	...	...	(225.57)

350

(ii) Dollar repayments									(103.01)
Subtotal									916.02
b. Foreign aid[f]			1.65			22.61	.48	30.89	55.53
8. Removal of surplus agricultural commodities[g]							63.60	338.72	402.32
9. a. Special milk program							90.92		90.82
b. Child nutrition									519.94
c. Food stamp									1,567.77
10. Total expenditures for all programs	1,300.94	1,433.03	744.11	(575.36)	188.82	244.88	507.50	841.28	6,942.63
11. Credit for nonfarm benefits (one-half of cost)									
a. CCC donations[h]	4.53	18.31				5.70	80.37	11.50	120.44
b. Removal of surplus agricultural commodities							31.80	169.36	201.16
c. Special school milk							45.46		45.46
d. Child nutrition									259.97
e. Food stamp									783.89
f. P.L. 480	49.39	250.18	63.35	.01	12.97	87.88	59.18	99.34	622.30
g. Foreign aid	.83					11.30	.24	15.45	27.82
h. Total credits	53.92	269.32	63.35	.01	12.97	104.88	217.05	295.65	2,061.01
12. Total farm program costs	1,247.02	1,163.71	680.76	(575.37)	175.85	140.00	290.45	545.63	4,881.62

[a]See table 8-20 (1967), footnote a.
[b]See table 8-22 (1969), footnote a.
[c]See table 8-15 (1962), footnote a.
[d]See table 8-18 (1965), footnote c.
[e]See table 8-20 (1967), footnote e.
[f]See table 8-16 (1963), footnote c.
[g]"Other" includes $12.8 million of grains.
[h]See table 8-20 (1967), footnote g.

Table 8-25. Government Cost (in Millions of Dollars) of Farm and Related Programs for Year ending June 30, 1972

Cost Item	Feed Grains	Wheat	Cotton	Soybeans	Tobacco	Rice	Dairy Products	Other	Total
1. CCC inventory and loan transactions for price support program[a]									
a. Sales plus loan re-payments	$ 733.86	$383.19	$183.76	$439.08	$272.29	$198.50	$225.46	$125.17	$2,561.31
b. Purchases plus loans made[b]	1,277.64	579.46	114.15	375.03	59.50	173.17	387.39	232.86	3,199.20
c. Gross loss on stocks	543.78	196.27	(69.61)	(64.05)	(212.79)	(25.33)	161.93	107.69	637.89
d. Storage, handling, transportation	131.53	108.33	.50	.23	...	4.80	12.30	9.03	266.72
e. Subtotal	675.31	304.60	(69.11)	(63.82)	(212.79)	(20.53)	174.23	116.72	904.61
2. Direct commodity payments[c]	1,053.31	878.08	823.95	...	...	...	...	198.90	2,954.24
3. CCC interest (net)	96.22	65.65	4.29	4.50	61.54	2.54	11.99	7.34	254.07
4. Operating expenses[d]	...	...	...	...	...	...	...	...	282.78
5. a. Long-term land retirement[e]	...	...		...	...	...	...	...	66.97
c. Agricultural conservation (REAP)	...	...	...	...	...	...	...	...	185.37
6. a. Commodity export program[f]	(.15)	64.72	...	...	26.73	25.34	...	(2.38)	114.26
7. a. P.L. 480[g]	106.45	509.60	88.97	.86	24.34	233.88	102.84	224.35	1,291.29
Less:									
(i) Sale of foreign currencies	...	...	...	...	...	...	...	...	(200.99)
(ii) Dollar repayments	...	...	...	...	...	...	...	...	(100.10)
Subtotal	...	...	...	...	...	...	...	...	990.20
b. Foreign aid[h]	...	1.27	...	4.32	...	21.93	2.56	36.44	66.52

8. Removal of surplus agricultural commodities[i]	1,931.14	...	...	...	...	...	16.00	577.22	593.22
9. a. Special milk program	...	...	...	...	...	...	93.55	...	93.55
b. Child nutrition	...	...	...	...	...	...	...	...	622.19
c. Food stamps	...	...	...	...	...	...	...	...	1,909.17
10. Total expenditures for all programs	1,931.14	1,823.92	848.10	(54.14)	(100.18)	263.16	401.17	1,158.59	9,037.15
11. Credit for nonfarm benefits (one-half of cost)									
a. CCC donations[j]	4.76	16.91	...	...	...	5.14	88.54	18.64	133.99
b. Removal of surplus agricultural commodities	...	...	...	...	...	...	8.00	288.61	296.61
c. Special school milk	...	...	...	...	...	...	46.77	...	46.77
d. Child nutrition	...	...	...	...	...	...	...	...	311.09
e. Food stamp	...	...	...	...	...	...	...	...	954.59
f. P.L. 480	53.23	254.80	44.48	.43	12.17	116.94	51.42	112.18	645.65
g. Foreign aid	...	.64	...	2.16	...	10.96	1.28	18.22	33.26
h. Total credits	57.99	272.35	44.48	2.59	12.17	133.04	196.01	437.65	2,421.96
12. Total farm program costs	1,873.15	1,551.57	803.62	(56.73)	(112.35)	130.12	205.16	720.94	6,615.19

[a] Unpublished CCC tables were used to separate costs of price support program operations from other program costs. (In earlier years the data were published separately.)

[b] See table 8-20 (1967), footnote a. Also included were corn purchases of $15.7 million under the CCC supply program.

[c] See table 8-22 (1969), footnote a.

[d] See table 8-15 (1962), footnote a.

[e] See table 8-18 (1965), footnote c.

[f] Unpublished CCC tables were used to separate costs of commodity export program from other program costs. (In earlier years data were published separately.)

[g] See table 8-20 (1967), footnote e.

[h] See table 8-16 (1963), footnote c.

[i] "Other" includes $13.9 million of grains.

[j] See table 8-20 (1967), footnote g.

Table 8-26. Government Cost (in Millions of Dollars) of Farm and Related Programs for Year ending June 30, 1973

Cost Item	Feed Grains	Wheat	Cotton	Soybeans	Tobacco	Rice	Dairy Products	Other	Total
1. CCC inventory and loan transactions for price support program[a]									
a. Sales plus loan repayments	$1,339.65	$984.91	$178.76	$222.91	$241.77	$141.11	$ 54.83	$206.39	$3,370.33
b. Purchases plus loans made[b]	550.35	203.43	176.73	202.16	51.43	139.95	162.12	214.95	1,701.12
c. Gross loss on stocks	(789.30)	(781.48)	(2.03)	(20.75)	(190.34)	(1.16)	107.29	8.56	(1,669.21)
d. Storage, handling, transportation	132.34	95.81	.10	.02	...	2.01	9.44	3.14	242.86
e. Subtotal	(656.95)	(685.66)	(1.93)	(20.73)	(190.35)	.85	116.73	11.69	(1,426.35)
2. Direct commodity payments[c]	1,846.34	855.46	813.49	...	...	...	...	155.12	3,670.41
3. CCC interest (net)[d]	82.07	43.56	2.01	1.09	41.92	.60	7.15	3.09	181.49
4. Operating expenses[d]	...	...	...	...	...	...	...	...	300.77
5. a. Long-term land retirement[e]	...	...	...	...	...	...	...	...	51.51
c. Agricultural conservation (REAP)	...	...	...	...	...	...	...	...	162.60
6. a. Commodity export program[f]	(.19)	295.09	...	...	27.81	20.79	...	(2.40)	341.10
7. a. P.L. 480[g]	121.88	429.48	103.92	.11	29.60	259.37	20.97	173.00	1,138.33
Gross program costs									
Less:									
(i) Sale of foreign currencies	...	...	...	...	...	...	...	...	(221.69)

354

	(1)	(2)	(3)	(4)	(5)	(6)	(7)	(8)	(9)
(ii) Dollar repayments	...	...	...	...	...	...	...	...	(164.95)
Subtotal	...	6.64	13.36	2.94	...	...	...	...	751.69
b. Foreign aid[h]	.01	...	...	...	.42	28.82	2.61	28.98	83.78
8. Removal of surplus agricultural.commodites[i]	...	...	...	...	...	...	16.00	724.22	740.22
9. a. Special milk program	...	...	...	...	...	...	90.86	...	90.86
b. Child nutrition	...	...	...	...	...	...	...	...	596.45
c. Food stamps	...	...	...	...	...	...	...	...	2,207.53
10. Total expenditures for all programs	1,393.16	944.57	930.85	(16.59)	(90.60)	310.43	254.32	1,093.70	7,752.06
11. Credit for nonfarm benefits (one-half of cost)									
a. CCC donations[j]	4.52	19.55	...	...	...	7.42	86.43	10.88	128.80
b. Removal of surplus agricultural commodities	...	...	...	...	...	...	8.00	362.11	370.11
c. Special school milk	...	...	...	...	...	...	45.43	...	45.43
d. School lunch	...	...	...	...	...	...	...	...	298.23
e. Food stamp	...	...	...	...	...	...	...	...	1,103.76
f. P.L. 480	60.94	214.74	51.96	.06	14.80	129.68	10.49	86.50	569.17
g. Foreign aid	.01	3.32	6.68	1.47	.21	14.41	1.30	14.49	41.89
h. Total credits	65.47	237.61	58.64	1.53	15.01	151.51	151.65	473.98	2,557.39
12. Total farm program costs	1,327.69	706.96	872.21	(18.12)	(105.61)	158.92	102.67	619.72	5,194.67

[a] See table 8-25 (1972), footnote a.
[b] See table 8-20 (1967), footnote a.
[c] See table 8-22 (1969), footnote a.
[d] See table 8-15 (1962), footnote a.
[e] See table 8-18 (1965), footnote c.
[f] See table 8-25 (1972), footnote f.
[g] See table 8-20 (1967), footnote e.
[h] See table 8-16 (1963), footnote c.
[i] "Other" includes $13.6 million of grains.
[j] See table 8-20 (1967), footnote g.

The Historical Record

Table 8-27. Agricultural Exports (in Millions of Dollars)
under Special Foreign Aid Programs, 1948–54

Year	Civilian Supplies[a]	Special Loans and Credits[b]	Adjusted Total Expenditures for All Programs[c]	Adjusted Total Farm Program Costs[d]
1948	$837	$306	$2,291	$1,280
1949	753	7	4,958	3,757
1950	461	46	3,860	2,845
1951	175	1	500	(251)
1952	68	184	1,330	807
1953	58	34	3,191	2,888
1954	24	. . .	3,980	3,640

[a] Government financed agricultural exports under Government and Relief in Occupied Areas (GARIOA).

[b] 1948: U.K. loan and USDA cotton credits; 1949–51: Natural-Fibers Revolving Fund; 1952: India grain loan, Spanish loan (wheat and cotton); 1953: India grain loan, Pakistan and Afghanistan wheat loans.

[c] Adjusted line 10, tables 8-1 to 8-7.

[d] Adjusted line 12, tables 8-1 to 8-7.

PART III

Consequences and Appraisal

CHAPTER 9

Program Analysis and Consequences

We turn in this chapter to a discussion of the principal consequences, or effects, of the programs of price and income support. We will inquire into and discuss the consequences of those programs under five categories: (1) farm prices and incomes; (2) the distribution of producer incomes and wealth; (3) resource allocation, efficiency, and output; (4) foreign trade; and (5) consumer welfare. As is well understood, these categories are highly interrelated. But, as is equally well understood, any effort to analyze them in one closed system would be extremely demanding in terms of modeling, estimation, and data, and probably destined to failure as far as policy results are concerned. Thus, we will analyze one category at a time, attempting in an *ad hoc* manner to take account of category interrelations.

Farm Prices and Incomes

It is clear that farm prices and incomes were higher in any given year between 1952 and 1972, as a result of the operation of government programs, than they would have been in the absence of those programs; it is not clear how much higher. A large number of studies were undertaken between 1959 and 1965 to measure the effect on farm prices and incomes of the operation of government programs in agriculture.[1] The assumptions on which these various studies were based vary considerably with respect to crop yields, levels of exports, elasticities of demand, and programs continued and programs dismantled; hence the production, price, and income results of the studies vary considerably. But for the most part all the studies were built around the following core assumptions: (1) price support and production control programs for the major commodities are eliminated,[2] (2) domestic and foreign surplus disposal programs are maintained, and (3) only those production adjustments that could be easily made in one to three years are made. Thus, these studies were typically short-run, quasi-free-market in their approach.

Given the assumptions noted directly above, the price-income results tend to fall in the following ranges. The index of prices received would fall between 10 to 20 percent; aggregate net farm income tends to fall between 20 and 50 percent. The studies consistently indicated that the price of wheat would fall by nearly 50 percent, feed grains by 20 to 30 percent, and whole milk by 10 percent or less.

In the period 1955–65 the senior author of this work made numerous estimates of how much the farm price level would have to fall in a completely free-market situation in order to eliminate the general excess production capacity in American agriculture. The results of these estimating efforts tended to scatter around a decline in the farm price level of 40 percent. These estimates were derived by aggregative methods, and described the free-market price response to producing at full production capacity at any one time.

The farmers who feared that farm prices would fall if farm price supports were lowered were right. The level of farm prices fell steadily from 1952 to 1960 as the level of support was lowered. And prices would have fallen further in any year from 1955 to 1965 if the price and income support programs in existence in those years had been eliminated: perhaps by only 10 percent as the most conservative estimate indicates or perhaps by as much as 40 percent as the most extreme estimate indicates. Because of the fixed input prices and production costs the decline in net farm income would be considerably greater than the decline in farm product prices in each case. Without doubt the dismantling of government programs in any year from 1955 to 1965 would have had horrendous short-run effects on farmers' income.

So much for the short run. What of the longer-run price and income consequences? Critics of government programs in agriculture typically have argued that once farmers had fully adjusted to the lower free-market prices, supplies would be reduced and farm prices would start moving up again. The argument runs as follows: Immediately following the elimination of government programs additional land would be brought into production, and probably additional labor, inputs of capital would hold about constant, output would increase, and farm prices decline; but in the longer run some of the poorer quality land would go out of production, labor would continue to leave agriculture, farmers would reduce their input of nonfarm capital items, and aggregate output would decline; this decline in aggregate output in conjunction with a growing demand would force farm prices to rise in the market and result in rising farm incomes. The argument is logical in its formulation. But several important questions regarding it remained unanswered for many years.

First, how long a time period would be required to achieve a reasonably full adjustment in productive resources and to start farm prices moving up once again? Second, how rough would the adjustment process be in terms of falling prices and incomes, numbers of farms going out of business, and reconsolidation into larger, more efficient farms? And third, what would be the characteristics of the farm price level after full adjustment — how high would it be and how stable would it be?

With the improvement of econometric methods, computer hardware, and techniques for simulating the operation of entire sectors of the economy in recent years, long-run studies of the operation of the agricultural sector have been made which provide answers, in part at least, to the questions raised above. We shall present the relevant results from two such studies.[3] Ray and Heady report their results as follows:

To see how agriculture would have fared under free market conditions, all government policy variables are set to zero in simulation 2. The estimated results, assuming no price supports, no diversions of excess production, no acreage allotments or diversions, and no government payments, are reported for selected variables. . . .

The initial or first-year response to the removal of government programs is an increase in crop acreage and production. As these additional supplies reach the market, crop prices decline. Inelastic demands cause prices to drop by a larger percentage than supplies increase resulting in lower gross incomes. Faced with lower prices and incomes, farmers begin to reduce production. Simulation results indicate this reduced production is not accomplished by taking land out of production, but rather by applying fewer resources to each acre. Reduced resource use is partially in response to lower crop prices, but capital limitations also play an important role. Typically, the level of resources used by farmers is not the quantity that sets the value of the marginal product for each resource equal to its price. While the reasons for this less-than-efficient use of resources are many, often times the equilibrium level of resource use is prohibited by capital limitations. The reduced incomes and lower land values in the absence of government programs decrease internally generated capital and erode farmers' borrowing base. This tightening of capital constraints reduces the quantity of resources farmers can afford. Farmers rely more on the nonpurchased inputs, such as land and labor, and less on fertilizer, pesticides, and more efficient machines in their production activities.

Even though production for most crops declines with the removal of government programs (after the second or third year), supplies are larger than will clear the market at prices that existed when the government programs were in operation. These lower prices depress incomes throughout the 1932–67 period of analysis.

In the Ray-Heady free-market simulation, resource adjustments take place — very great resource adjustments — in response to falling farm prices, but farm incomes never recover. After nearly 30 years of adjustment to a condition of no farm programs (1932–58), aggregate net farm income for the nation in constant dollars for the period 1959–67 is only about half as large under the free-market simulation as it was in actual fact. Ray and Heady reach the following conclusion: "the assumed removal of acreage diversions and allotments causes acreage increases for feed grains, wheat and cotton during the last period of analysis, 1958–67, to more than offset reductions in input use per acre. The resulting increase in supplies further depresses prices and gross incomes during the 1958–67 period."[4]

Nelson simulates the operation of the farm economy for the period 1953–72. He then asks the following questions of his simulation model. If government programs had been eliminated in 1953, how low would farm prices and incomes have gone and how long would they have stayed depressed? Would a supply response on the part of farmers eventually have resulted in a recovery of farm prices and incomes to their actual historical levels or higher?

Resource adjustments in the Nelson free-market simulation model are similar but not identical to those derived in the Ray-Heady model. The input of nonfarm-produced capital items declines drastically in the Nelson model during the period 1953–63; the input of crop land first declines, and then moves well above the actual input from 1957 to 1973. The index of agricultural productivity moves with the actual index from 1953 to 1965 and then declines significantly in the period 1965–73.

As a result of these and other resource adjustments, the simulated index of free-market prices for all farm products falls sharply in the early 1950s, remains well below the historical record of actual prices from 1955 to 1963, begins to rise in 1964–65, and then soars above the actual level of prices in the late 1960s and early 1970s. Net farm income moves in the same pattern: fluctuating below the actual level from 1953 to 1964, turning up in the period 1964–65, and then shooting well above the actual level in the late 1960s and early 1970s. The differences between the free-market results derived by Nelson in his basic simulation and the actual historical values are presented in table 9-1.

Two important points should be noted with regard to the Nelson free-market simulation model. First, abundant supplies and cheap feed in the period 1953–57 initiate a strong livestock production cycle, which in turn causes the level of farm prices and incomes to oscillate to an important degree over the entire period 1953–72. Second, the index of price level variability in the free-market situation is much greater in magnitude than that for the actual situation.

In the Ray-Heady simulation model farm prices and incomes never regain the actual level of prices and incomes following the elimination of government programs; in the Nelson model prices and incomes regain their actual levels after 12 to 14 years, and then soar well above their actual levels, but the variability in prices and incomes through time is much greater in the free-market situation than in the actual situation. Two carefully done historical

Table 9-1. Economic Consequences of Eliminating Farm Programs in 1953
on Selected Variables: five-year averages, 1953–72

Item	Percentage Change from Historical Value			
	1953–57	1958–62	1963–67	1968–72
Crop supply available to the market[a]	8.4	2.6	−4.3	−9.5
Livestock supply available to the market[a] ..	3.8	4.8	3.4	−3.9
Price index for crops	−28.2	−22.6	−8.1	31.7
Price index for livestock	−19.5	−25.8	−18.5	25.2
Price index for all agriculture products	−23.2	−24.4	−14.9	27.7
Total net farm income	−42.0	−37.7	−19.7	40.3
Total agricultural productivity index	1.5	3.7	2.4	−5.1
Agricultural price variability index	52.7	7.2	36.1	150.0

Source: Frederick Nelson, "An Economic Analysis of the Impact of Past Farm Programs on Livestock and Crop Prices, Production and Resource Adjustments," Ph.D. thesis, University of Minnesota, 1975.

[a] Supply includes production less government market diversions plus beginning-of-year private stocks plus net private imports for livestock and gross imports for crops.

simulation studies thus suggest that the elimination of government programs in the agricultural sector in the decades of the 1950s and 1960s would have resulted in extended periods of severely depressed farm prices and incomes, and would have introduced considerably more variability in the overall level of farm prices and incomes. Stated differently, government programs did support farm prices and incomes significantly above equilibrium levels in the short and intermediate runs; for the very long run there is still some question. But how many farmers could have survived — remained financially solvent — for an extended period with net incomes running as much as 30, 40, or 50 percent lower than they actually were in the period 1950–70? Not many. The programs enabled some commercial farmers — the fittest — to survive and grow in a classic Darwinian situation.

The Distribution of Producer Incomes and Wealth

Farm programs of price and income support were conceived and put into effect in the 1930s to assist the commercial farmer to survive the Great Depression. Farm programs were employed in the World War II period to induce commercial farmers to increase their output of needed commodities. Farm programs were continued in the post–World War II period to protect commercial farmers from a precipitous decline in the farm price level. Farm programs were operated throughout the 1950s and 1960s to support the incomes of commercial farmers plagued by the chronic problem of general excess production capacity.

During this entire period it was no secret in the Congress, in succeeding administrations, or among the many and varied interest groups operating in Washington whom the "farm programs" were designed to benefit; they were designed to benefit the commercial farmer; they were designed to benefit the fellow with something to sell, and obviously the more he had to sell the more he benefited. True, the protagonists of farm programs may have cheated somewhat in stating their case for farm programs by including subsistence farmers and farm laborers in their national averages as a way of demonstrating need. And it is also true that the number of commercial farms declined in number from 1933 to 1973, as the average commercial farm, most often a family farm, doubled or tripled or quadrupled in size. But the basic mission of the government price and income programs in agriculture did not change between 1933 and 1973; it was to protect and enhance the incomes of the relatively small businessmen engaged in farming (i.e., commercial farmers).

Most participants in the farm policy struggles, on all sides, understood full well that the price-income support programs that were being forged could not help the subsistence farmer who had no surplus product to sell. And most participants in the policy formulation process saw nothing improper or inequitable about such a situation. The programs, as they were perceived, were designed to assist the small farm businessman, not provide welfare. If the small businessman engaged in farming was to be helped, he had to have something to sell. But what was not understood by most participants in the farm policy struggles in 1933 or in 1948, or even by 1973 was that (1) it is next to impossible to raise, on a permanent basis, the net return of the average, or representative, farmer in an atomistic, competitive market through price-supporting, or direct payment, schemes, and (2) farm price and income support programs interacting with rapid commercial and technological development result in a situation in which the larger, more aggressive, more alert commercial farmers cannibalize the smaller, less aggressive, less alert commercial farmers. Let us explore these two propositions since they are critically important to the questions "who benefited?" and "how much?" from the farm programs.

If the price of a farm product rises as the result of a market force, say an increase in the demand for the product, all farmers seek to expand output; as output expands, the price of the product falls once again and will fall to a level where the average, the representative, farmer is earning a return just sufficient to keep him in business. Now if the price of a product is increased through a price-supporting action by government, all farmers again will seek to increase output. But this time price does not fall as output increases; the government continues to support the higher price and in the short run all farmers earn higher incomes. In this situation farmers begin to compete with one another for the limiting resource, typically land, to further increase output. In the competitive process land values rise and in turn drive up the costs of production to a level where the average, the representative farmer, once again is earning a return just sufficient to keep him in business. The average farmer in a competitive market is on a treadmill from which there is no escape.[5]

Does this mean that no farmer ever gains from a price increase? In the unlikely event that farm product prices rise continuously and relative to all other product prices, wherein the competitive process never catches up with the farm product price increases, all farmers could gain. And the efficient farmer, whose costs of production are lower than those of the average, or representative farmer, before the price rise, would still hold his profit advantage after the price rise. But to the extent that farmers are operating in an atomistic competitive market and nothing happens except one discrete price rise to which there is a full and complete resource adjustment, then the answer must be that no farmer ever gains from a product price rise.

But other things do happen. Farm technological advance was rapid and widespread in the United States in the 1950s and 1960s. The commercial and management skills of some farmers increased during these decades. The farmer with superior commercial ability and superior technical skill used the price-income stability provided by the government programs to borrow capital, invest in new and improved technologies, reduce unit costs, and increase his net return on each unit of product sold. The alert, aggressive farmer gained financially in two ways. As an early adopter of an improved technology, he realized increased net returns in the early phases of the adoption process.[6] And as an expanding operator, he experienced an appreciation in the value of his land as he and other superior farmers bid for additional land under a system of government-supported prices.[7]

In other words, given the price and income insurance provided by the government price support programs, the alert, aggressive farmers who adopted the new technologies early in the competitive process increased their net return, acquired additional crop land from their less successful neighbors, expanded their farming operations, increased their net return some more, and were the final beneficiaries of rising land values resulting from the competitive bidding for land in which they were the principal participants. Thus, the alert, aggressive farmers became even larger operators in the competitive process and the farmers lacking in commercial and technological skills fell by the wayside — their productive assets being consolidated into the enlarged farms of the alert, aggressive farmers. The government programs were not designed to produce this outcome; they were designed to help all farmers. But the stable economic environment which they provided, in the context of rapid technological advance, made it easy for the alert, aggressive farmer to invest, reduce costs, expand, increase his rate of return, and expand further. The alert and strong cannibalized the less adaptable and the weak.[8] Thus, it must be concluded that the operation of the government programs of price and income support in conjunction with rapid and widespread technological advance benefited the alert and the strong at the expense of the small and the weak.

What about the size and distribution of government payments to farmers? It will be recalled that income payments to farmers increasingly substituted for programs of price support throughout the 1960s. The steady rise in the total flow of payments to farmers may be observed in table 9-2; also the distribution of payments by commodities and programs may be seen in that table. Walter W. Wilcox presents data obtained from the U.S. Department of Agriculture on the size and distribution of payments to producers for the calendar year 1968 (see table 9-3). It is clear from table 9-3 that most farmers received small to medium-sized payments; some 65 percent received payments of less than $1,000. Only a few farmers, less than 1 percent, received payments of $15,000 or more. But the great bulk of the funds paid out as payments to producers (some 67 percent) went to 33 percent of the producers in payments ranging from $1,000 per year to $15,000 per year. It can only be inferred from these data that the great bulk of the payments were made to alert, aggressive family farmers who grew in numbers and grew in size during the 1950s and 1960s. The little fellows received very little; very few huge operations were involved. The alert, aggressive, larger family farmers were the chief beneficiaries.

Charles L. Schultze in a comprehensive study of "who gets the benefits of farm programs" provides some interesting quantitative answers to the question posed. He estimates the benefits of farm programs to farmers by economic class resulting from (1) price supporting actions and (2) direct payments; his findings for 1964 and 1969 are presented in tables 9-4 and 9-5. Schultze concludes from his study that "By their very nature, current farm programs tend to provide benefits — paid for by both consumers and taxpayers — primarily to those larger farmers who produce the bulk of agricultural output. Conversely, the very large number of small farmers, who in the aggregate produce only a modest fraction of total farm output, are helped relatively little by these programs."[9] In absolute terms Schultze is correct; the 568,000 farms in classes I and II in 1969 received program benefits estimated to be worth $4.6 billion while the 1,509,000 farms in classes V and VI received benefits amounting only to $0.7 billion. But in relative terms Schultze is not correct; farms in each commercial class I through V in 1969 received approximately one-half of their net income from farming through farm program benefits, and the story is almost the same for 1964. In other words, the little fellow benefited about as much as the big fellow from farm programs on each unit of product sold; his problem was that he did not have enough product to sell.

Table 9-2. Government Payments (in Million Dollars), by Programs, 1948–72

Year	Conservation[a]	Soil Bank	Sugar Act	Wool	Feed Grain	Wheat	Cotton	Cropland Adjustment	Total[b]
1948	$218	...	$39	...	...	...	...	...	$257
1949	156	...	30	...	...	...	...	...	185
1950	246	...	37	...	...	...	...	...	283
1951	246	...	40	...	...	...	...	...	286
1952	242	...	33	...	...	...	...	...	275
1953	181	...	32	...	...	...	...	...	213
1954	217	...	40	...	...	...	...	...	257
1955	188	...	41	...	...	...	...	...	229
1956	220	$243	37	$54	...	...	...	...	554
1957	230	700	32	53	...	...	...	...	1,016
1958	215	815	44	14	...	...	...	...	1,089
1959	233	323	44	82	...	...	...	...	682
1960	223	370	59	51	...	...	...	...	702
1961	236	334	53	56	$772	$42	...	...	1,493
1962	230	304	64	54	841	253	...	...	1,747
1963	231	304	67	37	843	215	...	...	1,696
1964	236	199	79	25	1,163	438	$39	...	2,181
1965	224	160	75	18	1,391	525	70	...	2,463
1966	231	145	71	34	1,293	679	773	$51	3,277
1967	237	129	70	29	865	731	932	85	3,079
1968	229	112	75	66	1,366	747	787	81	3,462
1969	204	43	78	61	1,643	858	828	78	3,794
1970	208	2	88	49	1,504	871	919	76	3,717
1971	173	...	80	69	1,054	878	822	67	3,143
1972	198	...	82	110	1,845	856	813	52	3,955

Source: *Farm Income Situation*, July 1973, p. 64.
[a] Includes Great Plains and other conservation programs.
[b] Because of rounding, totals are not equal to the sum of individual programs in all cases.

367

Table 9-3. Distribution of Producer Payments,[a] Excluding Wool and Sugar Program Payments, Calendar Year 1968

Size of Payment	Producers			Total Amount of Payments[b]		
	Number	Percentage Distribution	Cumulative Percentage Distribution	Million Dollars	Percentage Distribution	Cumulative Percentage Distribution
Less than $100	281,413	11.9%	11.9%	$ 13.6	0.4%	0.4%
$100 to $199	258,762	10.9	22.9	38.3	1.2	1.6
$200 to $499	543,822	22.8	45.7	182.8	5.7	7.3
$500 to $699	244,819	10.3	56.0	145.4	4.6	11.9
$700 to $999	257,576	10.9	66.9	216.3	6.8	18.7
$1,000 to $1,999	397,360	16.8	83.7	555.8	17.4	36.1
$2,000 to $2,999	154,187	6.5	90.2	376.0	11.8	47.9
$3,000 to $3,999	79,591	3.4	93.6	274.6	8.6	56.5
$4,000 to $4,999	46,359	2.0	95.6	206.9	6.5	63.0
$5,000 to $7,499	52,908	2.2	97.8	319.1	10.0	73.0
$7,500 to $9,999	21,342	.9	98.7	183.6	5.8	78.8
$10,000 to $14,999	17,290	.7	99.4	208.2	6.5	85.3
$15,000 to $24,999	10,320	.4	99.8	194.5	6.1	91.4
$25,000 to $49,999	4,611	.2	100.0	153.5	4.8	96.2
$50,000 to $99,999	1,010	c	100.0	66.7	2.1	98.3
$100,000 to $499,999	255	c	100.0	41.2	1.3	99.6
$500,000 to $999,999	6	c	100.0	3.9	.1	99.7
$1,000,000 and over	3	c	100.0	7.0	.2	99.9
Total	2,371,634	100.0%		$3,187.3	100.0%	

Source: Walter W. Wilcox, Economic Aspects of Farm Program Payment Limitations (Washington, D.C.: Library of Congress, Legislative Reference Service, November 6, 1969), p. 2.

[a]Includes payments under the following ASCS programs: cotton, feed grain, wheat, milk indemnity, agricultural conservation, emergency conservation, Appalachia, cropland conversion, conservation reserve, and cropland adjustment.

[b]The sum of individual percentages and individual total amounts of payments may differ from totals shown because of rounding.

[c]Less than 0.05 percent.

368

Table 9-4. Distribution of Farm Program Benefits and Income by Farm Economic Class,[a] 1964

Item	I	II	III	IV	V	VI	I & II	V & VI
Aggregate benefits (in billions)								
Price supports	$1.44	$0.66	$0.61	$0.37	$0.18	$0.14	$2.09	$0.32
Direct payments	0.34	0.44	0.58	0.38	0.19	0.26	0.78	0.45
Total supports and payments	1.78	1.10	1.19	0.75	0.37	0.40	2.87	0.77
Percentage distribution of benefits								
Price supports	42.3%	19.3%	17.9%	11.0%	5.3%	4.2%	61.6%	9.5%
Direct payments	15.4	20.3	26.4	17.4	8.6	12.0	35.7	20.6
Total supports and payments	31.8	19.7	21.3	13.4	6.6	7.2	51.3	13.8
Income and benefits per farm (in thousands)								
Farmer's net income	$27.3	$11.8	$8.0	$6.3	$5.0	$5.1	$17.3	$5.1
Net income from farming	23.3	9.5	6.0	3.5	2.0	1.0	14.4	1.2
Price supports	9.9	2.5	1.3	0.7	0.4	0.1	5.0	0.2
Direct payments	2.3	1.6	1.2	0.7	0.4	0.2	1.9	0.2
Total supports and payments	12.2	4.1	2.5	1.4	0.8	0.3	6.9	0.4
Net income per farm from farming under free-market conditions (in thousands)	$11.1	$5.4	$3.5	$2.1	$1.2	$0.7	$7.5	$0.8

[a] Economic classes of farms, as measured by gross sales, are defined as follows:

Class	Gross Sales (in thousands of dollars)
I	$40 and over
II	$20–$40
III	$10–$20
IV	$5–$10
V	$2.5–$5
VI	less than $2.5

369

Table 9-5. Distribution of Farm Program Benefits and Income by Farm Economic Class,[a] 1969

Item	I	II	III	IV	V	VI	I & II	V & VI
Aggregate benefits (in billions)								
Price supports	$1.90	$0.76	$0.55	$0.22	$0.08	$0.09	$2.66	$0.17
Direct payments	1.08	0.90	0.88	0.43	0.20	0.30	1.98	0.50
Total supports and payments	2.98	1.66	1.43	0.65	0.28	0.39	4.64	0.67
Percentage distribution of benefits								
Price supports	52.9%	21.0%	15.4%	6.1%	2.2%	2.4%	73.9%	4.6%
Direct payments	28.5	23.7	23.2	11.3	5.3	7.9	53.6	13.2
Total supports and payments	40.3	22.5	19.4	8.8	3.8	5.3	62.8	9.1
Income and benefits per farm (in thousands)								
Farmer's net income	$33.0	$13.7	$9.6	$8.1	$7.0	$8.1	$20.9	$7.9
Net income from farming	27.5	10.5	6.5	3.6	2.1	1.1	16.8	1.3
Price supports	9.0	2.1	1.1	0.6	0.3	0.1	4.7	0.1
Direct payments	5.1	2.5	1.7	1.1	0.7	0.2	3.6	0.3
Total supports and payments	14.1	4.6	2.8	1.7	1.0	0.3	8.3	0.4
Net income per farm from farming under free-market conditions (in thousands)	$13.4	$5.9	$3.7	$1.9	$1.1	$0.8	$8.5	$0.9

[a] Economic classes of farms, as measured by gross sales, are defined as follows:

Gross Sales
(in thousands of dollars)

Class	
I	$40 and over
II	$20–$40
III	$10–$20
IV	$5–$10
V	$2.5–$5
VI	less than $2.5

This latter point takes on greater significance when we consider what happened to numbers of farms in classes IV, V, and VI between 1949 and 1969. Farms in these classes went out of business in droves between 1949 and 1969, the total number declining from 4,750,000 in 1949 to 1,898,000 in 1969.[10] The net return was too small to enable the operators of some 2.8 million of these small farms to continue in the farming business. And, as discussed earlier, the assets of these little fellows who fell by the wayside were gobbled up by those alert, aggressive farmers on the way to becoming larger operators. The number of operators in classes I, II, and III increased from 497,000 in 1949 to 1,073,000 in 1969. Once again we conclude that the alert, aggressive farmers who used the income benefits and the insurance provided by the farm program in combination with technological advance to borrow, to invest, to get their unit costs down, and to expand the size of their operations were the chief beneficiaries of the farm programs. And as pointed out above, there were a sizable number of these alert, aggressive, expanding commercial farmers.

Finally, it should be recognized that the alert, aggressive, expanding farmers were able to hold the income gains accruing to them from the farm programs and technological advance in the competitive context in which they operated in the long run *only insofar as they were land owners*. The income gains accruing to them from the farm programs and technological advance were through the competitive process capitalized into land values, and their unit costs of production increased through this land capitalization process. Data presented by Wilcox, Cochrane, and Herdt (see the accompanying tabulation) illustrate this point.[11]

Time Period	Value of Land and Buildings per Acre	Net Farm Income per Acre
1946–50	66	12.86
1951–55	85	11.76
1956–60	109	10.68
1961–65	131	12.05
1966–70	174	14.42

Over the long period 1946–70, net farm income measured on a per acre basis for the United States held almost constant, but the value of farm land increased from $66 to $174 per acre. The ultimate gainer from a net income increase in agriculture, whether resulting from an increase in demand, a farm technological advance, or a farm program, is the land owner. Any income gain tends to get capitalized into the limiting input, land, through the competitive process. And that is where the income benefits of the farm programs had to come to rest.

Resource Allocation, Efficiency, and Output.

As discussed in chapter 1, the United States was confronted with a continuing problem of general excess production capacity in the agricultural sector throughout the 1950s and 1960s. Some 5 to 10 percent too many resources in the aggregate were engaged in producing agricultural products, or were available to produce agricultural products each year; there were 5 to 10 percent too many resources available to produce agriculture products in the sense that the product of these resources could not move through the commercial market at the existing price level. This estimate of 5 to 10 percent of the aggregate resources available to agricultural production thus constitutes a measure of the resource allocation problem confronting the nation. If these resources could have been transferred to other sectors and employed there without creating a surplus condition, product prices in the farm sector would have been maintained, output in the new sectors would have been increased at constant prices, and the real product of the nation would have been increased.

But the nation was unable to find policy solutions to the excess capacity problem in agriculture which would produce the happy result described above. More precisely, there was never an attempt to develop a nationwide systematic resource policy, or plan, to bring aggregate resources employed in agriculture in line with requirements. The exodus of workers from agriculture in this period was huge; the number of workers employed in agriculture declined from 8.7 million in 1945 to 3.5 million in 1970. But given the cost-reducing possibilities stemming from the technological advances of the period (e.g., new plant varieties, new fertilizing practices, new harvesting machinery) and the price insurance provided by the government programs, nonfarm-produced capital flowed into agriculture in vast amounts and offset the outflow of human labor. Thus, productive resources in the aggregate in agriculture remained in excess. And as we have already observed, framers of farm policy in this period were unwilling to cure the problem of resource malallocation by letting farm prices and incomes fall to free-market levels. The price-income consequences of the free-market solution were too terrible to contemplate.

Thus, a farm policy compromise was forged, evolving over time, to contain the excess capacity problem. This evolving compromise, which included various program instruments — price support, direct payments, production control, surplus disposal, stock accumulation — did not, we argue, create the excess capacity, or resource allocation, problem; it came about in response to the resource allocation problem. The farm policy compromise may, depending on one's point of view, have prolonged the problem. But it did not create it.

The chronic excess capacity, or resource allocation, problem grew out of the interaction of four circumstances, or socioeconomic elements, of American society: (1) the high value that American society placed on scientific research and technological development, and the generous public support provided these activities in the agricultural sector; (2) the atomistic, competitive market organization, or structure, within which farmers operate; (3) the extreme inelasticity of the aggregate demand for food; and (4) the inability of resources previously committed to farm production to shift easily and readily out of farming in response to low prices and incomes.[12] The interaction of these components caused aggregate supply to press relentlessly on an inelastic demand for food such that, in the absence of any countervailing action, the farm price level would have had to fall precipitously to clear the market of farm food products — to erase the excess capacity to produce farm food products. The farm policy compromise which evolved over the period 1948–73 was *the* solution that policy makers in the United States came up with for living with or containing the problem.

But the price and income insurance provided farmers, in conjunction with rapid technological advance, did result in important gains in productive efficiency in American agriculture. Changes in farm productivity may be seen in table 9-6. Over the period 1948–73 the aggregate input of resources holds almost constant and total output increases over 50 percent; hence output per unit of input increases by about 50 percent.

This great burst in production efficiency did not occur by magic. It occurred as farmers adopted new and improved technologies, invested in new and improved forms of capital inputs, and created new and improved production combinations on farms. The question might be asked — What did the price and income support programs have to do with these gains in agricultural productivity? They had a lot to do with it. They provided the stable prices, hence price insurance, to induce the alert and aggressive farmers to invest in new and improved technologies and capital items, and the reasonably acceptable farm incomes and asset positions to induce lenders to assume the risk of making farm production loans. This is a point of very great significance. Farmers like other businessmen tend to disinvest in periods of falling prices, are wary of making investments in situations of uncertainty, and invest heavily when the future is bright. The future did not exactly look bright in the 1950s and 1960s, but the farm programs put a floor under farm prices and incomes and enabled alert, aggressive farmers to take investment risks which otherwise would have been closed to them.

References to two historical situations help illustrate the point. The overall production efficiency of American agriculture does not increase during the long period 1924–36, despite the fact that important improvements were being made in tractor power, hybrid corn was available in the latter part of the

Table 9-6. Farm Productivity, 1948–73
(1950 = 100)

Year	Farm Output	Farm Input	Output per Unit of Input
1948	104	99	104
1949	101	100	101
1950	100	100	100
1951	103	103	100
1952	107	103	104
1953	108	102	105
1954	108	101	107
1955	112	101	110
1956	112	99	113
1957	110	97	113
1958	118	96	122
1959	120	98	123
1960	123	96	128
1961	124	96	129
1962	125	96	130
1963	130	97	134
1964	129	97	132
1965	133	97	136
1966	131	98	133
1967	137	100	137
1968	139	101	138
1969	141	101	139
1970	140	101	138
1971	151	102	148
1972	152	102	149
1973[a]	158	103	153

[a]Preliminary.

period, and knowledge regarding the use of commercial fertilizer was widespread. Important gains in productive efficiency did not take place during this period because farmers could not afford to purchase and adopt the new technologies or make the necessary investments. This was a period of hard times — low and unstable prices, negative incomes, eroded asset positions, and business failure. Farmers were not thinking about more efficient production combinations involving new and improved technologies and additional capital investments in the early 1930s; they were concentrating on how to survive till the next year.

The effect of the elimination of price risk on potato production in the 1940s through the introduction of a price support program was most dramatic. We quote from the Minnesota study *Impact of Government Programs in the Potato Industry:*

Beginning with the 1943 crop, potatoes were affected by a Steagall Amendment, which provided for price supports at not less than 90 per cent of parity. There were earlier efforts to improve the potato grower's market; such measures as marketing agreements, purchase programs, and soil conservation payments were tried, but none of them attacked the problem on anything approaching the scale of the price support program.

The price support program created an unlimited market for potatoes at approximately the average price (in relation to parity) which had prevailed for 30 years and virtually eliminated the risk of very low prices. Moreover, it came at a time when farm incomes were high and rising, so the alternative enterprises of the lake states' producers were exceptionally attractive. Thus, without guaranteeing high prices, but merely by guaranteeing something close to the average free market price, the support program helped change the outlook of the individual potato producer.

The response to the program was immediate and of such magnitude as to be unmistakable. Growers in the outlying specialist states increased their plantings by one-third in 1943 and maintained the new higher acreages until acreage restrictions were imposed. Growers in the lake states, on the other hand, were more hesitant in their response; they increased their acreage by only one-fifth in 1943 and reverted thereafter to the previous downward trend in acreage.

The typical grower in the specialist states had been in a position for some time to produce potatoes profitably at the average equilibrium price. But the risk was great in any given year, when he might decide to enlarge his operation, that the price might fall and imperil his investment. The expansion of production in the specialist areas was also impeded by the tenacity of the small commercial producers throughout the lake states, combined with the fact that there was no expanding market to absorb new production. With the government guaranteeing a market, the natural response of specialist producers was to expand and intensify potato production. . . .

The production of specialists did not, with the introduction of greater price certainty, expand by magic. There exists no direct but mysterious relationship between the degree of price variability and the output of potatoes. *The expansion occurred through production adjustments induced by — motivated by — the greater price certainty.* The introduction of price supports in 1942 and the greater price certainty which accompanied them induced specialized potato growers everywhere, and particularly in specialist areas, to (1) expand acreage, (2) apply more capital in the form of fertilizer and machinery and equipment, (3) adopt improved practices already known but not widely used because of the costs involved, and (4) adopt such new practices as DDT sprays and overhead irrigation more rapidly than otherwise would have been the case. Increased price certainty resulting from price supports created the favorable economic climate in which these changes in production occurred rapidly and dramatically. This is the way in which the reduction of price risk contributed to increased specialization in potato production.[13]

As we have already noted, aggregate farm output increased by over 50 percent between 1948 and 1973. This increase did not occur in response to a higher level of prices. It occurred through an irregular shifting of a highly inelastic short-run aggregate supply function to the right as farmers adopted new and improved technologies, invested in new and improved capital items, and created new and more efficient production combinations. These latter developments were made possible by the economic climate provided by the various government programs of price and income support. This climate involved stable but not high product prices, tolerable but not good incomes. It was a climate conducive to rapid farm technological advance. It did not guarantee any producer a good income, but it protected the producer against a price collapse in the coming year. Driven by the quest for improved incomes and protected against economic collapse, the alert, aggressive farmer jammed into practice every new and improved technology that he could lay his hands on, reduced his costs, expanded his output, and experienced short-run income gains. Others followed suit, some surviving, some failing financially. But in this harsh competitive process aggregate output expanded. For 25 years with two brief exceptions (about one year during the Korean War, and 1973) the nation experienced a pressure of food supplies on demand and enjoyed the luxury of chronic food abundance. The farm policy compromise in conjunction with rapid and widespread technological advance, operating in the context of an atomistically competitive industry, produced the important result — chronic food abundance.

Foreign Trade

In a recent book, D. Gale Johnson argues that world agriculture is in disarray. What is his evidence? His evidence is largely qualitative and is summarized by him as follows:

In general . . . the opportunities for producing farm products under lowest-cost conditions are being lost and . . . much of the growth in world farm output has been — and is — occurring in nations where policies are encouraging output expansion with little or no consideration of the long-run effects upon either their own citizens or the interests of agricultural producers in other countries. In short, a significant fraction of world farm output is being produced in the wrong place. If significant benefits of a permanent nature were being derived from the distortions in location of output, there might be a reasonable basis for such interferences. However, the benefits that have been, and are being, derived are minimal; and the costs to consumers and taxpayers in many industrial countries, and to the possibilities of the developing countries to use their own resources to best advantage and to earn foreign exchange required for rapid economic growth, far outweigh any possible gains.[14]

That the location of agricultural producers is different, to some degree, given past and present policies of governmental intervention in agriculture, than it would be in a free-market situation, and that consumers pay some real cost for the benefits they seek, minimal or otherwise, through governmental intervention in the economy, as compared with a free-trade situation, few people would deny. But to argue that world agriculture is in disarray, as Professor Johnson does, because the world economy does not conform to a free-trade model is to mislead. World agriculture in both the developed and less-developed segments has performed miraculously in the past two decades in the way of increasing production to meet the rapidly expanding demand for food.

The interesting question, in terms of the Johnson thesis and the impact of government programs of price and income support in the United States, is: "How much different would the location of agricultural production be in a worldwide free trade situation?" The next and more important question is: "What is the real cost to consumers in each particular country of the set of trade protectionist practices in each country, with respect to agriculture, as measured against a free trade situation?" Answers to these questions will help us begin to formulate some rough measures of the impact of programs of price and income support and their ancillary trade protection practices on foreign trade in agricultural products.

What would happen to patterns of crop and livestock production if all nations adopted a free-trade policy? But first, before we try to answer that question, it must be recognized that the Communist countries are not market economies and the concept of free trade is completely meaningless to them; given their present set of institutions, there is no way that they could implement a free-trade policy.[15] Thus, we must restrict our thoughts to what would happen to the location of agricultural production in the non-Communist world.

Based upon what we know about the location and levels of trade barriers and changing patterns of trade,[16] and what we think we know about comparative advantage in agricultural production, the following points can reasonably be made with respect to shifts in the location of agricultural production resulting from the adoption of a free trade policy by *all nations* in the non-Communist world:

1. A major part of sugar production in Western Europe and the United States could be expected to shift to the tropics.

2. Some grain production (how much is not clear) in Western Europe could be expected to shift to the major grain-exporting countries.

3. Some rice production in Japan could be expected to shift to more favorably endowed areas, and some rice production in the United States might shift to other areas.

4. Some milk production for manufacturing purposes in the United States could be expected to shift to New Zealand and possibly to specialized dairying areas in Western Europe.

5. The production of livestock products and the feed grain base could be expected to shift about modestly among countries. But at this level of generality it is not possible to indicate the direction of the commodity shifts.

6. The production of certain fruits, vegetables, and other specialty crops could be expected to shift about among countries. But it is not possible at this level of generality to name commodities and indicate the direction of shifts.

With the possible exception of sugar, the adoption of a policy of free trade throughout the world would not, given the situation of the 1970s, alter significantly existing patterns of crop and livestock production. Crop and livestock production areas would undergo some changes, but in the main the major crops and animal products would be produced in about the same areas as they are at present. The changes in the location of production that did occur, without a corresponding change in the location of population, would, however, have the effect of increasing the volume of foreign trade. As the Flanigan Report on Agricultural Trade Policy[17] points out, a general movement toward free trade in agricultural commodities in the non-Communist world would increase importantly the exports of the grain and oilseed and oilseed products from the United States and increase the imports of dairy products and sugar into the United States.

In other words, it is reasonable and logical to argue that the programs of price and income support in the United States and in *all other non-Communist countries*, together with the ancillary protectionist measures, have operated to make each country somewhat more self-sufficient in each major agricultural commodity line than would be the case without the programs, hence have operated to reduce the volume of trade in agricultural commodities among trading nations somewhat below what it would be without the programs.

What about the real costs to society of producing a product mix which varies from the solution that would obtain under a free-market situation as the result of pursuing a domestic policy of farm price and income support and the necessary adjunct protectionist measures? Professor Johnson inquires into the question first through a theoretical analysis, and second through a presentation of the results of several empirical studies, and he is forced to conclude that "at least in the short run the losses in national income or welfare from restrictions of trade are a small fraction of national output."[18] It seems fair to say that, where we are considering only the restrictions on trade in agricultural commodities, the loss to national income can only be a *very, very* small fraction of national output.

But the analysis of the impact of programs of price and income support on foreign trade has, to this point, assumed the adoption of a free trade by *all* nations in the non-Communist world. This is a useful assumption for conducting an analysis. It is not a realistic assumption in terms of what most nations in the non-Communist world were prepared to do about domestic support programs in the agricultural sector or with regard to trade policy in the period 1948–73. Most developed countries in the non-Communist world had comprehensive and effective programs for supporting and protecting their agricultural plants in the 1950s and 1960s; [19] and most less-developed countries were employing various levels of trade protection measures (e.g., import controls, state trading organizations).

An investigation of the consequences of programs of price and income support in the United States on foreign trade must then take account of the fact that almost every trading partner of the United States was engaged in supporting and protecting its agricultural production complex. We, therefore, ask this question: What would have happened to foreign trade in agricultural products involving the United States if the United States had adopted a free-market, free-trade policy in the early 1950s, and its trading partners had not? Logic suggests that the adoption of such policies unilaterally by the United States would have wiped out most, if not all, of the mainland production of sugar and severely damaged the dairy industry in the United States. How badly the dairy industry would have been damaged might be debated, since domestic feed prices would have declined in the absence of programs, but it would have been damaged. But since nothing had changed in the major grain and oilseed importing nations, there is no reason why exports of the grains, oilseed products, and other traditional exports to those nations from the United States would have increased over those amounts moving under export subsidy in the 1950s. In sum, it is reasonable to argue that, given the battery of programs supporting and protecting agricultural production in almost every developed country in the 1950s, the programs of price and income support in the United States did not reduce exports of commodities in which it had a trade advantage (i.e., the grains, oilseeds, and possibly meats and cotton), and the programs saved producers of sugar from certain destruction, and protected dairy farmers from reduced prices and incomes. Of course, as we already know, the farm programs operated to hold the retail prices of sugar, dairy products, *and every other food product* above the level they would have been without the programs.

With the reformulation of the programs of price and income support in the 1960s, wherein the level of price support was lowered to about world levels for wheat, feed grains, and cotton, it is again questionable whether exports of those commodities would have increased with a unilateral dismantling of price and income support programs in the United States. But again, it is clear that imports of sugar and dairy products would have increased with unilateral elimination of the programs to the certain income disadvantage of sugar and milk producers. [20]

We thus reach the following conclusion: First, adoption of a free-trade policy throughout the non-Communist world would have had a moderate, but noticeable, effect on the location of agricultural production, would have increased rather importantly trade in agricultural products involving the United States, and would have increased the real incomes of consumers in the United States by some modest amount. Second, the unilateral adoption of a free-market, free-trade policy by the United States would have resulted in considerable damage to the agricultural industry from increased imports and produced few, if any, benefits in the way of increased exports. Third, in the real world, then, the programs of price and income support, and the ancillary protectionist measures, were a part of a worldwide system of such policies and programs which did operate to reduce and restrict trade as the nations involved sought other and conflicting objectives; but no one country, such as the United States, could significantly expand its trade through the adoption unilaterally of free-trade policies.

Consumer Welfare

The price of food to consumers in the United States would, without question, have declined in almost any given year between 1948 and 1965[21] if the farm price and income support program had been eliminated for that year. This follows from the fact that farm prices were being held above equilibrium levels by government programs over this long period. Farm prices for most commodities approached world equilibrium levels in the United States after 1965 as levels of price support were lowered to world equilibrium levels in the basic compromise. Thus retail food prices would have fallen little if any by the elimination of farm programs after 1965, although in the case of wheat an excise tax remained in the program which had to be paid by domestic consumers.

But the price of food to consumers would almost certainly have declined for any intermediate period of three to five years any time during the long period 1948–65 with the elimination of the farm programs. In the longer run, with full resource adjustment, the evidence as we have already noted is inconclusive: one study suggests that farm prices, hence food prices, would have remained below the actual level of prices for the entire period 1948–73; the second study suggests that farm prices, hence food prices, would have shot above the actual level of prices in the late 1960s if government programs of price and income support had been eliminated in the early 1950s. But regardless of the long-run level of food prices realized, if government programs had been eliminated, prices of food to consumers by commodity and in the aggregate would have been much more unstable than they were with the programs of support.

How much food prices would have fallen during the period 1948–65 with the elimination of government programs of price and income support cannot be stated neatly or precisely. This is the case for a number of reasons. First, although all studies indicate that the level of farm prices would have fallen in the short run with the elimination of government programs, the results of those studies vary from 10 to 40 percent depending upon the assumptions made. Second, the decline in farm prices varies importantly by commodity: the greatest decline is likely to occur in wheat and the least decline in milk. Third, the percentage decline in food prices would depend upon the marketing margin for the food commodity involved. For example, the marketing margin for bread is very wide; thus it would take a very large decline in the price of wheat at the farm level to result in an important decrease in the price of bread. On the other hand, the marketing margin for eggs is rather narrow; hence a large decline in the price of eggs at the farm level would also lead to a relatively large decline in the price of eggs at retail.

We conclude that the elimination of government programs of price and income support in agriculture would have reduced the price of food to consumers in the short and intermediate runs during the period 1948–65. But on the average and relatively speaking, the reduction of food prices would have been only about one-half as great as the decline in farm prices. In the short and intermediate run consumers would have gained from the elimination of farm price and income support programs, but their gain from the resulting decline in prices would, in relative terms, have been only about half as great as the losses sustained by farm producers.

As was recognized above, the reduction in the level of farm price support to equilibrium levels in the middle 1960s and the substitution of income payment programs for price support programs in the 1970s operated to reduce the real price of food to consumers. In fact the retail price of food to American consumers from 1965 to 1973 must have been close to market equilibrium levels. The price gains to consumers were not great, since the farm price reductions were not great and the market margin argument is operative in this connection too. But the basic thrust of farm program changes in the 1950s and 1960s which resulted in the lowering of farm price support levels to world equilibrium levels all worked to the benefit of consumers in the United States. After 1965 government programs of price and income support in the United States, *and other exporting countries*, may have operated to hold world prices somewhat above what they otherwise would have been, but the U.S. programs no longer operated to discriminate against U.S. consumers with respect to the price of food.

The maintenance of large reserve stocks of grains and other storable commodities in the United States from 1952 to 1972, perhaps more by accident than by design, did have one important serendipitous effect: it protected the U.S. consumer against sharp and unanticipated price increases and against physical shortages of food. The U.S. consumer paid somewhat more for his food, at least in the short run, given the fact of the government support programs, but he received something in return; he received insurance against food shortages. Stated positively, the government programs of farm price and income support enabled the U.S. consumer to luxuriate in food abundance for two decades.

Many and varied consumer groups around the world also benefited from the surplus stocks accumulated under the farm price and income support programs in the United States. Millions of consumers in India lived through the severe drought of 1965–66 because surplus stocks were available in the United States and were shipped to India under P.L. 480; millions of children and nursing mothers in the less-developed world have received food supplements to their meager diets; and certainly the Soviet consumer benefited from bountiful supplies of grain in the United States in 1972–73. For two decades the large stocks of grain and other storable commodities in the United States protected consumers around the world from calamitous acts of God and from the consequences of extreme poverty. Partly by accident and partly by design the United States carried food reserves for the world for most of the period 1948–73.

In conclusion, the U.S. consumer paid a higher price for food, at least in the short and intermediate runs, under the programs during the period 1948–65 than he would have had to pay without the programs. For this he could look forward to and expect relatively stable food prices and the absolute guarantee of abundant supplies of food. Consumers around the world were protected against the worst physical catastrophes and the consequences of extreme poverty. Consumers in the United States paid the price premium for insurance against starvation in most parts of the world most of the time from 1948 to 1973. But after 1965 that price premium was not very large.

CHAPTER 10

Program Appraisal and Implications for the Future

If one takes the view that the government programs of price and income support were designed, or should have been designed, to correct the excess production capacity problem confronting commercial agriculture in one year, or even several years, then the programs obviously failed and the money costs involved were exorbitant. But if one takes the view, which we do, that there was no course of action socially or politically acceptable to the American people for correcting the excess production capacity problem in one year, or even several years, then one's perspective on the programs — what they did and what they cost — changes. In our view the programs were designed to *contain* the excess capacity problem and thereby *stabilize* the agricultural industry and enable it to *grow* and *restructure* itself in an orderly fashion. And this the programs did accomplish.

Perhaps the word "design" connotes more rigor and more purposefulness in the policy formulation process than was in fact involved. The programs were, as we have already learned, the product of a protracted struggle and a long series of compromises in which many, varied, and differing interest groups were involved. We do not suggest that each interest group had the national, or even the industry, well-being in mind as it battled and maneuvered to achieve its particular policy objective. But we do suggest that the national interest was protected and a public interest point of view emerged from struggles and compromises *among* the varied and differing contending interest groups. The action and interaction of the varied, contending, and conflicting interest groups in the policy formulation process tended to wash out the most crass demand of those interest groups and to push the public interest into the foreground.

In this kind of political environment, we argue, farm programs were forged that could and did assist the agricultural industry to grow and restructure itself in a period of rapid technological advance wherein the full and heavy cost of the growth and restructuring processes did not fall on farmer-producers alone, and in which the whole process moved smoothly without interruptions in the flow of food products to consumers and without severe and unpredictable fluctuations in the flow of earnings to producers. This is what the evolving farm policy compromise over the period 1948–73 was all about.

These accomplishments came at considerable cost — high money costs, increased prices of food products, and a high incidence of business failure among small farmers. But, in this formulation of the issue, we are, in our opinion, in a position to ask the right question — Were the accomplishments worth the costs? We are in a position to weigh the specific accomplishments of the programs against their costs and make a judgment regarding their goodness or badness to society. And to this process of appraisal and judgment we now turn.

Program Appraisal

The contributions and achievements. Without doubt the foremost achievement of the farm price and income support programs during the period 1948–73 was the protection that they provided farmer-producers against a calamitous price level decline during that period. The level of farm prices did not drop into the "sub-basement" with the contraction in the international demand for farm products at the end of the reconstruction period following World War II as it did following World War I; and the condition of chronic excess production capacity during the 1950s and 1960s did not result in a sharp and drastic decline in the level of farm prices. The price floor provided by the programs protected farmers against precipitous price level declines such as they had experienced in 1919–21 and 1929–34.

Farm prices sagged under the pressure of a contracting world demand in the early 1950s and general excess production capacity throughout the 1950s and 1960s, *but they did not break.* Thus farmers escaped a major economic depression during the long period 1948–73. For farm operators this achievement dwarfs all others.

In addition to the fact that the farm programs protected farm operators against precipitous declines in the level of farm prices, the programs operated to stabilize farm prices and incomes.[1] This may be seen in tables 10-1 and 10-2. For farm prices in the aggregate, subaggregates, and individual commodities, farm prices were more stable in the 1950s and 1960s than in earlier periods, or for the period which includes the early 1970s. The same is true with respect to net farm income.

Table 10-1. Instability Indices for Selected U.S.
Agricultural Price Series at the Farm Level

Item	Average Absolute Percentage Change from Previous Year					
	1921–30	1931–40	1941–50	1951–60	1961–70	1964–73
Prices received by farmers						
All farm products . . .	9.7%	15.2%	13.2%	5.6%	3.1%	7.9%
All crops	13.1	18.5	13.9	3.7	3.4	7.7
All livestock	8.1	14.0	13.5	8.5	5.6	9.9
Corn price	18.6	33.0	22.5	6.0	7.0	18.1
Wheat price	17.8	24.9	16.1	3.3	10.7	29.3
Soybean price	11.2	33.7	20.7	5.1	6.9	16.0
Cotton price	27.2	20.3	19.9	5.9	9.7	19.6
Cattle price	12.5	18.3	18.3	15.4	8.3	10.5
Hog price	17.2	27.0	21.8	14.8	11.1	21.1
Milk price	9.5[a]	11.7	13.0	5.2	3.8	5.9
Prices paid by farmers[b]	6.5	6.9	8.3	2.7	1.9	3.6

[a] 1925–34.
[b] All items used in production.

Table 10-2. Instability Indices for Net Realized U.S. Farm Income,
with and without Direct Government Payments

Item	Average Absolute Percentage Change from Previous Year					
	1921–30	1931–40	1941–50	1951–60	1961–70	1964–73
Net farm income including direct payments	14.0%	20.8%	19.0%	8.9%	6.6%	13.0%
Net farm income excluding direct payments	14.0	20.5	21.5	9.0	5.5	11.7

Farmers obviously would prefer to see their product prices rising steadily and persistently relative to all other prices. But since this is not a realistic possibility, the next best alternative is high and stable product prices. This they did not realize in the period 1950–70 either. But they did realize a reasonable and stable level of prices in the period 1950–70. This stable economic environment in conjunction with rapid technological development resulted in rapid adoption of new and improved technologies on farms, relatively heavy investments in nonfarm-produced inputs, increased production efficiency, and a rapid rate of growth in aggregate production capacity which exceeded aggregate demand. This development involving a restructuring of American agriculture and rapid growth in agricultural output benefited the U.S. and world economies in many ways: increased per capita real incomes in the United States, increased merchandise exports from the United States, provided food aid to poor and hungry people in the less-developed countries, and acted to dampen the rate of inflation in the United States. Increased price and income stability provided by the farm programs in conjunction with rapid technological development resulted in important real income gains to the people of the United States and the world.

The rapid rate of growth in aggregate farm output in combination with the loan and storage programs resulted in the U.S. government acquiring and holding large stocks of grains, cotton, and other storable commodities during most of the period 1948–73. These stocks, often in excess of the amounts required to protect U.S. consumers against unforeseen contingencies, operated to guarantee adequate supplies of food to U.S. consumers at all times and to stabilize the retail price of food.[2] American consumers could and did enjoy food abundance. This was a boon to U.S. consumers that was largely taken for granted in the decades of the 1950s and 1960s, but which was coming to be appreciated by 1973–74.

Finally, the stocks of grain and other storable commodities generated by the price and income support programs enabled the United States to provide food aid to the poor and the hungry around the world over most of the period 1948–73. The farm programs literally gave life itself to millions of impoverished, hungry people around the world, hence were of incalculable benefit to those millions in dire need. The food abundance resulting from the operation of the farm programs also contributed to the institutionalization of domestic food programs to assist the poor and ill-fed within the United States. To the poor and the impoverished at home and abroad the programs were a great blessing.

The shortcomings and costs. A major shortcoming of the programs of price and income support at least through 1960 was a failure to understand the nature of the problem confronting commercial agriculture, namely, the excess capacity problem. This failure to understand led to various mechanical weaknesses in the programs: (1) an unwillingness to impose strict production controls, (2) the tendency to impose production controls over only the commodity in most serious oversupply and permit the released resources to shift into the production of other commodities (e.g., the shift of released resources from wheat to grain sorghum), and (3) undue reliance on storage and surplus disposal programs.

As long as farmers, their leaders, and other interest groups were of the mind that the surplus problem was a temporary problem that would fade away in a year or two, or that it was a relative problem in which too many resources were devoted to the production of one commodity (e.g., wheat) and not enough to another commodity (e.g., soybeans), the framers of farm policy legislation would not and could not effectively cope with the basic problem confronting their constituents, namely, excess production capacity. Thus, for a long time, roughly 1948–60, farm policy makers treated the symptoms and ignored the cause; they were unwilling, or unable, to formulate and place in operation programs with the capacity to deal with the problems of too many resources in the aggregate producing too many agricultural products in the aggregate. As a result, government inventories of storable price supported commodities built up to excessive levels and the costs of government programs soared needlessly.

A second important shortcoming of the programs was the almost complete reliance on acreage controls as a means of controlling supply throughout the entire period 1948–73. Why this was the case is hard to understand. Perhaps because of the age-old tradition that land is the principal and limiting resource in agricultural production. Perhaps because farmers and their leaders understood that acreage control was a weak form of production control. Whatever the reason, total reliance on acreage control, as a means of controlling marketable supplies, led to various kinds of problems. First, acreage control is a weak and slippery form of control. Farmers tend to place their poorest acres under control and they adopt new and improved technologies when they are available (and they were available throughout the 1950s and 1960s). This enables them to increase output per unit of input on their remaining operation. As a result, total output is not reduced as much as was anticipated, more acres must be removed from production in succeeding years, and program costs rise. Second, reliance on acreage controls led to a skewed and socially undesirable allocation of resources. The control of production through the requirement that a farmer reduce his input of land, where each farmer is free to maximize his return through the substitution of other factors for the acres removed, must result in a nonoptimal combination of productive resources for each producer involved and some diminution in the total social product. On the American scene in the 1950s and 1960s this meant the substitution of fertilizer, pesticides, machinery, and power for land and labor — for the land removed from production under the program, and the labor input on each acre removed from production. As a result, the programs operated to increase the flow of human labor out of agriculture and to speed up the flow of nonfarm-produced inputs into agriculture. And for much of the labor so displaced, this meant moving to the city, living in a ghetto, and not finding a productive job. Third, the increased intensity of agricultural production induced in part by the programs contributed to the land and water pollution problems of modern agriculture.[3]

A third shortcoming of the programs and perhaps the most striking of all was the failure of policy makers to recognize and effectively deal with the special problems of medium to small commercial farmers and hired labor in the production revolution that occurred in American agriculture in the 1950s and 1960s.[4] As was discussed in the previous chapter, the economic stability provided by the programs in conjunction with rapid technological advance produced an economic environment ideally suited to the acquisition activities of the larger, more alert, more aggressive farmer — in this environment he could borrow, invest, intensify, reduce unit costs, grow larger, and as a result buy out and so acquire the assets of his smaller, less alert, less aggressive neighbor.

The medium to small commercial farmers needed technical assistance, commercial assistance, special credit, and perhaps some kind of special income subsidy; hired farm labor needed the same kinds of economic and social protection that urban labor was acquiring. But neither group received that needed aid. The farm price and income support programs consistently ignored the economic and social needs of small commercial farmers and hired farm labor.

A fourth shortcoming of the programs of price and income support involves the failure to develop a legitimate reserve stock program with the intended purpose of ensuring adequate supplies to regular claimants on U.S. production (e.g., domestic consumers, traditional foreign importers), and of maintaining stable food and agricultural prices. The programs did, of course, provide for a storage operation, but it was a residual operation. The storage operation acquired stocks whenever supplies exceeded demand at the announced price support level (i.e., the loan rate), and it disposed of stocks whenever the opportunity presented itself — usually through food aid shipments after 1954. The storage operation acquired those supplies not contained by a weak and slippery acreage control program. And as we know, inventories in the storage operation became mountainous in the 1950s because the acreage control programs were weak, on-again, off-again, and nonexistent.

The concept of a legitimate reserve stock program with specific and announced price stabilization and inventory goals was often discussed, in government and out, throughout the 1960s. But nothing concrete happened. Administrators preferred the freewheeling flexibility provided by the legislation authorizing the Commodity Credit Corporation, and farmers had no interest in a price stabilization activity which put a ceiling over farm prices. Thus, consumers in the United States in 1973 experienced the greatest increase in food prices in modern times as government storage bins were emptied to satisfy the demands of foreign buyers in a poor crop year abroad. The food abundance enjoyed by U.S. consumers for over 20 years disappeared in 1973 as the administration exploited the short world grain situation to divest itself of stocks. Government stock policy at the close of 1973 was a "bare-shelf" policy.

The fifth shortcoming is concerned with the impact of the programs on foreign trade. Without doubt the programs operated to restrict international trade so long as the prices of individual commodities were supported well above world levels. The high domestic prices tended to reduce the volume of foreign sales, and import restrictions employed to protect the high domestic price operated to restrict imports as was intended. The use of export subsidies and P.L. 480 helped to circumvent those features of the programs that operated to block exports during the 1950s and 1960s. Nonetheless the overall effect of the major commodity programs from 1948 to the middle 1960s was to hold domestic commodity prices above world levels, whatever the cost to international trade. Professor Schuh has further shown that an overvalued U.S. dollar during much of the period in question operated to limit the flow of agricultural exports.[5] As a result, U.S. consumers and consumers of the world suffered some loss in real income. How much we really do not know; as suggested in the previous chapter, probably not a large amount, but some.

In its own self-interest the United States lowered the level of price support to world levels for such commodities as wheat, feed grains, and cotton in the middle 1960s. As a result of this action commercial trade in these commodities was facilitated and expanded. But the support of commodity prices at higher than world levels and/or the use of import restrictions remains in effect for such commodities as dairy products, sugar, rice, and beef, and for many farm commodities of lesser commercial importance. Without doubt international trade in the commodities mentioned above involving the United States (primarily imports into the United States) would increase if the United States dismantled the programs and/or import restrictions for these commodities. But the increased trade would come at the expense of producers of these commodities, and exports of other agricultural commodities from the U.S. would not necessarily increase *unless trading partners of the United States also liberalized their trade policies on agricultural products.* Price and income support for domestic agricultural producers, involving the use of import restrictions, is commonplace around the world, and the United States cannot reap the full benefits of expanded trade unless trading partners also reduce their trade barriers.

In conclusion, the United States restructured its price and income support programs for such major export crops as wheat, feed grains, and cotton in the 1960s so as to facilitate the export of these commodities. And this action worked to the distinct advantage of the United States. The United States in its own self-interest might wish to explore the restructuring of its commodity programs for dairy products, sugar, rice, and beef, and certain other commodities, which would operate to lower the relative price of these commodities to U.S. consumers through their increased importation. But difficult questions remain unanswered. Should the United States pursue such a course of action unilaterally, or only in a situation in which trading partners also reduce their barriers to trade? And how is the United States to protect its producers and its consumers from extreme price instability, if it moves to an essentially free-trade position?

By their very nature, domestic programs of price and income support conflict with international trade, hence impede trade in agricultural commodities. Domestic programs of price and income support are concerned with isolating the farm sector from the world economy. International trade is concerned with integrating the farm sector with the world economy. Undue concern with the objective of domestic farm price and income support in the period 1948–65 caused international trade in agricultural products involving the United States to suffer. A compromise between the objectives of domestic price and income support and international trade following 1965 has led to expanded trade and possibly real income benefits to consumers. But the embarkation of the United States on a policy of free trade in agricultural products while its trading partners engage in state trading and the heavy protection of their farm producers can result in severe supply-price problems for the United States, as the year 1973 demonstrates.

The sixth shortcoming is concerned with the higher prices of food that consumers in the United States had to pay as the result of the workings of the farm programs. As we noted in the previous chapter, the retail price of food was held above market equilibrium levels from 1948 to 1965 as farm prices were supported above equilibrium levels. This deficiency in the programs was corrected in 1965 in the basic farm policy compromise when levels of price support were lowered to world equilibrium levels. Secretary Brannan tried to correct this shortcoming in the programs back in 1949, but it took about 15 years of struggle to do so.

It would be a mistake, however, to conclude that consumers in the United States paid prices for food greatly in excess of free-market levels in the 1950s and early 1960s. Levels of farm price support were gradually reduced in the 1950s and early 1960s so that the decline in the retail price of food was barely noticed as levels of price support were finally reduced to world market levels in the middle 1960s. Continuous changes in farm policy legislation were moving retail prices of food toward free-market levels from 1955 to 1965, and after 1965 retail prices of food were very close to free-market levels.

The seventh and final shortcoming of the programs must be the loss in money income sustained by American taxpayers to defray the money costs of the programs: the transfer payments flowing from taxpayers to commercial farmers and agribusiness firms. Some individuals may have objected less than others to paying taxes to defray the money costs of government programs of farm price and income support. But to all it was a burden, and the total burden for the 26-year period was large indeed. As we noted in chapter 8, U.S. taxpayers paid on the average $3.7 billion per year to support farm prices and incomes from 1948 to and including 1973. What more is there to say?

Striking a Balance

How does one weigh the contributions and achievements of the programs of price and income support against the shortcomings and costs and reach a precise, noncontroversial appraisal of the programs? There is no way. Different people with different value systems weight the contributions and shortcomings differently. For us, the shortcomings of the programs were numerous and their adverse impacts varied, but all may be summed into a concept of real social cost (but not an objectively measurable real social cost). The contributions were essentially of one kind: the protection of the vital economic interests of producers of food and agricultural products and the consumers of those products. For us, the gains to society from the programs in protecting the vital interests of producers and consumers outweigh the real costs to society.

Stated somewhat differently, the real costs of the programs to society may properly be viewed as the costs of achieving a rapid rate of technological advance in American agriculture, which resulted in a continuing food surplus and provided consumers with an abundant supply of food but which was not permitted to destroy farmers economically. Again, we believe the benefits to society, on balance, outweighed the costs.

But it may be argued that the appraisal above is simply the judgment of two people, and in our society is worth no more than two votes. In a sense this is a valid argument; certainly the appraisal is dependent to a large degree on our particular value systems.

Is there not a firmer foundation for the appraisal? We think there is. The Congress of the United States reviewed and acted on major pieces of farm legislation in almost every year from 1948 to 1965. During this 18-year period the programs evolved through struggle and compromise, as was recounted in chapter 3, but the basic objective of protecting farmer-producers against precipitous price and income declines never changed. The means evolved slowly, but the basic object did not change.

The Congress of the United States reaffirmed year after year the need for price and income programs to protect and support farm incomes. This it did after reviewing the consequences of the programs each year and evaluating the costs of the programs. Thus, we argue that the Congress, representing all the people, after reviewing and appraising the operation of the programs each year, *consciously and deliberately continued the programs in operation*. This is evidence that the people of the United States speaking through their elected representatives were of the collective judgment that the farm price and income programs were, on balance, in the public interest, were good for the country, and should be continued. This the Congress affirmed once again in 1973 when it passed the Agriculture and Consumer Protection Act of 1973 for the duration of four years.

Implications for the Future

Much was said and written in 1973, and continued to be said and written in the middle 1970s, about the deteriorating world food situation, about the strong commercial demand for U.S. grains and oilseed products, and about the need for farm programs of price and income support being a thing of the past. Such could be the case, but no one knows, or can know, that it is the case. If agricultural prices should trend up gradually, as illustrated by the line OA in figure 10-1, throughout the 1970s and 1980s as the consequence of a steadily growing aggregate demand pressing modestly against a steadily growing aggregate supply, U.S. farmers would indeed be happy, consumers would not be too unhappy, and the need for farm programs would be a thing of the past. But farm prices in the United States could trend upward rather sharply, as illustrated by line OB in figure 10-1, as a consequence of a continued strong demand for grains and oilseed products by both the developed nations and the less-developed nations and a slow to stagnate rate of farm technological advance in the United States and other important exporting nations.[6] In such an event the clamor on the part of consumers in the United States for farm policies to increase food production and for food policies to distribute equitably the short food supplies would be terrific. On the other hand, farm prices could trend downward as illustrated by lines OC and OD in figure 10-1, if the demand for U.S. grain and oilseed products should slacken in the developed and less-developed nations and farm technological advance should once again become rapid and widespread in the United States and other exporting nations. And any trend in farm prices falling between lines OO and OD in figure 10-1 would bring strong pressure from farmers in the United States to make the Agricultural and Consumer Protection Act of 1973, and its successors, operative.

We are of the opinion that there is a greater likelihood of the long-run trend in farm prices falling between lines OO and OB in figure 10-1 than of the trend falling between lines OO and OD.[7] But the long-run future is not knowable; hence no one can do more than express an opinion about the future trend of farm prices.

There is a second aspect of future farm price developments in the United States which is even more uncertain and more precarious than the possible trend developments. It is short-run fluctuations in market supplies, hence fluctuations in the farm price level around trend in a free-market situation. In the absence of government programs to support and stabilize farm prices, the level of farm prices can gyrate in an extreme fashion in the United States; the events of 1972–73 make this clear. Possible patterns of year-to-year fluctuations in the level of farm prices about trend in the United States in a free-market situation are illustrated in figure 10-2 (to repeat, the annual observations presented in figure 10-2 are illustrative only; they are not predictions). The year-to-year fluctuations can be very great, and they are unpredictable because changes in the world supply situation are unpredictable.

Why should this be the case? The explanation flows from the following set of circumstances:

1. The world demand for grain is highly inelastic: this means that for any nation linked to the world grain market any small change in the supply of grain translates first into a relatively large change in the price of the grains, second, and after the appropriate lag, a significant change in the price of livestock products, and third, into an important change in the price of food product substitutes.

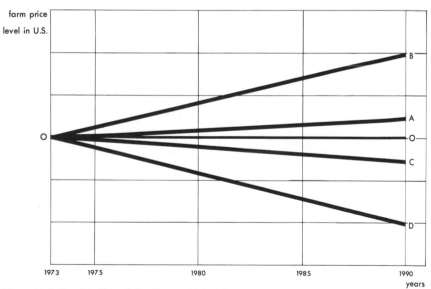

Figure 10-1. Possible Farm Price Trends, United States, 1973–90

2. The United States is linked to the world market as the largest supplier of grains to that market.

3. Supplies of grain on the world market can change significantly in any particular year, and unpredictably, as the result of (a) a change in the climate in any major exporting or importing region, (b) a change in food and trade

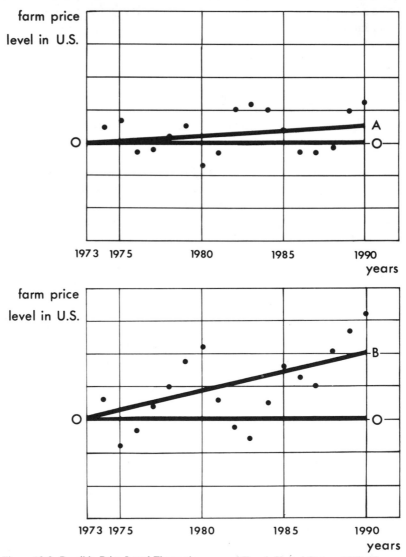

Figure 10-2. Possible Price Level Fluctuations around Trend, United States, 1973–90

policy on the part of any major nation-state (e.g., India, the Soviet Union), (c) a widespread crop infestation in a major exporting or importing region, or (d) a technical or resource change with a worldwide impact (e.g., an energy shortage, a new crop variety).

4. Given the facts of points 1 and 2 above and the possibilities of unpredictable changes in world grain supplies from point 3, it necessarily follows that the farm price level in the United States will fluctuate from year to year about trend in a wide and unpredictable fashion.

This is the type of farm price level behavior which the United States must expect in the future if it pursues an essentially free-market policy with respect to agriculture. We cannot predict the possible trend in the level of farm prices over the next two decades, or the pattern of price level fluctuation around this trend, but we can predict with certainty that some unknown pattern of price level fluctuations, sharp and wide, will emerge for the United States, if it pursues a free-market policy for agriculture.

It is further certainly predictable that there will be pressure, some of the time from consumers, and some of the time from producers, to even out supplies over time, stabilize farm and food prices, and provide income support and assistance to vulnerable groups of consumers and producers.[8] The pressure from consumers will, of course, come when food supplies are short and farm and food prices are high, as was the case in 1973–74. And the pressure from farmers will come when supplies of agricultural products are abundant and farm prices are low and falling.

Reconciling the opposing economic interests of consumers and producers in an effective and rational food and agricultural policy will not be easy. This is so because interest in achieving price stability will rarely if ever be concurrent with the two groups: when producers are seeking price stability consumers will be happy to let prices slide, and when consumers are seeking price stability producers will be happy to let prices soar. But an effective and rational integration of food and agricultural policies must be achieved because they are simply different aspects, or sides, of the same economic activity. An integrated food and agricultural policy will be necessary to keep food supplies flowing to consumers in the United States at stable prices, and in the right amounts and economic returns flowing to producers in the United States in stable and acceptable amounts, where the food-producing and distributive systems of the United States are operating in a worldwide market in which prices oscillate widely and sharply in response to unpredictable changes in marketable supplies. And, although the food aspects of farm policy became increasingly important in the 1960s and early 1970s, they will become even more important in the future and perhaps even dominate food and agricultural policy by 1980. We can be sure that the essentially urban society of the United

States will in the future develop and pursue policies designed to provide it with adequate supplies of food at as favorable a cost as possible — whether as consumers or as taxpayers.

It is reasonable to expect, then, that the Agriculture and Consumer Protection Act of 1973 will not be permitted to expire in 1977. In 1977, or perhaps earlier, it will be reviewed and refined by the Congress, with or without guidance from the administration, and new legislation will be passed designed to protect the vital economic interests of farm producers and consumers with regard to food.

It would be inappropriate in a volume such as this to attempt to spell out the specific content of the next piece of farm-food policy legislation. But it does seem appropriate to make use in some way of the lessons learned from the operation of past programs in the formulation and administration of future programs. This we will do by setting forth certain principles, gleaned from past experience, for guidance in the formulation and development of new programs. We advance ten such principles:

1. The programs must be highly flexible. They must have the capacity to move quickly from a surplus situation to a shortage situation, or vice versa, and deal effectively with the problems of either situation. If the programs lack this capacity they will, in the highly volatile world of food and agriculture, be out of phase and counterproductive much of the time.

2. Farm commodity prices should be stabilized at, or near, or approaching the world price level. If this principle is not observed a formidable program apparatus must be constructed and placed in operation to isolate the American farm economy from the world farm economy, and such a condition of isolation is in direct conflict with the necessity for the United States to be a major exporter of farm products.

3. A major reserve stock program, with or without the cooperation of other trading nations, is absolutely essential to the achievement of a tolerable degree of domestic price stability. In a world in which supplies of grain and other basic commodities change significantly and unpredictably from year to year there is no other way to even out supplies from year to year and thus stabilize the level of farm commodity prices within the United States.

4. A reserve stock program operating in the United States is unlikely to be successful in the intermediate and long run if it is not coupled with (a) an export policy designed to monitor and regulate the aggregate flow of basic commodities from the United States, and (b) a supply management policy designed to regulate the aggregate flow of basic commodities onto the domestic market. Point (a) above is necessary to protect domestic consumers in a period of critically short supply, such as was experienced in 1972–73. Point (b) is necessary to keep the storage bins from overflowing in a prolonged

period of excess production capacity, such as was experienced in the 1950s and 1960s.

5. Programs of supply management should cease to rely exclusively on acreage controls and move in the direction of negotiable marketing quotas. The latter type of supply control instrument would not operate to hinder or block the restructuring and reorganization of the agricultural industry, while at the same time controlling aggregate supply, and it would not tend to force producers to substitute nonfarm-produced inputs for land and labor.

6. Income assistance to farm producers should take the form of direct payments to producers made for specifically defined purposes and pinpointed with respect to recipients. The provision of income assistance through the use of direct payments enables society to know exactly who is being helped, in what amount, and at what cost. And product prices, stabilized within acceptable ranges, could do what they are supposed to do, namely, direct the use of productive resources.

7. Food assistance to domestic consumers should be based upon the needs of consumers and be achieved through specialized programs designed to meet the needs of consumers.

8. Food aid to the poor food-deficit nations should be a conscious policy in which the volume of that aid is based on (a) need in the food-deficit countries and (b) overt decisions in the United States about what share of that need should be met out of U.S. production. Foreign food aid should cease to be a residual claimant on U.S. production with aid being offered whenever a surplus exists in the United States. Foreign food aid, in whatever volume decided upon, should be built into total food requirements in the United States, along with such regular claimants as domestic consumers and regular foreign buyers.

9. The logic of assisting domestic and foreign consumers to meet their food needs, and of protecting farm producer incomes, should be extended to cover hired farm workers and low-production farmers. Hired farm workers merit the same kind of economic and social protection as urban workers, and low-production farmers may require *special* technical assistance, *special* production loans, and *special* income subsidies to enable them to become productive members of U.S. society.

10. If the world should move into a prolonged period of short food supplies, and the farm price level in the United States trends upward as illustrated by the line OB in figure 10-1, then a subpolicy on agricultural resource use may need to be developed as a means of increasing agricultural production. This subpolicy will need to consider the adequacy of the research and development effort, the need to expand irrigation and redirect water usage, the need to subsidize certain key inputs and the need to plan the use of productive land. Such a

subpolicy should be holistic in conception, and its scope will obviously depend upon the gravity of the world food situation. But it is just possible that the long period of excess production capacity in the United States has come to an end, and that food and agricultural policy must be reoriented to deal effectively with continuing food shortages.

These guiding principles taken as a package constitute a suggested food and agricultural policy for the United States in the late 1970s and 1980s. No single point is completely new, each is controversial, and the policy package has relevance only for the set of economic, social, and physical conditions that seem to be emerging in the United States, as a part of the larger world situation, in the 1970s. The policy package in reality evolves out of the policy ideas of the agricultural acts of 1965, 1970, and 1973, and should be thought of as the latest stage in an evolving policy which began as a strict farm policy, developed into an agricultural policy with important implications for consumers at home and abroad, and in the 1970s becomes an integrated food and agricultural policy.

This suggested food and agricultural policy recognizes the need for a prosperous agricultural sector which continues to grow, develop, and become increasingly productive. A number of the guiding principles presented above are included to ensure such a state of affairs. But the policy package also recognizes the needs of consumers at home and abroad and a number of the principles are included to ensure that those needs are met. Finally, the policy package attempts to make the food and agricultural policy of the United States consistent with its now dominant role, and possibly expanding role, in the world trade in agricultural products, while at the same time continuing to provide assistance and protection to both producers and consumers in the United States.

Achievement of this latter multiple objective will not be easy. And in all likelihood, we as a people will fail to achieve it in a manner which is satisfactory to all concerned. But it is predictably certain that events in the world of food and agriculture will force the United States to continue to strive to achieve that multiple objective over the next several decades.

NOTES

Notes

Chapter 1. The Agro-Economic Setting

1. See David Pimentel et al., "Food Production and the Energy Crisis," *Science*, 182:443–449 (November 2, 1973); and G. H. Heichel, *Comparative Efficiency of Energy Use in Crop Production*, Connecticut Agricultural Experiment Station, New Haven, Bulletin 739, November 1973.

2. This discussion of excess production capacity is based upon the discussion presented in a book by the senior author, *The City Man's Guide to the Farm Problem* (Minneapolis: University of Minnesota Press, 1965), pp. 110–116.

3. See U.S., Congress, Joint Economic Committee, "American Agriculture in 1965," *Policy for Commercial Agriculture, Its Relation to Economic Growth and Stability*, by James T. Bonnen, Joint Committee Print, 85th Congress, 1st session, November 22, 1957, p. 145; R. G. Bressler, Jr., "Farm Technology and the Race with Population," *Journal of Farm Economics*, 39:851 (November 1957); Nathan Koffsky, "The Long-Term Price Outlook and Its Impact on American Agriculture," *Journal of Farm Economics*, 36:797 (December 1954).

4. See Fred H. Tyner and Luther G. Tweeten, "Excess Capacity in U.S. Agriculture," *Agricultural Economics Research*, Economic Research Service, USDA, 16:23–31 (January 1964).

5. This analysis was first presented in a book by the senior author, *Farm Prices: Myth and Reality* (Minneapolis: University of Minnesota Press, 1958), pp. 105–107.

6. Murray R. Benedict, *Farm Policies of the United States, 1790–1950* (New York: Twentieth Century Fund, 1953).

Chapter 2. Policy Goals and Directions

1. The years of agricultural history before World War II are well documented in many sources. See, for example, Murray R. Benedict, *Farm Policies of the United States, 1790–1950* (New York: Twentieth Century Fund, 1953).

2. U.S., Department of Agriculture, *Agricultural Statistics 1967* (Washington, D.C.: Government Printing Office, 1967).

3. *Congress and the Nation 1945–1964* (Washington, D.C.: Congressional Quarterly Service, 1965), p. 684; and Benedict, *Farm Policies*, p. 472.

4. Association of Land-Grant Colleges and Universities, *Postwar Agricultural Policy*, Report of the Committee on Postwar Agricultural Policy, October 25, 1944; U.S., Department of Agriculture, *What Peace Can Mean to American Farmers*, 1945, published in four parts: *Post-*

War Agriculture and Employment, Misc. Pub. 562; *Maintenance of Full Employment*, Misc. Pub. 570; *Expansion of Foreign Trade*, Misc. Pub. 582; *Agricultural Policy*, Misc. Pub. 589; U.S., Congress, House, Special Committee on Postwar Economic Policy and Planning, *Postwar Economic Policy and Planning*, 79th Congress, 2nd Session, 1946, 10th Report; U.S., Congress, House, *Postwar Agricultural Policies*, 79th Congress, 2nd session, 1946, H. Rept. 2728.

5. L. J. Norton, "The Price Policy for Agriculture Contest," *Journal of Farm Economics*, 27:740 (November 1945).

6. Large potato surpluses under the price support program appeared in 1946 as an omen of future troubles. Perishable potatoes could not be exported readily; hence government purchases amounting to $91.3 million were necessary to maintain high support levels. Yet policy makers apparently did not perceive this situation as generally applicable to other commodities.

7. U.S., Congress, House, Committee on Agriculture, *Long-Range Agricultural Policy*, Hearings, 80th Congress, 1st session, pt. 1, April 21, 1947, pp. 2–4.

8. U.S., Congress, Senate, Subcommittee of Committee on Agriculture and Forestry, *Long-Range Agricultural Policy and Program*, Hearings, 80th Congress, 1st session, pt. 1, October 9, 1947, p. 8.

9. The struggles between those supporting O'Neal's view and Anderson's backers and the resulting compromise legislation are elaborated on in chapter 3.

10. "Resolutions Adopted at 30th Annual Convention," pamphlet of American Farm Bureau Federation, Chicago, Illinois, December 16, 1948, p. 10.

11. Patton later returned to his earlier position. He is quoted by Allen J. Matusow as saying: "When I went to report to the boys, I got worked over for compromising." *Farm Policies and Politics in the Truman Years* (Cambridge, Mass.: Harvard University Press, 1967), p. 192.

12. The 80th Congress also passed a piece of nonagricultural legislation, the Marshall Plan, which played a substantial role in maintaining foreign demand for U.S. agricultural products during the next few years. Adopted in 1948 to aid reconstruction of war-torn Europe, the Plan provided funds to dollar-short nations that stimulated demand for U.S. goods.

13. From the text of Truman's speech as published in the *New York Times*, September 19, 1948, p. 3.

14. *New York Times*, September 21, 1948, p. 1.

15. From the text of Thomas E. Dewey's speech as published in the *New York Times*, September 21, 1948, p. 20.

16. Components of the Brannan Plan and the unsuccessful efforts to enact it are treated in the next chapter.

17. Mimeographed copy of "Statement by Secretary of Agriculture Charles F. Brannan at a Joint Hearing of the House Committee on Agriculture and the Senate Committee on Agriculture and Forestry, Thursday, April 7, 1949, 10:00 a.m.," pp. 1–2.

18. American Farm Bureau Federation, "Resolutions Adopted at the 32nd Annual Convention," Dallas, Texas, December 14, 1950, p. 16.

19. "Letter from Secretary Benson to Senator Ellender," May 2, 1957, USDA mimeographed item 1377–57, p. 1.

20. Ezra Taft Benson, *Freedom to Farm* (Garden City, N.Y.: Doubleday, 1960), p. 181.

21. Republican platform as printed in the *New York Times*, September 7, 1952, p. 71.

22. Ibid.

23. *New York Times*, September 7, 1952, p. 1.

24. Ibid., p. 70.

25. An address by Secretary Benson to the Central Livestock Association in St. Paul, Minnesota, reported in the *New York Times*, February 12, 1953, p. 20.

26. "General Statement on Agricultural Policy," by Secretary Benson, February 5, 1953, USDA mimeographed item 273–53, pp. 1–3.

27. See chapter 3 for a more thorough discussion of the Eisenhower-Benson programs.

28. Farm address by President Eisenhower in Indianapolis, October 15, 1954, reported in the *New York Times*, October 16, 1954, p. 8.

29. *Congress and the Nation 1945–1964* (Washington, D.C.: Congressional Quarterly Service, 1965), p. 707.

30. U.S., Congress, House, Committee on Agriculture, *General Farm Legislation*, Hearings, 85th Congress, 1st session, pt. 1, May 16, 1957, p. 32.

31. U.S., Congress, Senate, Committee on Agriculture and Forestry, *Farm Program*, Hearings, 85th Congress, 2nd session, pt. 1, 1958, p. 8.

32. *Congressional Record*, 85th Congress, 1st session, vol. 103, August 29, 1957, p. A7219.

33. Ibid.

34. "1955 Policies of the American Farm Bureau Federation," pamphlet of American Farm Bureau Federation, Chicago, Illinois, December 16, 1954, p. 18.

35. "Farm Bureau Policies for 1960," pamphlet of American Farm Bureau Federation, Chicago, Illinois, December 17, 1959, p. 11.

36. "Farmers Union Program for 1954–1955," pamphlet of Farmers Educational and Cooperative Union of America, Denver, Colorado, March 15–19, 1954, p. 8.

37. "National Farmers Union Program for 1956–1957," pamphlet of Farmers Educational and Cooperative Union of America, Denver, Colorado, March 23, 1956, p. 8.

38. "Where We Stand: A Report to the American People by the Secretary of Agriculture," USDA mimeographed press release, July 19, 1960.

39. Willard W. Cochrane, "A Price Policy for Agriculture, Consistent with Economic Progress, That Will Promote Adequate and More Stable Income from Farming," *Journal of Farm Economics*, 27:813–820 (November 1945).

40. Willard W. Cochrane, "An Appraisal of Recent Changes in Agricultural Programs in the United States," *Journal of Farm Economics*, 39:288 (May 1957).

41. For a more detailed description see Willard W. Cochrane, *Farm Prices: Myth and Reality* (Minneapolis: University of Minnesota Press, 1958).

42. U.S., Congress, Joint Economic Committee, *Policy for Commercial Agriculture — Its Relation to Economic Growth and Stability*, Committee Print, 85th Congress, 2nd session, February 10, 1958, p. 17.

43. Ibid., p. 19.

44. U.S., Congress, Joint Economic Committee, *Economic Policies for Agriculture in the 1960's: Implications of Four Selected Alternatives*, Joint Committee Print, 86th Congress, 2nd session, November 26, 1960, p. iv.

45. See Don Paarlberg, "In Support of the Administration's Farm Policy" (paper presented at the joint meetings of the American Farm Economic Association and Allied Social Science Associations, Washington, D.C., December 27–30, 1959), published in *Journal of Farm Economics*, 42:401–412 (May 1960).

46. Robert L. Clodius, "Market Structure, Economic Power and Agricultural Policy: A Proposal for Forward Production Control" (paper presented at the joint meetings of the American Farm Economic Association and Allied Social Science Associations, Washington, D.C., December 27–30, 1959), published in *Journal of Farm Economics*, 42:413–425 (May 1960).

47. James T. Bonnen, "The Farm Policy Debate: Discussion" (paper presented at the joint meetings of the American Farm Economic Association and Allied Social Science Associations, Washington, D.C., December 27–30, 1959) published in *Journal of Farm Economics*, 42:429–434 (May 1960).

48. Don F. Hadwiger and Ross B. Talbot, *Pressures and Protests: The Kennedy Farm Program and the Wheat Referendum of 1963* (San Francisco: Chandler Publishing Co., 1965), p. 7.

49. Robert K. Buck, "Farm Agencies Must Face a New Direction," an address at the National Farm Institute, Des Moines, Iowa, February 19, 1960, published by the Greater Des Moines Chamber of Commerce.

50. Writings of T. W. Schultz and D. Gale Johnson and publications by the Committee for Economic Development during this period continued to stress a gradual return to free-market pricing tempered by special programs to mitigate transitional hardships.

51. *Washington Farmletter*, October 1, 1960, pp. 1–2.

52. John F. Kennedy, *Agricultural Policy for the New Frontier* (pamphlet), p. 7.

53. *Washington Farmletter*, October 1, 1960.

54. *Congress and the Nation*, p. 711.

55. From Vice President Nixon's address at the National Plowing Contest at Sioux Falls, S.D., as reported in the *New York Times*, September 24, 1960, p. 14.

56. Kennedy, *Agricultural Policy for the New Frontier*, pp. 12–13.

57. From a press release issued by the press office of Senator John F. Kennedy, Democratic National Committee, September 22, 1960, entitled "Following are excerpts from the remarks of Senator John F. Kennedy at the National Plowing Contest, Sioux Falls, S.D., Thursday, September 22, 1960."

58. Kennedy, *Agricultural Policy for the New Frontier*, pp. 11–12.

59. Key features of this and other farm legislation of the Kennedy-Freeman administration, and the struggles leading to enactment, are detailed in chapter 3.

60. *The American Farm Bureau Federation's Official News Letter*, August 7, 1961, p. 1.

61. "Statement by Secretary Freeman on the Signing of the Agricultural Act of 1961," August 8, 1961, USDA mimeographed item 2511–61, p. 1.

62. *Washington Farmletter*, August 12, 1961.

63. "Farm Bureau Policies for 1963," resolutions adopted at 44th Annual Meeting of American Farm Bureau Federation (pamphlet), Atlanta, Georgia, December 13, 1962, p. 8.

64. From the National Grange Pamphlet "How Will You Vote in the Wheat Referendum?" as printed in Hadwiger and Talbot, *Pressures and Protests*, p. 270.

65. Hadwiger and Talbot, *Pressures and Protests*, p. 251.

66. Ibid., p. 316.

67. Ibid., p. 318.

68. *Congress and the Nation*, p. 723.

69. "President Johnson's Message on Agriculture," transmitted to 88th Congress, 2nd session, January 31, 1964, printed in *Congressional Quarterly Almanac* (Congressional Quarterly Service, Washington, D.C.), 20:887 (1964).

70. *Congressional Quarterly Almanac*, 20:98 (1964).

71. *New York Times*, September 20, 1964, pp. 1 and 70.

72. U.S., Congress, House, *Message from the President of the United States Relative to Farm Program*, 89th Congress, 1st session, February 4, 1965, House Doc. 73, pp. 6 and 2.

73. Ibid., pp. 6–7.

74. *Kiplinger Agricultural Letter*, February 12, 1965.

75. "Farm Policy Issues during the Next Decade," Special Report of the Georgia Agricultural Experiment Station, College of Agriculture, University of Georgia, August 1965, p. 9.

76. Harold B. Meyers, "It's Time to Turn the Farmers Loose," *Fortune*, December 1966, pp. 145 and 232.

77. "The Crisis of the Agricultural Establishment," paper presented at American Farm Economic Association, Stillwater, Oklahoma, August 23, 1965, p. 3.

78. "Some Observations of an Ex Economic Advisor: Or What I Learned in Washington," *Journal of Farm Economics*, 47:461 (May 1965).

79. "Food and People: What We Can Do," speech by Secretary of Agriculture Orville L. Freeman at the 25th Biennial Congress of the Cooperative League of the USA in St. Paul, Minnesota, October 13, 1966, USDA mimeographed release 3232-66, pp. 1–2.

80. "Agriculture/2000 — Growing Nations, New Markets," address by Secretary Freeman at the Overseas Press Club, New York City, February 15, 1967, USDA release 933-67, pp. 5–6.

81. *Food from Farmer to Consumer*, Report of the National Commission of Food Marketing (Washington, D.C.: Government Printing Office, June 1966), p. 100.

82. Ibid., p. 2.

83. *Food and Fiber for the Future*, Report of the National Advisory Commission on Food and Fiber (Washington, D.C.: Government Printing Office, July 1967), p. iv.

84. Ibid., p. 15.

85. Ibid.

86. Ibid., pp. 18–19.

87. Ibid., p. 16.

88. *The People Left Behind*, A Report by the President's National Advisory Commission on Rural Poverty (Washington, D.C.: Government Printing Office, September 1967), p. x.

89. "Priorities in Agricultural Policy" (paper presented at 11th Annual Agricultural Industries Forum, Urbana-Champaign, Illinois, January 29–30, 1969), printed in *Proceedings of the General Session*, AE-4206, Department of Agricultural Economics, University of Illinois, pp. 7–11.

90. *Congressional Quarterly Almanac*, 24:992 (1968).

91. *Farm Journal*, 93:14 (February 1969).

92. *The Farmer*, Minnesota ed., 16:12 (February 1, 1969).

93. Ibid.

94. *Farm Journal*, 93:102 (March 1969).

95. "Legislative Possibilities," *A Review of Agricultural Policy — 1970*, Series 43, published by the Agricultural Policy Institute, School of Agricultural and Life Sciences, North Carolina State University, Raleigh, April 1970, p. 65.

96. L. T. Wallace, "Agricultural Policy Formulation — A Different View," *Agricultural Policy Review*, 9:11 (1969).

97. "Legislative Possibilities," pp. 65–66.

98. Mimeographed Remarks of Secretary of Agriculture Clifford Hardin before the House Agriculture Committee, July 15, 1969.

99. *Minneapolis Tribune*, March 29, 1970, p. 10A.

100. *Kiplinger Agricultural Letter*, December 12, 1969.

101. USDA news release 4673, USDA mimeographed item no. 3755-70, December 8, 1970.

102. "Farm Bureau Policies for 1971," resolutions adopted at 52nd Annual Meeting of American Farm Bureau Federation, Houston, Texas, December 1970, p. 8. Pamphlet.

103. *Washington Farmletter*, November 6, 1970.

104. *Kiplinger Agricultural Letter*, November 27, 1970.

105. *St. Paul Dispatch*, March 17, 1972, p. 2.

106. *Congressional Quarterly*, July 21, 1973, p. 1929.

107. John Schnittker, "And Then They Grew Money," *Washingtonian*, January 1972, p. 76.

108. *Congressional Quarterly*, August 26, 1972, p. 2162.

109. *Congressional Record*, Senate, 93rd Congress, 1st session, Vol. 119, pt. 10, April 12, 1973, pp. S7205–S7214.

110. Joseph Albright, "The Full Story of How *Amepuka* Got Burned and the Russians Got Bread: Some Deal," *New York Times Magazine*, November 25, 1973, p. 36.

111. *Congressional Quarterly*, May 12, 1973, p. 1147.

112. Ibid., pp. 1147–1148.

113. Ibid., July 28, 1973, p. 2082.

114. See chapter 3 for a more detailed discussion of the act.

115. For President Nixon's statement to the Congress on March 25, 1971, dealing with reorganization of the executive branch, see *Congressional Quarterly Almanac*, 27:73A–74A (1971).

116. National Planning Association, *Looking Ahead* (Washington, D.C.), 20 (December 1972).

Chapter 3. The Evolution of Policies and Programs

1. See the Glossary of Terms for definitions of terminology commonly used in connection with farm price and income programs of the United States.

2. The support level for cotton was raised to as high as 95 percent of parity for the 1944 crop, for example.

3. For a full description and analysis of the potato program see Roger W. Gray, Vernon L. Sorenson, and Willard W. Cochrane, *An Economic Analysis of the Impact of Government Programs on the Potato Industry of the United States*, Technical Bulletin 211, Agricultural Experiment Station, University of Minnesota, June 1954.

4. An excellent discussion of this period is to be found in Allen J. Matusow, *Farm Policies and Politics in the Truman Years* (Cambridge, Mass.: Harvard University Press, 1967).

5. George E. Brandow, "The Future Role of Support Prices," *Pennsylvania Farm Economics*, Agricultural Extension Service, no. 33, School of Agriculture, Pennsylvania State College, December 1948.

6. John D. Black, "Production Adjustment, 1950," an address to the USDA Graduate School, December 5, 1949, mimeographed. By "firm" achievements Dr. Black was referring to the flexible price support provisions of the act of 1948.

7. Bushrod W. Allin, "Agricultural Policy — Past, Present, and Future," the fourth in a series of four talks given before the Oklahoma Agricultural Cooperative Council at Lake Carl Blackwell, Oklahoma, July 24, 25, 26, 1953, mimeographed.

8. For a good brief discussion of these various agricultural acts see Wayne D. Rasmussen and Gladys L. Baker, "A Short History of Price Support and Adjustment Legislation and Programs, 1933–65," *Agricultural Economics Research*, Economic Research Service, USDA, 18:69–78 (July 1966).

9. For extended discussions of the Brannan Plan and Benson's policies see the sections "The Brannan Effort" and "The Benson Effort" which appear later in this chapter.

10. Refer to chapter 7 for a discussion of the operation of the Soil Bank.

11. Increased government budgets, galloping inflation, and rising food costs since 1970 render that understanding suspect.

12. For those who would like to review this period in some detail see the readable and accurate account by Don F. Hadwiger and Ross B. Talbot, *Pressures and Protests: The Kennedy Farm Program and the Wheat Referendum of 1963* (San Francisco: Chandler Publishing Co., 1965).

13. See table 4-8, chapter 6, for the complete provisions of the feed grain program.

14. Or because of it, as a few critics have claimed.

15. See chapter 2 for a discussion of the campaigns to support and defeat the referendum and for an analysis by political analysts.

16. The strange and unlikely interest groups involved in some way in farm policy formation are described and dissected by Wesley McCune in his little book *Who's Behind Our Farm Policy* (New York: Praeger, 1956).

17. Matusow, *Farm Policies and Politics*, p. 172.

18. R. M. Christenson provides the names of the officials participating and some insight into the nature of their discussions in his book. *The Brannan Plan: Farm Politics and Policies* (Ann Arbor: University of Michigan Press, 1959), pp. 26–30.

19. Those men were Wesley McCune, special assistant to the secretary; O. V. Wells, chief of the Bureau of Agricultural Economics; Ralph S. Trigg, administrator of the Production and Marketing Administration; Maurice Du Mars, an information specialist and an excellent writer; and John A. Baker, a trained economist with much experience in government.

20. Statement by Secretary of Agriculture Charles S. Brannan, *Congressional Record*, 81st Congress, 1st session, Vol. 95, pt. 3, April 7, 1949.

21. When we say "new ideas" we must be clear about what we mean. Each new idea in the Brannan Plan had been discussed to some degree by agricultural economists and farm leaders before the Brannan statement, but none had earlier received serious consideration by the administration or the Congress.

22. The senior author of this volume knows that, as a young professional, he was, and the record speaks for such giants of the profession as John D. Black and T. W. Schultz.

23. Matusow, *Farm Policies and Politics*, pp. 200 and 201.

24. For a discussion of the political struggles over the Brannan Plan see ibid., chapter 9.

25. U.S., Department of Agriculture, *General Statement on Agricultural Policy* by Ezra Taft Benson, USDA mimeographed item 273-53, February 5, 1953.

26. Paraphrased from the *Congressional Quarterly Almanac*, 10:103 (1954).

27. See chapter 2.

28. *U.S. Agricultural Policy in the Postwar Years, 1945–1963* (Washington, D.C.: Congressional Quarterly Service, 1963), p. 49.

29. The wheat program operated through a cumbersome set of certificates in which participating farmers redeemed those certificates at the Commodity Credit Corporation for their face value. The wheat farmer in reality received an income payment, but part of the revenue raised to pay for the wheat certificates came from a special excise tax rather than all from general revenues.

30. For greater detail on program expenditures see tables 8-1 to 8-26 in chapter 8. Specific loan rates and payment rates may be gleaned from the chapters on program operation, 6 and 7.

31. Although the size of the demand and supply adjustment programs in any particular year was related to the known and anticipated surplus problem, the operation of those adjustment programs in any given year was not a function of the level of prices. The adjusted supply and demand curves, D_aD_a and S_aS_a in figure 3-1, are thus positioned in the figure with slopes identical to the original demand and supply curves DD and SS. This we recognize as an oversimplification. The mode of operation of the adjustment programs no doubt had some influence on the slopes of the adjusted curves. But in a general sense we do not know how the slopes of the adjusted curves were affected. Such information regarding the slopes of the adjusted curves is not, however, central to this analysis. All that the logic of the adjustment programs requires, in the context of this analysis, is that the demand curve expand and that the supply curve contract; this is illustrated in figure 3-1 by curve D_aD_a lying to the right of curve DD, and curve S_aS_a lying to the left of curve SS.

Chapter 4. A Look at The Legislative and Administrative Processes

1. The charge to the commission and its principal findings may be reviewed in summary form in Murray R. Benedict, *Farm Policies of the United States, 1790–1950* (New York: Twentieth Century Fund, 1953), p. 200.

2. Those views are well stated in U.S., Department of Agriculture, *Economic Bases for the Agricultural Adjustment Act*, by Mordecai Ezekiel and Louis H. Bean (Washington, D.C.: Government Printing Office, December 1933).

3. This process, as well as the subject of this entire chapter, is discussed in some depth in Ross B. Talbot and Don F. Hadwiger, *The Policy Process in American Agriculture* (San Francisco: Chandler Publishing Co., 1968), chapters 6–10.

4. John Fischer, "Unwritten Rules of American Politics," *Harper's Magazine*, 197:27 36 (November 1948).

5. Clement W. Miller, *Member of the House: Letters of a Congressman*, edited and with added text by John W. Baker (New York: Scribner, 1962), p. 110.

6. For greater detail on the composition of the House and Senate committees on agriculture and their workload in the 92nd Congress see *Congressional Index, 92nd Congress, 1971–72* (Washington, D.C.: Commerce Clearing House, Inc.).

7. The activities of special interest groups may be reviewed in current issues of the *Congressional Quarterly*. A place to begin is with the *Congressional Quarterly* for August 25, 1973, pp. 2314–15.

8. There are some exceptions. Certain aspects of P.L. 480 have been administered in the U.S. Department of State, for example.

9. For a good discussion of the function of various agencies within the USDA, see Wayne D. Rasmussen and Gladys L. Baker, *The Department of Agriculture* (New York: Praeger, 1972).

10. It is perhaps too flexible and too unrestricted with respect to the use of funds to provide proper accountability to the Office of the President and the Congress.

11. This discussion is adapted from U.S., Department of Agriculture, Agricultural Stabilization and Conservation Service, "Commodity Credit Corporation," ASCS Background Information, BI 2, February 1971; and U.S., Department of Agriculture, *Summary of 30 Years of Operations of the Commodity Credit Corporation with Report of the President of the Commodity Credit Corporation, 1964*, May 1965.

12. U.S., Department of Agriculture, *Summary of 30 Years of Operations of the Commodity Credit Corporation with Report of the President of the Commodity Credit Corporation, 1964*, pp. 4 and 5.

Chapter 5. Farm Price and Income Legislation

1. The acts cited in this chapter were selected on the basis of their importance to U.S. farm prices and income. Excluded are acts whose impact is indirect or slight either because of the small number of farmers affected or because of the small degree of change. Extensions and amendments to acts are included only if they contain provisions that markedly alter the effects of the original measure or that indicate an important change in policy — for instance, a doubling or halving of

appropriation levels. For a complete listing and summaries of all agricultural legislation, see *Digest of Agricultural Legislation* for each session of each Congress, prepared by the U.S. Department of Agriculture, Office of Budget and Finance.

2. More detailed précis of the principal farm bills are available in microfiche or photocopy form from Microfiche Publications, Division of Microfiche Systems Corporation, 440 Park Avenue South, New York, N.Y. 10016, telephone (212) 679-3132. The bills cited in this chapter for which a more detailed summary is available are designated by an asterisk as here.

3. Beginning with this act, citations are to titles and sections of the U.S. Code, 1946 edition and supplements, that contain the provision of the acts described. These same title and section numbers are retained in subsequent editions of the code, thus permitting use of these citations for reference to updated versions of the codified law.

Objectives of the acts are quoted as they appear in the U.S. Statutes at Large. The volume and page in the Statutes at Large and the date the original act was signed into law appear after the U.S. code notation.

4. See CCC Charter Act of 1948, later in this chapter, for a more complete description of the purposes and powers of the corporation.

5. This measure and the one which follows are commonly referred to as "Section 22" and "Section 32," respectively. In the remainder of this book such a practice is followed.

6. Conservation features of the act amended the Soil Conservation and Domestic Allotment Act, described earlier.

7. Beginning with this citation, references are to the public law (P.L.) number, the volume and page in the U.S. Statutes at Large, and the date each act was signed into law. The Statutes at Large reproduce each law in the form enacted by the Congress. After each congressional session, laws of that session are incorporated with previous legislation into the U.S. Code or supplements thereto.

Quotations are from the acts as they appear in the U.S. Statutes at Large.

8. Because no official name was given this act, a descriptive title is employed here for the purpose of identification. Such a practice is followed throughout this chapter whenever an act lacks an official name.

9. Subsequent agreements extended coverage through 1967. From 1968 to 1971 wheat trade was guided by the International Grains Arrangement (June 15, 1968); a new IWA became effective July 1, 1971.

10. For fiscal 1954, $100 million to $250 million was specified for this purpose. The sum was raised to $350 million for the next year (P.L. 665, 83rd Congress), lowered to $300 million for fiscal 1956 (P.L. 138, 84th Congress), and then continued at a level of $175 million through fiscal 1961 (P.L. 141 and P.L. 477, 85th Congress, and P.L. 108 and P.L. 472, 86th Congress).

11. In 1956 the special milk program was extended for two years, authorizations were increased to $75 million yearly, and the list of eligible organizations was expanded (P.L. 465 and P.L. 752, 84th Congress). When due to expire, the program was further extended, until June 30, 1961, with no change in the level of authorized funding (P.L. 478, 85th Congress). Annual funding authorizations were later raised to $78 million for fiscal 1959 (P.L. 10, 86th Congress), and to $85 million and $95 million for fiscal years 1960 and 1961 (P.L. 163 and P.L. 446, 86th Congress).

12. Subsequent acts continued this amendment for additional years and extended coverage to durum areas in California.

13. U.S., Congress, House, "The Agricultural Act of 1958," *Congressional Record*, 85th Congress, August 20, 1958, vol. 104, pp. 18851–18852.

14. Adapted from U.S., Congress, House, *Congressional Record*, 87th Congress, 1st session, March 21, 1961, vol. 107, pt. 4, p. 4410.

15. Adapted from U.S., Department of Agriculture, "The Food and Agriculture Act of 1962: A Descriptive Summary," September 1962, mimeographed.

16. Adapted from U.S., Congress, Senate, *Feed Grain Act of 1963*, 88th Congress, 1st session, May 9, 1963, S. Rept. 172, pp. 1–2.

17. This program replaced the mandatory program authorized under the Food and Agriculture Act of 1962 which was not approved by wheat growers in the May 1963 referendum.

18. Adapted from U.S., Congress, House, *Congressional Record*, 88th Congress, 2nd session, March 26, 1964, vol. 110, pt. 5, p. 6394.

19. U.S., Congress, Senate, *Food Stamp Act of 1964*, 88th Congress, 2nd session, June 29, 1964, S. Rept. 1124, pp. 1–2.

20. U.S., Congress, House, Committee on Agriculture, *Agricultural Legislation in the 88th Congress*, Committee Print, 88th Congress, 2nd session, December 31, 1964, pp. 11–12.

21. Adapted from U.S., Department of Agriculture, Office of Budget and Finance, "Digest of Agricultural Legislation Enacted," 89th Congress, 1st session, December 3, 1965, p. 2, mimeographed.

22. All titles except IV are quoted from U.S., Congress, Senate, *Explanation of the Food and Agriculture Act of 1965*, Committee Print, 89th Congress, 1st session, October 12, 1965, pp. 1–3. Title IV — Cotton is quoted from Wayne D. Rasmussen and Gladys L. Baker, "A Short History of Price Support and Adjustment Legislation and Programs for Agriculture, 1933–65," *Agricultural Economics Research*, 18:78 (July 1966).

23. U.S., Department of Agriculture, Office of Budget and Finance, "Digest of Agricultural Legislation Enacted," 89th Congress, 2nd session, December 1, 1966, p. 3, mimeographed.

24. Adapted from, U.S., Department of Agriculture, "The New Food Aid Program," November 1966, mimeographed.

25. U.S., Congress, House, Committee on Agriculture, *Agricultural Legislation in the 90th Congress*, Committee Print, 90th Congress, 2nd session, November 9, 1968, p. 7.

26. Adapted from Gordon Gunderson, *The National School Lunch Program: Background and Development*, FNS-63, Food and Nutrition Service, U.S. Department of Agriculture, 1971, pp. 20–21.

27. This citation is to the volume and page in *U.S. Treaties*, the number in *Treaties and Other International Acts Series*, and the ratification date.

28. Adapted from U.S., Department of Agriculture, Agricultural Stabilization and Conservation Service, *Price-Support and Related Legislation through the Years*, ASCS Background Information, BI 11, December 1970, pp. 11–13.

Chapter 6. Program Operations: Major Commodities

1. A necessary adjunct to the price support programs were commodity storage and disposal programs operated by the Commodity Credit Corporation. Because CCC operations are similar for several commodities, they are discussed in a separate section in chapter 4.

2. The USDA defined the commercial corn-producing area as "(a) all counties in which average production of corn (excluding corn used as silage) during the preceding 10 calendar years, after adjustment for abnormal weather conditions, is 40 bushels or more per farm, and 4 bushels or more per acre of farm land in the county, and (b) all counties bordering on the commercial corn-producing area which the Secretary finds will likely produce a comparable amount of corn during the year for which such area is determined."

3. Exports were stimulated by shipments under concessional terms of P.L. 480. This government program is described in chapter 7.

4. Neither oats nor rye was in the feed grain program but many wheat farmers planted one or both of these crops on some of their cropland. By establishing a base for oats and/or rye, determined from his historical planting practices, a farmer had the option of expanding his wheat acreage and reducing his oats or rye acreage while retaining benefits from the government program.

5. Only programs for upland cotton, which accounts for more than 95 percent of cotton acreage and production, are discussed here. Price supports and acreage allotments, based on upland cotton program provisions, have also applied to extra long staple cotton.

6. "Cotton yields have trended downward since reaching a peak in 1965. Yields exhibited a fairly strong upward trend from the early 1950's through the mid-1960's. The interruption in the long-term upward trend appears to have been the result of several factors. First, growing conditions generally have not been as favorable in recent years. Second, some decline in skip-row planting has probably reduced yields. And third, producers may no longer find it as profitable to

devote the increasing quantities of inputs needed to raise yields. This may partly reflect a change in the price support program. For instance, since 1966, the basic price support loan level and the market price have dropped to near 20 cents, compared with about 30 cents or more in earlier years." U.S., Department of Agriculture, Economic Research Service, *Cotton Situation*, 243, October 1969, p. 5.

7. A detailed description of 1949–68 dairy programs is contained in U.S., Department of Agriculture, Agricultural Stabilization and Conservation Service, *Dairy Price Support and Related Programs, 1949–1968*, Agricultural Economic Report 165, July 1969; 1969–1972 programs are summarized in U.S., Department of Agriculture, Agricultural Stabilization and Conservation Service, *Operations and Accomplishments, 1969–1971*, May 1972, pp. 44–50.

8. Government programs for most other tobacco varieties were similar to flue-cured and burley programs.

9. Average yields per acre had more than doubled in the two decades under consideration here.

10. Detailed discussions of sugar programs are available in U.S., Department of Agriculture, Economic Research Service, *A History of Sugar Marketing*, Agricultural Economic Report 197, February 1971, and in U.S., Department of Agriculture, Agricultural Stabilization and Conservation Service, *The United States Sugar Program*, ASCS Background Information, BI 14, March 1972. The summary presented here is adapted from these sources.

Chapter 7. Program Operations: Land Retirement, Exports, and Food

1. A detailed summary of program accomplishments through 1970 is available in U.S., Department of Agriculture, Agricultural Stabilization and Conservation Service, *Agricultural Conservation Program 35 Year Summary: Practice Accomplishments by States*, October 1971.

2. For a more detailed discussion see Doris Detre Rafler, "Government Financing of Farm Exports in the Postwar Period," *Agricultural Economics Research*, 7:91–100 (October 1955).

3. The term "food aid" is used as a matter of convenience; it includes all agricultural exports financed under specific government programs including fiber, feed, and other nonedible agricultural products.

4. The history and achievements of P.L. 480 are detailed in two publications of the U.S., Department of Agriculture, Economic Research Service: *12 Years of Achievement under Public Law 480*, Foreign 202, November 1967, and *P.L. 480 Concessional Sales*, Foreign Agricultural Economic Report 65, September 1970.

5. The exceptions were the first two years of operation — because of the time required to work out procedures and negotiate agreements — and the years following 1968 when foreign currency sales were being phased out.

6. A "surplus agricultural commodity" as defined by the act was not required to be in government stocks. Any privately or publicly owned commodity qualified, if the secretary of agriculture declared it to be in excess of "domestic requirements, adequate carryover, and anticipated exports for dollars." When government-owned surpluses were specifically referred to, as in Title II, the term "CCC Stocks" was used.

7. The original congressional intent that P.L. 480 aid should be additional to aid under the Mutual Security Act apparently did not persist. A National Planning Association study noted that as early as 1958 the foreign aid budget request was adjusted to take account of the amount of economic aid generated by Title I operations. See U.S., Congress, National Planning Association, "Agricultural Surplus Disposal and Foreign Aid," *Foreign Aid Program*, Study 5, S. Doc. 52, 85th Congress, 1st session, July 1957, p. 378.

8. Title III authority included donations for domestic uses as well, since it was merely an enlargement of the existing program under Section 416 of the Agricultural Act of 1949; the domestic aspect is treated later in this chapter.

9. The agency responsible for economic aid was called Agency for International Development (AID) from 1962 to 1973; predecessor agencies were International Cooperation Administration (ICA) from 1956 to 1961, Foreign Operations Administration (FOA) from 1953 to 1955, and Mutual Security Agency (MSA) from 1951 to 1952.

10. A certificate of additionality is a document which certifies that the proposed barter transaction will have no effect on dollar purchases.

11. The original authorization was under a newly created Title IV; but in the Food for Peace Act of 1966 all sales provisions — whether for foreign currency, dollar credit, or "convertible currencies" credit — were combined in a revised Title I.

12. The material in this section draws heavily upon Gordon Gunderson, *The National School Lunch Program: Background and Development*, FNS-63, Food and Nutrition Service, U.S. Department of Agriculture, 1971, other published and unpublished FNS documents, and consultation with FNS staff. In the 1970s the commodity distribution program was more commonly known as the food distribution program.

Chapter 8. Program Interrelations and Costs

1. The economics of the interaction of efforts to expand demand and control supply under four sets of policies are illustrated in chapter 3, figures 3-1, 3-2, 3-3, and 3-4.

2. Some of these expenditures were made to pay for services needed by society (e.g., storage of products required by the economic system), but the great bulk of expenditures were made to achieve the price-income purposes of the programs.

Chapter 9. Program Analysis and Consequences

1. Some of the more important include the following: U.S., Congress, Senate, *Report from the United States Department of Agriculture and a Statement from the Land Grant Colleges, IRM-1 Advisory Committee on Farm Price and Income Projections, 1960–65, under Conditions Approximating Free Production and Marketing of Agricultural Commodities*, S. Doc. 77, 86th Congress, 2nd session, January 20, 1960; K. L. Robinson, "Possible Effects of Eliminating Direct Price Supports and Acreage Control Programs," *Farm Economics*, Department of Agricultural Economics, Cornell University, Ithaca, N.Y., 1960, pp. 5813–5820; U.S., Congress, Joint Economic Committee, *Economic Policies for Agriculture in the 1960's — Implications of Four Selected Alternatives*, by George Brandow, Joint Economic Committee Print, 86th Congress, 2nd session, December 1960; Luther G. Tweeten, Earl O. Heady, and Leo V. Mayer, *Farm Program Alternatives*, Report 18, Center for Agricultural and Economic Development, Iowa State University, Ames, Iowa, 1963; Luther G. Tweeten and Fred H. Tyner, "Excess Capacity in U.S. Agriculture," *Agricultural Economics Research*, 16:23–31 (January 1964); U.S., Congress, Senate, Committee on Agriculture and Forestry, *Farm Program Benefits and Costs in Recent Years*, by Walter W. Wilcox, Committee Print, 88th Congress, 2nd session, October 6, 1964; James Herendien, *Effects of National Farm Programs on Farm Prices and Incomes in the United States and the Northeast*, Experiment Station Bulletin 716, College of Agriculture, Pennsylvania State University, March 1965.

2. Tobacco is the consistent exception. The mandatory program works for a product deemed not to be a necessity; hence the program is left alone in fact and in assumption.

3. Daryl! E. Ray and Earl O. Heady, *Simulated Effects of Alternative Policy and Economic Environments on U.S. Agriculture*, Center for Agricultural and Rural Development, Report 46T, Iowa State University, Ames, Iowa, March 1974; and Frederick Nelson, "An Economic Analysis of the Impact of Past Farm Programs on Livestock and Crop Prices, Production and Resource Adjustments," unpublished Ph.D. thesis, University of Minnesota, 1975.

4. Ray and Heady, *Simulated Effects*, pp. 38–40.

5. See Willard W. Cochrane, *Farm Prices: Myth and Reality* (Minneapolis: University of Minnesota Press, 1958), chapter 5, "The Agricultural Treadmill."

6. Ibid., chapter 5.

7. Robert W. Herdt and Willard W. Cochrane, "Farm Land Prices and Farm Technological Advance," *Journal of Farm Economics*, 48:243–263 (May 1966).

8. For the results of the process on farm size see table 1-2, chapter 1, and for the theory of the process see Roger W. Gray, Vernon L. Sorenson, and Willard W. Cochrane, *An Economic*

Analysis of the Impact of Government Programs on the Potato Industry of the United States, Technical Bulletin 211, Agricultural Experiment Station, University of Minnesota, June 1954.

9. Charles L. Schultze, *The Distribution of Farm Subsidies: Who Gets the Benefits?* A staff paper. (Washington, D.C.: Brookings Institution, 1971), p. 30.

10. Refer again to table 1-2, chapter 1.

11. Walter W. Wilcox, Willard W. Cochrane, and Robert W. Herdt, *Economics of American Agriculture*, 3rd ed. (Englewood Cliffs, N.J.: Prentice-Hall, 1974), p. 362.

12. Adapted from the discussion on excess production capacity in chapter 1.

13. Gray, Sorenson, and Cochrane, *Impact of Government Programs on the Potato Industry*, pp. 6, 87.

14. D. Gale Johnson, *World Agriculture in Disarray*, Fontana World Economic Issues (London: Fontana/Collins, 1973), pp. 22–23.

15. We assume here only a free movement of products and services — not a free movement of people. The latter is a logical extension of the free-trade concept, but usually is not included as a part of it because most people living in the developed world shudder when they consider the implications to themselves of such a logical extension.

16. *International Trade, 1972* (Geneva: GATT, 1973); *Trade Yearbook, 1972* (Rome: FAO, 1973).

17. *Congressional Record*, 93rd Congress, 1st session, Senate, April 12, 1973, p. S7201.

18. Johnson, *World Agriculture in Disarray*, p. 246.

19. See U.S. Department of Agriculture, Economic Research Service, *Agricultural Policies of Foreign Governments, Including Trade Policies Affecting Agriculture*, Agriculture Handbook No. 132, 1964.

20. In the short run the damaging consequences to the U.S. dairy industry of a unilateral discontinuance of dairy import quotas are clearly shown in a recent publication: U.S. Department of Agriculture, Economic Research Service, *The Impact of Dairy Imports on the U.S. Dairy Industry*, Agricultural Economics Report 278, January 1975.

21. The year 1951 is a possible exception.

Chapter 10. Program Appraisal and Implications for the Future

1. For an examination of price and income stabilization in post–World War II agriculture in the United States, see James P. Houck, "Some Economic Aspects of Agricultural Regulation and Stabilization," a paper presented at the annual meetings of the American Association of Agricultural Economists, College Station, Texas, August 21, 1974.

2. Except in 1972–73 when the disposal of government-held food stocks became official government policy.

3. We do not catalogue the capitalization of program benefits into land values as a weakness or failure of the programs. We simply recognize it as a fact of life. *Any circumstance which increases the incomes of producers in a competitive situation will be capitalized into the fixed, or limiting, input whether that limiting factor be land or a franchise or something else.* Insofar as the programs increased the incomes of farmers, those program benefits in a competitive situation had to be capitalized into the fixed or limiting resource.

4. We do not refer to the low-production, subsistence farms here; we refer to the medium to small commercial farms with a production surplus for sale — farmers with gross receipts of $5,000 to $10,000 per year, for example. The noncommercial, subsistence farms had nothing to sell, hence could not benefit from the programs.

5. G. Edward Schuh, "The Exchange Rate and U.S. Agriculture," *American Journal of Agricultural Economics*, 58:1–13 (February 1974).

6. In this discussion we often shift back and forth between the concepts of the aggregate demand and supply of farm products and the demand and supply of grains. This is not inappropriate since grains are the principal food product moving in international trade and through the process of substitution influence all other farm product prices. In the world economy grains are synonymous with food. Thus in this discussion we use the terms almost interchangeably.

7. The senior author explores the policy alternatives confronting the nation where farm prices trend upward in the article "Food, Agriculture and Rural Welfare: Domestic Policies in an Uncertain World," *American Journal of Agricultural Economics*, Proceedings Issue, 56:989–997 (December 1974).

8. It is even possible that food-processing and food-marketing firms will add to the pressure for increased stabilizing of farm product prices over time. Parts of the industry swung over to this position in 1973–74.

INDEX

Index

Acreage allotments: Hardin's proposal of, 60; for wheat, 80, 81, 83, 204–209 *passim*, 220, 221, 222; for cotton, 82, 83, 223, 226, 228, 229, 230, 233, 234; suspension of, 83; for feed grains, 83, 176, 182, 186, 187; legislation concerning, 132, 134, 139–173 *passim*; defined, 134; for tobacco, 241, 244; for rice, 244; for peanuts, 244, 248

Acreage controls, 28: during Roosevelt administration, 23; during Eisenhower administration, 33, 77–78; farmers' interest in, 35, 78; during Kennedy administration, 41, 42, 79, 80; during Johnson administration, 47, 81, 82, 95, 96; during Nixon administration, 60, 61, 82–83, 84; during Truman administration, 75; shortcomings of, 387; recommendation against future use of, 397

Acreage diversion payments: during Roosevelt administration, 23; during Nixon administration, 60, 61, 83–84; during Kennedy-Johnson administrations, 79–82 *passim*, 96; distinguished from price support payments, 156, 157, 199, 200, 202; defined, 188; for feed grains, 188, 199, 200, 201; for wheat, 158, 209, 220, 222; for cotton, 230, 232

Acreage diversion program: for feed grains, 188, 199–201; for wheat, 208, 209, 220, 221, 222; for cotton, 230, 232, 234; and farm program costs, 304

Acreage-poundage quotas, 162, 241

Acreage reserve program: legislation of, 147, 149; termination of, 187, 257–258; described, 257–258, 260

Act of July *1, 1941*, 134–135

Act of October *2, 1942*, 134–135

"Advocates of abundance," 26–27

Agency for International Development (AID), 273, 410n9no.2

Agricultural Act of *1938*, 23, 78

Agricultural Act of *1948* (Hope-Aiken bill), 29, 139, 141, 145: policy debates on, 26–28; objectives and provisions of, 74, 137–138; evaluated, 75–76

Agricultural Act of *1949*, 29, 131, 142, 145, 148, 410n8no.2: objectives and provisions of, 126, 139–140, 268

Agricultural Act of *1954*, 32, 77, 91, 92: objectives and provisions of, 145–146. *See also* National Wool Act of *1954*

Agricultural Act of *1956*, 77: provisions of, 147–148

Agricultural Act of *1958*, 149–150

Agricultural Act of *1961*, 41, 80, 154: objectives and provisions of, 152–153

Agricultural Act of *1962*, *see* Food and Agriculture Act of *1962*

Agricultural Act of *1964*: discussed, 81, 220–221, 229; objectives and provisions of, 158–159

Agricultural Act of *1965*, *see* Food and Agriculture Act of *1965*

Agricultural Act of *1970*, 67, 103: described, 61; new concepts in, 82–83, 96; objectives and provisions of, 168–170; extension of, 172

417

Agricultural Act of *1973*, *see* Agriculture and Consumer Protection Act of *1973*

Agricultural Adjustment Act of *1933*, 18, 105: reenactment and amendment of, 132–133, 137

Agricultural Adjustment Act of *1938*, 131: objectives and provisions of, 133; amendment of, 138, 139, 140, 143, 144, 146, 147, 149

Agricultural Adjustment Administration, 105

Agricultural Conservation Program (ACP), 257

Agricultural Extension Service, 125

Agricultural Marketing Act of *1929*, 105

Agricultural Marketing Agreement Act of *1937*, 93, 131: objectives and provisions of, 132–133. *See also* Section *22*; Section *32*

Agricultural Marketing Service, 121, 124

Agricultural resources: substitution among, 4–5, 12, 299–300, 361, 372, 373–374, 387, 397; inelasticity of, 15–17, 372, 373; shift to uncontrolled commodities, 295–299, 386; adjustment of in free-market situation, 360–362; problem of allocation of, 372–373, 386–387; recommendations for future policies on, 397–398

Agricultural Stabilization and Conservation Service (ASCS): and price support operations, 123, 124–125; and storage operations, 126

Agricultural Trade Development and Assistance Act of *1954* (P.L. *480*), 131: objectives and provisions of, 144–145; amendment of, 147, 148, 149, 151, 153–154, 155, 157, 160–161, 163, 164–165, 167, 168, 172, 173. *See also* P.L. *480* programs

Agriculture, commercial: restructuring of, 7, 10, 12, 14, 364, 365–366, 371, 383, 385–386, 397; and farm ownership, 7, 10, 12, 366, 371; and classification of farms, 10, 412n4; market structure of, 15–17, 365, 373, 376; study on needs of, 52; industry-wide assets of, 68; benefit of USDA to, 70; and farm size, 364

Agriculture and Consumer Protection Act of *1973*, 103, 131: discussed, 67–69, 71, 83–85, 96; objectives and provisions of, 172–173; as affirmation of farm programs, 392; future of, 396

Aid, foreign, *see* Foreign economic aid; foreign food aid programs

Aiken, George, 74

Albright, Joseph, 66–67

Allin, Bushrod W., 76

Allotments, acreage, *see* Acreage allotments

American Farm Bureau Federation, 54: free-market philosophy of, 19, 34, 35, 61, 86; views on price supports, 27, 34, 73, 77, 86, 91; objectives of during Korean War, 29; against Food and Agriculture Act of *1962*, 42, 43, 44; proposal of land retirement scheme by, 58; composition and influence of, 116, 117

American Farm Economic Association, 25, 38

Anderson, Clinton P., 28, 87: farm policy of, 26, 74

Apples, 110: marketing orders for, 80, 153

Area Redevelopment Program, 93

Association of Land-Grant Colleges and Universities, report of, 24–25

Baker, John, 88

Bargaining, collective, 17, 35, 53–54

Barley: price support programs for, 73, 176; loan rates for, 182, 186, 187, 188, 199, 201; output and stocks of, 182, 186, 187, 188, 199, 201; market prices for, 182, 187, 188, 199, 200, 201; and acreage diversion, 199, 200; production control of, 199, 299; and set-aside, 201; acres planted to, 296–297, 299. *See also* Feed grains

Basic commodities, defined, 72

Beans, 72, 152

Beef: import restrictions on, 45, 46, 65, 159, 389, 390; export of, 65. *See also* Meats

Belcher, Page, 59

Benedict, Murray, 18

Benson, Ezra Taft, 34, 38, 39, 42, 46, 59: farm policy of, 30, 77–79, 89–92, 94; philosophy of, 31; cost of farm programs under, 35–36, 45; economic effects of programs of, 97, 101

Black, John D., 74, 76, 119

Bonnen, James T., 38, 49

Bonus coupons, 291, 293, 294

Brandow, George E., 75, 119

Brannan, Charles F.: appointments held by, 26, 28; philosophy of, 29; farm policy of, 29, 33, 87–89, 94

Brannan Plan, 29, 30, 31, 49: and production payments, 77, 94; radical features of, 87, 88; reasons for defeat of, 88–89

Bread, 381

Bread tax, *see* Domestic certificate payment

Bureau of Agricultural Economics (BAE), 26, 105
Bureau of Labor Statistics, 294
Bureau of the Budget, 108
Butterfat products, *see* Dairy products
Butz, Earl L., 68, 69: appointment of, 61; on farm policy, 61, 84; on Soviet grain deal, 66, 67

Calhoun, John C., 111
Certificate of additionality, 411*n*10
Certificate payments, *see* Domestic certificate payment; Export certificate payment
Chemicals: use of, 4–5, 299, 372, 375, 387; environmental effects of, 53, 387; cranberry growers' use of, 265
Cherries, 80, 153
Chicken: *1940*s price support of, 72, 74, 138; subsidized export of, 265
Child Nutrition Act of *1966*: objectives and provisions of, 165; amendment of, 166, 167–168, 170, 171–172, 173–174
Child nutrition programs: school lunch program, 23, 73, 85, 265, 280, 281, 283–285, 289; milk program, 23, 146, 289; school breakfast program, 289–290; nonschool food programs, 290–291; and calculation of farm program costs, 301. *See also* Child Nutrition Act of *1966*; National School Lunch Act
Clodius, Robert L., 38
Cochrane, Willard W.: on free-market situation, 36–37, 360; public utility approach of, 37, 38, 40; on program costs *vs.* budget limitations, 49; influence of, 119; on land capitalization, 371
Collective bargaining, 17, 35, 53–54, 118
Colmer, William, 24: and Colmer committee, 23, 24, 25
Committee for Rural Development, 33
Commodity Credit Corporation (CCC): purpose of, 23, 123; value of stocks owned by, 32; charter of, 123–124; financing of, 124; management of, 124; price support activities of, 124–125; inventory operations of, 125–127, 300; disposal of commodities by, 126–127; purchase of dairy products by, 126, 235, 236, 240; legislation concerning powers of, 132, 134, 137, 138, 140, 145, 147, 148, 151, 159, 161, 170; corn acquired by, 176, 182; sale of grains by, 188; and domestic food aid, 235, 236, 240, 281–283; role in tobacco price operations, 241, 244; role in peanut

programs, 248; and foreign food aid, 268–269, 272–277 *passim*; barter of goods held by, 268–269, 273; and subsidized exports, 269, 275, 276, 277; Export Credit Sales Program of, 274; and calculation of farm program costs, 301–305 *passim*; reserve stock program of, 388; role in wheat program, 406*n*29. *See also* Storage programs
Commodity Credit Corporation Charter Act: provisions of, 137; amendment of, 138, 140, 145; barter activities under, 273
Commodity distribution program: *1930*s version of, 23; use of Section *32* funds for, 265, 281, 283; eligibility for, 281; administration of, 281, 282; participation in, 282, 283, 292; purpose of, 283; foods distributed by, 283; discontinued, 283, 291–292
Commons, John R., 76
Communist countries: trade with, 44, 64, 66–67, 157–158, 223, 274; excluded from export programs, 161, 164, 165, 167, 270; economies of, 377
Congress, *see* U.S. Congress
Conservation, *see* Land retirement and conservation programs
Conservation reserve: legislation of, 147; described, 260, 262
Consumers: benefits of farm programs to, 42, 306, 381–382, 384, 386, 391; in free-market situation, 380–381, 390; interests of forwarded, 383, 391–392; effect of *1973* grain deals on, 388–389; disadvantages of farm programs for, 389, 390; future needs of, 392, 395, 396, 397
Controls, acreage, *see* Acreage controls
"Convertible local currency credit" (CLCC) sales, 274
Cooley, Harold, 34, 150
Coolidge, Calvin, 23, 105
Cooperative marketing associations, 125
Corn, 28, 93, 110, 373: yield per acre, 3; Kennedy administration and, 40, 79, 80, 81; Nixon administration and, 61, 63, 66; export of, 66, 276; levels of price support for, 72, 74, 77, 78, 79, 81, 90, 91; Truman administration and, 74; Eisenhower administration and, 77, 90, 91; supply management and, 80; price support programs for, 176; CCC acquisition of, 176, 182; acreage allotments for, 176, 182, 186, 187; market prices for, 177, 182, 187, 188, 199, 200, 201; output and stocks of,

178, 182, 183, 186–187, 188, 199, 200, 201; loan rates for, 182, 186, 187, 188, 199, 200, 201; production controls for, 182, 204, 296, 297; Soil Bank and, 186, 187, 257; and acreage diversion, 188, 200; and set-aside, 201; acres planted to, 296–297, 299; definition of commercial producing area for, 409n2. *See also* Feed grains
Corn Belt, 295, 299
Cost-sharing payment, 260, 262
Cotton, 24, 26, 27, 93, 110, 295, 298: yield per acre, 3; Kennedy-Johnson administrations and, 45, 47, 48, 81, 82; Nixon administration and, 61, 68, 83; levels of price support for, 72, 74, 77, 78, 81, 82, 90, 92; Truman administration and, 74; Eisenhower administration and, 77, 78, 90, 92; output and stocks of, 77, 78, 97, 224, 226, 228–234 *passim*, 300, 386, 409n6; acreage allotments for, 82, 83, 223, 226, 228, 229, 230, 233, 234; limit on government payments for, 83, 233; congressional support for, 114; lobbyists for, 117; administration of government programs for, 125, 126; CCC disposal of, 126; legislation concerning, 133–150 *passim*, 158–162 *passim*, 169, 172–173; type of price support program for, 223; programs during *1948–63*, 223–224, 226, 228–229; loan rates for, 223, 226, 228–233 *passim*; marketing quotas and penalties for, 223, 226, 233; production controls for, 223, 230, 233, 234, 296, 297; market prices for, 226, 228–234 *passim*; export of, 226, 228–234 *passim*, 265, 268, 274, 276, 277, 305; Soil Bank programs for, 228, 257; programs during *1964–65*, 229–230; equalization program for, 229–230, 232; domestic allotment program for, 230; program during *1966–70*, 230, 232–233; eligibility for program benefits, 230, 232, 233; acreage diversion program for, 230, 232, 234; computation of acreage diversion payment for, 232; price support payment for, 232, 233–234; price support at world levels, 232, 305, 379, 389; programs during *1971–73*, 233–234; set-aside payments for, 233, 234; acres planted to, 296–297, 299; and calculation of farm program costs, 305–306; in free-trade situation, 379
Cottonseed and cottonseed oil, 145, 148

Council of Economic Advisers (CEA), 57, 108
Coupons, bonus, 291, 293, 294
Cranberries, marketing orders for, 80, 153
Cranberry growers, Section *32* payments to, 265
Cropland Adjustment Program (CAP), 262–263
Cropland Conversion Program (CCP), 262
Cuba: sugar from, 136, 142, 148, 151, 155, 171, 252; trade restrictions against, 161, 164

Dairy products, 54: used in domestic food program, 23, 146, 236, 240, 289; Kennedy administration and, 42, 93; Johnson administration and, 47; importation of, 65, 234, 378, 389, 390; in free-trade situation, 65, 377, 378, 379, 389, 390; levels of price support for, 72, 74, 235, 236, 240; Truman administration and, 74; congressional support for, 114; lobbyists for, 117; administration of government programs for, 125, 126; government purchase of, 126, 235, 236, 240, 263, 265; legislation concerning, 133, 139–146 *passim*, 150, 153, 162, 165, 169–173 *passim*; type of price support used for, 234, 235; marketing orders for, 234–235; export of, 234, 236, 240, 276, 277; fixing of prices for, 235; production of, 236, 240; market prices for, 240, 360; in free-market situation, 360
Dairy program, special (special milk program): described, 23, 289; legislation concerning, 146, 150, 153, 165, 173–174
DDT, 118, 375
Defense Production Acts, 76, 141, 142
Deficiency payments: Nixon administration and, 69, 84, 96; as part of basic farm policy compromise, 96; defined, 172
Democrats, 34: on flexible price supports, 27, 29, 30, 32; southern, 27, 29, 33, 45, 68, 111, 114; *1948* party platform of, 28; *1952* party platform of, 30–31; *1956* party platform of, 33; *1960* party platform of, 39, 40; against Benson's policies, 42; for wheat supply management, 44; midwestern, 45; *1964* party platform of, 46; *1968* party platform of, 55; *1972* party platform of, 64; and USDA, 103–104; Farmers Union and, 117
Depression, 23, 363
Development Loan Fund, 161

Dewey, Thomas E., 28
Direct payments: Roosevelt administration and, 23; proposals concerning, 25, 26, 27, 29, 52–53, 77, 88, 94; Truman administration and, 29; limitation on, 33, 60–61, 71, 82, 83, 84, 88, 96, 168, 173, 201, 222–223, 233; Eisenhower administration and, 33, 77, 94; under various administrations compared, 45; Kennedy-Johnson administrations and, 48, 79–82 passim, 94, 96; Nixon administration and, 60, 61, 69, 83, 84, 96; and calculation of farm program costs, 301–306 passim; size and distribution of, 366; recommendations for future policy on, 397. See also Parity; Acreage diversion payments; Deficiency payments; Domestic certificate payment; Domestic equalization payment; Export payment; Land-rental payment; Per-acre rental payment; Storage payment; Sugar Act payments; Wool, payments to producers of
Diversion payments, see Acreage diversion payments
Diversion program, see Acreage diversion program
Diversion programs under Section 32, 266
Doctrine of the Concurrent Majority, 111
Domestic certificate payment: defined, 158; computation of, 220, 221, 222
Domestic equalization payment, 159
Domestic food programs, see Food programs, domestic

"Economic Cooperation Act of 1948," see Marshall Plan
Eggs: levels of support for, 72, 74, 138; market margin on, 381
Eisenhower, Dwight D., on price supports, 31
Eisenhower administration: farm policy during, 30–35, 38, 89–92, 94; stocks of wheat and feed grains during, 45; farm programs during, 76–79, 94; economic effects of programs of, 97, 101
Ellender, Allen: on Benson's policies, 34; on wheat referendum, 44
Employment, see Labor, farm, employment situation for; Labor, farm, exodus of
Employment, full, effect of on agricultural sector, 24, 26, 36
Employment Act of 1946, 26
Environment, 53, 387
Environmental groups, 118

Europe, 65, 66, 265, 377
Export certificate payment: defined, 158; computation of, 220; discontinued, 221
"Export differential," 275
Export-Import Bank, described, 268, 274
Export programs: Communist countries excluded from, 161, 164, 165, 167, 270; subsidized, 263, 265, 269, 274–277; scope of, 266, 277; during 1948–54, 266, 268–269; during 1955–73, 269–270, 272–277; payments of subsidies in, 274–277; and calculation of farm program costs, 301, 305; recommendations for future policy on, 396. See also Exports; Marshall Plan; P.L. 480 programs
Exports, 15; and reduction of stocks, 14, 73, 77; effect of McNary-Haugen proposal on, 22–23; demand for, 22, 68; Eisenhower administration and, 32, 35, 74–75, 76–77; Kennedy administration and, 41, 42, 44, 79; Johnson administration and, 44, 51; to Communist countries, 44, 64, 66–67, 157–158, 223, 274; concern about, 46, 65; Nixon administration and, 60, 64–67; value of, 64–67; in free-trade situation, 65, 378, 379, 380; Truman administration and, 75; increase in due to stable farm economic environment, 385–386; restructuring price and income support programs for, 389; effect of subsidies for, 389. See also Export programs

Family planning, 164, 167
"Famine Relief and Other Assistance," 144
Famine Relief Bill, 144
Farm Bureau, see American Farm Bureau Federation
Farm income: World War I and, 22, 23; evolving policy on protection of, 25, 26, 27, 29, 52–53, 69, 71, 77, 82, 83, 84, 88, 94, 95, 96; Eisenhower administration and, 31, 32, 35, 45, 77, 78; as 1960 campaign issue, 39–40; comparison of during different administrations, 45; Kennedy administration and, 45; Korean War and, 45; Johnson administration and, 50, 55; Nixon administration and, 68, 69; in free-market situation, 359–363; benefits of increase in, 364–366, 371; effect of farm programs on, 384; stability of, 384, 386
Farm labor, see Labor, farm
Farm organization, see Agriculture, commercial, restructuring of
Farm policy: farmers' influence on, 17–20,

35, 53–54, 63, 68, 70–71; overall goal of, 21–22; report of commission study on, 52–53; outside U.S., 65, 389, 390; basic compromise on, 95–96, 100, 101; recommendations for future, 396–398
Farm prices, *see* Prices, farm
Farm programs: farmers' demand for, 17–20; attempt to lower cost of, 35, 40, 45, 47–48, 49, 68; benefits of to consumers, 42, 306, 381–382, 384, 386, 391; cost of, 45, 49, 96, 114–115, 301–307, 366, 390–391; administration of, 121, 123–127; interrelationships of, 175, 295–300; success of, 295–300; definition of, 301; studies on effect of removal of, 359–363; intent of, 363, 364, 383, 391–392; benefits of to farmers, 364–366, 371, 384–385, 391; effect of on productivity, 373–376; outside U.S., 377–381 *passim*; shortcomings of, 386–391; impact of on foreign trade, 389–390; future of, 392–398
Farm-retail price spread, 51, 381
Farmers: decline in number of, 7, 10, 14, 16–17, 46, 68, 371; low-production, 10, 25, 33, 115, 116, 364, 397; classification of, 10, 412n4; influence of, 17–20, 35, 53–54, 63, 68, 70–71, 85–87, 116–118; tobacco, 22, 27, 110, 241; needs and problems of, 25, 33, 388, 395, 397; benefits of farm programs for, 364–366, 371, 384–385, 391
Farmers' Day, 63
Farmers Home Administration loans, 155
Farmers' movements, 17–20
Farmers Union, *see* National Farmers Union
Federal Farm Board, 23, 74
Feed Grain Act of *1963*, 157
Feed grains: Kennedy-Johnson administrations and, 40–48 *passim*, 79–81 *passim*, 92, 93; government stocks of, 45, 77–80 *passim*, 92, 300; Nixon administration and, 61, 64–66 *passim*, 68, 83; Eisenhower administration and, 76, 77, 78; levels of price support for, 76, 78, 79, 80, 81, 379, 389; production payments for, 81; price support at world levels, 81, 379, 389; acreage allotments for, 83, 176, 182, 186, 187; limit on payments for, 83, 201; congressional support for, 114; CCC handling of, 126, 300; legislation concerning, 138, 139, 142, 145, 150–157 *passim*, 162, 169–173 *passim*; type of price support used for, 176; programs during *1948–58*, 176–178, 182, 186–187; market prices for, 176–178, 182, 187, 188, 199,

200, 201; loan rate for, 176, 178, 182, 186, 187, 188, 199, 200, 201; type of production controls used for, 176, 182, 187, 188, 199, 200, 201, 204, 296, 297, 299; programs during *1959–60*, 187; programs during *1961–70*, 187–188, 199–200; acreage diversion programs for, 188, 199–201; relation of price support payment to loan rates for, 199; computation of acreage diversion payment for, 199, 200; price support payment for, 199, 200, 201; set-aside program for, 201; and wheat substitution provision, 221; subsidized export of, 276; acres planted to, 296–299 *passim*; and calculation of farm program costs, 305–306; in free-trade situation, 377. *See also* Barley; Corn; Grain sorghum; Grains; Oats
Feed Grains Bill, 40, 41, 79–80
Fertilizer: substituted for other inputs, 4–5, 299, 372, 375, 387; affordability of, 361, 374
Findley, Paul, 69, 82
Flanigan, Peter, 64: Flanigan Report on Agricultural Trade Policy, 64–66, 378
Flaxseed, 72
Food Aid Convention, 166, 167, 171
Food and Agriculture Act of *1962*: debate on, 42; described, 42, 80–81; defeat of mandatory control feature of, 81, 408n17; objectives and provisions of, 155–156; amendment of, 156
Food and Agriculture Act of *1965*, 81, 82, 103: legislative history of, 47–48; assessment of, 47–50, 95–96; extension of, 54–55, 167; objectives and provisions of, 162–163
Food and Nutrition Service, 123
Food for Peace, *see* P.L. *480* programs
Food for Peace Act of *1966*: features of, 164–165, 270, 272, 274, 411n11; and phasing out of foreign currency sales, 270
Food prices, *see* Prices, food
Food programs, domestic: commodity distribution program, 23, 281–283, 291, 292; as means of expanding demand for farm products, 42, 79, 85, 280; as outlet for surplus foods, 73, 234, 236, 240, 280, 386; legislation concerning, 135, 146, 151, 153, 156, 159–160, 165–166, 167–168, 170, 171–172, 173–174; Section *32* funds for, 170, 171, 263, 265; recommendations for future policy on, 397; and calculation of farm program costs, 301–305 *passim*. *See*

also Child Nutrition Programs; Food stamp program

Food programs, foreign, 42, 386: as surplus disposal, 14, 32, 35, 79, 266, 270, 272; for India, 141, 163–164, 165, 268, 382; for Pakistan, 142, 268; during famine, 143, 144–145; Food Aid Convention and, 166, 167, 171; and foreign policy, 266; from *1948–54*, 266, 268–269; from *1955–73*, 269–270, 272–277; new emphasis in, 270, 272, 274; cost of, 301–305 *passim*; and calculation of farm program costs, 301–305 *passim*; recommendations for future policy on, 397. *See also* Marshall Plan; P.L. *480* programs

Food Stamp Act of *1964*, 131: objectives and provisions of, 159–160; amendment of, 167, 170, 173

Food stamp program: *1930*s version of, 23; use of to gain support for farm legislation, 45, 58; expansion of, 45, 85; purpose of, 79, 291; pilot phase of, 151, 291, 292; product purchases disallowed under, 160; Section *32* funds for, 265; relation of to commodity distribution program, 283, 291–292; features of, 291–294

Foreign aid, *see* Foreign economic aid; Food programs, foreign

Foreign Aid Appropriations Act, 157

Foreign Assistance Act of *1948*, 136–137

Foreign Assistance Act of *1961*, 154, 157, 274

Foreign Assistance Act of *1963*, 157

Foreign Assistance Act of *1967*, 165

Foreign economic aid: programs for, 268; P.L. *480* as, 272; and food shipments, 272, 273; agencies responsible for, 410n9no. 2

Foreign food aid programs, *see* Food programs, foreign

Foreign Operations Administration (FOA), 410n9no.2

Free-market situation: debate on, 22, 27, 29, 31, 34, 36–37, 38, 86, 372; effect of on prices and income, 360–363, 372, 376, 379–381, 390; future developments under, 395

Free-trade situation: effect of on exports and imports, 65, 378, 379, 380, 389; for world agriculture, 376–380; for U.S., 379–380, 390; effect of on farm and food prices, 380–381

Freeman, Orville, 55: farm policies of, 40, 41, 92; on wheat referendum, 44; cost of price supports under, 45; on unlimited production, 50; on aid to developing countries, 50–51; farm programs of, 79–82; economic effects of programs of, 97, 100, 101

Fruits, 73, 133: marketing orders for, 80, 93, 153; Section *32* funds for purchase of, 263; Section *32* subsidized export of, 265; in free-trade situation, 378

Galbraith, J. K., 119

General Agreement of Tariffs and Trade (GATT), 66, 134

"General Statement on Agricultural Policy," 31, 89

Goldwater, Barry, 46, 47

Grain sorghum: Feed Grains Bill and, 40; price support programs for, 176–177; market prices for, 177, 182, 187, 188, 199, 200, 201; loan rates for, 182, 186, 187, 188, 199, 200, 201; output and stocks of, 182, 186, 187, 188, 199, 200, 201; and acreage diversion, 188, 200; and set-aside, 201; acres planted to, 296–297, 299, 386; use of production controls for, 299. *See also* Feed grains

Grain Terminal Association, 43

Grains: export of, 44, 64–67, 84, 378, 379; government costs in handling surpluses of, 45; government stocks of, 97, 386; administration of government programs for, 125, 126; storage of, 126; in free-trade situation, 377, 378, 379; value of reserve stocks of, 381; future demand for, 392, 393; unpredictability of supplies of, 394–395, 396; as principal food product in international trade, 412n6. *See also* Feed grains; Wheat

Grange: and National Wheat Committee, 43; coalition with Farmers Union and National Farm Organization, 54, 58, 60, 61; views on role of government in agriculture, 86; composition and influence of, 116, 117

Great Plains Conservation Act, 149, 153

Greenspan Program, 262–263

Gum naval stores, 125, 133

H.R. *12*, 91

Hadwiger, Don F., 44

Hardin, Clifford, 64, 82: policies of, 56–61; resignation of, 61; and legislative procedure, 106

Hay: conservation reserve program and, 260; acres planted to, 297

Heady, Earl O., 361–362

Herbicides, 299

Herdt, Robert W., 371
Hogs, 28: levels of price support for, 72, 74,
    138
Honey, 133, 139, 145
Hoover, Herbert, 105
Hope, Clifford, 73
Hope-Aiken bill, *see* Agricultural Act of *1948*
    (Hope-Aiken bill)
Hops, 133
House Appropriations Committee, 112, 115
House Committee on Agriculture, 28, 29, 60,
    68, 160: compared to USDA, 107;
    subcommittees of, 111; composition of,
    111, 114, 115–116
House of Representatives, and legislative
    process, 111, 115. *See also* House
    committees
Humphrey, Hubert H., 46, 55

*Impact of Government Programs in the Potato
    Industry*, 374
Imports: meats, 45, 46, 65, 159, 389, 390;
    dairy products, 65, 234, 378, 389, 390; in
    free-trade situation, 65, 378, 379, 380, 389,
    390; food stamp program regulation against
    purchase of, 160; restrictions on, 234, 389;
    wool, 250; sugar, 250, 252, 389, 390; rice,
    389, 390
Incremental approach to policy formulation,
    see Partial approach to policy formulation
Index of prices paid, 18
Index of prices received, 18
India, 50, 395: legislation of food aid to, 141,
    163–164, 165; grain loans to, 268;
    economic assistance loans to, 268; U.S.
    reserve stocks shipped to, 382
India Emergency Food Act of *1951*, 141
International Cooperation Administration
    (ICA), 410*n*9no.2
International Grains Agreement (IGA), 166
International Wheat Agreement (IWA), 139,
    166, 167, 171: exports under, 269, 275
Interest groups, *see* Special-interest groups
Iowa, 38, 110

Japan: farm policies of, 65; grain needs of, 66;
    cotton exports to, 274
Johnson, D. Gale: influence of, 119; study on
    state of world agriculture by, 376, 377, 378
Johnson, Lyndon B.: assumption of the
    presidency, 44, 45; farm issues in *1964*
    campaign of, 46; on farm objectives, 47
Johnson administration: and trade with
    Communist countries, 44; farm objectives

of, 45, 47; farm programs of, 47–55 *passim*,
    80–81, 95–96
Joint Commission of Agricultural Inquiry, 105

Kennedy, John F.: farm issues in *1960*
    campaign of, 39–40; on supply
    management, 40; outlines his program, 92
Kennedy administration: and supply
    management, 40–44; farm programs of,
    41–44, 79–81, 92–95 *passim*; policy views
    of, 92–94; economic effects of proposals of,
    97, 100, 101
Khrushchev, Nikita, 44
Kiplinger Agricultural Letter, The: on
    Johnson's programs, 48; on Hardin, 61
Kline, Allan B., 27
Korean War, 29, 31, 68: and farm prices, 5–7,
    18; and farm income, 45; emergency
    measures during, 141; output during, 182,
    244, 376; cotton prices during, 223, 232;
    profit from sale of surplus stocks during,
    307

Labor, farm, 364: nonfarm inputs substituted
    for, 5, 12, 299–300, 372, 387, 397; exodus
    of, 7, 10, 23, 30, 46, 68, 372; employment
    situation for, 12, 16–17; productivity of, 12,
    30, 35; needs and problems of, 115, 116,
    387, 388, 397; migrant, 116
Labor unions, 118
Lake states, 375
Land-rental payment: described, 258; limit on,
    260. *See also* Acreage diversion payments
Land retirement and conservation programs:
    during *1930*s, 23, 33; Eisenhower
    administration and, 33, 77–78; Kennedy
    administration and, 42; Johnson
    administration and, 47; Nixon
    administration and, 58; legislation
    concerning, 132, 133, 146–155 *passim*,
    163, 168, 173; intent of, 256; described,
    256–258, 260, 262–263; payments under,
    257, 258, 260, 262, 263; success of,
    298–299; and calculation of farm program
    costs, 304. *See also* Soil Bank
Legislative process, farms: Kennedy's
    proposed change in, 41; change in, 47; role
    of administration in, 103–109 *passim*; role
    of USDA in, 104, 107, 109; role of
    secretary of agriculture in, 105–109; role of
    congress in, 105–116; described, 105–121;
    special interests and, 113–119 *passim*; and
    implementation of programs, 121, 123–127;
    and amendment procedure, 131

Livestock products, 54: and international trade, 46, 63, 65, 377; Section *32* funds for purchase of, 263; price of keyed to price of grains, 393

Loan program: administration of, 125, 126. *See also* Price support loan rates

Low-production farmers, 364: decline in number of, 10; needs of, 25, 33, 115, 116; recommendations for protection of, 397

McCune, Wesley, 88

McNary-Haugen Bill, 19, 105: described, 18, 22–23

Market margin, 51, 381

Marketing agreements, defined, 133

Marketing certificate program, 158, 220, 221, 222

Marketing orders: for various products, 80, 90, 153; defined, 133; and dairy program, 162, 169, 234–236

Marketing quotas: use of in *1940*s, 73; emerging policy on, 92–93; defined, 92–93, 134; for wheat, 93, 204–208 *passim*, 220; for cotton, 93, 223, 226, 233; for tobacco, 93, 241; for rice, 93, 244; for peanuts, 93, 244; administration of, 125; legislation concerning, 134, 138–147 *passim*, 161–162, 171; recommendations for future policy on, 397

Marshall Plan: objectives and provisions of, 136–137; described, 268, 402*n*12

Meats: import quotas for, 45, 46, 65, 159, 389, 390; and food stamp program regulations, 160; in free-trade situation, 379

Midcontinent Farmers Association, composition and influence of, 116–117

Milk, *see* Dairy products

Murphy, Charles S., 127

Mutual Security Act of *1953*, 154: provisions of, 143; relation of P.L. *480* programs to, 144, 410*n*7no.2; and foreign currency sales, 269, 270

Mutual Security Agency (MSA), 410*n*9no.2

National Advisory Commission on Food and Fiber, 51: report of, 52–53

National Advisory Commission on Rural Poverty, 51: report of, 53

National Association of Wheat Growers, 43

National Commission on Food Marketing, 51: report of, 51–52

National Farm Institute, 38

National Farmers Organization (NFO), 86: withholding actions for milk and livestock by, 54; coalition with Grange and Farmers Union, 54, 58, 60, 61; composition and influence of, 116

National Farmers Union (NFU), 27: policies of during *1950*s, 34, 35; on supply management of wheat, 43; coalition with Grange and National Farmers Organization, 54, 58, 60, 61; composition and influence of, 86, 116, 117

National Grange of the Patrons of Husbandry, *see* Grange

National Planning Association: on reorganization of USDA, 70; study of P.L. *480* and Mutual Security Act by, 410*n*7no.2

National Plowing Contest, 30, 46, 47

National School Lunch Act: objectives and provisions of, 135, 283; amendment of, 156, 165–174 *passim*. *See also* School lunch program

National Wheat Committee, 43

National Wool Act of *1954*, 80, 131: provisions of, 146; extension of, 150, 153, 162, 170, 173

Nelson, Frederick, 362

New Deal, 19, 23: scarcity economics of, 27

New York Times, 28, 30: on Benson, 31; on Goldwater, 47

"*1949* Price Stabilization," 137

Nixon, Richard M.: farm addresses of, 39; farm issues in *1960* campaign of, 39–40; against trade with Communist countries, 44; farm issues in *1968* campaign of, 54, 55

Nixon administration, 21: farm policies of, 56–70; proposed government reorganization during, 69–70; farm programs of, 82–85

Nutrition programs, child, *see* Child nutrition programs

Nuts, 133, 139, 145

Oats: price support programs for, 73, 176; loan rates for, 182, 186, 187, 188; output and stocks of, 182, 186, 187, 188, 199; market prices for, 182, 187, 188, 199, 200; acres planted to, 296–299 *passim*. *See also* Feed grains

Office of Communication, 121

Office of Economic Opportunity, 59

Office of the General Counsel, 121

O'Hara, James G., 69

Oilseed and oilseed products: export of, 63, 64, 84, 378, 379; CCC disposal of, 127; in free-trade situation, 378, 379; future demand for, 392

O'Neal, Edward A.: on surpluses, 27; advocate of scarcity economics, 27, 73

P.L. *215*, *see* Trade Agreements Extension Act of *1953*
P.L. *480* programs, 244, 248, 409*n*3: and reduction of farm surpluses, 14, 32, 35, 51, 77, 269, 270; enactment of, 32; Kennedy administration and, 41, 79, 80, 85; Eisenhower administration and, 79; Nixon administration and, 85; total expenditures for, 85; relation of to programs under Mutual Security Act, 144, 410*n*7no.2; new direction of, 164, 266, 269, 270, 272; for concessional cotton sales, 228; for surplus dairy products, 236; and domestic aid, 236, 410*n*8no.2; described, 269–277 *passim*; total value of commodities exported under, 277; expenditures for and calculation of farm program costs, 301–305 *passim*; consumer benefits from reserve stocks under, 382; as aid to international trade, 389; administration of, 407*n*8; and definition of surplus agricultural commodity, 410*n*6. *See also* Agricultural Trade Development and Assistance Act of *1954* (P.L. *480*), Food for Peace Act of *1966*
Paarlberg, Don: on free-market, 38; on *1965* farm act, 48; on Hardin, 57, 58
Pace, Stephen, 73, 89
Pakistan: aid to, 142, 268, 270
Parity: defined, 134; computation of, 134, 137, 138, 140, 142, 145, 148
Partial approach to policy formulation, 112–114
Patton, James, 27
Payment in kind (PIK) assistance: legislation concerning, 151, 152, 159, 162; use of, 275–277
Peanuts, 110: levels of price support for, 72, 74, 77, 90; marketing orders for, 80, 153; marketing quotas for, 93, 244; congressional support for, 114; CCC disposal of, 127; legislation concerning, 133–145 *passim*, 153; price support and production control programs for, 125, 241, 244, 248; market prices for, 244, 248; quality regulations for, 248; role of CCC in programs for, 248; acreage reserve program and, 257
Per-acre rental payment, 260, 262
Pesticides, 299, 361, 387

Poage, William R., role of in program formulation, 58, 59, 60, 112
Pollution, modern agriculture and, 53, 387
Poor, rural: need for special programs for, 25, 33, 42, 45–46, 53; Eisenhower administration and, 33; Kennedy administration and, 42; Johnson administration and, 45–46, 47; report of study commission on, 53; Nixon administration and, 58; congressional responsiveness to, 115–116
Poor People's March, 54
Population control, 164, 167
Populists, 17, 19
Potatoes: levels of price support for, 72, 73; legislation concerning, 133, 139, 140, 145; diversion programs for, 266; surpluses of, 266, 402*n*6; impact of farm programs for, 374–375
Poultry, *see* Chicken, Turkey
President: role in policy formulation, 103–109 *passim*; legislation concerning powers of, 134, 139, 143, 144, 151, 154, 156, 158, 159, 165, 167
Price support loan rates: for feed grains, 176, 178, 182, 186, 187, 188, 199, 200, 201; relation of to market prices, 176, 223; at world levels, 199, 220, 232; for wheat, 201–202, 205–209 *passim*, 220, 221; for cotton, 223, 226, 228–233 *passim*; for tobacco, 241; for rice, 244; for peanuts, 244
Price support payments: Kennedy administration and, 81; distinguished from acreage diversion payments, 156, 157, 199, 200, 232; for feed grains, 199, 200, 201; for wheat, 209, 220; for cotton, 232, 233–234
Price supports: and government acquisition of stocks, 13, 14; and excess productive capacity, 13, 14, 17; effects of, 13, 14, 96, 100, 364–366, 374–375; farmers' demand for, 18–20; Steagall Amendment and, 18, 72–73; *1920*s program of, 23; *1930*s program of, 23; *1940*s theories on, 24–29 *passim*; high *vs.* variable (flexible), 24–29 *passim*, 36, 71; popularity of among various producers, 27; *1948* presidential nominees on, 28; "scarcity" approach and, 28; Korean War and, 29; Truman administration and, 29, 73–76; Eisenhower administration and, 32–35, 76–79, 90–92, 94; *1960* presidential nominees on, 39; Goldwater on, 47; Johnson administration and, 48, 49; report of study commission on, 53; Nixon administration and, 60, 61, 68, 84; during

World War II, 72; during *1941–48*, 72–73; Kennedy administration and, 79–81; at or near world levels, 82, 84, 96, 379, 380, 389, 390; on sliding scale, 90, 91, 94; Johnson administration and, 96; used to stabilize product prices, 100; and basic farm policy compromise, 100; administration of programs for, 124–125, 126; type of used in feed grain programs, 176; type of used in wheat programs, 201; type of used in cotton programs, 223; type of used in dairy products programs, 234, 235; type of used in tobacco programs, 241; type of used in rice programs, 244; type of used in peanut programs, 244, 248; type of used in soybean programs, 248; type of used in wool programs, 250; and calculation of farm program costs, 301, 305; impact of on potato industry, 374–375

Prices, farm, 67: effect of Korean War on, 5–7, 18; effect of world food situation on, 6–7, 18, 392–397 *passim*; effect of World War II on, 18, 23, 384; effect of World War I on, 22, 23, 384; relation of to food prices, 51, 381; effect of price freeze on, 62–63; stabilization of, 100, 373, 375, 376, 384, 385, 386, 396; effect of farm programs on, 100, 384; at world levels and cost of farm programs, 305; in free-market situation, 359–363, 380–381; during *1950*s, 360, 362; during *1960*s, 362; during *1970*s, 362; result of world levels for, 379–381, 389–390, 396; future of, 392–397 *passim*.; recommendations for future policy on, 396

Prices, food, 67: study commission report on, 51–52; during inflation, 51, 62–63; relation of to farm prices, 51, 381; effect of price freeze on, 62–63; in free-market situation, 380–381, 390; stabilization of, 386; history of, 390; future of, 395

Prices, target: problems with, 84; as part of basic farm policy compromise, 96; explained, 172

Production, *see* Productivity; Production control programs; Surplus production

Production control programs: Kennedy's supply management as, 39, 40, 92–93; Johnson administration stand on, 46; Nixon administration and, 69; during *1930*s and *1940*s, 75; success of, 75, 295–300, 386, 387; Eisenhower administration and, 76; use of in basic farm policy compromise, 95–96, 100; for feed grains, 176, 182, 187, 188, 199, 200, 201, 204, 296, 297, 299; for

wheat, 204, 207, 209, 220, 296; for cotton, 223, 230, 233, 234, 296; for tobacco, 241; for rice, 244; for peanuts, 244; for sugar, 250, 252; effect of on uncontrolled commodities, 295–298, 386; during *1950*s, 296–299, 300; during *1960*s, 299; during *1970*s, 300

Production payments: adoption of, 77, 81–82, 93, 94; under supply management, 81, 93; proposal of, 88; opposition to, 88

Productivity: increase in, 3–7, 12–17, 23, 28, 30, 35, 373–376 *passim*, 387; relation of to income, 7; excess capacity for, 12–17, 372–376; effect of farm programs on, 373–376; problems associated with increase in, 386–387. *See also* Surplus production

Puerto Rico, 142, 171, 284

Quotas, acreage-poundage, 162, 241
Quotas, marketing, *see* Marketing quotas

Ray, Daryll E., 361–362
Ray-Heady free-market simulation, 361–362
Reciprocal Trade Agreements Act of *1934*, 134

Republicans, 27, 28, 68: *1952* party platform of, 30–31; and price supports, 30, 32, 77; *1956* party platform of, 33; against Benson, 34; *1960* party platform of, 39–40; against Food and Agriculture Act of *1962*, 42; against trade with Communist countries, 44; *1964* party platform of, 46, 47; *1968* party platform of, 55; *1972* party platform of, 64; against Brannan Plan, 89; and USDA, 103–104; midwestern, 111, 114; and Farm Bureau, 117

Reserve program, acreage, *see* Acreage reserve program

Reserve stock program: need for, 83–84, 388, 396–397; current state of, 96; under CCC, 145, 388; under P.L. *480*, 382

Resource allocation, *see* Agricultural resources

Retail food prices, *see* Prices, food

Rice: Johnson administration and, 47, 48; levels of price support for, 72, 74, 76, 77, 91; Truman administration and, 74; Eisenhower administration and, 79, 91; marketing quotas for, 93, 244; legislation concerning, 133–150 *passim*, 163; price support and production control programs for, 241, 244; market prices for, 244; output of, 244; export of, 244, 273, 276, 277; acreage reserve program and, 257; in

free-trade situation, 377; import restrictions on, 389, 390
Roosevelt, Franklin Delano, 23, 105
Rural Areas Development Program, 155
Rural Development Act of *1972*, 131
Rural Environmental Assistance Program (REAP), 257
Rural Envionmental Conservation Program (RECP), 257
Rural poor, *see* Poor, rural
Russia, *see* USSR
Rye: *1940*s price support of, 73; legislation concerning, 148, 150, 157; and wheat substitution provision, 221

"Sales for Foreign Currency," 144, 147, 149, 270
Sapiro, Aaron, 17
Schnittker, John, 63–64, 119
School lunch program, 280, 281: *1930*s form of, 23; described, 73, 85, 283–284, 287–289; funding of, 284, 287, 288, 289; schools participating in, 284, 288; commodities used in, 287–288, 289; student eligibility for, 288. *See also* National School Lunch Act
Schuh, G. Edward, 389
Schultz, T. W., 119
Schultze, Charles L., 69, 366
Secretary of agriculture: role of in policy formulation, 87; role ofin farm legislative process, 105–109; and implementation of programs, 121, 124; legislation concerning powers of, 133, 135, 137, 138, 140, 146, 150, 154, 155, 157, 160, 161, 162, 169, 170, 171, 172; and dairy program, 235, 236
Section *22*: provisions of, 133; amendment of, 137, 138, 140–143 *passim*; and restrictions on dairy imports, 234
Section *32*: provisions of, 133; and export programs, 136, 263, 265, 269, 276; and use of customs receipts, 140, 147; and domestic food programs, 170, 171, 263, 265, 281, 283; funds for school lunch program, 170, 171, 265, 288; intent of programs under, 256; and commodity purchases, 263, 265; and purchasing power of cranberry growers, 265; and diversion programs, 266; expenditures and calculation of farm program costs, 301
Section *416*, 140, 145, 288, 410n8no.2
Senate: and legislative process, 111, 115; report on Food Stamp Act, 159. *See also* Senate committees

Senate Appropriations Committee, 115
Senate Committee on Agriculture and Forestry, 29, 68, 157, 161: subcommittees of, 111; composition of, 111, 114, 115–116
Senate-House Joint Economic Committee: report on rural problems, 37
Set-aside program: opposition to, 60; described, 60, 83–84, 96, 168; for feed grains, 201; for wheat, 222, 223; for cotton, 233, 234
Shuman, Charles, 59
Soil Bank: and *1930*s conservation programs, 23, 33; purpose of, 33, 147; reaction of farmers to, 35, 78; acreage reserve program of, 77–78, 147, 257–258, 260; conservation reserve program of, 78, 147, 260, 262; legislation concerning, 147, 148, 149; programs for allotment crops, 186, 187, 207, 228, 257, 260; and calculation of farm program costs, 304
Soil conservation, *see* Land retirement and conservation programs
Soil Conservation and Domestic Allotment Act of *1936*, 131, 149, 408n6: objectives and provisions of, 132
Soil Conservation Service, 256–257
Sorghum, *see* Grain sorghum
South, Lauren, 55
South, 73, 295: special interests of, 25, 27; cropping shifts to, 297, 298
Soy oils, 72, 277
Soybeans: Nixon administration and, 65, 66; export of, 65, 66, 248, 250, 277; *1940*s price support of, 72; legislation concerning, 133, 148, 153; price support programs for, 248; output of, 248, 250; market price of, 250; government ownership of, 250; acres planted to, 296–297, 299; undercommitment of resources to, 387
Special-interest groups: influence of on farm policy, 17–20, 63, 68, 70–71, 85–87, 112–119; and basic farm compromise, 85–87; and public interest, 115, 383
Statutes at Large, *see* U.S. Statutes at Large
Steagall Amendment: price supports under, 18, 72–73; purpose of, 24; provisions of, 134–135; effect of on potatoes, 375
Steagall commodities: defined, 72–73, 135; price support of, 72–73, 135, 138
Stevenson, Adlai, 30, 31
Storage payment, 125
Storage programs: costs of, 14, 35–36, 45, 79, 387; administration of, 23, 125–126; benefits of, 381, 386; shortcomings of, 386,

388; described, 388. *See also* Surplus
production
Sugar: congressional support for, 114;
lobbyists for, 117; beets, 117, 252;
production quotas for, 250, 252; payments
for growers of, 250, 252; importation of,
250, 252, 389, 390; acreage allotments for,
252; cane, 252; tax on, 252; increase in
marketings of, 252; stabilization of prices
for, 252, 255; in free-trade situation, 377,
378, 379. *See also* Sugar Act of *1937*; Sugar
Act of *1948*
Sugar Act of *1937*, 136
Sugar Act of *1948*, 125: objectives and
provisions of, 135–136; amendment of,
142, 148, 151–155 *passim*, 163, 171
Sugar Act payments, 250, 252
Sugar tax, 252
Supply control: during *1930*s, 23; Eisenhower
administration and, 29; Johnson
administration and, 48; Nixon
administration and, 61; Truman
administration and, 75; supply management
distinguished from, 92–93
Supply management, 45: Cochrane on, 37, 40;
as production control, 39, 40; economic
freedom and, 39–40, 42, 43; Kennedy
administration program of, 39, 40, 42–44
79–80, 92–94; Republicans against, 39, 42;
support for, 43, 48–49; distinguished from
supply control, 92–93; recommendations for
future policy on, 396–397
Surplus production: estimates of, 14–15;
export of, 14, 73, 77; growth in stocks of,
14, 79, 387; reasons for, 15–17; effect of on
farm prices and income, 16; types of
government programs, affecting, 17; during
Roosevelt administration, 23; during
Coolidge administration, 23; direct
distribution of, 23, 73; "advocates of
abundance" and, 26–28; during Eisenhower
administration, 30, 32, 35–36, 45, 77; *1960*
presidential nominees on, 39; during Kennedy
administration, 45, 79, 92; during
Johnson administration, 46; reduction in
stocks of, 46, 68; during Nixon
administration, 68; and need to develop
reserve stock program, 83–84, 96, 388,
396–397; economic effects of government
acquisition of, 97; and calculation of farm
program costs, 301–305 *passim*, 307;
during Korean War, 307; benefits of, 386;
misinterpreting problem of, 386–387. *See
also* Storage programs

Talbot, Ross B., 44
Talmadge, Herman E., 111
Target prices, *see* Prices, target
Tariff Commission, 143
Technological development: and increased
productivity, 3–5, 15–17, 23, 28, 30,
373–376 *passim*; substituted for land and
labor, 4–5, 12, 299–300, 361, 372,
373–374, 387, 397; and USDA, 70;
influence of on farm policy, 121; effects of
employment of, 364, 365, 371, 387; public
support for, 373; farm programs and, 375,
376, 385, 386; future of, 392
Tobacco, 411*n*2no.2: levels of price support
for, 72, 74, 76, 77, 91; Truman
administration and, 74; Eisenhower
administration and, 76, 77, 91; marketing
quotas and penalties for, 93, 241;
congressional support for, 114;
administration of government programs for,
125, 126; legislation concerning, 133, 139,
142, 144, 146, 147, 151, 161–162, 172; and
food stamp program regulations, 159; types
of price support for, 241; acreage-poundage
quotas for, 241; associations of farmers of,
241; types of production and marketing
controls for, 241; acreage allotments for
241, 244; CCC and, 241, 244; export of,
241, 265, 276; output of, 244; market prices
for, 244; acreage reserve program and, 257
Tobacco farmers, 22, 110: price supports and,
27; associations of, 241
Trade Agreements Extension Act of *1951*, 141
Trade Agreements Extension Act of *1953*,
142, 143
Trade Expansion Act of *1962*, 156
Transfer payments, 391: effect of, 306–307
Truman, Harry S., 24, 87: farm issues in *1948*
campaign of, 28; supports Brannan Plan, 89
Truman administration, 21: policies and
programs of, 73–76
Turkeys: *1940*s price support of, 72; marketing
orders for, 80, 153
Tweeten, Luther G., 15
Tyner, Fred H., 15

Union of Soviet Socialist Republics (USSR),
382, 395: trade with, 44, 64, 66–67,
157–158, 223, 274
United Nations Relief and Rehabilitation
Administration (UNRRA), 268
United Nations World Food Program, 165
United States: effect of adoption of
free-market situation by, 379–380, 390,

395; as largest supplier of grains to world, 394; exportation of farm products by, 396; suggested food and agricultural policy for, 396–398
U.S. Code (U.S.C.), 131, 408n7
U.S. Congress: and legislative process, 105–116; mentioned, *passim. See also* House of Representatives; Senate
U.S. Department of Agriculture: indexes of, 18; Bureau of Agricultural Economics (BAE) of, 26, 105; *1948* study of future trends by, 28; study of free-market prices by, 38; and policy formulation, 41, 87; benefits of to nonfarm people, 42; changing role of, 42, 71; and wheat referendum, 43; proposed reorganization of, 69–70; and implementation of programs, 71, 121; role in *1940*s price support programs, 72–73; and change in application of acreage controls, 82–83; relations between Democratic administrations and, 103–104; relations between Republican administrations and, 103–104; and legislative process, 105, 107, 109; agencies of, 121, 123, 137; and school lunch program, 135; and cotton credits, 268; and foreign food aid, 268, 273, 282; and commodity distribution, 281, 282; and food stamp program, 291. *See also* Secretary of agriculture
U.S. Department of Defense, 273
U.S. Department of Health Education and Welfare, 166
U.S. Department of State, 407n8
U.S. Statutes at Large (Stat.), 131, 408n7

Vegetables: Section *32* funds for purchase of, 263; in free-trade situation, 378

Wallace, Henry A., 105
Wallace, Henry C., 105
War on Poverty, 45
Washington, 110
Wells, O. V., 87, 88
Wheat, 24, 29, 93, 110, 295: yield per acre, 3; Kennedy-Johnson administrations and, 40–48 *passim*, 80, 81, 83, 93–94; referendums on, 42–44, 48, 81, 94, 204, 220; sales to USSR, 44, 66–67, 157–158, 223; government stocks of, 45, 77, 78, 300; Nixon administration and, 61, 63, 66, 67, 68; levels of price support for, 72, 74–81 *passim*, 90, 91; Truman administration and, 74; Eisenhower administration and, 76, 77, 78; acreage allotments for, 80, 81, 83,

204–209 *passim*, 220, 221, 222; production payments for, 81; limit on government payments for, 83, 222–223; marketing quotas and penalties for, 93, 204–208 *passim*, 220; congressional support for, 114; lobbyists for, 117; CCC disposal of, 126; legislation concerning, 133, 138–158 *passim*, 163, 166, 168–169, 170, 173; type of price supports used for, 201; programs during *1948–61*, 201–202, 204–208; loan rates for, 201–202, 205–209 *passim*, 220, 221; amount exported, 202, 204, 206, 208, 221, 222; market prices for, 202, 205, 206, 207, 209, 220–223 *passim*; subsidized export of, 202, 265, 269, 275–276, 277, 305; production controls for, 204, 207, 209, 220, 296; output and stocks of, 204–209 *passim*, 220–223 *passim*; eligibility for price support loans, 205, 209, 220, 221; Soil Bank programs for, 207, 257, 260; programs during *1962–63*, 208–209, 220; acreage diversion programs for, 208, 209, 220, 221, 222; computation of price support payment for, 209; computation of acreage diversion payment for, 209, 220, 222; and cross compliance among commodity programs, 220; programs during *1964–65*, 220–221; certificate payments for, 220, 221, 222; price support at world levels, 220, 305, 379, 389; and feed grain substitution provision, 221; programs during *1966–70*, 221–222, 406n29; programs during *1971–73*, 222–223; set-aside program for, 222, 223; for Pakistan, 268; acres planted to, 296–297; resources shift to grain sorghum, 297, 386; and calculation of farm program costs, 305–306; in free-market situation, 360; excise tax on, 380; 406n29; price *vs.* bread price, 381; overcommitment of resources to, 387. *See also* Grains
Wheat Trade Convention, 166, 171. *See also* International Wheat Agreement (IWA)
Wilcox, Walter W.: influence of, 119; and study on size and distribution of government payments, 366; on land capitalization, 371
Wilson, "Tama Jim," 105
Wool, 47, 48, 138: payments to producers of, 77, 250; importation of, 250; price support program for, 250; consumption of, 250. *See also* National Wool Act of *1954*
Wool Act of *1954, see* National Wool Act of *1954*
Wool Bill, 41

World food situation: implications of, 6–7, 18, 392–395, 397–398; in *1960*s and American farm policy, 50–51

World War I: price and income situation following, 22, 23; compared to World War II in effect on farm prices, 384

World War II: as reliever of agricultural crisis, 18, 23; price supports during, 72, 134–135; and foreign aid programs, 266, 268, 302; use of farm programs during and after, 363; compared to World War I in effect on farm prices, 384